Green Finance and Sustainable Development Goals

Transformations in Banking, Finance and Regulation

Print ISSN: 2752-5821
Online ISSN: 2752-583X

Series Editors: Sabri Boubaker
(*EM Normandie Business School, France*)
Duc Khuong Nguyen
(*EMLV Business School, France*)

Presently, the banking and finance sectors evolve within a globalized and highly uncertain environment. Each business and financial decision requires careful consideration of country-specific and international factors due to high levels of shock transmission and volatility spillovers. Furthermore, it would be remiss to omit the COVID-19 health crisis, which caused harmful effects to all areas of the real economy and made profound changes in the way our firms, economies, and markets used to function.

Many other already well-known aspects, including the repercussions of quantitative easing policies, disruptive technologies in finance (e.g., FinTech, Big Data, Data Analytics, Artificial Intelligence, and Blockchains), as well as innovative financing instruments for startups (e.g., ICOs and crowdfunding) are currently revolutionizing banking and finance and posing numerous challenges to regulatory bodies and policymakers. Climate change emergencies also put pressure on governments and firms worldwide to improve policy on governance, corporate social responsibility, and sustainability practices.

This book series "Transformations in Banking, Finance and Regulation" attempts to address these issues by focusing on transformative perspectives in banking and finance. Accordingly, it provides evidence-based guidance, recommendations, and pathways to assist businesses and policy decision-makers through an interdisciplinary and in-depth understanding of ongoing changes in the behavior of economic agents.

Published

Vol. 12 *Green Finance and Sustainable Development Goals*
edited by Sabri Boubaker and Thai-Ha Le

Vol. 11 *Handbook of Environmental and Green Finance: Toward a Sustainable Future*
edited by Sabri Boubaker and Thai-Ha Le

Vol. 10 *Banking Resilience and Global Financial Stability*
edited by Sabri Boubaker and Marwa Elnahass

Vol. 9 *Banking Resilience: New Insights on Corporate Governance, Sustainability and Digital Innovation*
edited by Sabri Boubaker and Marwa Elnahass

For the complete list of volumes in this series, please visit
www.worldscientific.com/series/tbfr

Transformations in Banking, Finance and Regulation
Volume 12

Green Finance and Sustainable Development Goals

Editors

Sabri Boubaker
EM Normandie Business School, France

Thai-Ha Le
VinFuture Foundation, Vietnam

World Scientific

NEW JERSEY • LONDON • SINGAPORE • BEIJING • SHANGHAI • HONG KONG • TAIPEI • CHENNAI • TOKYO

Published by

World Scientific Publishing Europe Ltd.

57 Shelton Street, Covent Garden, London WC2H 9HE

Head office: 5 Toh Tuck Link, Singapore 596224

USA office: 27 Warren Street, Suite 401-402, Hackensack, NJ 07601

Library of Congress Cataloging-in-Publication Data
Names: Boubaker, Sabri, editor. | Le, Thai-Ha, editor.
Title: Green finance and Sustainable Development Goals / editors: Sabri Boubaker, EM Normandie Business School, France, Thai-Ha Le, VinFuture Foundation, Vietnam.
Description: New Jersey : World Scientific, [2024] | Series: Transformations in banking, finance and regulation, 2752-5821 ; volume 12 | Includes bibliographical references and index.
Identifiers: LCCN 2023023146 | ISBN 9781800614475 (hardcover) | ISBN 9781800614482 (ebook) | ISBN 9781800614499 (ebook other)
Subjects: LCSH: Finance--Environmental aspects | Sustainable Development Goals.
Classification: LCC HG101 .G744 2024 | DDC 332--dc23/eng/20230717
LC record available at https://lccn.loc.gov/2023023146

British Library Cataloguing-in-Publication Data
A catalogue record for this book is available from the British Library.

For any available supplementary material, please visit
https://www.worldscientific.com/worldscibooks/10.1142/Q0427#t=suppl

Desk Editors: Sanjay Varadharajan/Rosie Williamson/Shi Ying Koe

Typeset by Stallion Press
Email: enquiries@stallionpress.com

https://doi.org/10.1142/9781800614482_fmatter

About the Editors

Sabri Boubaker is a professor of finance at EM Normandie Business School in Paris, France, and the University of Swansea, Wales, United Kingdom. Sabri holds a PhD in finance from the University of Paris Est (2006) and a HDR degree (habilitation for supervising doctoral research) awarded in 2010 from the same university. Professor Boubaker is the editor-in-chief of the *Journal of International Financial Management and Accounting*. Sabri Boubaker has published more than 100 academic papers in international refereed journals, including the *Journal of Corporate Finance*, the *Journal of Banking and Finance*, the *Journal of International Money and Finance, Financial Management*, the *Journal of Business Ethics*, the *Journal of Economic Dynamics* and *Control, Auditing: A Journal of Theory & Practice*, the *British Journal of Management*, and the *Journal of Financial Research.* Professor Boubaker has also edited many books on corporate finance and financial markets and serves on the editorial boards of several peer-reviewed finance journals. He is the co-founder and co-chair of the annual *Paris Financial Management Conference* (2013–), the *Vietnam Symposium in Banking and Finance* (2016–), and the *Annual Meeting of the International Society for the Advancement of Financial Economics* (2022–).

Thai-Ha Le is the managing director of the VinFuture Foundation, Vietnam. She holds a bachelor of arts (Hons) and PhD in economics from Nanyang Technological University, Singapore. Prior to joining VinFuture Foundation, Dr. Le was the director of research and a senior faculty member at the Fulbright School of Public Policy and Management, Fulbright University, Vietnam, and a tenured senior lecturer at RMIT University, Vietnam. Her primary research fields include energy economics, environmental economics, and applied economics. Dr. Le has published about 70 scholarly research articles in international, peer-reviewed journals, such as *Energy Economics, Energy Journal, Energy Policy, Renewable Energy, Resources Policy, Economic Modelling*, the *International Review of Financial Analysis, Empirical Economics, Annals of Operations Research, Applied Economics*, and the *Australian Tax Forum.* According to rankings compiled by Stanford University and published in PLoS Biology in 2021 and Elsevier in 2022 and 2023, Dr. Le is in the world's top 1 percent most influential scientists across all scientific fields. Dr. Le has consulted for the World Bank, UNDP, the Asian Development Bank (ADB), and the Economic Research Institute for ASEAN and East Asia (ERIA). She is a recipient of multiple competitive research grants and fellowships. She was an external reviewer for the Vici Social Sciences and Humanities program under the NWO Talent Programme and the Dutch Research Council (NWO). She was the founding editor-in-chief of the Fulbright Review of Economics and Policy and holds associate editor/editorial roles with several other scholarly journals, including the *Journal of Economic Asymmetries*, the *Journal of Economic Development*, and the *Singapore Economic Review.*

https://doi.org/10.1142/9781800614482_fmatter

About the Contributors

Boualem Aliouat is a professor of strategic management at the University Côte d'Azur, France. He supervises research at the Groupe de Recherche en Management — IAE de Nice (GRM) on the performance and governance of innovation networks and technological clusters. He holds a PhD in management sciences (1993) and a habilitation for supervising doctoral research (1998) at the University of Lille 2, France. He has published many scientific papers and books on the governance and performance of technological poles. His recent work focuses on performance and risk management, prospective and systemic performance, green finance, and the contribution of neuroscience to entrepreneurial decisions. He is also the translator to French of the Nobel Prize in Economics Ronald H. Coase (Ed. Eyrolles and Ed. Diderot) book, which was the winner of the Montesquieu Prize in 2010 and the EFMD-FNEGE Prize for Best Management Book in 2022. He is now the vice president of the African Council for Entrepreneurship and Innovation.

Silvio Andrae is an economist with most of his professional experience in the financial sector. Since 2000, he has been working as a senior adviser on various green finance projects across Latin America, Africa, and Asia. He has also spent several years working in the Brazilian Amazon, where one of his focus areas was the valuation of ecosystem services. Silvio Andrae studied and received his PhD at the Free University of Berlin in Germany.

Muhammad Azam has a PhD in economics. He is currently an assistant professor at the Department of Economics, Ghazi University, Dera Ghazi Khan, Pakistan. His research interests are environmental economics and sustainability. He has recently published papers in many top-ranked journals, such as the *International Review of Financial Analysis, Finance Research Letters*, and the *Journal of Environmental Management.*

Syed Abul Basher received a PhD in economics from York University, Canada, in 2007 for his work on oligopoly models. He is currently a professor at the Department of Economics, East West University, Dhaka, Bangladesh. Prior to joining East West University, he served as a senior research fellow at Fikra Research & Policy, Doha (2014–2016), as a research economist at Qatar Central Bank (2007–2013), and as an economic consultant to the Qatar National Food Security Programme (2010–2012). Professor Basher has published over 50 scientific papers in peer-reviewed academic journals and presented papers at international conferences, including the American Economic Association. His papers were published, among others, in the *Journal of International Money and Finance*, the *Journal of Banking and Finance, Energy Economics, Global Environmental Change, World Development Sustainability*, the *Journal of Forecasting*, and the *Journal of Time Series Econometrics*. His current research interests are in the areas of development macroeconomics and energy economics.

Kathrin Berensmann has worked as a senior research fellow and has been a project leader of various projects in international economics and development finance at the German Institute of Development and Sustainability (IDOS) in Bonn since 2000. Before joining IDOS, she was employed as an economist with a focus on international finance and trade as well as monetary policy at the Institute of German Economy in Cologne, Germany. She received her doctoral degree (equiv. PhD) and "Diplom" (equiv. master's degree) in economics from the University of Würzburg, Germany. Her main areas of specialization are debt policy, sustainable finance, international financial architecture, and financial sector development. For more than 20 years, she has conducted extensive policy advisory work for various public, national, and international institutions, including the German Federal Ministry for Economic Cooperation and

Development (BMZ), the Federal Ministry of Finance, the United Nations, the World Bank, and the German Agency for International Cooperation (GIZ).

Mita Bhattacharya is a senior lecturer in economics at Monash University, Australia. Her major research areas are energy economics, sustainability, and applied industrial organization. Mita has published extensively in peer-reviewed journals, including *Energy Economics*, the *International Journal of Industrial Organisation*, the *Oxford Bulletin of Economics and Statistics, World Economy*, the *Review of Industrial Organisation*, and *Applied Energy*. She has held visiting positions at the Australian National University, Curtin University, Doshisha University, University of East Anglia, and the OECD headquarters in Paris. Mita has received numerous internal and external grants from the Australian Research Council, Tyre Australia, and National Science Council (Taiwan). Mita is the recipient of the annual award in 2017 from the Applied Energy Society for her citations on a paper published in *Applied Energy*.

Eleonora Broccardo is an associate professor in finance at the Department of Economics and Management at the University of Trento, Italy, where she teaches corporate finance. She holds a PhD in markets and financial intermediaries from the Catholic University of Milan, Italy. Her main interests include credit risk management, small business finance, and sustainable and impact finance. Her research has been published in national and international peer-reviewed journals, such as the *Journal of Political Economy*, the *Journal of Banking and Finance, Corporate Social Responsibility and Environmental Management*, the *Journal of Financial Management, Markets and Institutions*, the *Journal of Risk Finance*, and *Public Money and Management*. She serves as associate editor of the *Journal of Risk Finance* and as a reviewer for several peer-reviewed finance journals.

Giovanni Cardillo is an assistant professor in economics of financial intermediation at the University of Bologna, Italy; a research associate at the Yunus Social Business Center of Bologna; and an upcoming SCANCOR visiting fellow at Harvard University's Weatherhead Center for International Affairs, USA. His research interests are related to the impact of government monitoring on banks, the impact of IFRS on European capital markets, the implications of monetary policies for the real economy and banking sector, the evaluation of the effects of corporate governance mechanisms on bank performance and policies, and sustainable finance. He holds a PhD from the University of Bologna, Italy. In the past, he also served as a research fellow at Aston University, United Kingdom, a research assistant at the University of Nottingham, United Kingdom, and a teaching associate at the University of Amsterdam, in the Netherlands. He was also one of the founders of South Guys Ltd. which was supported by the European Commission, and a scientific consultant for ABIFormazione.

Youngho Chang is an associate professor and head of business and management minors at the Singapore University of Social Sciences. He specializes in the economics of climate change, energy and security, oil and economy, and electricity market economics. He has published his research output in various internationally referred journals, such as *Energy Economics*, *Energy Policy, Empirical Economics, Resources Policy*, and *Econometrics Journal.* Prior to entering academia, Dr. Chang worked as a landscape architect for two years in Korea and Saudi Arabia and as a financial analyst for four years in Korea. He has taught at the National University of Singapore and Nanyang Technological University, Singapore. He received his PhD in economics (environmental and resource economics) from the University of Hawaii at Manoa, USA.

Mohamed Bechir Chenguel is an associate professor of finance at the Higher Institute of Computer and Management of Kairouan, University of Kairouan, Tunisia. He holds a PhD in finance from the University of Tunis Al Manar and an HDR degree (habilitation for supervising doctoral research) from the University of Kairouan, Tunisia. He has recently published many academic papers in international refereed journals. His research interests include blockchain and cryptocurrency, financial crisis, Islamic banking, banking risk, and corporate governance. He is also an active reviewer for many indexed peer-reviewed journals published by Scopus, Taylor & Francis, Emerald, Springer, etc.

Graziano Coller is an associate professor of business administration at the Department of Economics and Management at the University of Trento, Italy. He holds a PhD in economics and management from the Sant'Anna School of Advanced Studies in Pisa, Italy. His main research interests focus on management accounting, family firms, internationalization, and board composition. He has published many academic papers in international refereed journals, including *Family Business Review*, the *Journal of Management and Governance*, the *Journal of Applied Accounting Research*, and the *Journal of Management Control*. He serves as a reviewer for several peer-reviewed accounting journals.

Angela Coscarelli holds a PhD in demography from the University of Calabria, Italy, where she teaches statistics. Her main interests include data science and multivariate statistical analysis.

Damiana Giuseppina Costanzo is a full professor of statistics at the University of Calabria, Italy, where she teaches statistics and advanced inferential statistics. She holds a PhD in statistics from the Sapienza University of Rome, Italy. Her main interests include data science, multivariate statistical analysis, stochastic processes, and environmental statistical methods. She has published numerous papers in top-tier peer-reviewed academic journals.

Zheng Fang is an associate professor and the deputy director of the Office of Graduate Studies at the Singapore University of Social Sciences. Prior to this, she worked as a research fellow at Nanyang Technological University, Singapore; an associate professor at Southwestern University of Finance and Economics, China; and a consulting analyst at Mercer-HRBS, Singapore. She obtained her PhD in economics from Nanyang Technological University, Singapore, in 2012 and has published more than 20 articles in leading journals, including *Energy Economics, Energy Policy, Economics of Transition, World Economy, Applied Economics, Economic Modelling, Empirical Economics, Social Indicators Research*, the *Journal of Happiness Studies*, the *Asian Economic Journal*, and the *Singapore Economic Review*. She is the associate editor of the *Singapore Economic Review* and a GLO fellow.

Mokshada Foolchand is a former student of the University of Mauritius, holding a degree in accounting and business informatics. She worked as an auditor for Ernst and Young (Mauritius) before joining Vistra as an accounting associate.

Mahnoor Hanif holds a master of business administration (MBA) in finance from PMAS-Arid Agriculture University, Rawalpindi, Pakistan. Her areas of interest are corporate finance, corporate governance, and investment management. She is a referee for the *International Journal of Emerging Markets*, the *Journal of Sustainable Finance and Investment*, and *SAGE Open*.

Murad Harasheh is a senior assistant professor of finance at the University of Bologna, Italy, and a research associate at the Yunus Social Business Center of Bologna, Italy. He was awarded his PhD in 2014 in economics, law, and institutions from the School of Advanced Studies of Pavia (IUSS), Italy. In 2021, he obtained the Italian National Scientific Qualification (ASN) as a second-tier (associate) professor in "Economics of Financial Intermediaries and Corporate Finance." Previously, he collaborated with the Italian Authority for Energy Regulations (ARERA) as an economist and energy markets analyst. His primary research interests are corporate finance, firm valuation, energy and commodity finance, and sustainability economics. He is the author of the book *Global Commodities: Physical, Financial, and Sustainability Aspects* (2021) as well as many publications in international journals in finance, business, and energy.

Syeda Shehtaz Hasib is a strategic partnership development and non-profit management professional working at Friendship, an international social purpose organization widely recognized for its work with Bangladesh's marginalized and climate-vulnerable population. She has strong grassroots knowledge of climate migrants and refugee communities and experience in collaboration and co-development of projects to cater to target communities' needs. She completed her bachelor's in business administration (BBA) degree from the Institute of Business Administration, University of Dhaka, Bangladesh, followed by a master of social science (MSS) degree in economics from the Department of Economics, East West University, Bangladesh.

Mohammad Kabir Hassan is a professor of finance at the Department of Economics and Finance at the University of New Orleans, USA. He currently holds the three endowed chairs: Hibernia Professor of Economics and Finance, Hancock Whitney Chair Professor in Business, and Bank One Professor in Business at the University of New Orleans. Professor Hassan received his PhD in finance from the University of Nebraska-Lincoln, USA. He is a financial economist with consulting, research, and teaching experiences in development finance, money and capital markets, Islamic finance, corporate finance, monetary economics, macroeconomics, and international trade and finance. Professor Hassan is the editor-in-chief of the *International Journal of Islamic and Middle Eastern Finance and Management*, a senior editor of the *International Journal of Emerging Markets*, and an associate editor of the *Review of International Business and Finance*, the *International Review of Economics and Finance*, and the *Pacific-Basin Finance Journal.* He has also edited and published 17 books and over 350 papers published in top refereed academic journals.

Ahmed Imran Hunjra is an associate professor of finance at Rabat Business School, International University of Rabat, Morocco, and Ghazi University, Dera Ghazi Khan, Pakistan. Dr. Ahmed earned an MBA, MS, and PhD (finance) from Iqra University, Pakistan. Furthermore, Ahmed has completed his postdoctoral fellowship at the University of Waikato, New Zealand. Currently, Dr. Ahmed is working on corporate finance, corporate governance, and sustainability. Ahmed has published in top-ranked journals such as *Finance Research Letters*, the *International Review of Financial Analysis, Economic Modeling, Technological Forecasting and Social Change*, the *Journal of Environmental Management*, the *Quarterly Review of Economics and Finance*, and the *International Journal of Emerging Markets.* He is an associate editor for the *Journal of Sustainable Finance and Investment*, the *International Journal of Emerging Markets*, and *Heliyon*, and a regular referee for over 40 journals.

Maria Mazzuca is an associate professor of banking and finance at the University of Calabria, Italy, where she teaches financial system and financial institutions management. Maria graduated *summa cum laude* from the University of Calabria in 1997. Following a PhD in banking and finance, she was enrolled at her *alma mater* first as a research fellow and then as an assistant professor. Her main research interests include securitization, credit risk transfer activity, bank disclosure, corporate social responsibility, cooperative banks, social and impact finance, and non-performing loans. Her research has been published in prestigious journals, such as *Corporate Social Responsibility and Environmental Management, Sustainable Development*, the *European Journal of Finance, Business Ethics: A European Review,* and *Public Money and Management.* She acts as a reviewer for several international journals, and she serves as an editor for *Corporate Social Responsibility and Environmental Management* and *Business Strategy and Development.*

Michael L. Polemis is an associate professor of industrial economics at the Department of Economics and has been a member of the Hellenic Competition Commission since April 2017. He received his PhD in economics from the National and Kapodistrian University of Athens, Greece. Between 2008–2011, he served as a teaching assistant at the Economics Department of the University of Piraeus in Greece. From 2004–2014, he served as a scientific expert-economist and head of the unit at the Hellenic Competition Commission. His main research areas include industrial organization, competition policy and regulation, and energy and environmental economics. Based on IDEAS RePEc's ranking list, in March 2020 he was ranked in the top 10 percent of economists globally and in the top 5 percent of economists in Greece. He has published more than 80 papers in many distinguished scientific journals, some of which are leading in the field, such as the *European Journal of Operational Research, Economics Letters, Regional Studies, International Business Review, The Energy Journal, Energy Economics*, the *Journal of Environmental Management, Empirical Economics,* and *Economic Modelling.* He has written five scientific books and serves as a member of the editorial board of the *European Competition Journal.*

Dineshwar Ramdhony is a senior lecturer at the University of Mauritius. He holds a PhD from the University of Southern Queensland, Australia. Dinesh worked as a sessional lecturer at several Australian institutions, including Monash University, RMIT, Charles Sturt University, Melbourne Polytechnic, and Monash College. He is keen to research topics related to corporate reporting, CSR, corporate governance, and technology management. Dinesh has published in several prestigious journals, such as the *Journal of Accounting in Emerging Economies*, the *Journal of Applied Accounting Research*, and the *International Journal of Bank Marketing.*

Fateh Saci is an associate professor of finance at the University of Nîmes (Chrome EA 7352), France. He earned a PhD in finance from the University of Côte d'Azur, France, in 2013. He taught at the

University of Nice, the University of Toulouse Capitole, the University of Paris 2, the Renmin University of China, and the University of Perpignan and at Institut Paul Bocuse. His research fields are finance, accounting, corporate governance, and strategic alliances. In 2015 and 2017, Dr. Fateh Saci received a professor of excellence award from the Renmin University of China, and was awarded the best paper at the conference Management and Business Academy, at Brunel University, United Kingdom, in December 2015. He has recently published many academic papers in international refereed journals, including *Finance Research Letters, Australian Economic Papers, Research in International Business and Finance, Strategic Change*, the *International Journal of Economics, Finance and Management Sciences*, and the *Journal of Organisational Studies and Innovation*.

Boopen Seetanah is a professor at the University of Mauritius (UoM) with research interests in tourism and transport, international trade and finance, and development economics. He is currently the co-chair of the WTO Chair (UoM) and the director of research at the International Centre for Sustainable Tourism and Hospitality (ICSTH) at the UoM. He is also the director of the UoM Doctoral School. Prof. Boopen is an associate editor of *Tourism Review* (a tier-one journal) and an editorial board member for other tier-one journals, such as the *International Journal of Tourism Research* and the *Journal of Hospitality Marketing and Management*. He has been a consultant for the government and numerous international organizations, including the UNEP, UNECA, UNDP, UNCTAD, the World Bank, ADB, UNIDO, AgriCane, ILO, and RMCE.

Thanasis Stengos joined the Department of Economics at the University of Guelph, Canada, in 1984. He received his BSc and MSc in economics from the London School of Economics, United Kingdom, and his PhD from Queen's University, United Kingdom. He currently serves as editor-in-chief for the *Journal of Risk and Financial Management*, co-editor of the *Review of Economic Analysis*, and an associate editor of the *Journal of Applied Econometrics, Empirical Economics*, and *Economics Letters*. His research has been published in some of the top journals, including the *Review of Economic Studies*, the *European Economic Review*, the *International*

Economic Review, *The Economic Journal*, the *Journal of Monetary Economics*, the *Journal of Econometrics*, *Econometric Theory*, *The Review of Economics and Statistics*, the *Journal of Applied Econometrics*, the *Journal of Business and Economic Statistics*, and the *Journal of Economic Growth*.

Dilvin Taşkın is an associate professor of finance at Yasar University, Turkey. She received her PhD in 2011 at Dokuz Eylul University, Turkey. Her research interests include behavioral finance, energy economics, sustainability, financial intermediaries, and corporate governance. She is a scientific member of various organizations and serves as the manager of the Financial Economics Association, which has around 40,000 members worldwide. She has several publications in national and international journals.

Hai Hong Trinh is a doctoral researcher in sustainable and climate finance at the School of Economics and Finance, Massey University, New Zealand, where his PhD studies focus on the interactions between climate risks and financial markets. Hai is an executive board committee member of the Interdisciplinary Perspectives SIG of the British Accounting and Finance Association (BAFA). Also, he has been a regular organizing member of FMA International. His research papers have been published in several top-tier journals, such as *Energy Economics*, *Pacific-Basin Finance Journal*, *Applied Economics*, and *Business Strategy and the Environment* (BSE). His scientific engagement and memberships come across the world's leading associations, such as the BAFA, the American Finance Association (AFA), the British Academy of Management (BAM), the European Association of Environmental and Resource Economists (EAERE), and the Economic Research Forum (ERF). Hai is a member of AVSE Global, where he is also part of the economic advisory board, contributing to economic policies for Ho Chi Minh City, Vietnam, in financial centers, financial development, and the economy.

Diem Thi Hong Vo is a lecturer in economics at the Department of Economics and Finance, School of Business and Management, RMIT Vietnam. Before joining RMIT Vietnam, she worked as a lecturer in econometrics and economics at the University of Waikato, New Zealand, and for over three years as a teaching and research assistant at the University of Canterbury, New Zealand. Diem obtained her PhD in economics at the University of Canterbury, New Zealand. Her research interests include gender equality, public policy, energy economy, applied microeconomics, and blockchain economy. Her research papers have been published in several journals, such as *Energy Economics, Review of Development Economics, Global Economic Review*, and the *Singapore Economic Review*.

Eric Yan is a postdoctoral fellow at the Department of Economics at Feng Chia University, Tainan, Taiwan. Eric has published in *Energy Economics, Economics Letters, Economic Modelling, Applied Economics*, and the *Annals of Tourism Research*. Eric is an applied economist, with a research focus on environment and energy economics, political economy, economic growth, and health economics.

Yinghui Yu is an associate professor and the head of the master of finance program and the graduate diploma in financial technology program at the Singapore University of Social Sciences (SUSS). She obtained her PhD in finance from the University of Hong Kong in 2006, and before joining SUSS, she was a derivatives trader with a global investment bank for eight years. Her research interests include asset pricing, alternative investments, risk management, financial technologies, and innovations. Her research has been published in journals such as the *Journal of Finance*.

Qasim Zureigat is a professor of finance at the School of Business, Sulaiman Al Rajhi University, Saudi Arabia. His research interests include accounting, auditing, financial accounting, financial reporting, management accounting, corporate governance, and corporate social responsibility. Qasim has published papers in the *Journal of Sustainable Finance and Investment*, the *International Journal of Emerging Markets*, and the *Journal of Risk and Financial Management*, among others.

https://doi.org/10.1142/9781800614482_fmatter

Contents

Part I

Climate Change and Green Finance in Emerging Markets

https://doi.org/10.1142/9781800614482_0001

Chapter 1

The Impact of Globalization and Financial Development on Climate Change: Fresh Evidence from 60 Developing Countries

Michael L. Polemis[†,‡,§,||] **and Thanasis Stengos**[*,¶,**]

[†]*University of Piraeus, Department of Economics, Piraeus, Greece*
[‡]*Hellenic Competition Commission, Athens, Greece*
[§]*Hellenic Open University, Patras, Greece*
[¶]*Guelph University, Ontario, Canada*
[||]*mpolemis@unipi.gr*
[**]*tstengos@uoguelph.ca*

Abstract

The scope of this chapter is to investigate the causal effects of globalization and financial development on environmental degradation, proxied by the level of carbon dioxide emissions for 60 developing countries over the period 1970–2014. The econometric methodology accounts for the presence of cross-sectional dependence, while it employs proper cross-sectional augmented panel unit root tests to ascertain unit root properties and cointegration relationships. To secure the robustness of our findings, we employ both parametric and semi-parametric techniques. The empirical findings postulate, for the first time in the empirical literature, a non-monotonic inverted-U-shaped curve between globalization and environmental degradation, similar to the environmental Kuznets curve (EKC) hypothesis. This empirical analysis suggests insightful

[*]Corresponding author.

policy implications for managers and policymakers, as the reduction in CO_2 emissions can be achieved without a slowdown in economic activity and financial development.

1. Introduction

Over the past decade, with the gradual in-depth discussion of global climate change issues, more and more countries have begun to realize that carbon emissions caused by excessively fast globalization have jeopardized their sustainable development in the future. Countries' economic growth and prosperity depend on the efficient use of energy consumption, and a large amount of fossil energy consumption has also aggravated anthropogenic greenhouse gas emissions, which runs counter to global climate change. To fine-tune their financial and economic goals with the greenhouse gas emissions reduction targets set by legally binding international agreements (such as the Paris Agreement and the Kyoto Protocol), countries have taken the development of clean energy and renewable energy as national strategic goals, considering the extensive globalization process. As a result, energy transition to clean energy forms (renewables, hydropower, geothermal energy, natural gas, hydrogen, etc.) has become a key strategy for countries to deal with climate change and sustainable green development in the future.

The financial sector, on the other hand, has made significant contributions in terms of economic growth, education, and health, but it can also promote the process of the energy transition to a certain extent. With the popularization of internet mobile payments and the improvement of income levels, financial development can effectively improve the efficiency of energy allocation, expand the capital acquisition and investment of renewable-energy-related firms and individuals, and accelerate the energy transition. Therefore, it is crucial to apply novel research methods to shed light on the financial development and green energy nexus in light of the imminent globalization process.

Most of the ongoing research investigates the impact of globalization on the environment by considering CO_2 emissions as a measurement of environmental degradation over the years, while a limited number of studies investigate the effect of globalization on NO_x (nitrogen oxides) and SO_x (sulfur oxides) emissions as indicators of environmental quality.

Specifically, several studies argue that globalization may enhance environmental quality through trade liberalization, as globalization enables emerging economies to gain access to eco-friendly technologies, leading to a reduction of greenhouse gas emissions (see Werner *et al.*, 2001). On the contrary, it is argued that globalization amplifies economic activities, which in turn leads to environmental degradation. This statement can be explained by the fact that emissions increase as the economy evolves from the agricultural to the industrial era and then decrease as there is a shift from the industrial to a technology-intensive phase (see Liddle, 2001).

Overall, globalization is classified into three main dimensions: economic, social, and political globalization. Numerous studies have investigated the impact of each category on the environment. Regarding economic globalization, research has shown that it is negatively correlated with emissions; therefore, it is assumed that this category improves environmental performance (Tisdell, 2001). On the contrary, concerning social globalization, it is found that it increases carbon emissions and threatens environmental quality due to human activities, such as tourism and transportation (see, for example, Shahbaz *et al.*, 2018). Moreover, political globalization has a positive upward correlation with emissions. This fact is also confirmed by Shahbaz *et al.* (2018), who investigated the relationship between overall globalization and CO_2 emissions in G7 countries (Canada, France, Germany, Italy, Japan, the United Kingdom, and the United States), taking into consideration annual data from 1980 until 2014 and applying the generalized method of moments (GMM).

The empirical literature focusing on the impact of financial development on environmental degradation does not provide a clear consensus among researchers and academicians on the magnitude of this nexus. This is so because researchers acknowledge that financial development generates positive as well as negative effects on environmental pollution (He & Wand, 2012; Omri *et al.*, 2015). The effects of financial development on environmental degradation can be broken down into three different elements, accounting for the scale, technique, and composition effect (see, among others, Grossman and Krueger, 1995).

In a closely related study, Halkos and Polemis (2017) argue that local and global pollutants redefine the validity of the environmental Kuznets curve (EKC) hypothesis when financial development indicators enter the model.[1] This study uses an unbalanced panel dataset covering the OECD countries over the period 1970–2014. By relying on parametric panel data techniques (i.e., OLS fixed effects, dynamic GMM, and MLE), this study finds non-monotonic relationships between financial development and environmental degradation. Specifically, an N-shaped relationship is observed for both global and local pollutants, while in the dynamic framework, a monotonic relation is present in the case of NO_x, rejecting the validity of the EKC hypothesis. The adjustment coefficients are estimated at very low levels of 0.28–0.7. Moreover, the effect of financial development on pollution using a constructed financial index as proxy results in a positive sign and a magnitude equal to 0.021.

Thus, the current study has several novelties contributing to the existing literature. First, compared to the existing empirical studies, it uses non-parametric techniques to reveal possible non-monotonic relationships between globalization, financial development, and environmental degradation. Consequently, this work employs flexible (semi-parametric) techniques that do not rely on specific functional forms. Second, it employs second-generation panel unit root testing that accounts for the presence of cross-sectional dependence to examine the order of integration between the main variables of the model. Third, panel-cointegration tests are also employed to account for the slope heterogeneity and dependence in the cross-sectional units to ascertain the long-term relationship between globalization, financial development, and carbon dioxide emissions. Finally, important policy implications are also discussed.

The empirical findings unravel a non-monotonic inverted-U-shaped curve between globalization and environmental degradation, similar to the EKC hypothesis. This empirical analysis suggests insightful policy implications for managers and policymakers, as the reduction in CO_2 emissions can be achieved without a slowdown in economic activity and financial development.

The rest of this chapter is structured as follows. Section 2 briefly reviews the existing empirical literature, while Section 3 describes

[1]The EKC hypothesis implies a concave curve between environmental degradation and economic growth (Grossman & Krueger, 1995).

the data and the sample selection. Section 4 presents the research design and the necessary preliminary testing (stationarity and cointegration tests) performed to secure the validity of the econometric results. Section 5 discusses the parametric and non-parametric empirical findings of the study, while Section 6 concludes the chapter, encapsulating the main findings while offering some useful policy implications.

2. Literature Review

Several studies attempted to dissect the relationship between CO_2 emissions and globalization through the employment of several models (see Table 1). Dinda (2006) conducted panel data analysis by using fixed effects (FE) and random effects (RE), considering annual data from 54 countries for the period 1965–1990, to investigate how economic globalization affects the "pollution level, pollution intensity and relative change of pollution." To examine this relationship, they use CO_2 emissions, which are the dominant GHG emissions, as the measurement criterion, and the data panel technique was applied to three categories of countries (developed, developing, and the world as a whole). The findings revealed that in the case of developed countries, globalization contributed to the reduction of CO_2 emissions, while in developing countries, a sharp increase in emissions has been observed.

Furthermore, Abdallh and Abugamos (2017) used a DOLS model in conjunction with panel data and semi-parametric panel fixed effects regression to examine the impact of globalization and urbanization on CO_2 emissions for 20 countries in the MENA region during the period 1980–2014. They reached two main conclusions: that an inverted-U-shaped relationship is detectable and that both economic growth and energy usage constitute the largest contributors to carbon emissions.

The relationship is also proven by the findings of the study conducted by Kalayci and Hayaloğlu (2019). They examined the effect of economic globalization in conjunction with trade openness on CO_2 emissions in NAFTA countries for the period 1990–2015 by adopting panel data analysis and the Durbin Watson effect to carry out an

Table 1. Summary of related studies.

Study	Countries	Period	Method	Effect on the environment
Shahbaz *et al.* (2018)	G7	1980–2014	GMM	Negative
Dinda (2006)	54 countries	1965–1990	OLS-FE OLS-RE	Negative for developing countries; positive for developed
Abdallh & Abugamos (2017)	MENA	1980–2014	OLS-FE	Negative
Kalayci & Hayaloğlu (2019)	NAFTA	1990–2015	Pooled OLS	Negative
Managi (2004)	63 countries	1960–1999	Pooled OLS	Negative
Baek *et al.* (2009)	50 countries	1960–2000	VAR	Negative for developing countries; positive for developed countries
Shahbaz *et al.* (2017a)	25 developed countries	1970–2014	CIPS	Negative
Bu *et al.* (2016)	166 countries	1990–2009	OLS-FE 2SLS	Negative for non-OECD countries; positive for OECD countries
You & Lv (2018)	83 countries	1985–2013	Spatial panel model	Positive
Bernard & Mandal (2016)	60 countries	2002–2012	GMM	Positive
Shahbaz *et al.* (2013)	Turkey	1979–2010	VECM	Negative
Ahad & Khan (2016)	Bangladesh	1972–2015	ARDL	Negative
Shahbaz *et al.* (2018)	Japan	1970–2014	NARDL	Negative
Solarin *et al.* (2017)	Malaysia	1970–2014	ARDL FMOLS	Negative
Leitão *et al.* (2014)	Portugal	1970–2010	VECM GMM	Positive
Khan & Khan (2018)	USA	1990–2014	2SLS FE RE	Negative
Shahbaz *et al.* (2016)	Australia	1970–2012	ARDL VECM	Positive

autocorrelation analysis. During panel data analysis, two models were developed in which the CO_2 emissions were the dependent variable, and the economic globalization, international trade, GDP, and energy consumption per person were used as independent variables. The results indicated that there is a strong correlation between the two economic variables. At this point, it is necessary to mention that several studies employ trade openness as an indicator to measure globalization. According to the pollution haven hypothesis proposed by Copeland and Taylor (2003), trade liberalization can be beneficial to environmental quality through the implementation of robust environmental policies. Managi (2004) focused on the impact of trade openness on emissions through the application of panel data in 63 countries, both developed and developing, for the period 1960–1999. The study argues that trade openness creates impediments to environmental quality.

However, Baek *et al.* (2009) proposed a VAR model for the examination of the effect of trade liberalization on the environmental quality for 50 developed and developing countries over the period 1960–2000. The empirical results suggest that globalization ameliorates the environmental conditions in developed countries by lowering SO_2 emissions, while many emerging economies are negatively affected, a fact that supports the pollution haven hypothesis. In addition to all the above, their research also proved that there is a unidirectional causality running from trade liberalization to SO_2 emissions concerning developed countries. While for developing economies, the causal relationship runs from SO_2 emissions to trade liberalization, resulting in a change in the latter.

Shahbaz *et al.* (2017a) investigated the spillover effects between globalization and CO_2 emissions in 25 developed countries over 44 years (1970–2014) by employing both time series and panel data analysis. They used several tests (CIPS) to check cross-sectional dependence in the panel, while they conducted several cointegration tests to determine the relationship between emissions and globalization. They concluded that globalization increases emissions for the majority of the countries under study. Finally, and most importantly, they implemented Granger causality panel estimates, and the findings showed that globalization and environmental change are strictly related.

The impact of globalization on the environment has also been examined in the study by Bu *et al.* (2016). The study was mainly based on FE and two-stage least squares (2SLS) models, which were applied to a panel data of 166 countries for the period 1990–2009. The empirical results revealed that there is a negative relationship between globalization and emissions for the OECD countries, while there is a positive association between the two for the non-OECD countries. On the contrary, You and Lv (2018) performed spatial panel data analysis on 83 countries for the period 1985–2013 to point out the association between globalization and emissions. The results showed that there is an indirect correlation between the two aforementioned variables, indicating that globalization lowers CO_2 emissions. These findings are in line with the results derived from the research conducted by Bernard and Mandal (2016). They applied dynamic panel data and specifically GMM to a group of 60 countries, incorporating both developed and emerging economies, from 2002 until 2012, considering the Environmental Performance Index (EPI) and CO_2 emissions as indicators for environmental performance. They concluded that political globalization reduces CO_2 emissions and improves EPI.

Except at the international level, it should be stressed that numerous studies have been focused on the implications of globalization on the environment at a national level. Shahbaz *et al.* (2013) explored the association between the above-mentioned variables, concentrating on the Turkish economy using data over the period 1979–2010, through the employment of the unit root test and cointegration approach, and the direction causality was tested by the VECM Granger causality approach. The findings imply that globalization increases emissions. According to Ahad and Khan (2016), globalization, together with economic growth, energy consumption, and other variables, has negative effects on the environment. More precisely, they applied the ARDL bound test in conjunction with Bayer–Hanck combined cointegration to investigate the long-term association between the variables and CO_2 emissions for Bangladesh from 1972 until 2015. The findings imply that globalization is detrimental to environmental performance in Bangladesh both in the short and long runs. The above-mentioned results are also confirmed by Shahbaz *et al.* (2018) through the employment of a threshold NARDL (TNARDL) cointegration model by considering the case of Japan for the period 1970–2014. They concluded that globalization aggravates environmental degradation. Solarin *et al.* (2017) applied the ARDL and FMOLS models based on data from Malaysia for the period 1970–2014 to assess the effect of globalization on the environment, and they concluded that globalization plays a pivotal role in CO_2 emissions. The research concluded by proposing to change the country's energy sector through the adoption of renewable energy resources.

Leitão *et al.* (2014) explored the effects of globalization on the Portuguese economy through the application of time series for the period 1970–2010. More specifically, the VECM and GMM methods were used, and the findings revealed that globalization lowers carbon emissions, demonstrating that the former is negatively correlated with the latter. On the other hand, Khan and Khan (2018) employed four different approaches to investigate the relationship between economic and environmental performance. More precisely, they employed 2SLS, FE, RE, and pooled OLS to annual panel data from 1990 to 2014 for the US, and the results indicated that globalization has a detrimental impact on environmental quality.

Lastly, Shahbaz *et al.* (2016) focused their research on emissions in Australia for the period 1970–2012. The methodology involved panel data techniques. Specifically, they applied ARDL combined with VECM. The empirical findings support the hypothesis that globalization negatively affects the level of CO_2 emissions, especially in the long run.

3. Data and Sample Selection

We use a yearly balanced panel dataset of 60 developing countries ($N = 60$) over the period 1970–2014 ($T = 45$), yielding 2,700 observations. The reason we restrict our sample to this period is strictly dictated by severe data discrepancies in most of the sample variables. Table 2 presents the summary statistics of the sample variables.

4. Research Design and Preliminary Testing

This section discusses the estimation strategy and methodology applied to empirically estimate the relationship between globalization and environmental degradation. Specifically, we first perform the

Table 2. Summary statistics.

Variables	Obs	Mean	Standard deviation	Min	Max
GI	2,700	45.53	12.60	14.29	80.78
GI^2	2,700	2,231	1,193	204.3	6,525
TrGI	2,700	38.61	14.17	11.15	83.09
FiGI	2,700	45.61	14.70	7.016	81.99
SoGI	2,700	37.47	15.99	8.129	81.11
IpGI	2,700	36.42	15.99	6.406	81.51
InGI	2,700	40.53	18.50	6.353	93.17
PoGI	2,700	56.81	17.44	13.32	92.82
TrGI2	2,700	1,691	1,227	124.3	6,903
log(CO2)	2,700	−0.359	1.501	−4.536	2.967
log(GDP)	2,700	7.568	1.143	5.335	10.58
log(TRADE)	2,700	4.003	0.550	1.593	5.617
log(POP)	2,700	3.657	1.309	0.102	6.255
log(CREDIT)	2,745	4.895	0.222	3.040	6.061

necessary unit root testing to check for the order of integration of our sample variables, and then, we proceed with the panel cointegration testing to uncover possible structural relationships and secure the validity of our findings.

4.1. *Estimation strategy and empirical methodology*

The modeling approach considers the following generic parametric specification:

$$\log(\mathrm{CO}_{2it}) = \mathrm{Constant} + GI\alpha_{it} + GI^2\beta_{it} + Z'_{it}\gamma_{it} + \delta_i + v_t + e_{it} \quad (1)$$

where CO_{2it} stands for the carbon dioxide emissions of country i at time t, expressed in metric tonnes per capita. The relevant variable includes those emissions stemming from the burning of fossil fuels and the manufacture of cement. They include CO_2 produced during the consumption of solid, liquid, and gaseous fuels and gas flaring. GI_{it} denotes the globalization index of country i at time t, which was originally developed by Dreher (2006) and derived from the KOF Swiss Economic Institute (Gygli *et al.*, 2019). The globalization index is constructed as an overall globalization index from three sub-indices:

economic globalization, social globalization, and political globalization. The index is generated with weights of 36, 38, and 26 percent for the economic, social, and political indices, respectively.[2]

The relevant index covers all aspects of globalization (economic, social, and political) and is widely used in the existing literature (see, for example, Shahbaz *et al.*, 2017b). Z'_{is} is the column vector of time-varying explanatory variables, including GDP per capita (GDP_{it}) in constant 2010 USD; trade openness (TRADE_{it}), measured by the logged sum of imports and exports over GDP; domestic credit (CREDIT_{it}), provided by the financial sector as a percentage of GDP to account for the effect of financial development on CO_2 emissions; and population density (POP_{it}). All the variables are expressed in natural logarithms. Population density is the midyear population divided by land area measured in square kilometers.[3] Domestic credit provided by the financial sector includes all credit to various sectors on a gross basis, except for credit to the central government, which is net.[4]

The sample variables, except for the globalization index (GI), are drawn from the World Bank (World Development Indicators). Finally, the model accounts for country and year fixed effects (δ_i, v_t) to allow for time-invariant unobserved heterogeneity, and finally, e_{it} is the i.i.d. error term.

We also use Baltagi and Li's (2002) flexible semi-parametric fixed-effects estimator. This approach considers a linear fixed-effects model, allowing for a non-parametric specification for one particular

---

[2]The data are extracted from the following website: http://globalization.kof.ethz.ch/.

[3]Population counts all residents regardless of legal status or citizenship, except for refugees not permanently settled in the country of asylum, who are generally considered part of the population of their country of origin. Land area is a country's total area, excluding area under inland water bodies, national claims to the continental shelf, and exclusive economic zones.

[4]The financial sector includes monetary authorities and deposit money banks, as well as other financial corporations where data are available (including corporations that do not accept transferable deposits but do incur such liabilities as time and savings deposits). Examples of other financial corporations are finance and leasing companies, money lenders, insurance corporations, pension funds, and foreign exchange companies.

regressor (e.g., globalization).[5] In this way, our model avoids any predetermined assumption regarding the functional form (e.g., "inverted U" or "N shape") of the environment–globalization nexus, while it allows the data to guide the empirical research.

Let the model be given by the following equation:

$$y_{it} = a_i + x^T \beta_{it} + w\gamma_{it} + f(z_{it}) + \varepsilon_{it} \tag{2}$$

where $f(\gamma)$ is an unknown function of zz_{iiii} (globalization), entering the model in a non-parametric way. yy_{iiii} is the dependent variable, namely the CO_2 emissions. xx_{iiii} is the vector of exogenous linear regressors, including the control variables described above, while the w-vector includes the year dummy variables, and $\varepsilon\varepsilon_{iiii}$ are zero-mean i.i.d. innovations. Moreover, we assume that the error term is uncorrelated with the unknown function $f(\gamma)$.

Following Baltagi and Li (2002), we approximate $f(z_{it})$ by series differences $p^K(z_{it})$, where the latter is the first k terms of a sequence of functions $[pp_1(zz), pp_2(zz), \ldots]$.

By taking the first differences to remove fixed effects, we end up with the following equation:

$$\Delta(y_i) = \Delta(x_i^T)\beta + \Delta(w_i)\gamma + \Delta\{p^k(z_i)\}\delta + \Delta(\varepsilon_i) \tag{3}$$

In the next step, we use the fitted fixed effects $\hat{a}_i$ to estimate the error component residual of Equation (3). Thus, we have

$$\hat{u}_{it} = y_{it} - x^T \hat{\beta}_{it} - w_i\hat{\gamma}_{it} - \hat{a}_i = f(z_{it}) + \varepsilon_{it} \tag{4}$$

The non-parametric part (fz_{it}) is approximated by a spline interpolation, which yields similar results to the classical Epanechnikov-kernel-weighted local polynomial fit but is recommended to approximate complex nonlinear shapes and does not suffer from Runge's phenomenon (Li & Racine, 2006; Newson, 2000).

Lastly, it is important to use both time and individual (country) fixed effects in our analysis to mitigate biases that stem from two potential sources (see also Kasioumi and Stengos, 2020). Our analysis controls for some unobserved factors which differ over time but are constant over space (e.g., countries), such as different globalization levels (time effects), as well as for factors that vary across countries but are constant over time (individual effects).

[5] We used the "*xtsemipar*" command in STATA ver. 15 developed by Libois and Verardi (2013).

4.2. Stationarity and cointegration testing

Before applying unit root tests, we need to check for the applicability of the first- or second-generation unit root tests. Specifically, one of the additional complications that arise when dealing with panel data compared to the pure time-series case is the possibility that the variables or random disturbances are correlated across the panel dimension. The early literature on unit root and cointegration tests adopted the assumption of cross-sectional independence (Pesaran, 2015).

In this pursuit, we must check the possibility of cross-sectional dependence in the data. This is straightforward since the implementation of second-generation panel unit root tests is desirable only when it has been established that the panel is subject to a significant degree of residual cross-section dependence (Apergis, 2018). In doing so, we have applied Chudik and Pesaran's (2015) weak cross-sectional dependence test. The null hypothesis reveals that cross-sections of the panel data are weakly dependent on each other. The empirical results of the Chudik and Pesaran (2015) cross-section test are reported in Table 3.

We find that cross-sectional dependence is significantly present between the variables in the model. As is evident from Table 2, the

Table 3. Cross-section dependence tests.

	Pesaran (2004)		**Chudik & Pesaran (2015)**		
Variables	**Test statistic**	***p*-value**	**Variables**	**Test statistic**	***p*-value**
$\log(CO_2)$	69.38***	0.000	$\log(CO_2)$	17.660***	0.000
GI	264.01***	0.000	GI	280.831***	0.000
GI^2	263.68***	0.000	GI^2	277.664***	0.000
log(GDP)	97.33***	0.000	log(GDP)	281.893***	0.000
log(TRADE)	64.55***	0.000	log(TRADE)	280.875***	0.000
log(CREDIT)	41.01***	0.000	log(CREDIT)	282.015***	0.000
log(POP)	270.89***	0.000	log(POP)	280.697***	0.000

Notes: Under the null hypothesis of cross-sectional independence, the Pesaran test (also known as "CD test") follows a two-tailed standard normal distribution. The Chudik and Pesaran (2015) test checks the residuals for weak cross-sectional dependence in a panel data model. Under the null hypothesis, the residuals are weakly cross-sectional dependent. ***1 percent level of statistical significance.

relevant test strongly rejects the null hypothesis of cross-section independence (p-value = 0.000). In light of this evidence, we proceed to test for unit roots using tests that are robust to cross-section dependence (i.e., second-generation tests for unit roots in panel data). The presence of cross-sectional dependence leads us to apply the second-generation unit root tests to test the stationarity properties of the variables.

To check the order of integration of the variables, we have applied the cross-sectional Im–Pesaran–Shin (CIPS) and cross-sectionally augmented Dickey–Fuller (CADF) unit root tests developed by Pesaran (2007). These tests are second-generation unit root tests assuming cross-sectional dependence in a panel dataset. The CIPS test is an extension of Im–Pesaran–Shin (IPS) (2003), with a single factor containing heterogeneous loading across the cross-sections. It is a cross-sectionally augmented IPS Dickey–Fuller-type test, considering the cross-sectional means of the level and lagged differences to IPS-type regression. In this case, the null hypothesis of homogeneous non-stationarity is tested against the hypothesis of heterogeneous alternatives. On the other hand, the PESCADF test is based on the mean of the augmented Dickey–Fuller (ADF) t-statistic of every panel member. The null hypothesis is that all of the variables in the panel are non-stationary, against the alternative hypothesis that only a section of the series is stationary.

The empirical results of the CIPS and PESCADF tests are reported in Table 4. We find that all the variables contain unit roots at the level in the presence of cross-sectional dependence. After the first difference, all the variables are stationary. This reveals that all the variables are integrated into order one (I-1).

After confirming the integrating order of the variables, we employ Westerlund's (2007) cointegration test. This test is applicable in the presence of cross-sectional dependence in the panel data. The empirical results of the panel cointegration test are reported in Table 5. We find that the null hypothesis of no cointegration is rejected at the 1 percent level of significance. This indicates the presence of cointegration between the sample variables.

However, the unobserved nonlinearity is not considered by Westerlund and Edgerton's (2007) cointegration test, which is covered by the continuously updated FMOLS test developed by Bai *et al.* (2009). This test is an extension of the two-stage fully modified estimator

Table 4. Second-generation panel unit root tests.

	CIPS test		**CIPS*test**		**PESCADF test**	
Variables	**Level**	**First difference**	**Level**	**First difference**	**Level**	**First difference**
$\log(CO_2)$	−1.356	−5.744***	−0.851	−5.536***	−2.063 [0.991]	−3.609*** [0.000]
GI	−1.789	−5.855***	−1.399	−5.716***	−2.286 [0.652]	−3.989*** [0.000]
GI^2	−1.024	−5.805***	−1.313	−5.680***	−2.292 [0.630]	−3.924*** [0.000]
log(GDP)	−1.312	−5.118***	−1.274	−4.690***	−2.239 [0.789]	−3.556*** [0.000]
log(TRADE)	−1.186	−5.953***	−1.898***	−5.813***	−1.653 [0.999]	−3.867*** [0.000]
log(CREDIT)	−1.098	−5.609***	−1.584**	−5.461***	−1.749 [0.999]	−3.527*** [0.000]
log(POP)	−1.124	−2.13**	−1.275	−1.947***	−1.950 [0.999]	−2.723*** [0.000]

Notes: CIPS estimates the cross-sectional Im, Pesaran, and Shin (2003) test for unit roots in heterogeneous panels developed by Pesaran (2007). Rejection of the null hypothesis indicates homogenous stationarity at least for one country. CIPS* denotes the truncated CIPS test. PESCADF performs the t-test for unit roots in heterogeneous panels with cross-sectional dependence, proposed by Pesaran (2003). The null hypothesis assumes that all series are non-stationary at least for one country. Both a constant and a time trend are included in the PESCADF test. The lag order for both tests is set at $L = 6$. The numbers in brackets denote p-values. **5 percent level of statistical significance, ***1 percent level of statistical significance.

proposed by Bai and Kao (2006) for the case of non-stationarity of the unobserved common components and in the presence of cross-member cointegration.

The empirical results of the continuously updated FMOLS cointegration approach are reported in Table 6. To test the robustness of the cointegration results, least-square dummy variable (LSDV) and Bai and Ng's (2006) two-step fully modified estimators are also presented (CUP-FM and CUP-BS). The empirical results confirm the existence of cointegration between the variables. This implies that long-term equilibrium is present between the variables for the period 1970–2014 in the 60 sample developing countries.

Table 5. Westerlund panel cointegration tests.

	Statistic			
Equation	G_τ	G_α	P_τ	P_α
$\log(CO_2) = f(GI)$	-2.672^{***}	-15.089^{***}	-20.473^{***}	-12.881^{***}
	(0.001)	(0.000)	(0.000)	(0.000)
$\log(CO_2) = f(GI^2)$	-2.719^{***}	-15.564^{***}	-21.112^{***}	-13.519^{***}
	(0.000)	(0.000)	(0.000)	(0.000)
$\log(CO_2) = f(\log(GDP))$	-3.022^{***}	-17.236^{***}	-21.640^{***}	-13.876^{***}
	(0.000)	(0.000)	(0.000)	(0.000)
$\log(CO_2) = f(\log(TRADE))$	-2.787^{***}	-15.560^{***}	-21.225^{***}	-13.513^{***}
	(0.000)	(0.000)	(0.000)	(0.000)
$\log(CO_2) = f(\log(CREDIT))$	-2.566^{**}	-14.553^{***}	-20.111^{***}	-12.596^{***}
	(0.022)	(0.001)	(0.000)	(0.000)
$\log(CO_2) = f(\log(POP))$	-3.294^{***}	-4.543	-22.772^{***}	-8.246
	(0.000)	(0.999)	(0.000)	(0.820)

Notes: The optimal lag/lead length is determined by the Akaike information criterion (AIC), with a maximum lag/lead length of 6. The width of the Bartlett kernel window is set to 3. Bootstrapped p-values were based on 500 replications. The null hypothesis assumes that there is no cointegration. p-values are reported in parentheses, and bootstrapped p-values (allowing for cross-sectional dependence) are reported in square brackets. **5 percent level of statistical significance, ***1 percent level of statistical significance.

5. Results and Discussion

5.1. *Parametric results*

Table 7 reports the main results of interest using a battery of parametric techniques, including the dynamic generalized method of moments (GMM) developed by Arrelano and Bover (1995). This parametric technique makes use of the GMM method to avoid the case of endogeneity, as we expect the level of environmental degradation expressed by the CO_2 emissions to affect globalization, leading to a reverse causality bias.

As is evident from the relevant table, the estimates are statistically significant and robust.[6] The OLS fixed-effect model in

[6]We have also estimated the relevant models using time dummies to control for seasonal effects. The estimation results are qualitatively similar in all cases and are available upon request.

Table 6. Continuously updated FMOLS analysis.

Variables	LSDV	Bai-FM	CUP-FM	CUP-BC
$\log(CO_2)$	0.02535[a]	0.02389[a]	0.03430[a]	0.01927[a]
	[4.59887]	[8.03192]	[10.23470]	[6.61517]
GI	0.02368[a]	0.01853[a]	0.01631[a]	−0.00637[b]
	[4.14913]	[6.26917]	[4.88146]	[−2.18529]
GI^2	0.02049[a]	0.02324[a]	0.02638[a]	0.00015
	[3.69964]	[8.70966]	[8.51821]	[0.05613]
log(GDP)	0.01860[a]	0.02785[a]	0.02249[a]	0.00631[b]
	[3.60327]	[11.13760]	[7.80769]	[2.58273]
log(TRADE)	0.02311[a]	0.01761[a]	0.00652[b]	0.00301[c]
	[4.96995]	[8.10824]	[2.51107]	[1.33172]
log(CREDIT)	0.02276[a]	0.01640[a]	0.00351[c]	−0.00321[c]
	[4.67752]	[7.37628]	[1.29633]	[−1.37990]
log(POP)	0.02320[a]	0.02303[a]	−0.00004	−0.01207[a]
	[4.51471]	[10.21955]	[−0.01480]	[−4.92452]

Notes: [a]Significant value at 1 percent; [b]Significant value at 5 percent; [c]Significant value at 10 percent, and t statistics are within brackets.

Column 1 reveals that state aid is negatively and statistically significantly correlated with economic growth (−0.00667). Moreover, we obtain nonlinear effects since the estimated negative quadratic term is statistically significant at the 10 percent level of significance (see Column 2), indicating an inverted-U-shaped relationship between globalization and environmental degradation. As is also evident, financial development is positively correlated with the level of CO_2 emissions, though this relationship is not statistically significant.

Columns 3 and 4 present the dynamic GMM panel data estimators, where the (lagged) linear and quadratic terms of globalization are treated as endogenous variables instrumented by their lags, while the rest of the variables are assumed to be predetermined.[7] The point estimates of the GI coefficient are smaller than the ones obtained by OLS, ranging within a close interval (0.00737–0.0494). The empirical

[7]The results drawn from the two-step dynamic GMM estimator are similar to the ones presented in Table 7 and are therefore available from the authors on request.

Table 7. Parametric results.

Variables	(1) OLS-fixed effects model	(2) OLS-nonlinear model	(3) Difference-GMM	(4) Difference-GMM-nonlinear model
$\log(CO_{2it-1})$	—	—	0.252***	0.271***
			(0.0235)	(0.0238)
GI_{it}	0.0121***	0.0186***	0.00737**	0.0494***
	(0.00223)	(0.00467)	(0.00317)	(0.00466)
GI^2_{it}	—	−0.00006*	—	−0.000416***
		(0.00004)		(3.35e-05)
$\log(GDP_{it})$	0.803***	0.807***	0.196***	0.167***
	(0.0264)	(0.0265)	(0.0602)	(0.0608)
log(TRADE)	0.00851	0.00375	0.0868***	−0.00495
	(0.0248)	(0.0250)	(0.0273)	(0.0285)
$\log(CREDIT_{it})$	0.0180	0.0135	0.275***	0.351***
	(0.0423)	(0.0424)	(0.0663)	(0.0672)
$\log(POP_{it})$	0.447***	0.416***	0.134*	−0.393***
	(0.0599)	(0.0628)	(0.0687)	(0.0812)
Constant	−8.592***	−8.627***	−4.232***	−2.833***
	(0.369)	(0.369)	(0.724)	(0.739)
Country FE	Yes	Yes	Yes	Yes
Year FE	Yes	Yes	Yes	Yes
Observations	2,700	2,700	2,640	2,640
R-squared	0.530	0.530	—	—
AR(1) p-value	—	—	0.000***	0.000***
AR(2) p-value	—	—	0.210	0.220
Sargan-Hansen test	—	—	81.22	98.53

Notes: p-values in brackets. Standard errors clustered at the country level are in parentheses. $^{***}p < 0.01$, $^{**}p < 0.05$, $^{*}p < 0.1$.

results also suggest the presence of nonlinear (quadratic) effects (concave curve). The rest of the covariates, when significant, are properly signed. Specifically, economic growth is positively correlated with environmental degradation, while trade openness and financial development seem to increase the level of carbon dioxide emissions.

Tests reported at the bottom of the table show that the instruments are exogenously alleviating the concern of possible severe bias due to the presence of weak instruments. Furthermore, the Sargan–Hansen tests confirm the validity of the overidentifying restrictions, while based on the AR(2) testing, the GMM models do not suffer from serial correlation since we cannot reject the null hypothesis.

5.2. *Non-parametric results*

Figure 1 portrays the graphical representation of the relationship between climate change as expressed by the logged CO_2 emissions and globalization as proxied by the competent index. In this figure, we add a locally weighted regression line, represented by the curve, to provide a first analysis of the visualization of the relationship between globalization and environmental pollution proxied by the level of CO_2 emissions. Specifically, the estimated regression line is used to predict the smoothed value of the independent variable (GI) for each value of environmental degradation only (the dependent variable).

As it is evident from the relevant figure, the relationship between climate change and globalization appears to be non-monotonic. A careful look at the curvature reveals an almost inverted-U-shaped curve.

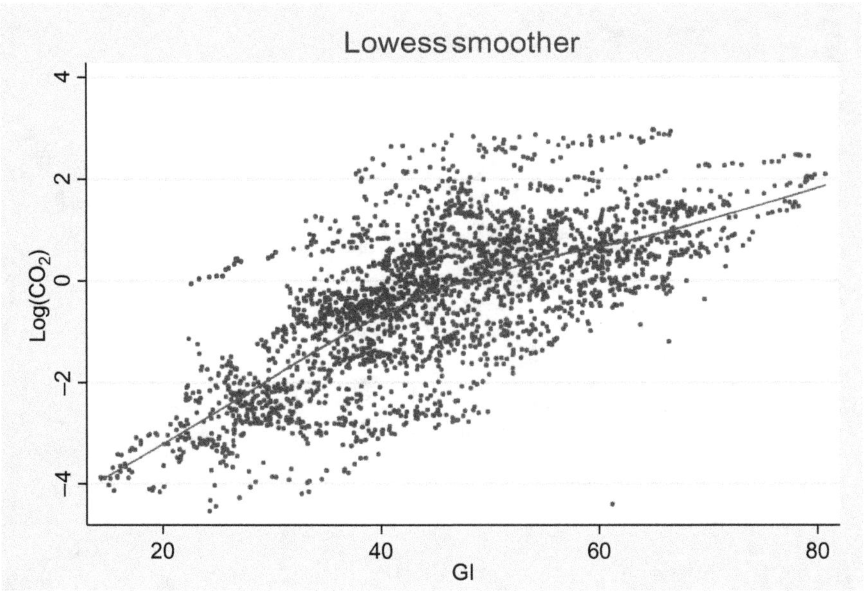

Figure 1. Non-parametric regression line between globalization and carbon emissions.

Note: The relevant figure provides the locally weighted scatterplot smoothing. The locally weighted regression line is represented by the curvature. The bandwidth is set to 0.8.

Similar results are obtained if we focus on the impact of financial development on environmental degradation (see Figure 2). Specifically, the "hump-shaped" curve between financial development and environmental degradation is evident. When the economy starts to grow, the government tries to support industrial growth by providing them with domestic credit. In such a situation, when the economy opens, the domestic industries encounter stiff competition from their global rivals. Therefore, while facilitating the economy to grow, globalization helps the domestic industries become stronger, and the flow of domestic credit plays a crucial role in strengthening them. This justifies the increasing part of the curve. However, when these industries start to mature and self-sustain, they try to attract foreign investments, and thereby, their reliance on domestic credit goes down. As the attractiveness of these industries rises with the rise in globalization, the flow of domestic credit to the native industries starts to come down, justifying the decreasing part of the curve.

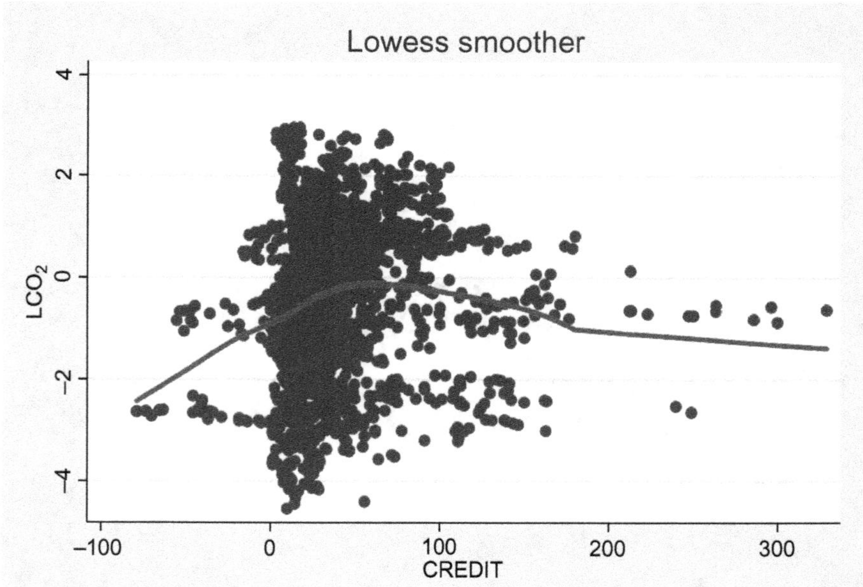

Figure 2. Non-parametric regression line between globalization and financial development.

Note: The relevant figure provides the locally weighted scatterplot smoothing. The locally weighted regression line is represented by the curvature. The bandwidth is set to 0.8.

Figure 3 plots the estimates of the impact of the globalization index (horizontal axis) on carbon dioxide emissions (vertical axis) along with 99 percent confidence bands (gray shaded area). As it is evident from the relevant figure, which is based on the semi-parametric panel data fixed-effects estimator developed by Baltagi and Li (2002), it seems that globalization exhibits very weak nonlinear effects on environmental degradation. However, we must mention that most of the estimated effect is not significantly different from zero, as the 99 percent confidence band includes zero, except for some outliers at the center of the distribution.

It is worth mentioning that, when we employ the financial development indicator (LCREDIT), the same weakness of the nonlinear relationship as well as the lack of statistical significance between financial development and environmental degradation remain intact (see Figure 4). These findings partially confirm earlier studies, where it is argued that the finance–pollution relationship appears to be

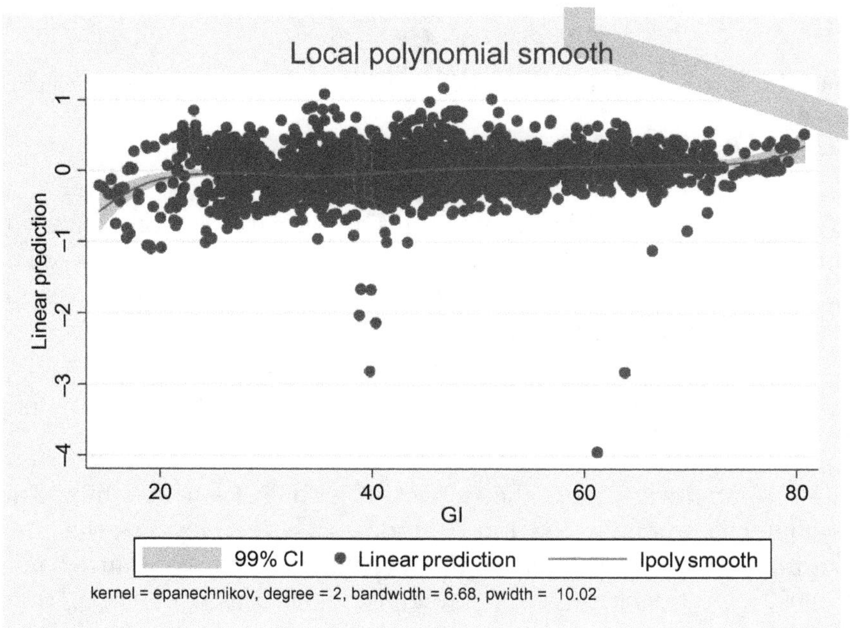

Figure 3. Non-parametric estimates of globalization on environmental degradation.

Note: Gray shaded area denotes the 99 percent confidence bands.

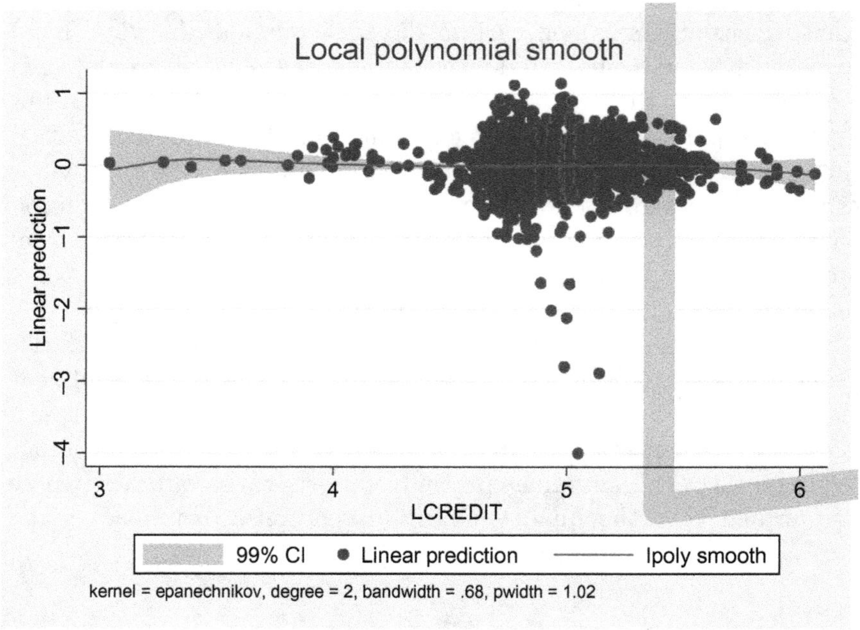

Figure 4. Non-parametric estimates of financial development on environmental degradation.

Note: Gray shaded area denotes the 99 percent confidence bands.

linear when nonlinearities between initial per capita income, human capital, and economic growth are considered, but not in terms of its statistical significance. In our case, we find that such a relationship is very weak, if it exists at all.

6. Conclusion

This chapter investigates the impact of globalization and financial development on environmental degradation by employing a flexible semi-parametric fixed-effects estimator, along the lines of Baltagi and Li (2002), to a sample of 60 developing countries over the period 1970–2014.

The econometric methodology accounts for the presence of cross-sectional dependence, while it employs proper cross-sectional augmented panel unit root tests to ascertain unit root properties and cointegration relationships. To secure the robustness of our findings, we employ both parametric and semi-parametric techniques. The empirical findings unravel a non-monotonic inverted-U-shaped curve between globalization and environmental degradation, justifying the EKC hypothesis.

Lastly, the empirical findings reveal that the impact of financial depth, proxied by the level of domestic credit, on climate change appears to be very weak and tentative, despite showing mild nonlinearity. However, the absence of strong and statistically significant nonlinearities is consistent with most of the existing studies.

This finding has important implications to policymakers and government officials since a better functioning of the financial intermediaries, such as commercial banks, investment banks, mutual funds, and pension funds, will tend to accelerate globalization and thus environmental damage.

Appendix: List of Sample Countries

Argentina, Armenia, Aruba, Austria, Australia, Azerbaijan, Bahamas, Bahrain, Barbados, Belarus, Belgium, Belize, Benin, Bhutan, Bolivia, Bosnia-Herzegovina, Botswana, Brazil, Brunei, Bulgaria, Burkina Faso, Burundi, Cambodia, Cameroon, Canada, Central African Republic, Chad, Chile, China, Colombia, Costa Rica, Cote d'Ivoire, Croatia, Cuba, Cyprus, Czech Republic, Denmark, Djibouti, Dominican Republic, Ecuador, Egypt, El Salvador, Estonia, Ethiopia, Fiji, Finland, France, Gabon, Gambia, Georgia, Ghana, Grenada, Guatemala, Guinea, Guyana, Haiti, Honduras, Hungary, Iceland, India, Indonesia, Iran, Iraq, Ireland, Israel, Italy, Jamaica, Japan, Jordan, Kazakhstan, Kenya, Kuwait, Laos, Latvia, Lebanon, Liberia, Libya, Lithuania, Luxembourg, Madagascar, Malawi, Malaysia, Maldives, Mali, Malta, Mauritania, Mauritius, Mexico, Moldova, Mongolia, Morocco, Mozambique, Namibia, Nepal, Netherlands, New Zealand, Nicaragua, Niger, Nigeria, Norway, Oman, Pakistan, Panama, Papua New Guinea, Paraguay, Peru, Philippines, Poland, Portugal, Qatar, Romania, Russia, Rwanda, Samoa, Sao Tome & Principe, Saudi Arabia, Senegal, Seychelles, Sierra Leone, Singapore, Slovakia, Slovenia, Solomon Islands, South Africa, South Korea, Spain, Sri Lanka, St. Lucia, St. Vincent

& Grenadines, Sudan, Suriname, Sweden, Switzerland, Tajikistan, Tanzania, Thailand, Togo, Tonga, Trinidad & Tobago, Tunisia, Turkey, Turkmenistan, Uganda, Uruguay, Uzbekistan, Venezuela, Vietnam, Yemen, Zambia, Zimbabwe.

References

Abdallh, A. & Abugamos, H. (2017). A semi-parametric panel data analysis on the urbanisation-carbon emissions nexus for the MENA countries. *Renewable and Sustainable Energy Reviews*, *78*, 1350–1356.

Ahad, M. & Khan, W. (2016). Does globalization impede environmental quality in Bangladesh? The role of real economic activities and energy use. MPRA Paper 76278, University Library of Munich, Germany, pp. 258–279.

Apergis, N. (2018). Education and democracy: New evidence from 161 countries. *Economic Modelling*, *71*, 59–67.

Arrelano, M. & Bover, O. (1995). Another look at the instrumental variables estimation of error components models. *Journal of Econometrics*, *68*, 29–51.

Baek, J., Cho, Y., & Koo, W. (2009). The environmental consequences of globalization: A country-specific time-series analysis. *Ecological Economics*, *68*(8–9), 2255–2264.

Bai, J. & Ng, S. (2006). Evaluating latent and observed factors in macroeconomics and finance. *Journal of Econometrics*, *131*, 507–537.

Bai, J., Kao, C., & Ng, S. (2009). Panel cointegration with global stochastic trends. *Journal of Econometrics*, *149*(1), 82–99.

Bernard, J. & Mandal, S. (2016). The impact of trade openness on environmental quality: An empirical analysis of emerging and developing economies. *Environmental Impact III*, *203*, 195–208.

Baltagi, B. (Ed.). (2002). *Recent Developments in the Econometrics of Panel Data, Books*. Edward Elgar Publishing, p. 2701.

Baltagi, B. H. & Li, D. (2002). Series estimation of partially linear panel data models with fixed effects. *Annals of Economics and Finance*, *3*(1), 103–116.

Blundell, R. & Bond, S. (1998). Initial conditions and moment restrictions in dynamic panel data models. *Journal of Econometrics*, *87*, 115–143.

Bond, S., Clive B., & Windmeijer, F. (2001). Criterion-based inference for GMM in autoregressive panel data models. *Economics Letters*, *73*(3), 379–388.

Bu, M., Lin, C., & Zhang, B. (2016). Globalization and climate change: New empirical panel data evidence. *Journal of Economic Surveys*, *30*(3), 577–595.

Chudik, A. & Pesaran, M. H. (2015). Common correlated effects estimation of heterogeneous dynamic panel data models with weakly exogenous regressors. *Journal of Econometrics, 188*(2), 393–420.

Copeland, B. & Taylor, M. (2013). *Trade and the Environment: Theory and Evidence.* Princeton: Princeton University Press.

Dinda, S. (2006). Globalization and environment: Can pollution haven hypothesis alone explain the impact of globalization on environment? MPRA Paper 50590, University Library of Munich, Germany.

Dreher, A. (2006). Does globalization affect growth? Evidence from a new index of globalization. *Applied Economics, 38*, 1091–1110.

Grossman, G. M. & Krueger, A. B. (1995). Economic growth and the environment. *Quarterly Journal of Economics, 110*(2), 353–377.

Gygli, S., Haelg, F., Potrafke, N., *et al.* (2019). The KOF globalisation index — Revisited. *Review of International Organizations, 14*(3), 543–574.

Halkos, G. & Polemis, M. (2017). Does financial development affect environmental degradation? Evidence from the OECD countries. *Business Strategy and the Environment, 26*(8), 1162–1180.

He, J. & Wang, H. (2012). Economic structure, development policy and environmental quality: An empirical analysis of environmental Kuznets curves with Chinese municipal data. *Ecological Economics, 76*, 49–59.

Im, K. S., Pesaran, M. H., & Y. Shin. (2003). Testing for unit roots in heterogeneous panels. *Journal of Econometrics, 115*, 53–74.

Kalayci, C. & Hayaloglu, P. (2019). The impact of economic globalization on CO_2 emissions: The case of NAFTA countries. *International Journal of Energy Economics and Policy, 9*(1), 356–360.

Kasioumi, M. & Stengos, T. (2020). The environmental Kuznets curve with recycling: A partially linear semiparametric approach. *Journal of Risk and Financial Management, 13*(11), 1–26.

Khan, H. & Khan, O. (2018). Income-FDI-environmental degradation nexus for developing countries: A panel analysis of America continent. MPRA Paper 88154, University Library of Munich, Germany.

Li, Q. & Racine, J. (2006). *Nonparametric Econometrics: Theory and Practice.* Princeton University Press, edition 1, number 8355.

Libois, F. & Verardi, V. (2013). Semiparametric fixed-effects estimator. *The Stata Journal, 13*(2), 329–336.

Leitão, N. (2014). Economic growth, carbon dioxide emissions, renewable energy and globalization. *International Journal of Energy Economics and Policy, 4*(3), 391–399.

Liddle, B. (2001). Free trade and the environment-development system. *Ecological Economics, 39*(1), 21–36.

Managi, S. (2004). Trade liberalization and the environment: Carbon dioxide for 1960–1999. *Economics Bulletin, 17*(1), 1–5.

Newson, R. (2000). sg151: B-splines and splines parameterized by their values at reference points on the x-axis. *Stata Technical Bulletin, 57*, 20–27. Reprinted in Stata Technical Bulletin Reprints 10, pp. 221–230. College Station, TX: Stata Press.

Omri, A., Daly, S., Rault, C. H., *et al.* (2015). Financial development, environmental quality, trade and economic growth: What causes what in MENA countries. *Energy Economics*, *48*, 242–252.

Pesaran, M. H. (2004). General diagnostic tests for cross section dependence in panels' Cambridge Working Papers in Economics 0435, Faculty of Economics, University of Cambridge.

Pesaran, M. H. (2007). A simple panel unit root test in the presence of cross-section dependence. *Journal of Applied Econometrics*, *22*, 265–312.

Pesaran, H. (2003). A simple panel unit root test in the presence of cross section dependence. Cambridge Working Papers in Economics 0346, Faculty of Economics, University of Cambridge.

Shahbaz, M., Ozturk, I., Afza, T., *et al.* (2013). Revisiting the environmental Kuznets curve in a global economy. *Renewable and Sustainable Energy Reviews*, *25*, 494–502.

Shahbaz, M., Bhattacharya, M., & Ahmed, K. (2016a). CO_2 emissions in Australia: Economic and non-economic drivers in the long-run. *Applied Economics*, *49*(13), 1273–1286.

Shahbaz, M., Mallick, H., Mahalik M. K., *et al.* (2016b). The role of globalization on the recent evolution of energy demand in India: Implications for sustainable development. *Energy Economics*, *55*, 52–68.

Shahbaz, M., Shahzad, S., & Mahalik, M. (2017a). Is globalization detrimental to CO_2 emissions in Japan? New threshold analysis. *Environmental Modeling & Assessment*, *23*(5), 557–568.

Shahbaz, M., Shahzad, S., Mahalik, M., *et al.* (2017b). Does globalisation worsen environmental quality in developed economies? *Environmental Modeling & Assessment*, *23*(2), 141–156.

Shahbaz, M., Balsalobre, D., & Shahzad, S. (2018a). The influencing factors of CO_2 emissions and the role of biomass energy consumption: Statistical experience from G-7 countries. *Environmental Modeling & Assessment*, *24*(2), 143–161.

Shahbaz, M., Shahzad, S., Alam, S., *et al.* (2018b). Globalisation, economic growth and energy consumption in the BRICS region: The importance of asymmetries, *The Journal of International Trade & Economic Development*, *27*(8), 985–1009.

Solarin, S., Al-mulali, U., & Sahu, P. (2017). Globalisation and its effect on pollution in Malaysia: The role of Trans-Pacific Partnership (TPP) agreement. *Environmental Science and Pollution Research*, *24*(29), 23096–23113.

Tisdell, C. (2001). Globalisation and sustainability: Environmental Kuznets curve and the WTO. *Ecological Economics*, *39*(2), 185–196.

Werner, A., Copeland, B., & Taylor, M. (2001). Is free trade good for the environment? *American Economic Review*, *91*(4), 877–908.

You, W. & Lv, Z. (2018). Spillover effects of economic globalization on CO_2 emissions: A spatial panel approach. *Energy Economics*, *73*, 248–257.

https://doi.org/10.1142/9781800614482_0002

Chapter 2

Green Finance and Sustainable Development in India: Current Status and Challenges Beyond the COVID-19 Period

Mita Bhattacharya[*,†,§] **and Eric Yan**[‡,¶]

[†]*Department of Economics, Monash University, Melbourne, Australia*

[‡]*Department of Economics, Feng Chia University, Tainan, Taiwan*

[§]*mita.bhattacharya@monash.edu*

[¶]*ericyan@o365.fcu.edu.tw*

Abstract

A sustainable development pathway requires a significant shift in investments away from greenhouse gases, fossil fuels, and natural-resource-intensive industries and toward more renewable sources, as well as changes in business models. The financial sector will play a greater role in this movement toward sustainable, green growth. This chapter provides an overview of the need for green finance and the role of financial governance. It reviews the state of green lending and investment in India and provides an overview of the country's green financial governance initiatives. We recommend that continued market innovations and financial assistance are necessary for achieving sustainable development.

[*]Corresponding author.

1. Green Finance and Sustainable Development: An Introduction

Society expects much more from enterprises today, and enterprises are required to assume greater responsibilities to meet social expectations. Some of the expectations include how an enterprise plays a role in the supply chain, the interplay between ecological and economic systems, and how it addresses its relationship with stakeholders. The environmental, social, and governance (ESG) criteria are a well-known set of standards for the operations of organizations, and additional criteria are developed on this basis.

The rising importance of the ESG criteria reflects the prominence of the issues they address. The criteria per se are further developed to fit the demands of different professions for them. The recent development of green finance is one such example. While developing sound financial institutions, climate-proofing and climate resilience measures are needed, as suggested by the UNFCCC (2015, Section 44). This has also been recognized in the Paris Agreement. The ESG criteria are widely applied in the formation of green financial systems (Volz, 2018). Under the criteria of green finance, a firm's non-compliant behavior may negatively impact its business. An example of this is the Malaysian palm oil firm IOI's non-compliance with the standards of the Roundtable on Sustainable Palm Oil (RSPO), which caused the temporary suspension of the firm's sustainability certification. The disposal measures taken by the RSPO resulted in the cancellation of contracts between the Malaysian company and its international customers (Taufik, 2016).

According to Investopedia (2021a), the environmental criteria of ESG are concerned with an enterprise's energy efficiency, pollution emissions, resource conservation, and even its treatment of animals. They are crucial for evaluating any environmental risks that an enterprise might face and how it manages those risks.[1] Nevertheless,

[1]Environment is one perspective of the ESG criteria, while the other two perspectives of the ESG are social and governance criteria. Social criteria are concerned with whether an enterprise consistently holds the values it claims to its suppliers, donates a portion of its profit to social causes, encourages its employees to participate in volunteer work, shows high regard for the health and safety of its employees, and takes account of the interests of other stakeholders. Governance criteria are concerned with the enterprise's adoption of transparent and accurate

despite the influence of ESG criteria on the development of green finance, the definition of green finance remains unclear. This is because sustainability has a variety of meanings. Under the well-known definition of sustainability proposed by the United Nations, the global goals of sustainable development have 17 perspectives: (1) No Poverty, (2) Zero Hunger, (3) Good Health and Well-being, (4) Quality Education, (5) Gender Equality, (6) Clean Water and Sanitation, (7) Affordable and Clean Energy, (8) Decent Work and Economic Growth, (9) Industry, Innovation, and Infrastructure, (10) Reduced Inequality, (11) Sustainable Cities and Communities, (12) Responsible Consumption and Production, (13) Climate Action, (14) Life Below Water, (15) Life On Land, (16) Peace, Justice, and Strong Institutions, (17) Partnerships for the Goals.[2]

The broad definition of green finance is associated with "the overall goal of the financial system in terms of sustainability and provide a means to assess its effectiveness" (Zhang *et al.*, 2015a, p. 18). From this perspective, green finance almost serves the purposes of all the above 17 goals. For this reason, RBI Bulletin (2021) specifies the definition of green finance as "the financial arrangements that are specific to the use for projects that are environmentally sustainable or projects that adopt the aspects of climate change." Zhang *et al.* (2015a) narrow the definition of green finance by considering green finance to be "what proportion of a particular set of financial assets or institutions can be considered green, for example, to measure volumes of 'green investment' or to act as eligibility criteria for particular labels such as for 'green bonds'."

The government's fiscal expenditure and the financing channels to support sustainable development can be labeled "broadly defined green finance." The government can support green finance through (1) establishing and securing funding for green growth and green industries, (2) developing new financial products to support low-carbon, green growth, (3) strengthening corporate disclosure of green management practices, (4) helping to build and sustain green infrastructure by attracting private investments, and (5) setting up markets for environmental goods and services, such as carbon markets

accounting methods and its involvement of stakeholders in the decision-making process on important issues (Investopedia, 2021a).

[2]See the 17 goals at https://sdgs.un.org/goals.

featuring carbon credits (Soundarrajan, 2016). On the other hand, the funding supports for sustainable development from the United Nations, its affiliated institutions (for example, Food and Agriculture Organization of the United Nations and the International Fund for Agricultural Development) and regional international financial institutions, such as the Asian Development Bank (ADB), can also be labeled "broadly-defined green finance".

Recently, the roles of bank loans, corporate bonds, equity, insurance, and other financial instruments in green finance have gained greater prominence. When serving the purposes of sustainable development, these may be classified as financial tools for "narrowly-defined green finance."

From the perspective of an enterprise, a bank loan is a firm's borrowing that will be repaid to the bank in the form of interest. Usually, the bank will see the business' accounts, business plan, balance sheet, etc., and study the firm's credit history before determining whether to lend them money. If the firm receiving the loan fails to repay the interest to the bank, the bank may request collateral from the firm. The green credit policy in China is a specific policy of bank loans that calls on banks to approve loans or offer credit based on environmental laws and regulations (Zhang *et al.*, 2015b, p. 6). A corporate bond is a debt security issued by a firm and sold to its investors for financing purposes. The investors are either retail or institutional investors that provide the company with debt financing (Investopedia, 2021b). They can request either fixed or variable values of a pre-established number of interest payments from the firm before the bond expires. Once the bond expires, interest payments will cease, and the original investment will be returned all at once. Green bonds are now being issued to meet the need for green finance for infrastructure (Zhang *et al.*, 2015b, p. 15). An equity entitles a firm's shareholders (stockholders) to a fraction of its earnings, proceeds from the liquidation of assets, or voting power, depending on the amount of money each shareholder invested. It represents an ownership stake in the firm. If the firm goes bankrupt, equity holders are last in line to receive money (Investopedia, 2021b). Venture capital firms or funds are a financial source that supports companies in their early stages in exchange for their equities or ownership stakes. A green venture capital fund is a specific "financial instrument that guides funds to the SMEs that have started green projects but are not qualified to be listed" (Zhuo & Zhang, 2015, p. 40). As for insurance, its presence can help compensate for a firm's property loss due to an unexpected event; while the firm cannot effectively reduce its potential property loss, hiding it in its planning horizon using its managerial sophistication. The insurance does not trigger a firm's speculative behavior because, under the fat-tail risk feature of a property loss, a firm's speculative behavior is not unprofitable (Aunon-Nerin & Ehling, 2008). In the age of climate change, green insurance can be used to build resilience against the long-term risks of natural disasters, sea-level rise, floods, windstorms, etc., due to climate change (Ma & Lan, 2015, p. 77).

How firms finance projects (whether by loans, bond, equities, insurances, etc.) impacts how they evaluate their repayment projects and optimization. Meanwhile, firms and industries receiving subsidies from the government for sustainability to different degrees may develop their technologies in different directions, and the differences in their technological levels may grow with the subsidies (Acemoglu *et al.*, 2012). This means that, even if firms share an identical goal of green finance, their policy-making and technological development may differ due to their different sources of green finance.

In the age of global warming, the importance of green finance is apparent, particularly so in the ASEAN region, where member countries are becoming more and more vulnerable to the increasing frequency of typhoons, rising sea levels, a long, exposed coastline, and urban water shortage due to climate (Mehta *et al.*, 2020, p. 6). Furthermore, in the current post-COVID-19 world, in addition to global warming, there are also other challenges to economic recovery. The foreword in Mehta *et al.* (2020) stresses that a country must not recover its economy at the expense of its environment, nor should the country reverse all of its past gains made for environmental protection and carbon reduction. They stress the importance of countries' endeavors to recover their economies without harming sustainability. For example, policies have already been put in place for post-COVID-19 recovery goals in the ASEAN region, setting a target for enterprises to generate 23 percent of their primary energy from renewable sources by 2025, as opposed to a 9.4 percent share in 2014.

2. Current Initiatives in India

The current initiatives in green finance in India are deployed in two respects. One is the initiative under the government's funding support, subsidies, etc. The Five-Year Plan of India provides a framework where relevant policies direct some industries' technical change toward greater sustainability. The other is the development of bank loans, bonds, equity, etc., with the aim of having more meaningful sustainability goals. In contrast to the initiatives under the Five-Year Plan framework, the development of green bonds, loans, and equity is more accounted for by the private sector.

With the second-largest population in the world, India has yet to achieve complete industrialization.[3] Thus, the sustainability volume of the Twelfth Five-Year Plan specifically stresses food security to minimize the downside effects of economic growth (Twelfth Five Year Plan, 2012–2017, p. 4). This is observed from the fact that the plan puts the agricultural sector of India on a trajectory of 4 percent annual growth and 9.1 percent growth by the end of the Plan period (Twelfth Five Year Plan, 2012–2017, p. 81). Under this goal, the central government is expected to subsidize state governments with 63,246 crore for agriculture and 91,435 crore for irrigation, respectively, representing 7.37 percent (= 63,246/857,786) and 10.7 percent (= 91,435/857,786) of the central government's full subsidy (Twelfth Five Year Plan, 2012–2017, p. 83). The emphasis on agriculture can also be observed in the allocation of the central government's gross budget support to develop agriculture and villages. Moreover, the central government's budget support for the agriculture and water resources sectors increased from 7.33 percent of the total in the Eleventh Plan to 7.96 percent of the total in the Twelfth Plan. Relevant policies, such as the budget support for rural development and Panchayati Raj, occupy 25.01 percent of the total in the Eleventh Plan and 18.86 percent of the total in the Twelfth Plan. For more details, see Table 3.13 of the Twelfth Five Year Plan (2012–2017).

[3]China is the country with the largest population in the world.

However, the focus of sustainability is more on carbon emissions reduction when it comes to global warming. Indian Prime Minister Narendra Modi committed to achieving net-zero emissions by 2070 during the brainstorming session at COP26 in Glasgow. He also promised to reduce carbon intensity to 45 percent and outlined a lofty aim for India to produce 500 GW of energy from non-fossil sources by 2030 as part of the five-pronged commitment "Panchamrit." Moreover, he committed to lowering the projected carbon emissions in India by 1 billion tonnes between 2021 and 2030 (Chaudhry, 2022), raised India's 2030 target for low-emission energy capacity to 500 GW from 450 GW, and wanted the country to generate half its electricity using renewable energy (Chaudhary, 2021).

While most of the demand for infrastructure investment in Asia comes from the electricity industry (Figure 1), the Indian government has also stressed the fact that electricity generation is primarily accountable for carbon emissions. According to the Twelfth Five Year Plan (2012–2017, p. 89), the investment in electricity increased from 728,494 crore under the Eleventh Plan to 1,501,666 crore under the Twelfth Plan. The effort toward carbon emissions

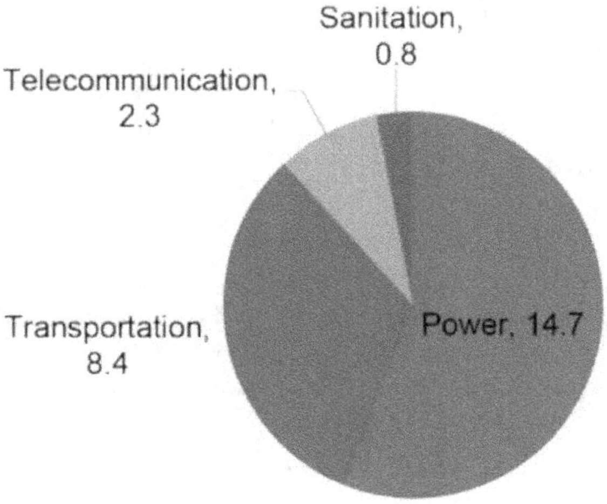

Figure 1. Asia infrastructure investment needs by sector, 2016–2030 (in trillion dollars).

Source: ADB (2017) and Volz (2018).

reduction in the energy sector is reflected in the substantial increase in total projected investment in renewable energy from 89,220 crore under the Eleventh Plan to 318,626 crore under the Twelfth Plan. During the period of the Twelfth Plan, the investment in renewable energy was 31,199 crore in 2012, 42,590 crore in 2013, 58,125 crore in 2014, 79,075 crore in 2015, and 107,637 crore in 2016. The annual growth rate of investment in renewable energy is around 36 percent.

In 2004, the Government of India launched a Viability Gap Funding (VGF) scheme for public–private partnerships in infrastructure projects. Under the project, 5,000 MW of grid-connected solar PV projects were set up (Climate Bonds Initiative, 2019). However, the Council on Energy, Environment, and Water (CEEW) estimated a need for investments upward of $10 trillion in order to achieve net zero by 2070. However, India could face a significant investment shortfall of $3.5 trillion in trying to achieve this goal of net-zero emissions, according to an estimate by the CEEW (Chaudhry, 2022). Also, there will be an extremely heavy fiscal burden on the government should its supports and subsidies be deemed the only sources of green finance for sustainability. The rising importance of the private sector in green finance compared to government support can be observed from the Twelfth Five Year Plan (2012–2017, p. 89). While the central and state governments' total investment in renewable energy was 4,375 (= 3,631 + 744) crore in 2012 and 11,914 (= 10,427 + 1,487) crore in 2016, the private sector's total renewable energy investment increased from 26,825 crore in 2012 to 95,724 crore in 2016.

Meanwhile, the role of banks in plugging any gaps and meeting these investment targets has gained greater importance. Banks are expected to help reduce the impacts of climate change, as it is estimated that the financial services industry would account for a massive 72 percent of the total potential financial impact of climate change (Chaudhry, 2022). In this vein, green bonds, green loans, and equity for green finance have become more important in the past decade. India started issuing green bonds in 2015. Yes Bank, Export-Import Bank of India, CLP Wind Farms, and IDBI were the first issuers. In February 2015, their total green bonds amounted to $1.1 billion (Kidney, 2016). The year 2020 marked a milestone in energy transition, as Indian lenders channeled more funds to clean energy projects than coal-based ones by a third. In 2020, the funding from financial institutions for clean energy projects amounted to 243.8 billion rupees ($3 billion), roughly 74 percent of the total funds from financial institutions. This amount grew from the clean energy projects of about 229.71 billion rupees in 2019, translating into a 6 percent rise. In contrast, 26 percent of the 2020 funds (or 85.2 billion rupees) from Indian lenders went to coal-fired plants, implying an 86 percent slump in approvals for coal plants (Chaudhary, 2021). While the amount of green bonds issued between 2018 and 2020 was about $8 billion, the outstanding amount of green bonds simultaneously increased to $16.3 billion by February 12, 2020. By 2021, green bonds accounted for about 0.7 percent of all bonds in India's financial market (RBI Bulletin, 2021).

Most of the green bonds issued in India are by public sector units or corporations with better financial health (RBI Bulletin, 2021). Table 1 lists green bond issuances in different countries since January 2018. According to this table, most of the world's green bonds are issued in the euro area, totaling US$196,854 million. China is in second, with an amount of $63,023 million. China is followed by the US, Japan, South Korea, and Central and South America. India is ranked seventh, with $7,992 million.

Green bond issuers in India include not only corporates and the government but also international organizations, such as the World Bank. The World Bank began issuing green bonds in India much earlier than corporates and the government. RBI Bulletin (2021) lists, in a table, the World Bank's green bond commitment to India. According to the table, green bonds issued by the World Bank in India target (1) renewable energy and energy efficiency, (2) clean transportation, (3) water and wastewater management, and (4) agriculture, land use, forests, and ecological resources. The first project was named "Rampur Hydropower Project," starting on September 13, 2007 and ending on December 31, 2014. As of January 2022, there were still outstanding green bonds of the World Bank, such as the Tamil Nadu Irrigated Agriculture Modernization Project and the Shared Infrastructure for Solar Parks Project.

Unlike professional investors, most people do not have the time to investigate the profitability or prospects of companies issuing green bonds or green equities. The development of green stock indices allows people to invest in green bonds or green equities at lower

Table 1. Green bonds issuance since January 1, 2018 (corporates and governments: all maturities).

Country	Amount issued ($M)	Number of bonds issued	Amount issued as percent of all bond issuance (percent)	Number of bonds issued as percent of all bond issuance (percent)
Euro area	1,96,854	594	1.7	0.4
China	63,023	183	0.3	0.2
USA	35,421	71	0.2	0.2
Japan	11,815	88	0.1	1.1
South Korea	11,781	44	1	0.4
Central and Southern America	8,869	53	0.5	1
India	7,992	22	0.7	0.3
Southeast Asia	7,208	86	0.6	1.4
Australia and New Zealand	5,878	15	1.1	0.8
UK	5,311	17	0.4	0.5
Hong Kong SAR	4,781	19	0.5	1
Singapore	496	9	0.05	1.2

Source: RBI Bulletin (2021), https://rbidocs.rbi.org.in/rdocs/Bulletin/PDFs/04AR_2101202185D9B6905ADD465CB7DD280B88266F77.PDF.

time costs. An example is the ESG leaders' stock price indices in India, designed for people seeking exposure to companies with relatively low tracking error to the underlying equity market and a strong sustainability profile (RBI Bulletin, 2021). Figure 2 shows a rising preference for ESG compared to the general stock index, manifesting the rising importance of this financial tool. India has various reporting mechanisms, including perform, achieve and trade (PAT) and renewable purchase obligations (RPOs), to monitor greenhouse gas emissions. However, like many other countries, India does not have a national measurement, reporting, and verification platform to track green finance (Jain, 2020). The development of green stock indices, to some degree, makes up for the deficiency of a green finance tracking mechanism in India.

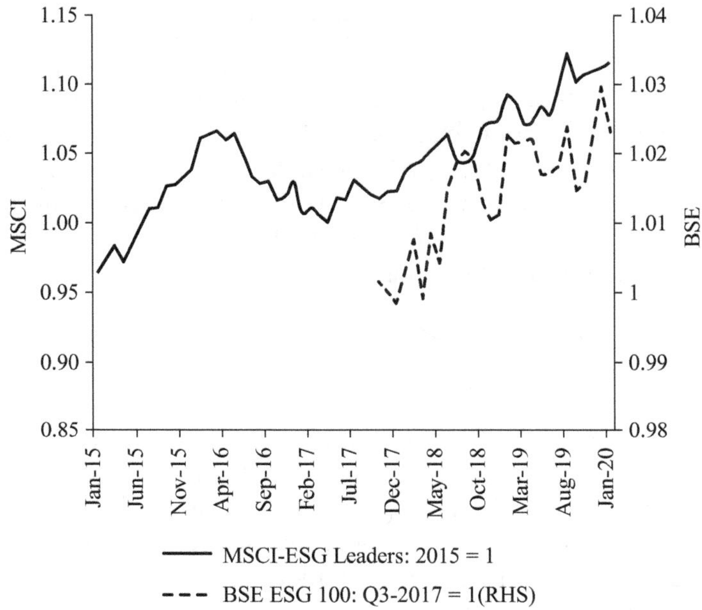

Figure 2. ESG compared to a general stock index.
Source: RBI Bulletin (2021), https://rbidocs.rbi.org.in/rdocs/Bulletin/PDFs/04AR_2101202185D9B6905ADD465CB7DD280B88266F77.PDF.

3. A Comparison with Other Asian Countries on the Progress of Green Finance

Sustainability has become an important issue in Asian countries, and Asia is expected to contribute roughly 60 percent of global growth by 2030 (Yendamuri & Ingilizian, 2019). While the development of green finance is a recent occurrence in many Asian countries, it has proceeded at a high pace in recent years (Volz, 2018). Asian countries that had green finance or were working on relevant policies for green finance by 2018 include Bangladesh, China, Hong Kong SAR, India, Indonesia, Japan, Mongolia, Singapore, Vietnam, Cambodia, Laos, Nepal, Pakistan, the Philippines, Sri Lanka, and Thailand (Volz, 2018). In the following paragraphs, we discuss the development of green finance in Asian countries in general and China in particular.

3.1. *Green finance in Asian countries*

The tools of green finance include bank loans, bonds issued by corporates, governments, and international organizations, equities, insurances, and even foreign exchanges. In this section, we first introduce the recent developments in green finance in Asia in these respects. Then, we narrow our focus on green finance in China, the world's largest carbon dioxide emitter (World Bank, 2022), as well as its counterpart in India, which has a large population second only to China.

3.1.1. *Green loan markets*

According to the World Bank (2021), US$1.6 billion of the estimated $33 billion in outstanding green loans is accounted for by developing countries. The World Bank Group's International Finance Corporation (IFC) is the leading global provider of green loans among international development banks, while in Asia, the ADB plays an equally important role in providing green loans alongside the IFC. For example, the ADB's Green Loan for Renewable Energy and Electric Vehicle Charging Network entails a corporate loan with a three-year tenor to finance two of Energy Absolute's operating solar and wind projects in Thailand (ADB, 2020a).

Alongside the green loan policies of the IFC and ADB, some Asian countries have also put forth relevant policies to legitimize the green loan business of domestic banks. For example, "Mandatory Green Finance Credit Targets l" was issued in Bangladesh in 2015; "Green Credit Policy" was launched by the China Banking Regulatory Commission (CBRC), People's Bank of China (PBoC), and the Ministry of Environmental Protection (MEP) in China in 2007; "Directive on Promoting Green Credit Growth and Managing Environmental and Social Risks in Credit Extension" was issued in Vietnam in 2015 (Volz, 2018).

3.1.2. *Green bond markets*

The development of the green bond market is a recent event in Asia (Volz, 2018). As another tool of green finance, green bonds can be traded domestically or internationally. The Export-Import Bank of Korea was the first Asian bank to issue green bonds in 2013

(Allens Linklaters, 2015). Indonesia saw its first green bond launch in April 2014 to combat climate change with the support of the IFC (IFC, 2018). In China, the first corporate green bond was issued offshore in Hong Kong SAR in 2015 (Kidney, 2016); in the same year, the Agricultural Bank of China issued the first green bond of a Chinese bank in London (Reuters, 2015); and, in 2016, under the authority of the Green Financial Bond Guidelines, China Industrial Bank (CIB) and Shanghai Pudong Development Bank issued the first two domestic green bonds in China (Volz, 2018). After issuing €250 million in October 2014, the Development Bank of Japan became the first Japanese green bond issuer (Allens Linklaters, 2015). In India, the first bank to issue a green bond was Yes Bank in 2015 (Kidney, 2016), while IFC purchased the issuance of Yes Bank in the same year through the first green bond issued in the offshore rupee markets (IFC, 2015). The ADB issued its first green bond for water and clean energy in 2010, and the size of bond issuance was over $500 million in March 2015 and reached $1.3 billion and $1.25 billion in August 2016 and August 2017, respectively (Volz, 2018). While most green bonds in Asia were issued with public support, the issuance of corporate green bonds by Advanced Semiconductor Engineering in Taiwan in 2014 was the first exception (Münzer-Jones & Johnson, 2016).

Although green loans and green bonds are similar in their role of raising capital for eligible green projects, a green loan typically has a smaller scale and lower transaction costs than a green bond. Moreover, a green loan is usually a private operation, while a green bond can be issued with public support. Green bonds and green loans follow different principles of issuance too. The issuance principle of green loans is the Green Loan Principles of the International Capital Market Association (ICMA), while that of green bonds is the Green Bond Principles (GBP) of the ICMA (World Bank, 2021).

3.1.3. *Green insurance markets*

Facing more serious problems of climate change, some Asian countries have also started to issue catastrophe bonds (or cat bonds). For example, in 2018, the Monetary Authority of Singapore funded 100 percent of the upfront issuance costs of cat bonds in Singapore (Ralph, 2017). However, different from green bonds, cat bonds are used to create risk-linked securities which transfer a specific set of risks (typically catastrophe and natural disaster risks) from an issuer or sponsor (ceding company) to capital market investors (Artemis, 2022). In 2013, the former State Environmental Protection Administration (SEPA) and China Insurance Regulatory Commission (CIRC) jointly released the Guiding Opinions on Environmental Pollution Liability Insurance to actively promote environmental pollution liability insurance (Ma & Lan, 2015, p. 77) in China.

3.1.4. *Green equity markets*

In 2022, sustainable stock indices became available in the Dhaka Stock Exchange in Bangladesh; the Shanghai Stock Exchange, the Shenzhen Stock Exchange, and HKEX in China; the Bombay Stock Exchange in India; the Indonesia Stock Exchange; the Japan Exchange Group in Japan; Bursa Malaysia; the Philippine Stock Exchange; the Qatar Stock Exchange; the Saudi Exchange; the Singapore Exchange; the Colombo Stock Exchange in Sri Lanka; the Stock Exchange of Thailand; Borsa Istanbul in Turkey; the Abu Dhabi Securities Exchange and Dubai Financial Market in the UAE; and the Hanoi Stock Exchange and the Ho Chi Minh Stock Exchange in Vietnam (Sustainable Stock Exchanges Initiative, 2022).

3.1.5. *Green foreign exchange markets*

Finally, in addition to loans, bonds, equity, and insurance mentioned above, foreign exchange is also used in some countries as a funding source for green investments. For example, the ASEAN Infrastructure Fund (AIF), established by the ADB and ASEAN members, is an institution that plays a role in mobilizing foreign exchange reserves to fund infrastructure projects for sustainability (Climate Bonds Initiative, 2019).

3.2. *Green finance in China*

Among Asian countries, we aim to further introduce green finance in China to compare it with India. This is because China is the world's largest emitter of carbon dioxide (World Bank, 2022). Its energy infrastructure is heavily focused on fossil fuels, coal, and other industries contributing heavily to carbon emissions. Meanwhile, water scarcity and soil contamination remain threats to the health and livelihoods of China's population (Maizland, 2021). All of these environmental issues have forced China to implement various measures to mitigate or ameliorate the problems it faces. The government's efforts in response to the problems have made China a notable pioneer in green banking in Asia (Volz, 2018).

3.2.1. *Green loans/credits and bonds*

The first "green credit" product was inaugurated by the CIB and IFC in May 2006 for energy conservation and emission reduction projects. One year later, in July 2007, the then SEPA, the PBoC, and the China Banking Regulatory Commission jointly released the "Opinions on Implementing Environmental Protection Policies and Regulations and Preventing Credit Risk." In China, banks directly or indirectly also control financing and transactions in the bond, trust, and shadow banking markets (Ma & Lan, 2015, p. 76). Thus, the "Opinions" is used as a guideline not only for green loans/credits but also for green bonds.

The "Opinions" aimed to curb the expansion of energy-intensive and high-pollution industries. However, it has more positive implications in that it urges banking and financial institutions to carefully implement national macroeconomic control policy, fulfill the social responsibilities of the financial sector, innovate loan provision services, reduce credit origination to energy-intensive and high-emission industries, and support industrial restructuring (Ma & Lan, 2015, p. 76).

3.2.2. *Green equities*

China has already linked the ESG criteria to the performance of the green stock market index. The Shanghai Index is the world's first urban sustainable development index system based on the five-pronged performance in economy, society, culture, environment, and governance. The index, used to evaluate a city's sustainable development and promote the concept of "people-oriented" urban development, was jointly designed with the UN-Habitat, the UN agency for human settlements (CGTN, 2021).

Moreover, in February 2008, the former SEPA, together with the China Securities Regulatory Commission and other departments, released the "Guiding Opinions on Strengthening Supervision and Management of Environmental Protection by Listed Companies" to make environmental auditing a compulsory initial public offerings (IPOs) requirement.

3.2.3. *Green insurances*

Green insurance in China began in 2007, when the former SEPA and the CIRC jointly released the "Guiding Opinions on Environmental Pollution Liability Insurance" to actively promote environmental pollution liability insurance. Jiangsu, Hubei, Hunan, Chongqing, and Shenzhen are the provinces where the national environmental pollution liability insurance pilots started in 2008. In February 2013, the MEP and the CIRC jointly released the "Guiding Opinions on Carrying out Pilots of Compulsory Environmental Pollution Liability Insurance" to guide local governments in promoting the pilot work of compulsory environmental pollution liability insurance in heavy-metal-related industries and industries with high environmental risks, such as petrochemicals (Ma & Lan, 2015, p. 77). Before 2017, the system was piloted at the local level in 30 provinces (UNEP, 2017).

4. Challenges of Green Finance in India

Green finance is still in its nascent stage in India. Government supports to industries in the form of subsidies or fiscal expenditures under the framework of the Twelfth Five Year Plan are the primary source of achieving sustainability. The challenges facing India are institutional. India is known for its high levels of corruption and venality in public life. Beyond these, its state capacity is limited, which is reflected in the incompetence of policy design, formulation, and implementation. For these reasons, India, as a member of the G20, has had a lower performance in shaping its business environment. As can be seen in the 2016 edition of the "Doing Business" report, India ranks 130th out of 189 countries in the overall ease of doing business, 178th in enforcing contracts, 183rd in getting a construction permit, and 155th in the ease of starting a business (Vaishnav *et al.*, 2017).

Compared to India, China acted on green finance earlier and has more diversified tools of green finance, including bonds, loans, insurances, and equities. Nevertheless, as both China and India have the world's largest populations and the world's largest bureaucratic and administrative systems, the experience of China can be a good example for India, an institutional latecomer. Tian *et al.* (2015) listed the deficiencies of green finance in China, which can be valuable lessons for an emerging economy such as India. We abstract five of them as follows.

First, a country's national strategy for green and sustainable development may not be fully and effectively implemented to develop financial policies. For example, banks may have a wider range of credit for projects other than green finance and thus allocate more credit to firms applying for loans for non-green-finance use.

Second, relevant entities do not share the same definitions of green finance. As noted, green finance can be broadly defined to include fiscal expenditure or subsidies supportive of clean industries, in addition to loans, bonds, insurance, equities, etc. It can also be narrowly defined to include the financial systems' tools of loans, bonds, insurance, and equities for sustainability. Moreover, the goals of sustainability have a very wide range, from energy efficiency improvements, pollution mitigation, etc., to climate change and catastrophe adaptations. Failing to define green finance will result in difficulties in setting standards and criteria.

Third, there are coordination difficulties among government departments of ecological protection, financial reform, and supervisory authorities. The difficulties arise from an incomplete implementation of the information-sharing mechanism, an ineffective flow of information among institutions, and a lack of an effective external supervisory mechanism to facilitate coordination among the entities.

Fourth, financial institutions often lack the scientific knowledge or techniques needed for investigating firms applying for green loans. Meanwhile, they are less motivated to lend to firms pursuing greener production or higher energy efficiencies. These may result in the misallocation of green credits, thus lowering the efficiency of resource use.

Fifth, the implementation of green finance policies actually involves the complexities of institutional design, given that green finance concerns many different entities with no coinciding interests. The entities include the central government and its departments, local governments, financial regulatory authorities, banks, insurance companies, securities companies, venture capital firms, individual investors, and businesses. The difficulties of institutional design can be even higher in federal India than in centralized China.

Wang (2015) shares some views similar to those of Tian *et al.* (2015) and further highlights the following institutional drawbacks of green finance in an emerging economy.

First, there is no complete legal system in place for implementing green finance policies, as sustainability is still a less concerning issue than economic growth in many developing economies. For this reason, laws made for green finance are usually at lower legal levels, making it difficult for relevant entities to coordinate. Institutional defects may also arise due to a lack of a higher authority to supervise violations by a financial institution or government department. Moreover, many regulations under the guidance of green finance are merely directive rather than mandatory.

Second, there are no sufficient relevant policies to implement green finance. For example, while green finance policies aim to support the development of energy conservation and environmental protection enterprises or projects, the government often demonstrates little effort in motivating financial institutions to develop the products and capacities needed for policy implementation.

Third, even if policies are developed, professional service providers may not be ready to enter the field of green financial services. Professional service providers include credit rating agencies, asset appraisal institutions, accounting firms, law firms, and consulting companies. The cultivation of professionals in these respects is of equal importance in forming green finance policies.

Some of the above viewpoints are especially stressed in RBI's recent study (2019) on India's green financial system. For example, it is suggested that the authority needs to remove the problem of asymmetric information between investors and recipients and that the definition of green finance needs to be clear and consistent. Meanwhile, RBI (2019) argues the importance of financial market deepening alongside the implementation of green finance policies.

Jain (2020) points out the pervasive short-termism and profit motive in Indian markets. He realizes the difficulties in creating a new system for environmental risks. Thus, he suggests that the government should develop an environmental stress test to make incorporating environmental risk into India's risk management system more effective, as China does. On the other hand, Jain (2020) also emphasizes the importance of a government-supported green bank under the Indian Renewable Energy Development Agency (IREDA) in promoting domestic and international capital and better financing terms, including lower interest rates with longer lending terms. A government-supported green bank under this framework can be helpful for leveraging private investments in green technologies.

4.1. *A comparison between India and other Asian markets in the post-COVID-19 world*

Today, the world is facing difficulties in recovering from the COVID-19 pandemic under the constraints of global warming. On the one hand, there have been substantial losses, requiring governments to implement policies to address the issues of economic life. Table 2 details the estimates of ADB (2020b), focusing exclusively on the world in total, Asia, China (PRC), Southeast Asia, and South Asia (mainly India). According to the table, the world's economic losses due to COVID-19 can decelerate GDP at a rate ranging from 6.4 percent to 9.7 percent in short and long containment scenarios respectively. Similarly, in Asia, the deceleration of GDP could be at a rate between 6.2 and 9.3 percent; in China, between 7.5 and 11.2 percent; in Southeast Asia, between 4.6 and 7.2 percent; and in South Asia, between 3.9 and 6 percent. On the other hand, investments for economic recovery that hide potential environmental risks should be evaluated more prudently before they are conducted, as stressed in the foreword in Mehta *et al.* (2020). These manifest the rising importance of green finance in recovering the economy post-COVID-19.

Figure 3 illustrates the three pillars to balance for a green recovery strategy. The first is to leverage scarce government funds as best as possible. While many emerging and developing countries face onerous debt repayment obligations and a dearth of capital sources due to the increased sovereign risk, a government recovery strategy for attracting capital must plan to better leverage their resources from various non-public sources and the capital markets. The second is to mitigate market participants' project risk perceptions that can be heightened during the COVID-19 pandemic period. Risk perception

Table 2. GDP impact (excluding policy measures): Deviation from the non-COVID-19 baseline.

	GDP($M)		GDP (percent)	
	Short containment	**Long containment**	**Short containment**	**Long containment**
Global	−5,796,893	−8,789,852	−6.4	−9.7
Asia	−1,667,824	−2,529,112	−6.2	−9.3
Australia and New Zealand	−91,156	−139,456	−4.6	−7.0
Central Asia	−21,070	−33,978	−3.4	−5.5
East Asia ex-PRC	−164,085	−256,741	−6.0	−9.3
PRC	−1,083,078	−1,623,381	−7.5	−11.2
Southeast Asia	−163,223	−252,899	−4.6	−7.2
South Asia	−141,938	−217,646	−3.9	−6.0
Pacific	−3,275	−5,010	−4.6	−7.0
G3	−3,528,842	−5,327,954	−7.3	−11.0
USA	−1,485,318	−2,226,466	−7.1	−10.7
Japan	−324,483	−491,035	−5.9	−8.9
European Union + UK	−1,719,041	−2,610,453	−7.7	−11.7

Source: ADB (2020b).

is a subjective judgment made by people regarding the characteristics and severity of a risk. Mitigating this kind of subjective judgment is crucial for sustainable development because the presence of such a perception can lead to lower capital flows. The third is to accelerate the protection of natural resources and improve climate resilience. According to Mehta *et al.* (2020, p. 6), while green infrastructure for a green recovery is an especially critical area to focus on, the estimate of the Global Commission on Adaptation suggests that $7.1 trillion in total new benefits can be generated by investing $1.8 trillion globally from 2020 to 2030 in resilience-building measures.

Currently, ASEAN member states implementing green packages for post-COVID-19 recovery include the Philippines, Indonesia, Thailand, Malaysia, Vietnam, and Cambodia. In the Philippines, the "Build, Build, Build" program is a plan that provides $160 billion to foster economic recovery while simultaneously considering the creation of green jobs. The Action Plan to Reduce Plastic Pollution,

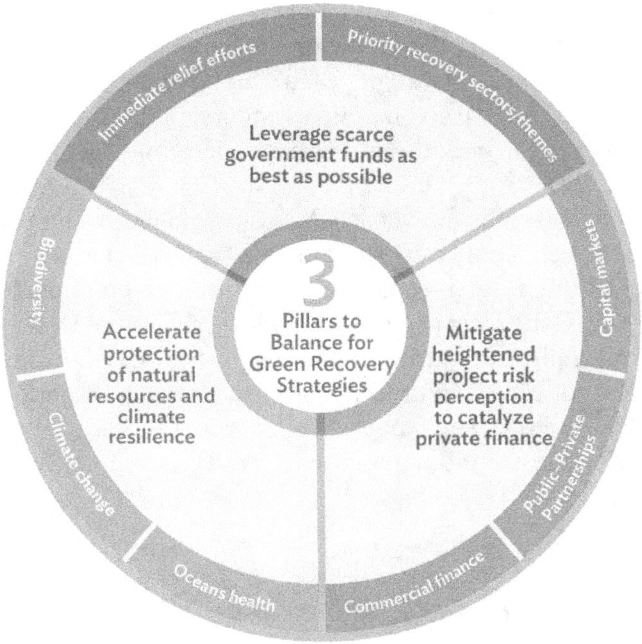

Figure 3. Balancing relief, recovery, and rejuvenation.
Source: Mehta *et al.* (2020)

unveiled in April 2020, is expected to have a society-wide and long-lasting green economic impact on Indonesia. It is expected that this will be achieved by channeling investments into green small- and medium-sized enterprises, sustainable infrastructure for recycling, and new technologies for packaging and recycling, along with waste disposal facilities. In contrast to the Action Plan to Reduce Plastic Pollution, Indonesia's National Economic Recovery Program is implemented to inject capital into state-owned enterprises. Thailand wants to implement a plan for 92 PPP projects worth 1.09 trillion baht ($33.39 billion) from 2020 to 2027 and has embarked on issuing sovereign sustainability bonds to fund green infrastructure projects in August 2020. Malaysia has supported an ASEAN economic recovery plan to ensure critical infrastructure for trade and trading routes via air, land, and sea. Vietnam's National Strategy on Green Growth aims to provide a strong framework through the development of investment guidelines. It is implemented to mobilize public and private finance for green economic recovery projects. Cambodia's National Strategic Plan on Green Growth prioritizes green incentives for catalyzing investments, including green taxes, green finance, green credit, and green microfinance (Mehta *et al.*, 2020, pp. 22–23).

The above cases in Southeast Asia are pioneering governmental projects for green finance in the post-COVID-19 period. Currently, there is no similar large-scale governmental green finance project for post-COVID-19 recovery in India. Nevertheless, ADB's sovereign loan of $200 million to support lending by the IREDA can achieve the same goal of green finance in the post-COVID-19 period (Mehta *et al.*, 2020, p. 31), and the same is true for China's Shandong Green Development Fund, created with ADB's support (Mehta *et al.*, 2020, p. 28).

5. Concluding Remarks

The importance of green finance is fast emerging in the public policy arena. This chapter reviewed the developments of green finance in India compared to other Asian countries and identified some challenges in achieving sustainable development beyond the COVID-19 period. Better information management systems and increased coordination among stakeholders are needed for sustainable long-term development. Investment in green finance will play a greater role in the post-COVID-19 world in facilitating a shift toward sustainable economic development. An increase in fiscal and financial incentives is necessary for these purposes.

References

Acemoglu, D., Aghion, P., Bursztyn, L., *et al.* (2012). The environment and directed technical change. *American Economic Review, 102*(1), 131–166.

ADB (2017). *Meeting Asia's Infrastructure Needs.* Manila: Asian Development Bank.

ADB (2020a). Green loan for renewable energy and electric vehicle charging network: Report and recommendation of the President, Asian Development Bank. Retrieved from https://www.adb.org/projects/documents/tha-54268-001-rrp.

ADB (2020b, May). An updated assessment of the economic impact of COVID-19. ADB Brief No. 133. Manila. Retrieved from https://www.adb.org/sites/default/files/publication/604206/adb-brief-133-updated-economic-impact-covid-19.pdf.

Allens Linklaters (2015). *Green Bonds: Emergence of the Australian and Asian Markets.* Melbourne and Hong Kong: Allens Linklaters.

Aunon-Nerin, D. & Ehling, P. (2008). Why firms purchase property insurance. *Journal of Financial Economics, 90*(3), 298–312.

Artemis (2022). What is a Catastrophe Bond (or Cat Bond)? Artemis. Retrieved from https://www.artemis.bm/library/what-is-a-catastrophe-bond/.

CGTN (2021). Shanghai index to help build sustainable and resilient cities faster. Retrieved from https://news.cgtn.com/news/2021-11-01/Shanghai-Index-to-help-build-sustainable-and-resilient-cities-faster–14PVIcEAZfa/index.html.

Chaudhary, A. (2021). India's clean energy got more loans than coal for third year. Bloomberg Green. Retrieved from https://www.bloomberg.com/news/articles/2021-12-15/india-s-clean-energy-got-more-financing-than-coal-for-third-year.

Chaudhry, A. (2022). Green finance can Bolster India's transition to Net-Zero. Here's How. World Economic Forum. Retrieved from https://www.weforum.org/agenda/2022/01/green-finance-bolster-india-transition-net-zero/.

Climate Bonds Initiative (2019). *ASEAN Green Financial Instruments Guide.* Climate Bonds Initiative, England and Wales (no. 1154413).

IFC (2015, August). IFC issues first green masala bond. Retrieved from http://www.ifc.org/wps/wcm/connect/news_ext_content/ifc_external_corporate_site/news+and+events/news/ifc+issues+first+green+masala+bond+on+london+stock+exchange.

IFC (2018). IFC's Pioneering Komodo Green Bond raises $134 million for climate investments in Indonesia. International Finance Cooperation. Retrieved from https://pressroom.ifc.org/all/pages/PressDetail.aspx?ID=24852.

Investopedia (2021a). Environmental, Social, and Governance (ESG) Criteria. Investopedia. Retrieved from https://www.investopedia.com/terms/e/environmental-social-and-governance-esg-criteria.asp.

Investopedia (2021b). Debt Financing. Investopedia. Retrieved from https://www.investopedia.com/terms/d/debtfinancing.asp.

Jain, S. (2020). Financing India's Green Transition. ORF Issue Brief No. 338, January 2020, Observer Research Foundation.

Kidney, S. (2016, January 11). 2015 Year End Review — From Tall Trees to Many Green Shoots: The Evolution of the Green Bond Market Continues with 2015 Seeing $41.8bn Green Bonds Issued — That's the Biggest Ever! Retrieved from https://www.climatebonds.net/2016/01/2015-year-end-review-tall-trees-many-greenshoots-evolution-green-bond-market-continues-2015.

Ma, Zhong & Lan, Hong (2015). Environmental and industrial policy environment for the development of green finance in China. In Section 2 of "Greening China's Financial System". International Institute for Sustainable Development (IISD), The Development Research Center of the State Council. Retrieved from https://www.iisd.org/system/files/publications/greening-chinas-financial-system.pdf.

Maizland, L. (2021). China's Fight against Climate Change and Environmental Degradation. Council on Foreign Relations. Retrieved from https://www.cfr.org/backgrounder/china-climate-change-policies-environmental-degradation.

Mehta, A., Crowley, S., Tirumala, R. D., *et al.* (Eds.). (2020). Green Finance Strategies for Post COVID-19 Economic Recovery in Southeast Asia: Greening Recoveries for Planet and People. Asian Development Bank.

Münzer-Jones, V. & Johnson, D. (2016, February). Recent Developments in the Asian Green Bond Markets. Retrieved from http://www.nortonrosefulbright.com/knowledge/publications/137413/recent-developments-in-the-asian-green-bond-markets.

Ralph, O. (2017). Singapore seeks to muscle in on market for catastrophe bonds. *Financial Times*, 1 November. Retrieved from https://www.ft.com/content/55229b4c-befd-11e7-b8a3-38a6e068f464.

RBI (2019). Opportunities and challenges of green finance. Report on Trend and Progress of Banking in India (2018–2019), pp. 17–18.

RBI Bulletin (2021). Green finance in India: Progress and challenges. Reserve Bank of India. Retrieved from https://rbidocs.rbi.org.in/rdocs/Bulletin/PDFs/04AR_2101202185D9B6905ADD465CB7DD280B88266F77.PDF.

Reuters (2015, October 14). China agricultural bank sells $1 billion debut 'Green Bond' in London. Retrieved from https://uk.reuters.com/article/uk-china-bonds-offshoreidUKKCN0S807Q20151014.

Soundarrajan, P. (2016). Green finance for sustainable green economic growth in India. *Agricultural Economics, 62*(1), 35–44.

Sustainable Stock Exchanges Initiative (2022). Exchanges with Guidance. ESG Disclosure Guidance Database. Retrieved from https://sseinitiative.org/esg-guidance-database/.

Taufik, K. (2016). Unilever Palm Oil Supplier Must Suspend All Plantation Expansion to Save Reputation. *The Guardian*. Retrieved from https://www.theguardian.com/sustainable-business/2016/apr/09/ioi-malaysian-palm-oil-company-unilever-mars-kellogg-rspo-deforestation.

Tian, Hui, Ning Chen, Liping Zhang *et al.* (2015). Lessons from the Development of Green Finance China. In Section 2 of "Greening China's Financial System, International Institute for Sustainable Development (IISD)". The Development Research Center of the State Council. Retrieved from https://www.iisd.org/system/files/publications/greening-chinas-financial-system.pdf.

Twelfth Five Year Plan (2012–2017). Faster, More Inclusive and Sustainable Growth, Volume I. Planning Commission, Government of India.

UNEP (2017). Establishing China's Green Financial System: Progress Report 2017. Geneva: UNEP Inquiry into the Design of a Sustainable Financial System.

United Nations Framework Convention on Climate Change (UNFCCC) (2015). T.I.A.S. No. 16-1104.

Vaishnav, M., Mehta, P. B., & Kapur, D. (2017). Weak public institutions behind India's low State capacity. Mint. Retrieved from https://www.livemint.com/Opinion/W5Fx1zCQNdnmCRDx9AAQ6O/Weak-public-institutions-behind-Indias-low-state-capacity.html.

Volz, U. (2018). Fostering green finance for sustainable development in Asia. ADBI Working Paper 814. Tokyo: Asian Development Bank Institute. Retrieved from https://www.adb.org/publications/fostering-green-finance-sustainable-development-asia.

Wang, Gang (2015). Problems and difficulties in the development of China's green finance. In Section 2 of "Greening China's Financial System, International Institute for Sustainable Development (IISD)," The Development Research Center of the State Council. Retrieved from https://www.iisd.org/system/files/publications/greening-chinas-financial-system.pdf.

World Bank (2021). What you need to know about green loans. World Bank. Retrieved from https://www.worldbank.org/en/news/feature/2021/10/04/what-you-need-to-know-about-green-loans.

World Bank (2022). DataBank — CO_2 emissions (metric tons per capita). World Bank. Retrieved from https://databank.worldbank.org/reports.aspx?source=2&series=EN.ATM.CO2E.PC.

Yendamuri, P. & Ingilizian, Z. (2019). In 2020 Asia will have the World's largest GDP. Here's what that means. World Economic Forum. Retrieved from https://www.weforum.org/agenda/2019/12/asia-economic-growth/.

Zhang, C., Zadek, S., Ning, C., *et al.* (2015). "Synthesis," in Section 1 of "Greening China's Financial System, International Institute for Sustainable Development (IISD)". The Development Research Center of the State Council. Retrieved from https://www.iisd.org/system/files/publications/greening-chinas-financial-system.pdf.

Zhang, C., Zadek, S., Ning, C., *et al.* (2015). Greening China's Financial System: Synthesis Report. Winnipeg and Beijing: Institute for Sustainable Development and Development Research Center of the State Council.

Zhuo, Xian & Zhang, Liping. (2015). A framework for green finance: Making clear waters and green mountains China's gold and silver. In Section 2 of "Greening China's Financial System, International Institute for Sustainable Development (IISD)". The Development Research Center of the State Council. Retrieved from https://www.iisd.org/system/files/publications/greening-chinas-financial-system.pdf .

https://doi.org/10.1142/9781800614482_0003

Chapter 3

Green Finance in China: Development and Impact Analysis*

Zheng Fang[†,‡], Youngho Chang[§], and Yinghui Yu[¶]

School of Business, Singapore University of Social Sciences, Singapore

[‡]*fangzheng@suss.edu.sg*

[§]*yhchang@suss.edu.sg*

[¶]*yhyu@suss.edu.sg*

Abstract

China's green credit balance has grown at a compound annual growth rate of 14 percent between 2013 and 2021, and its green bond market has seen a growth rate of 22 percent during the period 2016–2021. The Chinese carbon market, though developed much later, has become the world's largest carbon market since its nationwide market opened in July 2021. With the backdrop of fast development in green finance, this chapter reviews the policies of green finance development in China, focusing on the three areas of green credit, green bonds, and the carbon market. We empirically analyze the relationship between green finance development, carbon emissions, renewable energy, fossil fuel energy, and economic development, using data from 2000 to 2018. Green finance appears to stimulate renewable energy and economic development, but its effect on reducing carbon emissions may take more time to be seen.

*We thank the excellent research assistance provided by Siti Muneera.

[†]Corresponding author.

1. Introduction

Climate change is a global challenge that has drawn increasing attention from policymakers, scholars, and the public internationally. Under the 2015 Paris Agreement, 196 countries agreed to work together to limit the temperature rise to well below 2 degrees Celsius above its pre-industrial level, and aim to limit it to 1.5 degrees Celsius. The Glasgow Climate Pact signed at COP26 in 2021 finalized the Paris Agreement and maintains the 1.5 degree limit. Now, more than 90 percent of the world's GDP and around 90 percent of global carbon dioxide emissions are covered by net-zero commitments (UNFCCC, 2021). This is impossible without the participation of the two largest economies and emitters, the United States and China. This chapter focuses on China, the second-largest economy and top carbon emitter, which contributed 17.39 percent of the world's GDP in 2020 and 30.30 percent of global carbon dioxide emissions in 2018, according to recent data from the World Bank.

In September 2020, China made the announcement to peak its carbon dioxide emissions before 2030 and achieve carbon neutrality by 2060, a target which is known as "30–60," or "double-carbon". Environmental policies are expected to be critical in achieving the 30–60 target; especially, green finance has a crucial role to play. The term "green finance" dates back to the 1970s, but it only appeared frequently in reports of international organizations and national governments after 2010, when the Green Climate Fund was established (Zhang *et al.*, 2019). There is so far no commonly agreed definition of green finance. Klein *et al.* (2019) defined green finance as "financing of investments that provide environmental benefits," while the World Economic Forum introduced it as "any structured financial activity that's been created to ensure a better environmental outcome" (Fleming, 2020). As a result, green finance can sometimes be used interchangeably with environmental finance or, more broadly, sustainable finance.

The development of green finance has been accelerating since the Paris Agreement, and even more following COP26 which secured the global goal of achieving net zero emissions by 2050, with developed countries mobilizing at least $100 billion in climate finance by 2023 (COP26, 2021). In China, financial resources have been further encouraged to support green and low-carbon projects after the announcement of the double-carbon target. For example, in 2020,

China issued $44 billion in green bonds, making it the world's second-largest source of green bond issuance after the United States (Meng *et al.*, 2021). Due to the national push for net-zero emissions, the green bond issuance in China during the first nine months of 2021 reached a record of $63.16 billion. Green loans in China also rank as the largest in the world, with a value of $1.8 trillion in 2020 (Xinhua, 2021a). The Chinese carbon market, after a few years of piloting experience in seven provinces and cities, started trading on a national scale in July 2021 and immediately became the world's largest carbon market. The cumulative trading reached 107 million tonnes and 4.4 billion yuan in turnover in its first 102 days of operation (Xinhua, 2021b).

With the fast development of green finance practices, mostly driven by green finance policies in China, a growing body of green finance research in economics and finance has emerged recently (Chang, 2019; Chang *et al.*, 2021; Zhang *et al.*, 2021c). However, a comprehensive and up-to-date review of green finance development in China is lacking in the literature. This chapter, therefore, fills the gap by providing an overview of the development of green finance policies in China, as well as a comprehensive review of economic studies on green finance in China, particularly in the areas of green credit, green bonds, and the carbon market.

This chapter also attempts to empirically analyze how green finance affects economic development, environmental quality, and energy use in China and evaluates whether coordination between energy conservation and emissions reduction policies and economic growth is possible. Due to the short history of green finance development (relative to traditional finance), there are only a few studies that focus on China and examine the impact of green finance on the environment (Zhang *et al.*, 2021a; Zhang *et al.*, 2021b; Zhou & Xu, 2022) and economic development (He *et al.*, 2019). Even fewer studies are found to examine the nexus between green finance and energy consumption (Song *et al.*, 2021), let alone those that have examined the nexus between green finance, environment, and economic growth (Zhou *et al.*, 2020) or the nexus between green finance, environment, and energy (Ren *et al.*, 2020) at the same time. To the best of our knowledge, there are no existing studies that have examined how green finance affects environmental quality, energy conservation, and economic development simultaneously. This is, therefore, another contribution of this chapter. Unlike some of the above-mentioned impact analysis studies, we investigate green finance development as a whole based on the green finance framework proposed by the People's Bank of China (PBoC) in 2016 (People's Bank of China, 2016), rather than focusing on the impact of a specific area, such as green credit, green bonds, or the carbon market, separately.

Our analysis, based on data from 2000–2018, shows that a 1 percent increase in the green finance development index is associated with a 0.796 percent increase in carbon intensity, a 5.53 percent increase in renewable energy intensity, and a 4 percent increase in GDP per capita. Meanwhile, when the green finance development index increases by 1 percent, fossil fuel intensity will decrease by 2.86 percent. Granger causality, running from the variables of carbon intensity, renewable energy intensity, fossil fuel intensity, and GDP per capita to the green finance development index, is evidenced; however, green finance development is found to only Granger-cause fossil fuel intensity and GDP per capita, not carbon intensity and renewable energy intensity. These findings seem to indicate the important roles that green finance plays in stimulating renewable energy development and economic development, but its effect on reducing carbon emissions may take longer to be seen.

The rest of the chapter is organized as follows. Section 2 provides an overview of the development of green finance policies and the green finance market in China, especially the policies and market data of green credit, green bonds, and the carbon market. In addition, the literatures related to green finance, and the three areas of green finance, in China are reviewed. Section 3 empirically investigates the relationship between green finance development and the environment, energy, and economic development in China. Section 4 concludes.

2. Development of Green Finance in China

Green finance has an important role to play in achieving China's double-carbon target. In 2015, the State Council released their "Overall Plan for the Reform of the Ecological Civilization System," which, for the first time, identified an overall design for building a green financial system in China. The following year, seven ministries consisting of the PBoC, the Ministry of Finance, the National Development and Reform Commission (NDRC), the Ministry of

Environmental Protection (MEP), the China Banking Regulatory Commission (CBRC), the China Securities Regulatory Commission (CSRC), and the China Insurance Regulatory Commission (CIRC) issued the "Guidance on Building a Green Financial System," which laid out a clear framework for green finance development. In June 2017, green financial reform and innovation pilot zones were established in Zhejiang, Guangdong, Jiangxi, Guizhou, and Xinjiang, where the respective provincial governments made detailed implementation measures and guidelines in 2018. In March 2021, the PBoC established the "three functions" and "five pillars" policy ideas for the development of green finance. While the development of green finance appears to be recent in China, it actually dates back to the 1990s. In the following sections, we extend our discussion on the three areas of green finance: green credit, green bonds, and the carbon market.

2.1. *Green credit in China*

Green credit has played a central role in the early conceptualization and subsequent development of the green finance ecosystem in "China's banking-dominated system" (IISD, 2015). According to a 2020 report by the Climate Policy Initiative, the "big four" state-owned commercial banks in China were dubbed the "world's largest financiers of coal," having contributed $240 billion to the fossil fuel sector between 2016 and 2019 (Choi *et al.*, 2020). The need for a clampdown on the banking sector's unhindered financing of environmentally damaging projects, coupled with a recognition of the influential role that the country's state-owned banks play in providing finance to achieve the government's industrial policy objectives, necessitated a green financial reform of China's banking ecosystem (Naughton, 2021). Green credit in China, a green financial instrument that initially served to encourage banks to consider the environmental risks when lending, has since evolved into a comprehensive policy with regulatory pressure for implementation.

The early conceptualization of green credit in China, or for that matter, green finance itself, dates back to 1995, when the PBoC issued a policy document entitled "Notice on Issues Relating to Improving Environmental Protection in Credit Policy," a guideline for banks on how to incorporate environmental considerations into their credit decisions. This policy, however, was not successfully implemented as it was introduced at a period when "economic growth at any cost" was a top priority (Aizawa & Yang, 2010). It was in 2007 that China's Green Credit Policy was formally launched through the collaboration of three agencies — the MEP, the PBoC, and the CBRC — in the issuance of the "Opinions on Implementing Environmental Protection Policies and Rules and Preventing Credit Risks." Under this initiative, it was stipulated that banks were to make compliance with environmental laws a prerequisite for loan approval, thus encouraging loans for environmentally beneficial companies and restricting credit to "highly polluting and high energy-consuming enterprises and projects" (Aizawa & Yang, 2010). However, it still fell short of a clear implementation guide for the banks, resulting in the policy remaining at the theoretical stage (Zhang *et al.*, 2021b).

The Green Credit Policy was then further revamped in 2012 through the issuance of the "Green Credit Guidelines" by the CBRC. It served as the first comprehensive policy, providing specific guidelines for not only the development of green credit in banks but also the adoption of "sound governance and internal management" (Ho, 2018) to better manage environmental and social risks associated with their credit activities. In the following year, to make clear the need for adoption of the policy, the CBRC launched the green credit statistics system, which made the reporting of their green lending a requirement for the country's 21 main banks. Subsequently, to further reinforce the tracking and assessment of green credit performance, the CBRC introduced the Key Performance Indicators of Green Credit Implementation in 2014.

Another pivotal milestone in the development of green credit in China then came in 2016. The "Guidelines for Establishing the Green Financial System" was issued that year through the collaboration of seven government agencies, and it set out the necessary steps to be taken for the institution of China's green financial system and the overall promotion of an ecological civilization (People's Bank of China, 2016). This set of guidelines followed President Xi Jinping's remarks regarding the advancement of a green finance market and green credit in the country (Xie, 2021). The policy document outlined the government's plans to promote green credit, including the use of monetary policy to provide direct financial incentives (Choi *et al.*, 2020). Similarly, China's green credit policy has continuously evolved over the years to reach its current state, that is, fundamentally, a policy that: (a) puts a check on the financing activities of banks by requiring them to do due diligence to check the environmental performance of the projects they lend to; (b) encourages the development of eco-friendly enterprises and projects in the country while dissuading the persistence of highly polluting, high-energy-consuming industries and projects; and (c) necessitates the transparency and disclosure of environmental information by both the financial sector and the corporate sector.

Figure 1 shows the growth of green loans in China from 2013 to 2021. With the constant development and push for the issuance of green credit in China, by the end of 2020, outstanding green loans in the country had amounted to 12 trillion yuan ($1.8 trillion), making it the highest in the world (Xie, 2021). And with green loans accounting for 90 percent of all green financial products in China, just a year later, the outstanding green loans in the country saw a substantial growth to nearly 15 trillion yuan by the end of the third quarter in 2021. According to a Deutsche Bank analyst, between 2013 and 2019, there has been an average annual growth of 19 percent for green loans in China (Liu, 2020). Furthermore, the PBoC launched a monetary policy tool that offers cheap lending to banks, which

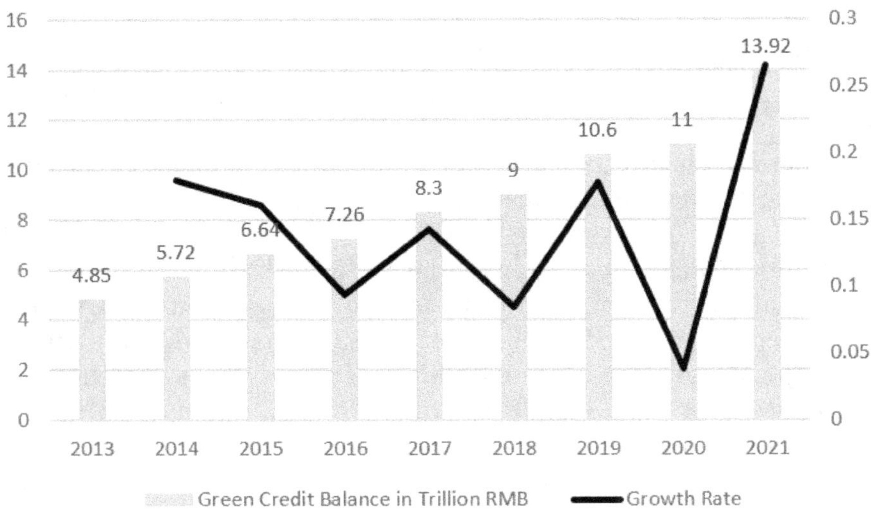

Figure 1. Growth of green credit balance in China.
Source: Adapted from Liu (2020, p. 37).

will in turn subsidize their lending to carbon reduction projects in 2021. This new policy tool is thus further expected to cause a boom in green loans and the growth of the green finance sector in China (Pang, 2021; Xue, 2021).

The literature on the effectiveness of China's green credit policy in executing the country's environmental goals largely yields positive findings while also revealing certain limitations. The existing literature seems to suggest that the green credit policy has successfully initiated a behavioral change in enterprises and corporations, with more Chinese companies recognizing that a shift toward eco-friendly conduct is becoming a survival imperative in the country. This is supported by a finding by Ji *et al.* (2021), which, using correlation and regression analysis, shows that the financial support provided by green credit caused a significant increase in "the scale of environmental protection investment of heavily polluting enterprises." This finding is especially compelling given that it demonstrates a promising shift in the behavior of businesses which are inherently highly polluting. The shift in behavior is also supported by another study which found that the green credit policy stimulates companies to behave in an environmentally friendly way, which then leads to the whole industry shifting toward green and sustainable development (Cao *et al.*, 2021c). Just like Cao *et al.* (2021c), who translated the behavior of individual companies to the advancement of their respective industries, Hu *et al.* (2020) also maintain that, indeed, green credit has promoted the transformation and optimization of the industrial structure, with a gradual expansion of green and environmentally friendly industries and a contraction of highly polluting, high-energy-consuming industries.

It is necessary to go one step further and analyze whether the behavioral changes of companies and the optimization of the overall industrial structure translate to concrete improvements in China's environmental conditions. Sun *et al.* (2019) observed that the green credit policy not only reduces pollution, but also helps prevent pollution at the source. Supporting this narrative, a study by Hu and Zheng (2021), based on the coupling coordination and PVAR models, observes that green credit has a significant inhibitory effect on carbon emissions. Song *et al.* (2021), using a spatial econometric model, find that green credit effectively promotes energy efficiency nationwide. A caveat is also added, though, about how this inhibitory effect has a long lead time but ensures a lasting impact; therefore, it is important for the policy to be consistent, stable, and durable (Hu & Zheng, 2021). Another limitation of the policy is pointed out by Zhang (2022), who expounds that, while green credit aids in reducing carbon emissions through increased pollution protection investments, the emission-reducing effect fades over time. He attributes this to the punitive effect that the policy has on a firm's investments dwindling over time Zhang (2022). Zhang *et al.* (2021b) also bring up a related drawback: the punitive effect, while effective on highly polluting, high-energy-consuming large-scale enterprises, is not a strong enough deterrent to have the same impact on the long-term financing of their small- and medium-sized counterparts. To summarize, the existing literature seems to agree largely on the effectiveness of China's green credit policy in bringing about positive changes and improvements in behaviors, industrial structure, and environmental outcomes. However, certain points for refinement do need to be considered to ensure the prevalence and longevity of the policy and its intended effects.

2.2. *Green bonds in China*

China's green bond market has displayed tremendous growth in the span of a few years since its inception. The country's decision to actively promote green bonds as a green financial instrument arose from a need for a more market-oriented mechanism, conducive to the efficient and sustainable allocation of capital in the industry. Green projects are novel and involve complex technology (IISD, 2015). Bank and government personnel may lack the knowledge or aptitude with regard to such matters to thoroughly assess the efficacy of a green project. Therefore, on top of the existing green credit market, which is "backed by implicit public funding and guarantees," there is a need for a direct financing market to provide a broader range of perspectives in the assessment of green projects, accurize risk evaluation and pricing, and, overall, increase the financing channels for green enterprises (IISD, 2015, p. 9).

A green bond is a direct financing instrument that entities such as government bodies, financial institutions, and businesses issue to raise funds for the sole purpose of supporting or investing in environmentally beneficial projects. Table 1 shows the timeline of

Table 1. A timeline of key regulations in China's green bond market.

Date of issuance	Issuing organization	Name of policy document	Main contents
December 2015	PBoC	Notice on Green Financial Bonds; Green Bond Endorsed Project Catalogue (2015 Edition)	An introduction to green bonds and its issuance in the interbank bond market, accompanied with a list of eligible green projects
January 2016	NDRC	Guidelines on Green Bond Issuance	Guidelines on the issuance of green bonds for non-listed companies
March 2016	Shanghai Stock Exchange	Notice on Launching the Pilot Programme of Green Corporate Bonds	Outline of the green bond regulations applicable to their respective markets
April 2016	Shenzhen Stock Exchange		
March 2017	CSRC	Guiding Opinions for Supporting the Green Bonds	An overarching regulatory framework for the trade of green bonds through stock markets
March 2017	NAFMII	Guidelines on Green Debt Financing Tools for Non-Financial Enterprises	Guidelines for non-financial enterprises, regulating their issuance of green notes in the interbank market
October 2017	CSRC	Green Bond Assessment and Verification Guidelines	Emphasized the quality and credibility of the green bond assessment and verification process
December 2017	PBoC		
July 2018	PBoC	Plan for green credit performance evaluation of banking depository financial institutions (trial)	Provided a basic reference for green credit performance evaluation of the PBOC branches
March 2019	NDRC, PBoC, and 5 other public institutions	Green Industry Guidance Catalogue	Clarified the definition of "green industry" and established clearer boundaries on what qualifies for a green project
June 2020	PBoC, CSRC, NDRC	Green Bond Endorsed Project Catalogue (2020 Edition)	Unification of green bond guidelines and the definition of green activities across market segments
April 2021	PBoC	Green Bond Endorsed Project Catalogue (2021 Edition)	Exclusion of coal and other fossil fuels from the list of approved green activities and adoption of the "no significant harm" principle

Source: Emmrich & Lütkehermöller (2021); policy documents from various government websites.

key regulations in China's green bond market. The inception of green bonds in China dates back to 2015, when the PBoC issued the "Notice on Green Financial Bonds" with the aim of "creat(ing) a financial channel for financial institutions to raise funds to support green industry projects through the bond market" (Peng *et al.*, 2018). Serving as the first formal introduction to green financial bonds in the Chinese market, the announcement specified the regulatory aspects of its issuance in the interbank bond market. It was accompanied by the Green Bond Endorsed Project Catalogue (2015 edition), which provided an outline of the projects that would qualify as green for the purpose of interbank green bond issuance. Within the following month, in January 2016, the NDRC released the "Guidelines on Green Bond Issuance," detailing corporate green bond issuance targeted at state-owned enterprises (SOEs). These guidelines had their own set of green bond requirements and eligible projects separate from those defined in the PBoC notice (New Climate Institute, 2021).

In 2016, the Shanghai and Shenzhen stock exchanges published the "Notice on Launching the Pilot Programme of Green Corporate Bonds," which contained regulations regarding green bond issuance through the stock exchanges. Then, in 2017, the "Guiding Opinions for Supporting the Green Bonds" was released by the CSRC, providing an "overarching regulatory framework for green bond trade through the stock exchanges" (Zhang, 2020, p. 1). The CSRC assumed the same green definitions as set out by the PBoC but "with a restrictive provision excluding high-polluting and high-energy consuming companies that conflict with the national industrial planning policy" (Green Finance Platform, 2017). The National Association of Financial Market Institutional Investors (NAFMII), shortly after and within that same month, issued the "Guidelines on Green Debt Financing Tools for Non-Financial Enterprises," applicable to non-financial institutions that issue bonds in the interbank market to raise funds for green projects (Zhang, 2020).

Within that year, to further bolster the country's green bond regulatory framework, the PBoC and CSRC issued the "Green Bond Assessment and Verification Guidelines," with regulatory stipulations for the verification of green bonds, including the "required qualifications and credentials, verification methods, and reporting requirements" (Green Finance Platform, 2018).

At this juncture, the different regulatory bodies each had their own set of rulings for green bond issuance for the respective market segments they were responsible for. Thus, there appeared to be a divergence even within the country on what qualifies as green. Therefore, "in a first effort to harmonize green bond regulations and the definition of green activities," the NDRC, along with six other public institutions, including the PBoC, launched the Green Industry Guidance Catalogue in 2019, establishing clearer boundaries on what qualifies for a green project and advancing the "harmonization of standards both within China and with international standards" (NCI, 2021, p. 8). Then, in June 2020, in alignment with the previous year's Green Industry Guidance Catalogue, the PBoC, CSRC, and NDRC jointly presented an updated version of the Green Bond Endorsed Project Catalogue (2020 edition), unifying the green bond guidelines and the definition of green activities across the market segments. The China Banking and Insurance Regulatory Commission (CBIRC), previously referred to as the CBRC, which merged with the CIRC in 2018, was also involved in this process of updating the catalogue in a bid to align green bond regulations with those of green credit. More recently, in April 2021, the PBoC further revised the catalogue to exclude coal and other fossil fuels from the list and adopted the "no significant harm" principle. These major exclusions were included in an effort to further align domestic standards with international standards and make Chinese green bonds appealing to international investors (SynTao Green Finance, 2021).

Despite its late start in the green bond market relative to other developed countries (Huang & Yue, 2019), China, in just a few years, has grown to become one of the largest green bond issuers in the world (Zhang, 2020). Just a year into the launch of the Chinese green bond market, it had already become the largest in the world by 2017, contributing 40 percent of total green bonds issued that year (Ma *et al.*, 2019). Since then, China has been closely competing with other countries to maintain its position as the largest green bond issuer globally. In 2019, China's green bond issuance reached a record of \$56.18 billion (Igno *et al.*, 2021). However, a slowdown due to the COVID-19 pandemic led to China issuing only a total of

$44 billion worth of green bonds in 2020, making it the second-largest green bond issuer that year (Jones, 2021). A recovery was evident the following year itself, with the issuance of Chinese green bonds surpassing the previous 2019 record within only the first nine months of 2021, "driven by nonfinancial companies such as those in the energy and consumer sectors as well as government-backed entities" (Igno *et al.*, 2021). In fact, the total volume of Chinese green bonds issued in 2021 was more than double that of the previous year, reaching a whopping figure of $94.77 billion (Isjwara & Ahmad, 2022). This figure is further estimated to grow by at least 80 percent in 2022 amidst "the government's initiatives to widen the investor base and encourage bank lending to energy transition projects" (Isjwara & Ahmad, 2022).

However, as seen in Figure 2, of the record volume of Chinese green bonds issued in 2021, more than half were not aligned with international standards. This has been a point of contention among

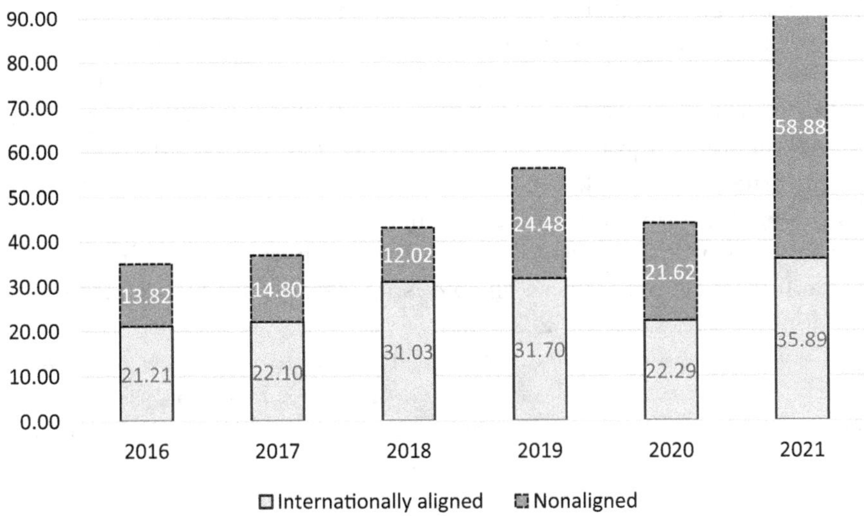

Figure 2. Volume of Chinese green bond issuance during 2016–2021 (US$ billion).

Note: Internationally aligned green bonds refer to those where at least 95 percent of proceeds are designated for green projects aligned with the Climate Bonds Taxonomy.

Source: Climate Bonds Initiative.

international authorities and investors. Some studies have been conducted on this matter to investigate whether the rapid growth and development of the Chinese green bond market over the few short years may be owed to the divergence in standards within the domestic market and across international markets. Based on a study conducted by Cao *et al.* (2021b), it is found that, instead of financing costs, it is regulatory arbitrage that motivates Chinese commercial banks to issue green bonds. The empirical results show that green bonds do not have lower financing costs than their non-green counterparts. Cao *et al.* (2021b), therefore, conclude that the rise in bank-issued green bonds in the country is owed to low-asset-liquidity banks supplementing their liquidity by "taking advantage of the convenient green bond financing permissions." This finding is corroborated in a study by Huang & Yue (2019), who explain the performance of green bonds in China as the outcome of financial repression. Issuers choose green bonds over other bonds because of the "convenient administrative procedures and lenient requirements" that come with issuing the former, as opposed to the latter's need for "permission from regulatory authorities and compliance with the requirements set by a variety of regulatory documents" (Huang & Yue, 2019). According to both studies, the lack of a uniform regulatory authority for green bonds and its unique rules system that is completely different from the international market are what have enabled the boom in the Chinese green bond market. This, therefore, points to a need for the Chinese green bond market to make further efforts to align itself both internally and externally so as to ensure its healthy and sustainable development (Cao *et al.*, 2021a).

There are some studies, however, that rebut this view, attributing the widespread uptake of green bonds in China to "greenium." Green-bond premium — or greenium in short — refers to the phenomenon where bonds designated for environmentally beneficial projects "command higher prices and lower yields than conventional bonds" (Bahceli, 2021), thereby lowering the cost of financing for issuers and serving as a motivating factor for their issuance. This phenomenon is highlighted in a study by Wang *et al.* (2020), who employed a univariate analysis to evaluate the difference in yield spreads between green bonds and their conventional counterparts. Their results show that the former's yield spreads are "significantly lower" than that of the latter's, leading to the conclusion that there is indeed a pricing premium of corporate green bonds relative to conventional bonds (Wang *et al.*, 2020). This finding is supported by another study by Jeong *et al.* (2021), who find the existence of greenium in Chinese green bond markets with statistical significance. Macaire & Naef (2021) also establish the existence of this phenomenon but with a focus on its more pronounced effect following a monetary policy reform by the PBoC. In June 2018, the PBoC introduced a policy allowing (and favoring) green financial bonds as collateral for its medium-term lending facility. According to Macaire & Naef (2021), this policy alone led to a further increase in greenium by 46 basis points post-reform. Li *et al.* (2020) also went a step further to verify the link between a firm's bond credit rating, green certification, and CSR score to its green bond yield spread; they find that a higher bond credit rating and CSR score and the presence of green certification help lower the cost of financing for a green bond issuer. Overall, the rapid boom of the Chinese green bond market over the course of a few years since its introduction cannot be owed to a single cause. Rather, it is the result of a number of factors at play.

2.3. *Carbon market in China*

China has become the largest carbon emitter since 2006 (BP, 2020). China's actions against climate change are therefore crucial for the world to achieve the two-degree-Celsius goal set in the Paris Agreement. Around the late 2000s, the Chinese government began to take various measures to promote sustainable economic development. In 2009, at the Copenhagen Global Climate Conference, China committed to reduce its carbon emissions per unit of GDP by 40–45 percent from its 2005 level by 2020 (Cui *et al.*, 2014). With great efforts spent nationwide, this commitment was achieved ahead of time, and by the end of 2017, China had lowered its carbon intensity by 46 percent from the 2005 level. Among the many policy measures taken to reduce carbon emissions, the carbon emission trading market is one that has seen increasing popularity globally and has been adopted by or is scheduled for implementation by 31 countries or regions.

The key events related to the development of a carbon market in China are summarized in Table 2. It is noted that seven carbon market pilots were proposed in 2011; in 2013, four of them, namely

Table 2. Timeline of carbon market development in China.

Year	Event
2011	China's 12th Five-Year Plan proposed to gradually establish a domestic carbon emissions trading market, and approved seven pilot areas in Beijing, Tianjin, Shanghai, Chongqing, Hubei, Guangdong, and Shenzhen.
2013	On June 18, 2013, Shenzhen started the first "cap-and-trade" ETS in developing countries. Quotas covered 635 industrial enterprises and 197 large-scale public construction enterprises. By the end of 2013, carbon price in the Shenzhen carbon market has increased from 28 yuan/ton to 80 yuan/ton.
	On November 26, 2013, Shanghai ETS was launched, and it published "Guidelines for China's Carbon Emission Accounting" and "China's Carbon Emission Accounting Methodology" and established a carbon market management system, which provided reference for other pilot areas.
	On December 19, 2013, Guangdong ETS was launched.
	On December 28, 2013, Beijing ETS was launched.
2014	By the end of 2014, all seven carbon market pilots had been launched.
2015	Before COP21 held in Paris in 2015, China made the announcement to reduce its carbon intensity by 60–65 percent from its 2005 level by 2030 and reach the carbon peak at the latest by 2030.
2017	In December 2017, the national ETS development was launched, a roadmap outlined and endorsed by the State Council. Eight industries, including petrochemicals, chemicals, building materials, steel, non-ferrous metals, papermaking, electric power, and civil aviation, will be gradually included in the national carbon market.
2018	Responsibility for climate change and the ETS was transferred from the National Development and Reform Commission (NDRC) to the Ministry of Ecology and Environment (MEE), which monitors GHGs alongside other pollutants at the enterprise level.
2020	President Xi Jinping announced at the UN General Assembly that China will achieve carbon neutrality by 2060.
	In December 2020, Administrative Measures for Carbon Emission Trading (Trial) were published (effective February 1, 2021).
2021	In February 2021, Interim Regulation for the Management of Carbon Emissions Trading (Draft) was published (Karplus, 2021).
	On July 16, 2021, the national carbon market started trading.

Source: Karplus (2021); policy documents from various government websites.

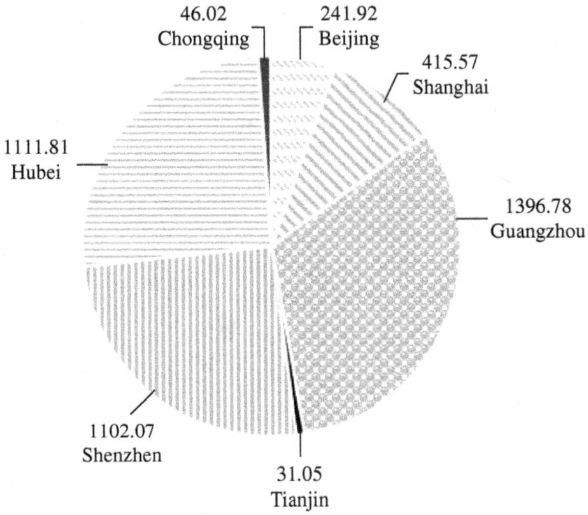

Figure 3. Carbon emission trading volumes of seven pilot markets in 2016 (unit: 10,000 tons).

Source: Tanpaifang.com.

Shenzhen, Shanghai, Guangdong, and Beijing, launched carbon markets, and in 2014, the other three in Tianjin, Chongqing, and Hubei started carbon emission trading markets as well. It is estimated that the seven carbon market pilots have covered 18 percent of the total population, 30 percent of GDP, and more than 7.43 million tons of carbon emissions from more than 2,000 enterprises in China (Zhou & Li, 2019). However, as seen in Figure 3, trading volumes were quite different in the seven pilot areas for two possible reasons: first, the quota allocation methods were different; second, the emission reduction targets were different.

In 2015, one year after China launched the seven pilot carbon markets, it promised to further reduce its carbon intensity by 60–65 percent from its 2005 level by 2030, a renewed target from its commitment made in 2009. This reduction target was further strengthened to "more than 65% by 2030" in December 2020 (Reuters, 2020), the same month when President Xi Jinping announced the target of carbon neutrality by 2060 at the UN General Assembly. After many years of carbon market pilot experience, a national carbon market officially started trading on July 16, 2021, even though its development had started as early as December 2017. A few development milestones that were reached during 2017–2021 are noteworthy:

A roadmap of a national emissions trading system (ETS) development was endorsed by the State Council in 2017. The regulatory responsibility was transferred from the NDRC to MEE in 2018. Two important policy documents, the "Administrative Measures for Carbon Emission Trading (Trial)" and the "Interim Regulation for the Management of Carbon Emissions Trading (Draft)" were published in December 2020 and February 2021, respectively, giving detailed guidelines on the trading administration and regulation. The national carbon market trading center is located in Shanghai, and the carbon quota registration system is located in Wuhan, Hubei. By the end of 2021, the cumulative trading volume of carbon emission allowances had reached 179 million tons, with a cumulative transaction value of 7.661 billion yuan; the compliance rate was 99.5 percent. The closing price on December 31, 2021, was 54.22 yuan/ton, an increase of 13 percent from the opening price on the first day of July 16, 2021.

As China's carbon market is a quota-based trading market like the EU Emissions Trading System, quota allocation is crucial for successful carbon trading. There are many studies that have examined the quota allocation in China (Han *et al.*, 2016; Qin *et al.*, 2017). There is also a large body of research that has examined the impacts of carbon market pilots in China (Munnings *et al.*, 2016; Cheng *et al.*, 2015; Hu *et al.*, 2017). Some studies find that carbon markets are effective in reducing carbon emissions in China (Wang *et al.*, 2015; Zhang *et al.*, 2017); however, the reason may not be due to efficiency improvements. For example, Cao *et al.* (2021a) investigate the effectiveness of China's carbon market pilots in reducing carbon emissions in the electricity sector. They find that coal consumption has decreased significantly due to reduced electricity production from coal-fired power plants rather than improved coal efficiency. Meanwhile, electricity production from non-coal-fired power plants has significantly increased in the ETS regions of China.

While many studies find that carbon market pilots are conducive to low-carbon economic development and China's transition to a low-carbon economy (Jiang *et al.*, 2016; Wang *et al.*, 2019), the negative impacts of these pilots on GDP, household consumption, investment, and innovation are evidenced by others (Lin & Jia, 2019a, 2019b; Shi *et al.*, 2018; Zhang & Wang, 2021). For instance, Zhang and Wang (2021) use data from A-share-listed companies in eight energy-intensive industries in China during 2009–2018 and the difference-in-differences approach to examine the investment impact of CET pilot policies. They find that the policy has reduced the investment expenditure of carbon emissions trading (CET)-covered enterprises by 0.24 percent, but the effects are heterogeneous across industries and regions. Shi *et al.* (2018) find that the ETS pilots in China have reduced innovation not only in regulated enterprises but also in non-regulated enterprises in the ETS region. As for the factors driving the carbon prices in China, Wen *et al.* (2022) find the main ones that vary across markets. Specifically, the carbon prices in the Hubei market are mainly affected by the electric power index, while the carbon price dynamics in the Guangdong and Shenzhen markets are mostly driven by market sentiment and air quality, respectively.

It is worth noting that almost all the existing studies on the carbon market in China are about the seven carbon market pilots since the nationwide carbon market only started in July 2021. One exception is the work by Fan *et al.* (2016), who used a multi-regional CGE model to evaluate the effects of a nationwide ETS policy in China, and their results show that the nationwide ETS policy can reduce emissions reduction cost, reduce regional development disparities, and improve the welfare of the whole society. After the nationwide carbon market operates for some time and data become available, we can expect that more studies will emerge to examine the effectiveness and efficiency of the nationwide carbon market as well as its impacts on various areas in the next few years.

3. Impact Analysis

3.1. *Data and econometric methods*

The green finance development index is taken from the work of Ren *et al.* (2020). It is constructed from four indicators: green credit, green securities, green insurance, and green investment, which are based on the green finance framework proposed by the PBoC in 2016 (People's Bank of China, 2016). Carbon intensity, GDP, and GDP per capita were extracted from the World Development Indicators (WDI) of the World Bank. Energy consumption data on coal, oil, natural gas, and renewables come from the BP Statistical Review of World Energy 2020 (BP, 2020). The consumptions of coal, oil, and natural gas are

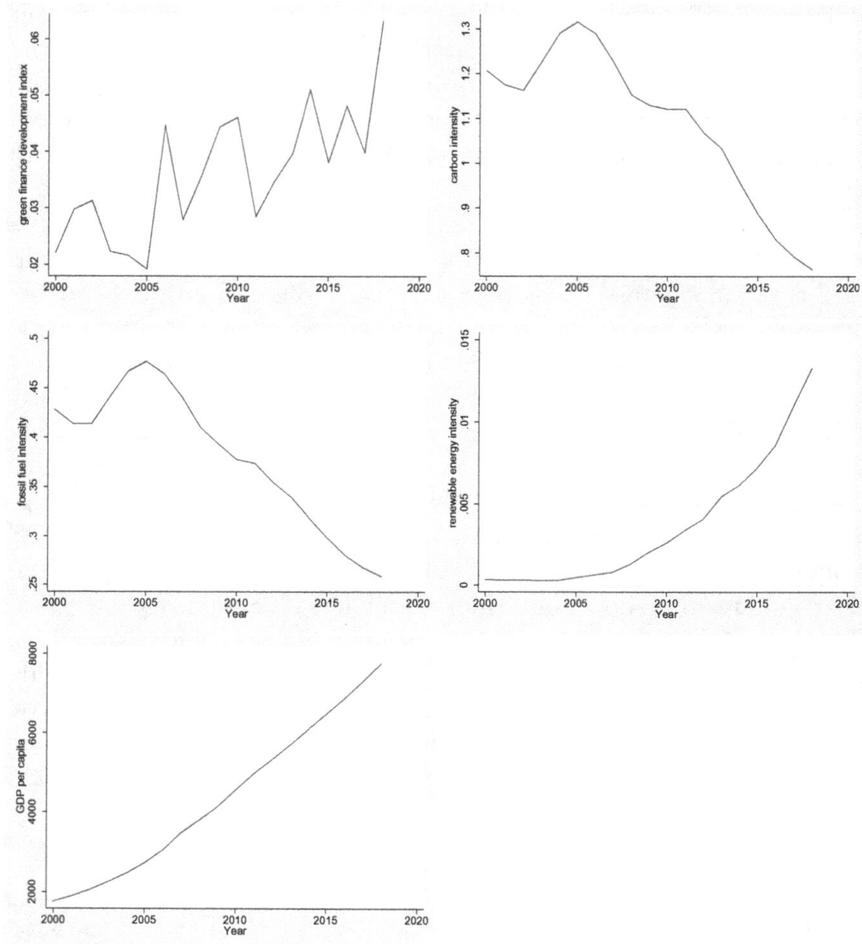

Figure 4. Time series plots of variables.

summed up to create the variable of fossil fuel consumption, which is then divided by GDP to create the variable fossil fuel intensity. Renewable energy intensity is generated from the ratio of renewable energy consumption to GDP. This study covers the period of 2000–2018. Figure 4 shows the time series plots of five variables. It is found that green finance development, renewable energy intensity, and GDP per capita are trending upward, while carbon intensity and fossil fuel intensity are trending downward, especially after 2005, which suggests that the effectiveness of the energy conservation

Table 3. Variable definitions and descriptive statistics.

Variable	Definition	Source	Mean	S.D.	Min	Max	N
log_gf	Green finance development index in logarithm	Ren *et al.* (2020)	−3.368	0.330	−3.953	−2.761	19
log_carbon	Carbon intensity in logarithm (kg CO_2 emissions per 2015 US$ of GDP)	WDI	0.076	0.168	−0.269	0.275	19
log_fossil	Fossil fuel intensity in logarithm (kg oil equivalent per 2010 US$ of GDP)	BP (2020); WDI	−0.985	0.194	−1.353	−0.740	19
log_renewable	Renewable energy intensity in logarithm (kg oil equivalent per 2010 US$ of GDP)	BP (2020); WDI	−6.406	1.408	−8.200	−4.321	19
log_gdp	GDP per capita in logarithm (constant 2010 US$)	WDI	8.274	0.485	7.478	8.956	19

and emission reduction policy started from the 11th Five-Year Plan (2016–2020). All variables used for empirical analysis are converted into logarithmic form. The definitions and descriptive statistics of the variables are presented in Table 3.

Since the time series is short with only 19 years' data, we decided to use a bivariate framework to examine the relationship between green finance and each of the four variables: carbon intensity, fossil fuel intensity, renewable energy intensity, and GDP per capita, specifically. First, unit root tests are employed to examine whether the series are stationary. When all the series are found to be integrated of order one, the cointegration test is next applied to check whether there is a long-term equilibrium relationship between green finance and each of the other four log variables. Subsequently, according to the Granger representation theorem, cointegrated variables can be represented by an error correction model. We proceed to estimate the vector error correction (VEC) models and perform Granger causality tests to identify the existence and direction of potential Granger causal relationships. The results of the empirical analysis are discussed next.

3.2. *Results and discussions*

Table 4 shows the unit root test results of the ADF test and the KPSS test for both the level variables and the variables after the first difference. Two models are considered, with one including only the intercept and the other including both the intercept and trend in the model specification. Results from the ADF unit root tests show that all five variables are not stationary at level but become stationary after the first difference (except GDP per capita) at least at the

Table 4. Unit root test results.

	Level		First difference	
	Intercept	Intercept and trend	Intercept	Intercept and trend
ADF test				
log_gf	−1.192	−3.147	−6.491***	−6.259***
log_carbon	1.318	−0.927	−2.042	−3.843**
log_fossil	0.500	−2.642	−3.049**	−2.359
log_renewable	−0.331	−2.641	−2.665*	−2.479
log_gdp	−2.588	−0.614	−1.077	−2.603
KPSS test				
log_gf	0.633**	0.083	0.144	0.134*
log_carbon	0.612**	0.177**	0.391*	0.055
log_fossil	0.634**	0.170**	0.363*	0.076
log_renewable	0.713**	0.096	0.192	0.150**
log_gdp	0.730**	0.179**	0.408*	0.144*

Note: $^{***}p < 0.01$; $^{**}p < 0.05$; $^{*}p < 0.10$.

significance level of 10 percent. Results from the KPSS tests show that the null hypothesis of stationarity is rejected at the significance level of 5 percent for the level variable in the model that contains only the intercept. However, after first differencing the variables, the stationarity hypothesis cannot be rejected at the 5 percent significance level in at least one of the model specifications. Combining the results from both the ADF and KPSS tests, we conclude that all five variables are integrated of order one. Therefore, we proceed with the Johansen cointegration test next.

Since the Johansen cointegration test is sensitive to the choice of lag order in the model, we first determine the optimal lag order based on the criteria of AIC, HQIC, and SBIC. The results are not shown but are available from the authors upon request. Table 5 reports trace statistics from the Johansen cointegration tests for four bivariate models (i.e., the models of green finance and one of the four variables, carbon intensity, fossil fuel intensity, renewable energy intensity, and GDP per capita, separately) in two model specifications with and without the trend term. The critical values at the significance level of 5 percent are also shown in the last column. Results show that

Table 5. Johensen cointegration test results.

	(1)	(2)	(3)	(4)	(5)
	log_gf and log_carbon (lag = 4)	**log_gf and log_fossil (lag = 4)**	**log_gf and log_renewable (lag = 3)**	**log_gf and log_gdp (lag = 3)**	**5 percent critical value**
(A) Model with only intercept					
$r = 0$	13.420*	15.433	19.757	40.021	15.41
$r = 1$	0.686	0.266*	1.430*	10.903	3.76
(B) Model with both intercept and trend					
$r = 0$	21.590	27.217	25.036	25.677	18.17
$r = 1$	2.058*	13.180	8.257	0.193*	3.74

Notes: Columns (1)–(4) list the Johansen cointegration test results for four bivariate models; the optimal lag order for each model is shown in the bracket. The last column lists critical values at the significance level of 5 percent. Panel A lists trace statistics for the model specification including only the intercept; Panel B lists trace statistics for the model specification including both the intercept and trend terms. $^{***}p < 0.01$; $^{**}p < 0.05$; $^{*}p < 0.10$.

Table 6. Cointegration equations for the four bivariate models.

$\ln\text{ci} = 0.796\ln\text{g}f - 0.050t + 3.224$	$\ln\text{fossil} = -2.860\ln\text{g}f - 10.877$
(0.103)	(0.484)
$\ln\text{renew} = 5.530\ln\text{g}f + 12.771$	$\ln\text{gdp} = 4.000\ln\text{g}f - 0.075t + 22.398$
(0.586)	(0.659)

there is one cointegrating relationship between green finance and carbon intensity and between green finance and GDP per capita when the model specification includes both the intercept and trend terms; while for the models of green finance and fossil fuel intensity as well as green finance and renewable energy intensity, there is one cointegrating relationship when the model contains only the intercept. Based on the findings of the existence of a long-term relationship in the four bivariate models, we can proceed to estimate the VEC model.

The long-run cointegration equations for the four bivariate models are shown in Table 6. In parentheses are the standard errors of the estimate of interest. It is found that green finance development is significantly and positively related to carbon intensity, renewable energy intensity, and GDP per capita and negatively related to fossil fuel intensity. Specifically, a 1 percent increase in green finance development index is associated with a 0.796 percent increase in carbon intensity, a 5.53 percent increase in renewable energy intensity, and a 4 percent increase in GDP per capita. Meanwhile, when the green finance development index increases by 1 percent, fossil fuel intensity will decrease by 2.86 percent. The relationships between green finance and fossil fuel intensity, renewable energy intensity, and GDP per capita are within expectations, as green finance is likely to direct finance and resource allocation to clean energy projects more efficiently. Therefore, green finance development is expected to help reduce fossil fuel consumption and increase renewable energy consumption per unit of GDP and, at the same time, stimulate the economic development. However, the positive relationship between the green finance development index and carbon intensity is unexpected, highlighting the difficulty of achieving the 30–60 target through the development of green finance. However, it should be noted that the data used here cover the period of 2000–2018, while green finance is expected to develop more quickly and at a larger scale only after the

Table 7. Granger causality test results based on VECM.

	(A) log_gf Granger causes ___:			(B) ___Granger causes log_gf:		
	Short-run	Long-run		Short-run	Long-run	
		CI	Short-run + CI		CI	Short-run + CI
log_carbon	5.98	1.09	6.06	10.79**	3.58*	16.98***
log_fossil	9.67**	5.65**	10.38**	27.95***	6.57**	29.55***
log_renewable	0.70	0.01	0.99	30.14***	21.34***	101.49***
log_gdp	14.74***	1.36	16.83***	8.01**	29.07***	31.37***

Notes: Column (A) tests whether log_gf Granger-causes each of the four variables: log_carbon, log_fossil, log_renewable, and log_gdp; Column (B) tests whether each of the four variables Granger-causes log_gf. Each row represents one vector error correction model of log_gf and the specific variable. Three tests are performed for each direction of Granger causality, namely, the short-run Granger causality test on the differenced terms, the long-run Granger causality test on the error correction term, and another long-run Granger casualty test on both the error correction term and the differenced terms. The χ^2 test statistics are shown in the table. $^{***}p < 0.01$; $^{**}p < 0.05$; $^{*}p < 0.10$.

double-carbon target was raised in 2020. Therefore, we speculate that the relationship may evolve in the future with the fast development of green finance in China over the next 10 or even more years.

Lastly, we try to identify the Granger causal relationships among the four pairs of variables based on the VEC model. Results are shown in Table 7. The short-run Granger causality is tested on the coefficients of differenced terms, while the long-run Granger causal relationships include two tests: one on the coefficient of the error correction term, and the other, a joint test, on both the coefficient of the error correction term and the coefficients of the differenced terms. Each row of variables represents one VEC model of the bivariate framework for the green finance development index and the specific variable. It is found that all four variables Granger-cause green finance in both the short run and the long run significantly. However, green finance development only Granger-causes fossil fuel intensity and GDP per capita in both the short term and the long term, while there is no Granger causality running from green finance development to carbon intensity and renewable energy intensity. These findings suggest that, statistically, many factors appear to play a role in the development of green finance; nevertheless, though green finance may inhibit fossil fuel consumption, its impacts on reducing carbon emissions and promoting renewable energy consumption are not strong enough. The finding of the existence of unidirectional Granger causal relationships of carbon intensity and renewable energy intensity with green finance is different from that reported by Ren *et al.* (2020), which supports bidirectional Granger causal relationships. Nevertheless, they do note that green finance may not "play an important role in promoting the development of new energy," which is in line with our findings.

4. Conclusion

This chapter reviewed the green finance policies and the recent developments in green credit, green bonds, and carbon markets in China. Green finance in China has undergone rapid development since the 2010s, when environmental and climate change issues had drawn growing attention domestically. China's green credit balance has grown at a compound annual growth rate (CAGR) of 14 percent during the period of 2013–2021, even though COVID-19 has significantly and negatively affected its growth in 2020 with only a 3.8 percent growth. China's green bond market has also displayed tremendous growth since its inception and has seen a CAGR of 22 percent during 2016–2021, even with a negative 21.8 percent growth in 2020. The carbon market, though developed much later, has become the world's largest carbon market, immediately after the nationwide market opened in July 2021.

With the rapid economic development in China, there have been many studies on various issues related to green finance development in China. Most studies seem to agree on the effectiveness of China's green credit policy in that it has brought about a positive change and improvement in behaviors, industrial structures, and environmental outcomes, though there are points for improvement to ensure the prevalence and longevity of the policy and its intended effects. Studies on the Chinese bond market find that there are many factors at play to explain its boom in a short time span, and it is crucial to have a unified and clear guideline on the definition and verification of green projects to ensure the healthy and sustainable development of the green bond market. In regard to the literature on the

Chinese carbon market, studies in general agree that it has a conducive impact on the low-carbon economic development, or the green transition of China, though some negative impacts were identified by some studies.

This chapter empirically investigated the relationship between green finance development and carbon emissions, fossil fuels, renewable energy, and economic development in China. The cointegrating analysis shows that green finance development is significantly and positively related to renewable energy intensity and GDP per capita and negatively related to fossil fuel intensity. The Granger causality analysis finds that green finance development Granger-causes fossil fuel intensity and GDP per capita in both the short run and the long run; however, no Granger causality is found from green finance development to carbon intensity and renewable energy intensity. Our results are consistent with the findings of most studies, which found that green finance plays a positive role in stimulating green investments in research and development of renewable energy or clean technology in the fossil fuel industry. The unexpected association between green finance and carbon intensity as well as the absence of a Granger causal relationship between green finance and carbon and renewable energy intensity may be partly due to the shortness of the period 2000–2018 considered in this chapter, which does not reflect the recent and rapid development since 2020.

References

Aizawa, M. & Yang, C. (2010). Green credit, green stimulus, green revolution? China's mobilization of banks for environmental cleanup. *The Journal of Environment & Development, 19*(2), 119–144.

Bahceli, Y. (2021, June 2). Analysis: 'Greenium' shrinks as climate bond sales swell to record. Reuters. Retrieved from https://www.reuters.com/business/sustainable-business/greenium-shrinks-climate-bond-sales-swell-record-2021-06-02/.

BP (2020). *BP Statistical Review of World Energy 2020.* London, UK: BP.

Cao, X., Jin, C., & Ma, W. (2021b). Motivation of Chinese commercial banks to issue green bonds: Financing costs or regulatory arbitrage? *China Economic Review, 66*, 101582.

Cao, J., Ho, M. S., Ma, R., *et al.* (2021a). When carbon emission trading meets a regulated industry: Evidence from the electricity sector of China. *Journal of Public Economics*, *200*, 104470.

Cao, Y., Zhang, Y., Yang, L., *et al.* (2021c). Green credit policy and maturity mismatch risk in polluting and non-polluting companies. *Sustainability, 13*(7), 3615.

Chang, Y. (2019). Green Finance in Singapore: Barriers and Solutions. *ADBI Working Paper 915.* Tokyo: Asian Development Bank Institute.

Chang, Y., Ji, Q., & Zhang, D. (2021). Green finance and energy policy: Obstacles, opportunities, and options. *Energy Policy, 157*, 112497.

Cheng, B., Dai, H., Wang, P., *et al.* (2015). Impacts of carbon trading scheme on air pollutant emissions in Guangdong Province of China. *Energy for Sustainable Development, 27*, 174–185.

Choi, J., Escalante, D., & Larsen, M. L. (2020). Green Banking in China — Emerging Trends. Climate Policy Initiative.

COP26 (2021). COP26 the Glasgow climate pact. In *UN Climate Change Conference UK 21.* Retrieved from https://ukcop26.org/wp-content/uploads/2021/11/COP26-Presidency-Outcomes-The-Climate-Pact.pdf.

Cui, L. B., Fan, Y., Zhu, L., *et al.* (2014). How will the emissions trading scheme save cost for achieving China's 2020 carbon intensity reduction target? *Applied Energy, 136*, 1043–1052.

Emmrich, J. & Lütkehermöller, K. (2021). China: Transforming the finance sector with technical assistance. *SNAPFI Case Study*, Project Number 820043.

Fan, Y., Wu, J., Xia, Y., *et al.* (2016). How will a nationwide carbon market affect regional economies and efficiency of CO_2 emission reduction in China? *China Economic Review, 38*, 151–166.

Fleming, S. (2020, November 9). What is green finance and why is it important? World Economic Forum. Retrieved from https://www.weforum.org/agenda/2020/11/what-is-green-finance/.

Green Finance Platform (2017). China Securities Regulatory Commission Green Bond Assessment Guidelines for Listed Companies. https://www.greenfinanceplatform.org/policies-and-regulations/china-securities-regulatory-commission-green-bond-assessment-guidelines

Green Finance Platform (2018). China's Green Bond Verification Guidelines. https://www.greenfinanceplatform.org/policies-and-regulations/china's-green-bond-verification-guidelines

Han, R., Tang, B. J., Fan, J. L., *et al.* (2016). Integrated weighting approach to carbon emission quotas: An application case of Beijing-Tianjin-Hebei region. *Journal of Cleaner Production, 131*, 448–459.

He, L., Zhang, L., Zhong, Z., *et al.* (2019). Green credit, renewable energy investment and green economy development: Empirical analysis based on 150 listed companies of China. *Journal of Cleaner Production, 208*, 363–372.

Ho, V. H. (2018). Sustainable finance & China's green credit reforms: A test case for bank monitoring of environmental risk. *Cornell International*

Law Journal, 51. Retrieved from https://ww3.lawschool.cornell.edu/research/ILJ/upload/Ho-final.pdf.

Hu, Y. & Zheng, J. (2021). Is green credit a good tool to achieve "Double Carbon" goal? Based on coupling coordination model and PVAR Model. *Sustainability, 13*(24), 14074.

Hu, Y. J., Li, X. Y., & Tang, B. J. (2017). Assessing the operational performance and maturity of the carbon trading pilot program: The case study of Beijing's carbon market. *Journal of Cleaner Production, 161*, 1263–1274.

Hu, Y., Jiang, H., & Zhong, Z. (2020). Impact of green credit on industrial structure in China: Theoretical mechanism and empirical analysis. *Environmental Science and Pollution Research, 27*(10), 10506–10519.

Huang, T. & Yue, Q. (2019). How the game changer was generated? An analysis on the legal rules and development of China's green bond market. *International Environmental Agreements: Politics, Law and Economics, 20*(1), 85–102.

Igno, A. C., Isjwara, R., & Ramos, M. (2021, October 26). China green bond market breaks record with policy push, offshore interest. S&P Global Market Intelligence. Retrieved from https://www.spglobal.com/marketintelligence/en/news-insights/latest-news-headlines/china-green-bond-market-breaks-record-with-policy-push-offshore-interest-67105182.

International Institute for Sustainable Development (IISD) (2015). Greening China's financial system. Retrieved from https://www.iisd.org/system/files/publications/greening-chinas-financial-system.pdf.

Isjwara, R. & Ahmad, R. (2022, January 19). China green bond issuances set to cross $100B mark in 2022. S&P Global Market Intelligence. Retrieved from https://www.spglobal.com/marketintelligence/en/news-insights/latest-news-headlines/china-green-bond-issuances-set-to-cross-100b-mark-in-2022-68453272.

Jeong, H., Hyun, S., & Li, C. (2021). Exploring Greenium in the Chinese green bond market: Focusing on the primary market. Retrieved from SSRN: https://ssrn.com/abstract=3962807 or http://dx.doi.org/10.2139/ssrn.3962807.

Ji, L., Jia, P., & Yan, J. (2021). Green credit, environmental protection investment and debt financing for heavily polluting enterprises. *PLoS One, 16*(12), e0261311.

Jiang, J., Xie, D., Ye, B., *et al.* (2016). Research on China's cap-and-trade carbon emission trading scheme: Overview and outlook. *Applied Energy, 178*, 902–917.

Jones, L. (2021, September 30). China totalled USD44bn in labelled green bonds during 2020: Second largest country for green issuance. Climate bonds initiative. Retrieved from https://www.climatebonds.

net/2021/09/china-totalled-usd44bn-labelled-green-bonds-during-2020-second-largest-country-green.

Karplus, V. J. (2021). China's CO_2 Emissions Trading System: History, Status, and Outlook. Cambridge, Mass.: Harvard Project on Climate Agreements.

Klein, A., Widge, V., Bergedieck, L., Maheshwari, A., & Avendano Ugaz, F. (2019). Green Finance: A Bottom-up Approach to Track Existing Flows (Vol. 2): Full Report (English). Washington, D.C.: World Bank Group.

Li, Z., Tang, Y., Wu, J., *et al.* (2020). The interest costs of green bonds: Credit ratings, corporate social responsibility, and certification. *Emerging Markets Finance & Trade, 56*(12), 2679–2692.

Lin, B. & Jia, Z. (2019a). Impacts of carbon price level in carbon emission trading market. *Applied Energy, 239*, 157–170.

Lin, B. & Jia, Z. (2019b). What will China's carbon emission trading market affect with only electricity sector involvement? A CGE based study. *Energy Economics, 78*, 301–311.

Liu, L. (2020). China: Green finance to green transition. In Reid, J. (Eds.), Konzept #19: What We Must Do to Rebuild (pp. 35–39). Deutsche Bank Research.

Ma, J., Liu, J., Chen, Z., *et al.* (2019). China's Green bond market. Retrieved from https://hkgreenfinance.org/wp-content/uploads/2019/12/China%E2%80%99s-Green-Bond-Market.pdf.

Macaire, C. & Naef, A. (2021). Greening monetary policy: Evidence from the People's Bank of China. *Working Papers.* Retrieved from https://publications.banque-france.fr/sites/default/files/medias/documents/wp812_0.pdf.

Meng, A., Xie, W., Shao, H., & Shang, J. (2021). China Green Bond Market Report 2020. Climate Bonds Initiative.

Munnings, C., Morgenstern, R. D., Wang, Z., *et al.* (2016). Assessing the design of three carbon trading pilot programs in China. *Energy Policy, 96*, 688–699.

Naughton, B. (2021). *The Rise of China's Industrial Policy, 1978 to 2020.* Mexico City: Buena Onda, S.A. de C.V. Retrieved from https://dusselpeters.com/CECHIMEX/Naughton2021_Industrial_Policy_in_China_CECHIMEX.pdf.

New Climate Institute (NCI) (2021). China: Transforming the finance sector with technical assistance. Retrieved from https://newclimate.org/wp-content/uploads/2021/06/SNAPFI.-Transforming-Chinas-Financial-Sector.pdf.

Pang, I. (2021, November 9). China offers cheaper green loans. ING Bank. Retrieved from THINK Economic and Financial Analysis: https://think.ing.com/articles/china-offers-cheaper-green-loans/.

Peng, H., Luo, X., & Zhou, C. (2018). Introduction to China's Green Finance System. *Journal of Service Science and Management, 11*(1), 94–100.

People's Bank of China (2016, September 1). The People's Bank of China and Six Other Agencies Jointly Issue "Guidelines for Establishing the Green Financial System". Retrieved from http://www.pbc.gov.cn/english/130721/3131759/index.html.

Qin, Q., Liu, Y., Li, X., *et al.* (2017). A multi-criteria decision analysis model for carbon emission quota allocation in China's east coastal areas: Efficiency and equity. *Journal of Cleaner Production, 168*, 410–419.

Ren, X., Shao, Q., & Zhong, R. (2020). Nexus between green finance, non-fossil energy use, and carbon intensity: Empirical evidence from China based on a vector error correction model. *Journal of Cleaner Production, 277*, 122844.

Reuters (2020, December 13). China's Xi targets steeper cut in carbon intensity by 2030. Retrieved from https://www.reuters.com/world/china/chinas-xi-targets-steeper-cut-carbon-intensity-by-2030-2020-12-12/.

Shi, B., Feng, C., Qiu, M., *et al.* (2018). Innovation suppression and migration effect: The unintentional consequences of environmental regulation. *China Economic Review, 49*, 1–23.

Song, M., Xie, Q., & Shen, Z. (2021). Impact of green credit on high-efficiency utilization of energy in China considering environmental constraints. *Energy Policy, 153*, 112267.

Sun, J., Wang, F., Yin, H., *et al.* (2019). Money talks: The environmental impact of China's green credit policy. *Journal of Policy Analysis and Management, 38*(3), 653–680.

SynTao Green Finance (2021). Highlights of China's new green catalogue 2021. SynTao Green Finance. Retrieved from http://www.syntaogf.com/Uploads/files/Highlights%20of%20China%E2%80%99s%20New%20Green%20Catalogue%202021.pdf.

UNFCCC (2021). COP26 the Glasgow Climate Pact.

Wang, J., Chen, X., Li, X., *et al.* (2020). The market reaction to green bond issuance: Evidence from China. *Pacific-Basin Finance Journal, 60*, 101294.

Wang, P., Dai, H. C., Ren, S. Y., *et al.* (2015). Achieving Copenhagen target through carbon emission trading: Economic impacts assessment in Guangdong Province of China. *Energy, 79*, 212–227.

Wang, G., Deng, X., Wang, J., *et al.* (2019). Carbon emission efficiency in China: A spatial panel data analysis. *China Economic Review, 56*, 101313.

Wen, F., Zhao, H, Zhao, L., *et al.* (2022). What drives carbon price dynamics in China? *International Review of Financial Analysis, 79*, 101999.

Xie, E. (2021, April 2). What is green finance, and why is it important to China's carbon neutral goal? South China morning post. Retrieved from https://www.scmp.com/news/china/politics/article/3128167/what-green-finance-and-why-it-important-chinas-carbon-neutral?module=perpetual_scroll_0&pgtype=article&campaign=3128167.

Xinhua (2021a, July 02). China boosts green finance in pursuit of carbon neutrality. The State Council of the People's Republic of China. http://english.www.gov.cn/statecouncil/ministries/202107/02/content_WS60df0eaec6d0df57f98dc53f.html.

Xinhua (2021b, December 15). China's carbon market sees trading volume top 100 million tonnes. Xinhua Net. http://www.news.cn/english/2021-12/15/c_1310374653.htm.

Xue, Y. (2021, November 11). Cheap green loans funded by China's Central Bank could accelerate clean, energy saving projects, analysts Say. South China Morning Post. Retrieved from https://www.scmp.com/business/article/3155733/cheap-green-loans-funded-chinas-central-bank-could-accelerate-clean-energy.

Zhang, H. (2020). Regulating green bonds in the People's Republic of China: Definitional divergence and implications for policy making. Tokyo: Asian Development Bank Institute. *ADBI Working Paper 1072.*

Zhang, D. (2022). Does the green loan policy boost greener production? — Evidence from Chinese firms. *Emerging Markets Review, 51*, 100882.

Zhang, Y. J. & Wang, W. (2021). How does China's carbon emissions trading (CET) policy affect the investment of CET-covered enterprises? *Energy Economics, 98*, 105224.

Zhang, D., Zhang, Z., & Managi, S. (2019). A bibliometric analysis on green finance: Current status, development, and future directions. *Finance Research Letters, 29*, 425–430.

Zhang, D., Mohsin, M., Rasheed, A. K., *et al.* (2021a). Public spending and green economic growth in BRI region: Mediating role of green finance. *Energy Policy, 153*, 112256.

Zhang, K., Li, Y., Qi, Y., *et al.* (2021b). Can green credit policy improve environmental quality? Evidence from China. *Journal of Environmental Management, 298*, 113445.

Zhang, S., Wu, Z., Wang, Y., *et al.* (2021c). Fostering green development with green finance: An empirical study on the environmental effect of green credit policy in China. *Journal of Environmental Management, 296*, 113159.

Zhang, Y. J., Peng, Y. L., Ma, C. Q., *et al.* (2017). Can environmental innovation facilitate carbon emissions reduction? Evidence from China. *Energy Policy, 100*, 18–28.

Zhou, K. & Li, Y. (2019). Carbon finance and carbon market in China: Progress and challenges. *Journal of Cleaner Production, 214*, 536–549.

Zhou, H., & Xu, G. (2022). Research on the impact of green finance on China's regional ecological development based on system GMM model. *Resources Policy, 75*, 102454.

Zhou, X., Tang, X., & Zhang, R. (2020). Impact of green finance on economic development and environmental quality: A study based on provincial panel data from China. *Environmental Science and Pollution Research, 27*(16), 19915–19932.

https://doi.org/10.1142/9781800614482_0004

Chapter 4

Green Financing and Its Future Prospects in Climate-Vulnerable Asian Countries: The Case of Bangladesh

Syeda Shehtaz Hasib[*,†,‡] **and Syed Abul Basher**[*,§]

[*]*Department of Economics, East West University, Dhaka, Bangladesh*

[†]*Partnership Development Team, Friendship, Dhaka, Bangladesh*

[‡]*shetaj28@gmail.com*

[§]*syed.basher@gmail.com*

Abstract

We discuss the various approaches the Bangladesh Bank has taken to address climate risks in the financial system of Bangladesh, one of the countries most vulnerable to climate change. To understand the forces reshaping green financing in Bangladesh, we provide a systematic account of the green financing initiatives being considered by the Bangladesh Bank to help tackle climate issues. We also review recent empirical studies that offer solution-oriented policy pathways for reducing carbon emissions and preventing climate change. In this context, we discuss how Bangladesh Bank can step up its climate change efforts in response to global warming taking place more rapidly than was predicted.

[*]Corresponding author.

1. Introduction

Mark Carney's[1] landmark speech at Lloyd's of London sparked a global conversation about how climate change could undermine the financial stability of the banking system (Carney, 2015). He identified three channels[2] through which climate change shocks can affect financial stability. His speech also raised an important question regarding what central banks can do to tackle climate change. Back in 2015, it might have seemed odd for a central bank to be talking about climate change, as its job is typically to worry about the price and financial stability of an economy. In fact, Carney's speech spurred backlash, rather unsurprisingly, from oil companies (*The Economist*, 2016). Several studies have questioned whether the task of climate mitigation should be delegated to technocratic institutions such as central banks (Demekas & Grippa, 2021). Nevertheless, over the past couple of years, there has been an intense debate about why central banks should care about climate change.

Although little known internationally, Bangladesh Bank — the central bank and financial sector regulator of Bangladesh — started greening the banking system in 2011, roughly half a decade earlier than developed-market central banks. What is unique about Bangladesh Bank's green initiative is that it started before its citizens and businesses demanded sustainability as a part of economic development. In the parlance of the environmental Kuznets curve, Bangladesh has not yet reached the turning point where concerns over environmental degradation, such as carbon dioxide (CO_2) emissions per capita, outweigh the growth in gross domestic product (GDP) per capita. However, being identified as one of the most vulnerable countries to climate change, addressing the environmental and social risks associated with climate change has become a more urgent priority for Bangladesh Bank. As we elaborate in the following, Bangladesh Bank has promulgated a range of sustainable and inclusive banking policy initiatives in the past decade.

---

[1]Former governor of Bank of England.

[2]Briefly, these are physical risks (e.g., the loss of financial assets due to floods or storms), liability risks (e.g., an individual or a business seeking compensation from an allegedly responsible party), and transition risks (e.g., the financial risks involved when a country moves toward a lower-carbon economy).

Bangladesh is not the only country in the region to be an early mover in sustainability banking; neighboring developing countries in South and Southeast Asia have also taken similar steps in the past as they share the common existential threat of climate change. Moreover, the carbon intensity of developing Asian countries is far higher than that of their developed counterparts. For example, as of 2018, the levels of carbon intensity — measured as CO_2 emissions (kg per 2015 US$ of GDP) — were 0.8 and 0.7 in South and East Asia and the Pacific (excluding high-income countries), respectively (Volz, 2018). By comparison, the carbon intensities in the euro area and North America are 0.2 and 0.3, respectively. In other words, the developing Asian countries emit far more CO_2 to produce one dollar of GDP than the developed European and North American countries. Against the backdrop of climate vulnerability and the need for reducing carbon intensity, central banks in selected Asian countries have systematically integrated sustainability into the lending and investment decision-making process (Volz, 2018). In fact, as noted in Volz's publication, both Bangladesh Bank and the People's Bank of China have been pioneers in green finance in Asia.

The main findings presented in this chapter are summarized as follows: (i) Bangladeshi banks and insurers may be unable to deal with the potential financial consequences of climate change due to rising non-performing loans and inadequate governance. Conducting "climate stress tests" may be a solution. (ii) Just as monetary policy is rendered ineffective when commercial banks keep excess reserves, central bank measures will fail to boost the green economy unless banks and financial institutions (FIs) mobilize money for retail investors. Intermediary groups play an essential role in connecting green initiatives with appropriate finance and filling gaps for the government to meet its goals. (iii) Bangladesh Bank's green policies must strengthen climate readiness, adaptation, and mitigation efforts. (iv) Green loans provide both direct and indirect advantages. Local banks in the nation can be encouraged to learn from overseas banks about the most effective ways to incentivize green lending.

This chapter reviews the progress made so far in greening the financial sector in Bangladesh. In so doing, following the introduction, Section 2 presents a brief overview of Bangladesh's climatic and economic conditions. Section 3, the core and longest part of the chapter, presents an in-depth analysis of the green banking initiatives from their inception to the present. Section 4 reviews the findings of selected studies on green financing. Section 5 provides a discussion of major policy issues related to green financing. Section 6 concludes the chapter.

2. A Brief Overview of the Climatic and Economic Conditions of Bangladesh and Its Neighboring Countries

2.1. *Account of the global climate risks*

The citizens of Bangladesh are at the forefront of fighting the consequences of disasters brought about by climate change. Bangladesh, a low-lying delta with two-thirds of the land below five-meter sea level (The World Bank, 2016), is also one of the world's most densely populated countries, with a significant dependency on agricultural activities in disaster-prone areas. With the unpredictable shifts in climatic conditions, the last-mile disadvantaged communities living in the rural areas, including those living on shifting river islands with no regular connectivity with the mainland, bear the brunt of the climate-related calamities at least once a year. According to the Global Climate Risk Index 2021 (Eckstein *et al.*, 2021), Bangladesh ranks seventh on "The Long-Term Climate Risk Index (CRI): 10 countries most affected from 2000 to 2019," with a CRI score of 28.33 and 185 occurrences of climate disasters in the past 20 years.

Other nearby developing and least developed countries also shoulder climate change risks. India, Myanmar, Nepal, Pakistan, Thailand, and the Philippines are also in the top 10 list of the Long-Term Climate Risk Index. Even though Vietnam is not in the top 10, it has a CRI score of 35.67, putting it in the 13th position (Eckstein *et al.*, 2021).

The Intergovernmental Panel on Climate Change (IPCC) identifies unmanageable urbanization due to rising domestic fragility and climate-driven migration as the key contributing factor to the threat of climate change in Bangladesh (Hasan & Macdonald, 2021). Dhaka's[3] high population density problem is intensifying in the face

[3]Dhaka is the capital city of Bangladesh.

of a continual influx of migrants due to climate-related displacement. On top of that, the influx of nearly one million Rohingya refugees in a concentrated area in Bangladesh's coastal district has led to several environmental problems, including deforestation and groundwater depletion.

The erratic weather patterns due to evolving climatic conditions affect people's physical and mental health. In a survey of 15,000 people across 3,600 households in Bangladesh, Mahmud *et al.* (2021) found that a 1 degree Celsius increase in temperature increases the probability of contracting a respiratory infection by 5.7 percent (Mahmud *et al.*, 2021). Similarly, an increase in humidity is associated with higher rates of waterborne diseases, such as diarrhea and cholera, and increases the risk of the spread of dengue in the capital city. Moreover, the study also sought to elucidate the impact of weather change on mental health and found that rising temperatures are negatively correlated with depression and anxiety.

2.2. *Economic perspectives*

According to the Ministry of Finance in 2021, the growth rate in Bangladesh reached, on average, 8.15 percent in the fiscal year 2018–2019. However, the COVID-19 pandemic affected economic conditions severely. Now, in 2022, Bangladesh is recording a recovery from the pandemic, and its economy is expected to improve in a short period. In the provisional records of the review document, the GDP per capita in the fiscal year 2020–2021 is $2,097 (an increase of $167 from the previous year), and the national income per capita is $2,227 (an increase of $203 from the previous year). With Bangladesh in line to gain the status of a middle-income country, the social, economic, and technological changes are swift and drastic. As such, it is very important to monitor and manage the methods of rapid industrialization and development to ensure minimal environmental dilapidation.

2.2.1. *Economic loss due to climatic risks*

In general, the effects of climate change observed worldwide are evident in Bangladesh, increasing the vulnerability of a country's economy. The monetary impacts occur through the loss and damage of resources and belongings and decreased sources of income. The other monetary implication includes the costs of mitigation, rehabilitation, and adaptation. So, increased global warming and climate-induced risks each year mean more significant future costs to be incurred.

According to the Global Climate Risk Index (2021), Bangladesh has incurred a loss of $13 million in purchasing power parity (PPP), equivalent to a 37 percent loss in GDP per unit, on average, in the past 20 years. The trends are similar for neighboring countries vulnerable to climate change, such as Pakistan, Myanmar, India, and Vietnam, with a loss per unit GDP summing up to 33, 19, 52, and 47 percent, respectively.

Ra and Li (2018) conducted an infrastructure gap assessment in developing Asia, recording an amount of $26.2 trillion between 2016 and 2030, or $1.7 trillion annually. The Asian Development Bank (ADB) quoted to invest $26.2 trillion in its 45 developing member countries (DMCs), out of which $3.6 trillion is specifically required for climate change mitigation and adaptation costs.

3. Green Financing Initiatives by Bangladesh Bank

As early as 1992, at an Earth Summit, the UN Environment Programme (UNEP) partnered with commercial banks to promote the environmental program in the banking sector, managed by the UNEP Finance Initiative (UNEP FI, 2020). There, the idea of green financing was born, with many institutions and banks restructuring their financial products and services to preserve the environment. Bangladesh joined the bandwagon at the central bank level to bring structural changes to the financial systems within the country.

The official journey to green banking started in 2011. Consequently, the Sustainable Finance Department was established at Bangladesh Bank to manage all green and sustainable initiatives under the umbrella of sustainable financing, categorizing it into three broad parts: green banking, corporate social responsibility (CSR), and financial inclusion. These initiatives are further categorized into four sections: (i) policy initiatives, (ii) monitoring of green banking practices of banks and non-banking financial institutions (NBFIs), (iii) refinance schemes for green products/initiatives, and (iv) in-house environmental management initiatives. The chronological order of policies since 2011 is provided in Appendix A. Currently,

Table 1. Breakdown of number of banks and financial institutions (FIs) in Bangladesh.

State-owned commercial banks (SOCBs)	6
Specialized development banks (SDBs)	3
Private commercial banks (PCBs)	43
Foreign commercial banks (FCBs)	9
Financial institutions (FIs)	34

Source: Bangladesh Bank.

the formal and semi-formal financial sectors of Bangladesh are structured as shown in Table 1.

Dang and Nguyen (2021) emphasized the importance of standardized guidelines[4] for assessing and managing risks and impacts on the social environment to ensure the performance of loans and the quality of the projects to be funded. Bangladesh Bank's first step toward green financing started with the issuance of the environmental risk management (ERM) guidelines for all the banks and FIs to encourage them to include ERM policies in their general credit risk management procedures (Bangladesh Bank, 2011). The target of the guidelines was mainly to (i) protect the financing bank or FI from the risks of increased climate change and environmental degradation and, in turn, reduce non-performing loans, (ii) ensure sustainable banking practices, (iii) standardize risk management, and (iv) encourage borrowers to adopt environmentally friendly and better management practices. The guidelines include environmental risk rating (EnvRR) and environment risk due-diligence (EDD) checklists to be performed before making financing decisions. Bangladesh Bank worked further on the ERM guidelines with the International Finance Corporation (IFC), resulting in a more robust system for banks and FIs to follow. An assessment was carried out on the ERM practices in the banks, based on which a new guideline was published in 2017, including the social risks in the credit management system, terming it as the Environmental and Social Risk Management (ESRM) Guidelines.

[4]For example, the Equator Principles and the Operation Standards of International Finance Corporation (IFC).

In a personal interview, Millat (2022)[5] shared that the checklists under the guidelines were made more comprehensive than before, and the measures were made more quantitative, making them easier for banks and FIs to use. Soon after, Bangladesh Bank issued a comprehensive green banking policy guideline and strategy framework for the banks to follow in three phases. Among the various activities, Phase I primarily deals with a financial entity's in-house environmental activities, including environmental risks in credit, climate risk funds, green marketing, employee training, and consumer awareness of green products. Phase II involves formulating sector-specific environmental policies, such as setting up green branches, formulating bank-specific ERM plans and guidelines, and publishing independent "Green Banking and Sustainability" reports. In Phase III, banks are requested to design and introduce innovative products and publish independent "Green Annual Reports." The same circular was issued for FIs in 2013. According to the policy for banks and FIs, a minimum of 10 percent of the total fund disbursement is expected to be in green finance (Bangladesh Bank, 2020).

3.1. *Initiation of sustainable finance*

To attain global targets under the United Nations Sustainable Development Goals (SDGs), Bangladesh Bank soon incorporated sustainability and social inclusion in the overall financing policies and activities. Bangladesh Bank then changed the name of its Green Banking and CSR unit to Sustainable Finance Department (SFD) in 2015 (SFD, 2022). In December 2020, SFD issued a comprehensive sustainable finance policy, aligned with the SDGs, to develop convergent key terminologies and policies for the stakeholders. Millat (2022) further stated that these decisions by Bangladesh Bank have made them a pioneer as a regulatory body in the financial sector. These policies and guidelines have helped banks and FIs address environmental, social, and governance (ESG) issues in their portfolios and credit management. Today, all banks and FIs have formed their own sustainable finance units, as mentioned in the Quarterly Review Report (SFD, October–December 2021).

[5]Khondoker Morshed Millat, General Manager, Sustainable Finance Department, Bangladesh Bank.

The categories under the Green and Sustainable Finance Taxonomy are presented in Appendix B.

The policy has a clear guideline on the types of projects under each sector (agriculture; cottage, micro, small & medium enterprises, or CMSME; and socially responsible finance). However, a significant portion of financing falls under term loans. This is primarily because term loans are easier for banks and FIs to manage due to their long-term commitments. Moreover, banks and FIs can transfer the liability of term loans to Bangladesh Bank under refinance schemes.[6] In addition, Bangladesh Bank does not issue refinancing loans multiple times. Thus, working capital is not dealt with under the sustainability umbrella. Bangladesh Bank expects businesses to have the capacity to finance their own working capital to be sustainable. According to Millat (2022), some businesses can take loans for working capital, such as selected solar energy manufacturing plants and other renewable energy plants, waste recycling plants, the establishment of green buildings, and environment-friendly brick production.

3.2. *Funds through corporate social responsibility*

In December 2014, Bangladesh Bank issued the first circular aligned with ensuring the maximization of the value of banks and FIs (SFD, 2022). The policies and guidelines have been planned, prioritizing national and international plans, such as the government's 8th Five Year Plan, the National Sustainable Development Strategy, the Perspective Plan of Bangladesh (2021–2041), Bangladesh Climate Change Strategy, the SDGs, and the National Financial Inclusion Strategy (NFIS). Initially, the funds under CSR were issued for various activities, such as relief and support programs for disaster management, "greening" programs, health, and education. The funding

[6]Bangladesh Bank's refinance schemes are only issued on term loans. Target attainment of all the refinances schemes together is a minimum of 20 percent of the total loan disbursement for sustainable finance and 5 percent of the total loan disbursement for green finance. Some notable schemes available for banks and FIs are (i) green transformation fund, (ii) refinance fund for technology development/upgradation of export-oriented industries, and (iii) *shariah*-based refinancing schemes for green products — see Sustainable Finance Policy (2020) for further details.

can be utilized by providing grants or financing at a concessional interest rate. A minimum of 30 percent of the total CSR expenditure has been allocated to education, with another 30 percent for health interventions and 20 percent for the environment and climate change mitigation and adaptation, i.e., a climate risk fund. Thus, in total, 80 percent of the funds are allocated to health, education, and climate change. Bangladesh Bank has issued a clear guideline for the product/initiative categories under each sector. Bangladesh Bank also published a list of products/initiatives on which banks and FIs can spend the remaining 20 percent of the funds, including women empowerment.

3.3. *Screening and monitoring*

Bangladesh Bank has issued individual guidelines and steps for screening for sustainable banking, including green banking, refinance schemes, and CSR projects. Some of the guidelines issued are the ESRM Guidelines, the off-site reporting format, the on-site checklist format, and the ESDD screening (SFD, 2020). The certification of green buildings and green industries are graded as "gold," "silver," or "platinum" by an approved organization, such as the Sustainable and Renewable Energy Development Authority (SHREDA) in Bangladesh. Bangladesh Bank has also provided the banks and FIs with guidelines for setting yearly targets on green finance and sustainable finance based on the previous year's net outstanding amount and requested disclosure of the targets at the beginning of the calendar year. Bangladesh Bank reviews the disclosures and issues achievable targets with justification for all banks and FIs. In one of his articles on green recovery, Rahman (2021)[7] said that rating the banks and FIs had provided recognition to those who chose green products, enhancing their reputational incentives to go green.

For the CSR activities of banks and FIs, Bangladesh Bank has imposed policies and monitoring initiatives to understand their social accountability. These activities are philanthropic and do not have the scope to be evaluated. However, a sustainability rating is used

[7]Bangabandhu Chair Professor, Dhaka University, and Former Governor of Bangladesh Bank.

to grade their performances. The rating includes a quantitative measure of the percentage spent under the following components: health, education, and climate. The qualitative measures are also in the form of a checklist measuring the policies implemented, disclosures, and in-house CSR activities. Lastly, the core banking activities are rated in the form of quantitative and qualitative factors, such as the total non-performing loan (NPL) rate, efficiency ratio, liquidity coverage ratio, return on assets, and equity (SFD, 2021).

3.4. *Roles of the government and other stakeholders*

Sustainable financing is an effort of several stakeholders to ensure that the objectives set are adequately met. Bangladesh Bank plays an essential role in this process as a regulator and a supervisor, guiding all other stakeholders to play their parts through comprehensive frameworks and guidelines. The circulars, policies, and guidelines set by Bangladesh Bank for banks and FIs are developed in consultation with the stakeholders and through surveys to support the discussions. The other government stakeholders involved in sustainable finance in Bangladesh are the Ministry of Finance, the Ministry of Environment, Forest and Climate Change, the Ministry of Commerce, and the Ministry of Industries. All these government bodies provide macro-level suggestions to guide the decisions taken by the SFD in Bangladesh Bank.

The Climate Fiscal Framework developed in 2014 supports the Sustainable Finance Initiative and the NFIS (Bangladesh Bank, 2020–2021). The Chittagong Stock Exchange and Dhaka Stock Exchange (acting as a secondary capital market) and the Bangladesh Association of Banks (BAB) are also part of the stakeholder groups promoting sustainable finance. The government created a climate change trust fund for green investment and has allocated nearly 7.26 percent of the annual budget for climate adaptation in various sectors in FY 2021–2022 (Antara, 2021).[8]

All the stakeholders are consulted before Bangladesh Bank develops any new policy or guideline. Bangladesh also involves

[8]Other important stakeholders include SHREDA, Bangladesh Institute of Bank Management (BIBM), and the National Security Board and the Security Exchange Commission.

international parties for consultation and technical assistance in the process. This includes membership in the Sustainable Banking Network (SBN) since 2012 and partnerships with multilateral agencies, such as the UNEP, the European Union Taxonomy, the Climate Bond Initiative's Climate Bond Taxonomy, and the United Nations Framework Convention on Climate Change (UNFCC).

3.5. *Latest trends of green financing in Bangladesh*

The trends described in the following exhibit the target attainments linked to sustainable finance. The data represented here have been collected from the quarterly and annual reports between 2016 and 2021.

3.5.1. *Refinance schemes*

In the third quarter of 2021, banks financed BDT 17.85 billion and FIs financed BDT 1.83 billion under green finance. As for sustainable finance, banks spent BDT 261.33 billion and FIs spent BDT 6.26 billion. According to the past half-yearly records, 65 percent of the borrowers were from sustainable agriculture, 34 percent from socially responsible financing, 0.5 percent from green finance, and 0.5 percent from sustainable CMSMEs. 38 percent of the borrowers were women this quarter (SFD, 2021).[9]

Observing the values and trends in Table 2 and Figure 1, loans disbursed under sustainable finance schemes show positive growth,

Table 2. Sustainable linked finance, 2021. $1 approximately equals to BDT 88.

	Banks	**FIs**	**Total**
Sustainable finance (billion BDT)	797.27	16.27	813.54
Percent of total loan disbursement	8.05	8.03	8.04
Green finance (billion BDT)	68.84	4.54	73.39
Percent of total loan disbursement	3.05	4.17	3.35
Sustainable linked finance (billion BDT)	866.12	20.81	886.94

Source: Quarterly Review Reports (2021).

[9]Includes four quarterly reports for the year 2021.

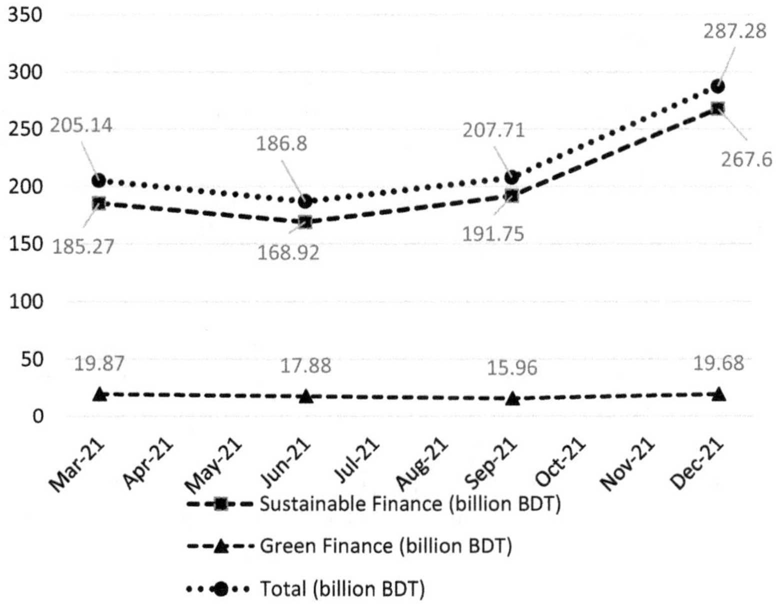

Figure 1. Quarterly trend under refinance scheme, 2021.

given that the sustainable financial policy guideline was published recently. The target attainment for green loans still seems unreachable, with almost no growth in 2021. The green loans issued for green infrastructures account for almost 50 percent of the total green loan disbursed (SFD, October–December 2021).

Khairunnessa *et al.* (2021) state that after including ESRM guidelines, a risk-rating model, practical regulations, and reporting requirements, a visible improvement in performance was recorded in bank and FI practices. The private commercial banks contributed the most to green finance. However, FIs have faced a negative growth rate from 2016 to 2018 and since 2020. The possible reasons for negative growth are that (i) the business lines for FIs are narrow, with the most concentration in the industrial sector, and (ii) most FIs conduct their merchant banking through separate subsidiaries, such as banks.

Banks' green financing has grown significantly over the years but saw a significant drop in 2021 (Table 3). The plausible reasons for this drastic drop can be the issuance of the Sustainable Taxonomy

Table 3. Green finance trend since 2016.

	2016	2017	2018	2019	2020	2021
Banks (billion BDT)	27.37	34.01	67.91	98.74	105.91	68.84
Relative changes (year wise, in percent)	3.60	24.20	99.70	45.40	7.25	−34.99
FIs (billion BDT)	5.94	4.63	3.38	6.49	5.29	4.54
Relative changes (year wise, in percent)	−28.50	−22.10	−26.80	91.80	−18.50	−14.11
Total green finance	33.32	38.64	71.30	105.24	111.20	733.39

Source: Khairunnessa *et al.* (2021) and SFD (2021).

and proper categorization of the products and services. Several previously considered green products/services now fall under sustainable financing.

3.5.2. *Climate risk fund*

In the said year, the total climate risk fund utilized stood at BDT 3,005 billion, given to 134,484 environmental risk-rated projects. The banks were swift to start online banking, with 99.28 percent of the banks having an online branch for services in the October–December 2021 quarter. The performance of the green investment scheme in Bangladesh is negligible, with no investments recorded in green bonds, green *sukuk*, or impact funds by banks and FIs in 2021.

4. Is Green Finance Working?

This section summarizes selected empirical studies from developed countries that investigate the role of green financing in addressing climate issues. Ehlers *et al.* (2020) find no clear evidence that issuing green bonds helps lower carbon intensities at the firm level over time. Their findings show that the types of firms involved matter. While financial firms, notably banks, are the least carbon-intensive firms compared to utility sectors, the investments of financial firms are heavily in carbon-intensive industries (Ehlers *et al.*, 2020). This is consistent with the fact that carbon-intensive sectors are heavily debt-financed (Delis *et al.*, 2018). So, are banks charging a premium on the loans provided to carbon-intensive, particularly fossil fuel, firms? Based on a cross-section of 72,742 loans over 2007–2016, Delis *et al.* find that banks are not charging significantly higher loan spreads to fossil fuel firms. However, in the post-2015 Paris Agreement period, there is evidence that banks raised loan spreads to fossil fuel firms that are significantly vulnerable to climate policy risk. Furthermore, Reghezza *et al.* (2021) document that, following the 2015 Paris Agreement, European banks reduced their loan shares to polluting firms by three percentage points (Reghezza *et al.*, 2021). These results suggest that international climate change initiatives and improved awareness will likely nudge banks to lower their exposure to carbon-intensive activities.

As carbon taxes and other climate measures are often deeply politically contentious, many companies embrace sustainable investing, encompassing the ESG considerations of emission-reducing policies. Based on a panel of 52 investor-owned firms in 20 countries accounting for nearly 30 percent of global emissions, Elmalt *et al.* (2021) find weak evidence that higher ESG investment reduces emission growth. Their results highlight an important issue: ESG scores are not necessarily related to companies' actual carbon footprints (Elmalt *et al.*, 2021). Regarding the difficulty in levying carbon taxes on polluting firms, research by Bolton and Kacperczyk (2020) suggests that increasing the cost of equity for polluting firms can be an alternative to carbon pricing for environment-minded investors. Examining data on 10,852 firms across 22 European emerging markets, De Hass *et al.* (2021) find that credit-constrained firms are 30 percent less likely to engage in green investment. However, credit constraints increase carbon emissions, but better green management reduces them. Their results highlight that delegating a manager in charge of climate issues can significantly improve a firm's green investments and lower emissions.

Several central banks in advanced countries have conducted stress tests on the impact of climate change on their banking systems. In a stress test by the Banque de France (2021), it was revealed that French banks and insurers are moderately exposed to the physical and transition risks of climate change. A study by the Reserve Bank of Australia documents that 1.5 percent of houses in the country would lose a tenth of their value by 2050 because of climate risks

(*The Economist*, 2022). A pilot study of climate stress tests in the Hong Kong banking sector reveals that participating banks' profitability is reduced due to an upsurge in expected credit losses (HKMA 2021). Jung *et al.* (2021) developed a methodology to stress test the resilience of FIs to climate-related risks. They used the method to measure the climate risk of 27 large global banks. Among other results, they find that banks with high exposure to the oil and gas industry tend to have higher climate betas.

Overall, the evidence presented above paints a mixed picture. On the positive side, investors are punishing polluting companies by increasing their cost of equity, while banks are slowly shying away from giving loans or charging higher loan spreads to carbon-intensive firms. On the skeptical side, neither green bonds nor ESG criteria are enough to lower firms' emissions growth.

5. Discussion

Sustainable Banking and Finance Network (SBFN) has reported Bangladesh's progress in the green and sustainable financing arena in March 2022, where Bangladesh climbed up the ladder to the "advancing" sub-stage of the "implementation" stage according to the Overall SBFN Progression Matrix along with Vietnam, with China and Indonesia in an advanced "consolidating" stage among all Asian countries (SBFN, 2022). In the recent Reserve Bank of India (RBI) Bulletin, a few of Bangladesh's green financing policies and guidelines were considered the best practices globally. Bangladesh's mandate on biannual reporting of CSR activities of commercial banks, incentivized environmental risk analysis under credit appraisal, assessment of social risks, and the uniformity of risk reporting format are considered good examples of sustainability disclosures. The report also mentioned that Bangladesh's refinance schemes and mandated lending guidelines exemplify an excellent policy framework (RBI Bulletin, 2021).

The trend of green finance in the past few years portrays that the mandate to record ESG risks and other regulatory policies has boosted the performance of the schemes. As reported in the SBFN-Bangladesh Country Progress Report (2022), as of July 2021,

$2.9 billion, or approximately 21 percent of banking assets, are covered by ESG integration requirements in the national sustainable finance framework, 100 percent of the banks have established internal ESG structures and/or policies, and 100 percent of the banks report their ESG activities timely.

Even with evolving and commendable policies and frameworks in place, the banking sector in Bangladesh faces undeniable risks and vulnerabilities for the non-performing loans, inadequate credit information, poor governance, lengthy legal procedures, and financial scams (Khairunnessa *et al.*, 2021). The COVID-19 pandemic has greatly affected the entire economy since 2020, including the financial system. The policies and procedures in Bangladesh are in place; however, along with the reduced performance of the schemes, environmental and social due diligence did not perform well. Rahman (2021) emphasized that "One of the common strategies must be accelerating green growth as a part of the recovery from the pandemic by focusing more sharply on sustainable finance." He discussed how the multi-pronged challenge, i.e., the COVID-19 pandemic and climate change, has made global leaders realize the need for strategies to accelerate green growth as part of recovery from the pandemic. With the drastic fall in the performance of the schemes due to the pandemic, Bangladesh Bank must now strongly think of methods such as the "climate stress test" to assess the financial risks on the banks and FIs. The Bank of England also recently initiated a pilot project to conduct a climate stress test among its banks and insurers to measure the resilience of the United Kingdom (UK) financial system to the risks (i.e., physical and transition risks mentioned earlier) (Bank of England, 2022).

Another major bottleneck in the system is the mobilization of funds by the banks and FIs toward potential investors. This bottleneck affects the proper utilization of funds under the schemes established by the Bangladesh Bank. In a personal interview, Rahman (2021)[10] appreciated the policies and frameworks of the Bangladesh

[10]Mr. Lutfor Rahman is the Founder and Chief Executive Officer of GreenTech Foundation, Bangladesh.

Bank, making Bangladesh a pioneer in green and sustainable financing. However, banks are often uninterested in venture capital funding. There is a strong need for intermediary organizations to act as mediators to link green projects with appropriate funding. For example, the Infrastructure Development Company Limited (IDCOL) acts as an intermediary in refinancing solar home energy systems, solar irrigation systems, and loans to microfinance intuitions. Similarly, the Green Tech Foundation — a local non-governmental organization (NGO) — initiated a project to build an ecosystem of green entrepreneurship and green enterprise, provides green technology support, green infrastructure, energy auditing, and, most importantly, conducts education and training programs. Several other NGOs and entities are working as intermediaries to provide incubation support, training, mentoring, and capacity building for new or small green and sustainable projects. These intermediaries work to link them to banks and FIs for funds and guide them throughout the project period for proper utilization and scale-up.

Banks and FIs are more interested in funding these projects as they go through a robust screening through the intermediaries. Intermediaries also share the risk of the projects they choose to assist. Rahman (2021) stated that "Planning for the long-term investment in large and small projects with the support of the corporates who can mobilize capital and transfer risk is at the core of this green transition." Proper coordination between these intermediaries and Bangladesh Bank must be developed to identify and mobilize green projects and ensure proper utilization of the schemes. One approach for Bangladesh Bank is to develop a sustainable financing forum, including government authorities, BIBM, banks, FIs, intermediaries, and potential borrowers. In the UK, the Bank of England established the Climate Financial Risk Forum (CFRF) to build capacity and share best practices across the financial system (Bank of England, 2022). This is a great approach to reducing stakeholder gaps, increasing information flow, and generating ideas for a comprehensive plan to meeting the national targets.

The banks' and FIs' initiatives to incentivize borrowers require further development. For example, foreign banks in Bangladesh, such as HSBC and Standard Chartered Bank (SCB), operate their sustainable financing activities following their global policies, frameworks, and guidelines, which are much stricter. For example, one of HSBC's recent KPIs is to ensure a net-zero carbon footprint across its customer base by 2050. This target has made the financing activities more robust at HSBC, making it easier for the bank to achieve the targets set by Bangladesh Bank. The foreign banks provide incentives against their loans given to assessed portfolios which exhibit consistent improvement in their business's sustainability or contribute to gender equality. The marketing of these incentives also plays a vital role in attracting potential borrowers.[11]

The capital market of Bangladesh, especially the market for green bonds, is at a very nascent stage compared with India and other countries promoting green financing. Hitherto, investments in green bonds, green *sukuk*, and impact funds are nonexistent in Bangladesh (SBFN, 2022).[12] While there is no doubt that the issuance of green bonds would contribute to the development of a much-needed debt market in Bangladesh, recent research suggests that the promise of green bonds is overrated. As already mentioned, Ehlers *et al.* (2020) find that green bonds do not necessarily lead to a material reduction in carbon emissions. Rather, the firm-level green rating system delivered better results in transitioning to a low-carbon economy.[13]

---

[11]During our interviews with several local banks, some of the identified problems were as follows: (i) there is a lack of knowledge and capacity of the local banks to develop a structured plan and implement it to roll out their sustainable financing, (ii) banks need structured auditing and "push" to increase their green portfolio, (iii) banks are not well connected with intermediary organizations to access projects with reduced risks, (iv) local banks do not usually have funds available to incentivize their clients and will incur loss otherwise, and (v) banks do not have any or enough sustainable products to offer. However, with Bangladesh Banks's newly formalized sustainable policy guideline and revised tools, these issues are expected to be resolved in the coming years. Adequate training, advocacy, and entrepreneurial motivation are needed to bridge the gap between banks and their green portfolio clients.

[12]In 2022, SCB and Sajida Foundation collaborated to arrange zero-coupon bonds of BDT 1 billion for environmentally friendly and energy-efficient initiatives of micro-credit and SME clients of Sajida Foundation. They are the first to set an example for other banks and institutions to follow.

[13]It is better to consider a firm-level rating rather than a project-based classification since firms are the ultimate decision-makers regarding the carbon footprint of an economic activity. Furthermore, it is easier to measure a firm's carbon intensity than a project or a sector.

A positive side effect of the green rating system is that investors can use it to rate stocks and evaluate firms' products (i.e., whether to buy products from a polluting firm or not).

In our view, Bangladesh Bank's green financing policy must focus on strengthening climate preparedness, adaptation, and mitigation activities. The steps to reduce carbon intensity are robust, and all that is needed now is an efficient rollout. Given that Bangladesh is already dealing with regular floods and cyclones, green rural infrastructure must be the next focus area, which should be supported by exploring "climate finance". Some organizations in Bangladesh are now working on mangrove afforestation in the southern coastal belt regions to reduce erosion and the impact of cyclones. Mangrove trees also improve biodiversity, provide protection from saline water, and capture five times the CO_2 compared to other trees. Funds ought to be directed toward climate-compatible infrastructures. Friendship, a social purpose organization in Bangladesh, has been working on innovative plinth structures for shifting river islands in the northern parts of Bangladesh, apart from its mangrove afforestation and other climate-compatible projects. The innovative oval-shaped plinth structure is a raised platform housing a community of people and providing shelter during flooding since the islands get inundated at the slightest floods, especially in the northern part of Bangladesh (Friendship, 2022). Bangladesh Bank needs to focus on such innovative projects that contribute to the preparedness and adaptation needed to fight climate change.

Besides the suggestions mentioned above, Bangladesh Bank needs to strengthen its international connections. Bangladesh Bank is recommended to conduct a study of standardized institutional frameworks, practices, and possible associations to check the feasibility of Bangladesh's frameworks. Bangladesh Bank could also explore ideas such as digital currency and polymer banknotes. Both China and India have approved digital currency in their economies, albeit on a limited scale. A digital euro is on its way, while the Federal Reserve is looking into the prospect of a digital dollar. Digital currency reduces paper usage and, most importantly, is an excellent monitoring tool for central banks across their financial systems.

On the other hand, Bangladesh Bank may also consider some sustainable and green ideas exercised by Bangko Sentral (Central Bank of the Philippines). Benjamin E. Diokno,[14] in a meeting, discussed the Philippines' digital payments transformation roadmap, the "no single-use plastic bottles policy," and long-lasting polymer banknotes with a low carbon footprint (Diokno, 2022). These ideas have the potential to add value to green initiatives.

6. Conclusion

In recent years, more and more central banks have been working to determine the channels through which climate change may affect the financial stability of the banking sector. The "greening" of monetary policy, which provides the legal mandate for central banks to favor green firms over polluters, is a step along the road toward sustainable economic growth. This chapter attempts to provide a systematic analysis of the green financing policies of Bangladesh Bank, the central bank of Bangladesh, one of the countries most vulnerable to climate change. Several significant points stand out. First, the ballooning non-performing loans and poor governance mean that Bangladeshi banks and insurers might be unprepared to cope with the potential financial fallout from climate change. To determine banks' vulnerability to climate-related financial risks, conducting "climate stress tests" is one way forward. Second, in the same way, monetary policy becomes ineffective when commercial banks hold excess reserves, and the central bank's policies will not improve the green economy unless banks and FIs mobilize funds toward retail investors. There appears to be a need for intermediary organizations (e.g., IDCOL, NGOs) to link green projects with appropriate funding. Third, the direct and indirect benefits of green loans are obvious. Local banks in the country can be encouraged to learn from foreign banks about incentivizing green loans in the most efficient way. Fourth, and most importantly, Bangladesh Bank's green policies must be geared toward strengthening climate preparedness, adaptation, and mitigation activities. In this regard, further discussion on climate finance is imperative.

[14]Governor of Bangko Sentral ng Pilipinas (BSP, the central bank of the Philippines).

Appendix A: Policy Initiatives: Chronological Order of Policies Since 2011

2011	• Issuance of Environmental Risk Management (ERM) Guidelines for banks and FIs	• Banking Regulation and Policy Department (BRPD) Circular No. 01/2011
	• Issuance of Green Banking Policy Guidelines for banks	• BRPD Circular No. 02/2011
2012	• Introduction of a uniform reporting format for green banking activities	• BRPD Circular No. 07/2012
2013	• Issuance of Green Banking Policy Guidelines for FIs and newly scheduled banks	• Green Banking and CSR Department (GBCSRD) Circular No. 04/2013
2014	• Minimum target of 5 percent of total funded loan disbursement/ investment was set for direct green finance, effective from January 2016 onward for all banks and FIs	• GBCSRD Circular No. 04/2014
2015	• Bangladesh Bank instructed banks and FIs to form a "climate risk fund," with allocation of at least 10 percent of their CSR budget	• GBCSRD Circular No.04/2015
2016	• Bangladesh Bank instructed banks and FIs to build solid waste management systems, rainwater harvesting, and solar power panel in	• SFD Circular No. 01/2016

(*Continued*)

	their newly constructed or arranged building infrastructure	
	• All banks and FIs are asked to ensure that possible clients receiving financing for establishing and operating effluent treatment plants (ETPs) in their businesses	• SFD Circular No. 03/2016
	• Bangladesh Bank instructed all banks and FIs to convert green banking and CSR units to sustainable finance units and sustainable finance committees	• SFD Circular No. 02/2016
2017	• SFD department issued Guidelines on Environmental and Social Risk Management (ESRM) for banks and FIs, along with an Excel-based risk-rating model	• SFD Circular No. 02/2017
	• SFD unit issued a comprehensive list of products/initiatives of green finance for banks and FIs	• SFD Circular No. 04/2017
2018	• SFD unit issued a new uniform reporting format of the quarterly review report on green banking activities for banks and FIs along with an environmental and social due diligence (ESDD) risk assessment tool aligning more with international standards to ensure the quality and uniformity of data shared	• SFD Circular No. 01/2018

(*Continued*)

(*Continued*)

2019	• SFD issued a circular stating that any investment by scheduled banks and FIs in any impact fund which is registered under BSEC (Alternative Investment) Rules, 2015 and formed for environment friendly sectors/ purposes (resource and energy efficiency, renewable energy, waste management and treatment, women and child right protection, etc.) will be considered green finance	• SFD Circular No. 01/2019
2020	• SFD unit set a minimum target of 5 percent for green finance from the total funded loan disbursement/ investment for all banks and FIs, effective from September 2020	• SFD Circular Letter no. 05/2020
	• SFD unit issued a new sustainable finance policy for banks and FIs along with a new quarterly report format on sustainable finance, including sustainable finance taxonomy and green taxonomy	• SFD Circular No. 05/2020
	• They also issued a sustainability rating methodology for banks and FIs	• SFD Circular No. 06/2020
2021	• SFD issued a fixed yearly "target and achievement" of green and sustainable finance for banks and FIs	• SFD Circular No. 01/2021 • SFD Circular Letter No. 03/2021
	• They also issued a sustainability rating methodology for banks and FIs	• SFD Circular Letter No. 05/2021
2022	• SFD issued policy guidelines on CSR for banks and FIs	• SFD Circular No. 01/2022

Source: Bangladesh Bank Circulars (2022).

Appendix B: Sustainable Finance Taxonomy

<table>
<tr><th colspan="2">Sustainable Finance Taxonomy</th></tr>
<tr><td rowspan="8">Green Taxonomy:
• Green banking activities
• Methodology of defining green finance
• Identification process of green products/projects/initiatives with norms, benchmark/ standards
• Policy activities toward green environment
• Economic activities for reducing negative impact of environment
• Screening and monitoring
• Developing a green bond standard
• Greening the polluting industries
• Carbon footprint reduction measures
• Technological advancements
• Green strategic planning
• Green marketing, awareness, and capacity development
• Research and development for green product innovation, green impact assessment/ review
• Green finance disclosure</td><td>Identification of sustainable-linked agriculture, CMSMEs, and socially responsible finance</td></tr>
<tr><td>Identification of other finances linked to sustainability</td></tr>
<tr><td>Inclusion of technological advancement</td></tr>
<tr><td>Screening and monitoring</td></tr>
<tr><td>Sustainable finance strategic planning</td></tr>
<tr><td>Research and development for sustainable product innovation, marketing, awareness, and capacity building</td></tr>
<tr><td>Impact assessment/review</td></tr>
<tr><td>Sustainable finance disclosure</td></tr>
</table>

Source: SFD (2020).

References

Antara, N. F. (2021, June 3). Budget FY22: Around Tk25,125cr Budget Proposed to Tackle Climate Change. Dhaka, Dhaka, Bangladesh. Retrieved from https://archive.dhakatribune.com/business/economy/2021/06/03/budget-fy22-around-tk25-125cr-budget-proposed-to-tackle-climate-change.

Bangladesh Bank (BB) (2020). *(BB) Annual Report 2019–2020*. Dhaka: Bangladesh Bank. Retrieved from https://www.bb.org.bd/pub/annual/anreport/ar1920/full_2019_2020.pdf.

Bangladesh Bank (2011, January 1). Environmental Risk Management (ERM) Guidelines for Banks and Financial Institutions in Bangladesh. *ERM Regulation Guideline*, 43. Dhaka, Dhaka, Bangladesh: Bangladesh Bank. Retrieved from https://www.bb.org.bd/aboutus/regulationguideline/jan302011erm.pdf.

Bangladesh Bank (2020–2021). Chapter 6: Sustainable and inclusive banking. In Bangladesh Bank, *Annual Report* (p. 18). Dhaka: Bangladesh Bank. Retrieved from file:///C:/Users/Shehtaz/Desktop/Book/full_2020_2021.pdf.

Bangladesh Bank Circulars (2022, May 23). Mediaroom Circulars. Retrieved from Bangladesh Bank: https://www.bb.org.bd/en/index.php/mediaroom/circular.

Bank of England (2022, April 25). Climate Change. Retrieved from Bank of England: https://www.bankofengland.co.uk/climate-change.

Banque de France (2021). A first assessment of financial risks stemming from climate change: The main results of the 2020 climate pilot exercise. No. 122-2021.

Bolton, P. & Kacperczyk, M. T. (2021). Global pricing of carbon-transition risk. *NBER Working Paper* No. 28510. https://www.nber.org/papers/w28510.

Carney, M. (2015, September 29). Breaking the Tragedy of the Horizon — Climate Change and Financial Stability — Speech by Mark Carney. (L. o. London, Interviewer). Retrieved from https://www.bankofengland.co.uk/-/media/boe/files/speech/2015/breaking-the-tragedy-of-the-horizon-climate-change-and-financial-stability.pdf?la=en&hash=7C67E785651862457D99511147C7424FF5EA0C1A.

Dang, T. T. & Nguyen, T. T. (2021, July 5). Developing green bank operation in India and Vietnam: Comparison. *Asian Journal of Business Environment*, *11*(3), 33–43. doi:10.13106/ajbe.2021.vol11.no3.33.

De Haas, R., Martin, R., Muûls, M., *et al.* (2021). Managerial and financial barriers to the net-zero transition. *CEPR Discussion Paper* No. 15886.

Delis, M., Greiff, K., & Ongena, S. (2018, May 15). Being Stranded on the Carbon Bubble? Climate Policy Risk and the Pricing of Bank Loans. *SSRN*, 65. Retrieved from https://papers.ssrn.com/sol3/papers.cfm?abstract_id=3178099.

Demekas, M. G. & Grippa, P. (2021, December 17). Financial Regulation, Climate Change, and the Transition to a Low-Carbon Economy: A Survey of the Issues. *International Monetary Fund (IMF) eLibrary, 2021*(296), 45. doi:https://doi.org/10.5089/9781616356521.001.

Diokno, B. (2022, January 17). Message — 73rd Inaugural Meeting of the Management Association of the Philippines, Manila, Manila, Philippines. Retrieved from https://www.bis.org/review/r220117c.pdf.

Eckstein, D., Künzel, V., & Schäfer, L. (2021). *Global Climate Risk Index 2021*. Berlin: Germanwatch E.V. Retrieved from www.germanwatch.org/en/cr.

The Economist (2016). How to deal with worries about stranded assets. *Special Report on Oil: Breaking the Habit.* London: The Economist. Retrieved from https://www.economist.com/sites/default/files/20161126_oil.pdf.

The Economist (2022). The Wish to Respond to Climate Change. Chicago: The Economist. Retrieved from https://www.economist.com/special-report/2022/04/20/the-wish-to-respond-to-climate-change.

Ehlers, T., Mojon, B., & Packer, F. (2020). *Green Bonds and Carbon Emissions: Exploring the Case for a Rating System at the Firm Level.* Basel: BIS. Retrieved from https://www.bis.org/publ/qtrpdf/r_qt2009c.pdf.

Elmalt, D., Igan, D., & Kirti, D. (2021). *Limits to Private Climate Change Mitigation.* London: Centre for Economic Policy Research. Retrieved from https://cepr.org/active/publications/discussion_papers/dp.php?dpno=16061#.

Friendship (2022, February 24). Climate Adaptation. Retrieved from Friendship, Retrieved from https://friendship.ngo/what-we-do/climate-adaptation/.

Hasan, M. & Macdonald, G. (2021, September 13). *How Climate Change Deepens Bangladesh's Fragility. Analysis and Commentary.* Washington D.C., USA: United States Institute of Peace. Retrieved from https://www.usip.org/publications/2021/09/how-climate-change-deepens-bangladeshs-fragility.

HKMA (2021, December). Pilot Banking Sector Climate Risk Stress Test. Hong Kong Monetary Authority, Washington D.C., USA.

Jung, H., Engle, R., & Berner, R. (2021). Climate stress testing. Staff Report No. 977, Federal Reserve Bank of New York.

Khairunnessa, F., Vazquez-Brust, D., & Yakovleva, N. (2021). *A Review of the Recent Developments of Green Banking.* Basel: MDPI. https://doi.org/10.3390/.

Mahmud, I., Raza, W. A., & Hossain, M. (2021). Climate Afflictions. Washington D.C.: International Development in Focus, the World Bank. doi: 10.1596/978-1-4648-1764-6.

Millat, K. M. (2022, March 10). Green and Sustainable Financing by Bangladesh Bank. (S. S. Hasib, Interviewer) Dhaka, Bangladesh.

The Ministry of Finance (2021). Chapter One: Macroeconomic Situation. In Finance Division, *Bangladesh Economic Review 2021* (p. 10). Dhaka, Bangladesh: Finance Division. Retrieved from https://mof.portal.gov.bd/sites/default/files/files/mof.portal.gov.bd/page/f2d8fabb_29c1_423a_9d37_cdb500260002/10.%20Chapter-01%20Eng%20Eng-21.pdf.

Ra, S. & Li, Z. (2018, June 1). Closing the financing gap in Asian infrastructure. *ADB South Asia Working Paper Series No. 57*, p. 35. http://dx.doi.org/10.22617/WPS189402-2.

Rahman, A. (2021, April 24). Sustainable Finance for Green Recovery. Dhaka, Dhaka, Bangladesh. Retrieved from https://thefinancialexpress.com.bd/views/sustainable-finance-for-green-recovery-1618584938.

Rahman, L. (2022, March 3). Green Financing and Green Tech Foundation. (S. S. Hasib, Interviewer) Dhaka, Dhaka, Bangladesh.

RBI Bulletin (2021). *Green Finance in India: Progress and Challenges.* Mumbai: Reserve Bank of India. Retrieved from https://rbidocs.rbi.org.in/rdocs/Bulletin/PDFs/04AR_2101202185D9B6905ADD465CB7DD280B88266F77.PDF.

Reghezza, A., Altunbas, Y., Marques-Ibanez, D., *et al.* (2021). *Do Banks Fuel Climate Change?* Frankfurt: European Central Bank. Retrieved from https://www.ecb.europa.eu/pub/pdf/scpwps/ecb.wp2550 24c25d5791.en.pdf.

SBFN (2022). *Bangladesh Country Progress Report — Supplement to the 2021 Global Progress Report of the Sustainable Banking and Finance Network.* Washington D.C.: IFC and SBFN. Retrieved from https://sbfnetwork.org/wp-content/uploads/pdfs/2021_Global_Progress_Report_Downloads/2021_Country_Progress_Report_Bangladesh.pdf.

SFD (2020). *Sustainable Finance Policy for Banks and Financial Institutions.* SFD. Dhaka: Bangladesh Bank. Retrieved from https://www.bb.org.bd/mediaroom/circulars/gbcrd/dec312020sfd05.pdf.

SFD (2021). *Quarterly Review Reports on Sustainable Finance of Banks and Financial Institutions.* SFD. Dhaka: Bangladesh Bank. Retrieved from https://www.bb.org.bd//pub/quaterly/greenbanking/jan_mar2021.pdf; https://www.bb.org.bd//pub/quaterly/greenbanking/

apr_june2021.pdf; https://www.bb.org.bd//pub/quaterly/greenbanking/sfr_jul_sep2021.pdf.

SFD (2021). *SFD Circular No. 06.* SFD. Dhaka: Bangladesh Bank. Retrieved from https://www.bb.org.bd/mediaroom/circulars/gbcrd/jan172021sfd02.pdf.

SFD (2022, January 9). Policy Guidelines on Corporate Social Responsibility for Banks and Financial Institutions. Dhaka, Dhaka, Bangladesh. Retrieved from https://www.bb.org.bd/mediaroom/circulars/gbcrd/jan092022sfdl01e.pdf.

SFD (2021, October–December). *Quarterly Review Report on Sustainable Finance of Banks and Financial Institutions.* Bangladesh Bank, Sustainable Finance. Dhaka: SFD. Retrieved from https://www.bb.org.bd/en/index.php/publication/publictn/2/39.

Sustainable Finance Department (SFD) (2022, May 24). Sustainable Finance Department. Retrieved from Bangladesh Bank: https://www.bb.org.bd/en/index.php/about/deptdtl/61#:~:text=Sustainable%20Finance%20Department%20was%20established,FIs%20through%20efficient%20and%20effective.

The World Bank (2016, October 9). Bangladesh: Building Resilience to Climate Change. Retrieved from The World Bank: https://www.worldbank.org/en/results/2016/10/07/bangladesh-building-resilience-to-climate-change.print.

UNEP FI (2020). *UNEP FI Annual Overview 2020.* Geneva: United Nations Environmental Programme Finance Initiative. Retrieved from https://www.unepfi.org/wordpress/wp-content/uploads/2021/07/2020-Annual-Overview.pdf.

Volz, U. (2018, March). Fostering Green Finance for Sustainable Development in Asia. *ADBI Working Paper 814*, 30. Retrieved from Asian Development Bank Institute.

https://doi.org/10.1142/9781800614482_0005

Chapter 5

Determinants of Green Banking Disclosures: Evidence from Mauritius

Dineshwar Ramdhony*,†, Mokshada Foolchand‡, and Boopen Seetanah§

University of Mauritius, Réduit, Mauritius
†*d.ramdhony@uom.ac.mu*
‡*mokshada.foolchand@umail.uom.ac.mu*
§*b.seetanah@uom.ac.mu*

Abstract

In annual reports, green banking practices and their disclosure have become prominent as they communicate how banks operate while considering the environment. This chapter investigates the factors influencing the extent of green banking disclosures (GBD) made in the annual reports of 16 banks in Mauritius from 2010 to 2019. We particularly focus on corporate governance practices, such as board size, board independence, institutional ownership, directors' ownership, multiple directorships, and profitability. A green banking disclosure index was constructed using content analysis to measure the extent of green banking disclosure. Using random effect estimates, panel data confirm that board size, board independence, institutional ownership, and profitability positively influence green banking disclosures. However, no significant relationship was found between directors' ownership, multiple directorships, and green banking disclosures. Our findings have implications for academics, regulators, and practitioners.

*Corresponding author.

1. Introduction

The world has experienced progress in terms of economic, technological, and social advances, many inhabitants have experienced immense comfort and an increase in inflows of income. However, this progress has come at the expense of the environment, causing several problems such as climate change, global warming, an increase in greenhouse gases, deforestation, and pollution (Tara & Singh, 2014). Environmental degradation has occurred due to the current unbalanced ways of production and consumption (Mehedi & Kuddus, 2017). All business sectors, including the banking sector, are responsible for this environmental degradation, as they use excessive electricity, fuel, gas, water, and paper for their operations. Pressure from stakeholders, such as the media and NGOs, is compelling banks to integrate sustainable practices into their day-to-day operations (Day & Woodward, 2009). The banking industry has recognized that the success and survival of banks depend not only on financial performance and efficiency but also on how banks embed green practices in their day-to-day operations (Coulson, 2009).

Our study aims to examine the determinants of green banking practices in a developing country, Mauritius. In this study, the phrase "green banking" refers to the adoption, support, and promotion of environmentally friendly policies and reducing a bank's carbon footprint in both internal and external operations (Green Banking Report, 2016). Mauritius is a small island in the Indian Ocean. The country has performed well economically and ranks first in country governance in Africa (Mo Ibrahim Index, 2020). Since 2008, Mauritius has embarked on an ambitious project to embrace sustainability in various sectors (Maurice Ile Durable, or MID). Banks have hopped on the bandwagon, and in 2009, the Mauritius Commercial Bank, the largest bank in the country, launched an internal program to reduce energy waste and pollution (*Lexpress*, 2009).

To the best of our knowledge, no prior study on green banking in Mauritius is available. Even in other parts of the world, studies on green banking are lacking. A recent study on green banking was undertaken by Bose *et al.* (2018) in Bangladesh. Other studies in the banking sector focused on other forms of disclosure, such as sustainability and CSR (Branco & Rodrigues, 2008; Day & Woodward, 2009; Khan *et al.*, 2013). We, therefore, extend the literature on green banking in a developing economy and small island developing state (SIDS) context.

The chapter is organized as follows. Section 2 reviews the literature and develops hypotheses related to this study. This is followed by the research methods section. The penultimate section shows the findings and discussion of this study. Finally, Section 5 concludes the study and explores avenues for future research.

2. Related Literature and Hypothesis Development

Several theories attempt to explain and describe the implementation and disclosure of green banking practices. They are the stakeholder theory (Freeman *et al.*, 2004; Michelon & Parbonetti, 2012; Hossain *et al.*, 2016), the legitimacy theory (Brown & Deegan, 1998; Mousa & Hassan, 2015), and the agency theory (Hill & Jones, 1992; Elshabasy, 2018). We shall, in what follows, rather focus on the determinants of green banking disclosures (GBDs) and develop hypotheses for our study. With empirical studies on GBDs being scarce, we borrow from other strands of related disclosure practices, such as sustainability reporting and CSR reporting. One of the rare studies on GBD (Bose *et al.*, 2018) associated it with corporate governance practices. It found that board size and institutional ownership have a positive and significant relationship with GBD. However, no association was found between independent directors and GBD. Ahmed (2021) investigated the attributes of banks linked to the disclosure of information rather than in a general sense. In a different study, Grassa *et al.* (2021) compared the disclosure practices of Islamic and conventional banks. Tran *et al.* (2021) examined the relationship between profitability and CSR disclosure and found that they are inversely related. Given the paucity of studies on GBD, we aim to provide more empirical evidence on the link between corporate governance practices and GBD.

2.1. *Hypotheses development*

2.1.1. *Board size*

The resource-based view and resource dependence theory posit that a large board size provides access to a larger human capital base and other resources, such as relationships (Jackling & Johl, 2009). Large boards are associated with better monitoring ability. As such, it is expected that a larger board size will lead to increased disclosure. De Villiers *et al.* (2011) argue that firms with large board sizes report their information more properly and provide more capital and finance to firms. However, having a larger board size may result in distortion of the power of managers. It may lead to some disadvantages such as an absence of communication, improper decision-making, excessive powers for managers, a lack of unity (Kiliç *et al.*, 2015). Disclosure about green practices occurs where the board has the power to set aims, targets, and guidelines for the firm to perform its operations within the environmental scope (Chan *et al.*, 2014).

Moreover, when board interests are associated with stakeholders, there is a greater possibility for firms to disclose GHG emissions and environmental practices (Ben-Amar & McIlkenny, 2015). Empirical evidence on the link between board size and corporate disclosure is mixed. For instance, Ntim and Soobaroyen (2013) find that board size has a significant positive influence on disclosure practices. In the same vein, Bose *et al.* (2018), in the Bangladeshi context, and Hermawan and Gunardi (2019), in the Indonesian one, concluded that board size and GBD share a positive relationship. However, Brammer and Pavelin (2008) found, in their research in the UK, that board size harms environmental disclosure, while Mooneeapen *et al.* (2021) find no relationship between board size and corporate disclosure. This study can shed some light on the association between board size and GBD in developing countries. We, therefore, put forward the following hypothesis.

H1: There is a relationship between board size and GBDs.

2.1.2. *Board independence*

Independent directors play an important role in monitoring the behavior of managers for the sake of both shareholders and stakeholders (Haniffa & Cooke, 2005). This monitoring role is effective when independent directors are present in large numbers and bring more awareness, relevance, and integrity to the information disclosed (Ghabayen *et al.*, 2016), leading to a fall in agency costs (Shamil *et al.*, 2014; Bose *et al.*, 2018). As opposed to executive directors, who are more concerned about the operating activities of the business, independent directors are focused on the disclosures of the firm's operations, which must respect the social and environmental norms (Khan *et al.*, 2013). It is observed that having a large number of independent directors helps further promote the quality of environmental disclosure by banks (Rupley *et al.*, 2012). Most past studies point toward a positive relationship between board independence and corporate disclosure (Hermawan & Gunardi, 2019; Ramdhony *et al.*, 2021; Khan *et al.* 2013). However, Bose *et al.* (2018) found that in Bangladesh, board independence has a negative effect on GBDs. Therefore, the following hypothesis is provided.

H2: There is a positive relationship between board independence and GBDs.

2.1.3. *Institutional ownership and influence of stakeholders*

The various institutional shareholders and stakeholders have different targets regarding the firms they are financing (Johnson & Greening, 1999). Institutional shareholders are considered strong pillars of organizations due to the ownership of a large number of shares and hence voting rights. Agency theory states that institutional shareholders and other stakeholders have the power to make decisions and control an organization's operations, thereby leading to greater disclosure of environmental activities (Masud *et al.*, 2018a; Matten & Moon, 2008; Bose *et al.*, 2018). These institutional shareholders usually need high-quality information about the operations of the firm due to the environmental risks that firms' operations pose. Stakeholder theory predicts that firms will cater to powerful stakeholders' needs, and as such firms are motivated to provide green disclosures. Bose *et al.* (2018) and Masud *et al.* (2018b) offered evidence that institutional shareholders positively influence GBDs. However, Htay *et al.* (2012) and Habbash (2016) concluded that there was no significant relationship between institutional ownership and GBDs. Therefore, the following hypothesis is proposed.

H3: There is a positive relationship between institutional ownership and GBDs.

2.1.4. *Directors' ownership*

Ownership of directors can be measured by the number of shares they hold in an organization compared to the total number of shares issued. Companies in which directors own a large number of shares tend to be less involved in environmental and green banking activities because public interest tends to be low in these companies (Ghazali, 2007). Additionally, owner-managers might be reluctant to disclose information, including environmental and green banking information, as they want to utilize it for their benefit (Htay *et al.*, 2012). In their studies, Oh *et al.* (2011), based on Korean companies, and Bae *et al.* (2018), based on South Asian countries, found that directors' ownership negatively influences environmental disclosures. Conversely, Htay *et al.* (2012) and Haji (2013) show that director ownership positively influences the extent of environmental disclosure. This can be achieved when owner-directors are involved in green and environment-friendly decisions and want to show how much they are interested in environmental issues, thereby attracting more stakeholders and investors (Masud *et al.*, 2018b). We hypothesize the following.

H4: Directors' ownership is negatively related to GBDs.

2.1.5. *Board of directors with multiple directorships*

Directors with multiple directorships, i.e., those performing duties as directors of other organizations, possess more expertise, experience, contacts, a better reputation, and greater stimulus for carrying out their responsibilities as directors (Lopez & Rodriguez, 2014). Multiple directorships are referred to as being the most important tool for stakeholders and organizations due to the influence that directors and the board as a whole have on the transactions of a company, which, in turn, affect the companies' ways of making environmental disclosures and their performance toward the environment (Deegan & Rankin, 1996; Courtois *et al.*, 2011). In the same vein, Courtois *et al.* (2011) show that multiple directorships contribute significantly to environmental disclosures. It is also noted that multiple directorships enable other board members to link with other directors of other organizations to disclose information about environmental activities. Therefore, there is a consensus that environmental disclosure is somehow linked to directors' expertise, status, contacts, and experience. In addition, research in Australia showed that directors with multiple directorships have more skills and experience. Based on this, they may realize the significance of disclosing critical environmental information (Elsakit & Worthington, 2014). Rupley *et al.* (2012) and Ali *et al.* (2016) found that multiple directorships positively influence environmental disclosure. We hypothesize the following.

H5: There is a positive relationship between multiple directorships and GBDs.

2.1.6. *Profitability: Return on assets*

Hackston and Milne (1996) argue that a firm's ability to make continuous profits largely depends upon how much it is associated with environmental and corporate social activities. The banking industry's fierce competitiveness forces bank executives to invest heavily in ecological practices to demarcate themselves from their competitors (Forgione & Migliardo, 2020). According to Birindelli *et al.* (2018) and Forgione and Migliardo (2020), environmental investment helps a bank establish its own brand identity and gain a long-term competitive advantage. Nawaiseh (2015) argues that organizations tend to disclose environmental and corporate social information in annual reports when they are profitable. Being profitable provides banks the flexibility to devote resources to green practices. Empirical evidence shows a positive relationship between profitability and corporate disclosure (Waddock & Graves, 1997; Haniffa & Cooke, 2002; McKendall *et al.*, 1999). We hypothesize the following.

H6: There is a positive relationship between profitability and GBDs.

3. Research Methodology and Analysis

The study principally aims to examine the corporate governance determinants and profitability factors that lead to the disclosure of green banking activities in the annual reports of the banks of

Mauritius. The study employs a panel data analysis over a ten-year period, from the year 2010 to the year 2019. The sample population consists of banks operating in Mauritius. The Mauritian banking sector currently consists of 19 banks, of which five are local, nine are foreign-based subsidiaries, one is a joint venture, and four are branches of foreign banks. However, the actual sample size consists only of 16 banks in Mauritius out of the 19 banks due to the unavailability of data. The list of banks for the target and existing population is shown in Appendix 2.

3.1. *Model specification*

Grounded on theoretical underpinnings and past empirical research (see Courtois *et al.*, 2011, Oh *et al.*, 2011, and Bae *et al.*, 2018, among others), the following regression model is subsequently specified:

$$\text{GBDI} = \alpha + \beta_1 \text{ BSIZE} + \beta_2 \text{ BIND} + \beta_3 \text{ DOWN} + \beta_4 \text{ INSOWN} + \beta_5 \text{ MULDIRECT} + \beta_6 \text{ ROA} + \varepsilon_t \quad (1)$$

where GBDI is the green banking disclosure index, which acts as a proxy for GBDs. Content analysis using a checklist (see Appendix 1) based on Bose *et al.* (2018) was used to measure GBDs. We apply a dichotomous approach, whereby each item disclosed on the checklist was given a score of either 1 or 0, which is widely used in the corporate disclosure literature (Ramdhony *et al.*, 2021). This unweighted approach assumes that all items in the disclosure checklist are equally important (Cooke, 1989). The GBDI for each company is the sum of all items disclosed divided by the maximum allowable score (21). More specifically, the GBDI for each company is calculated using the following equation:

$$\text{GBDI} = \frac{\sum_{t=1}^{nj} X_{ij}}{n_j}$$

where GBDI_i is the green banking disclosure index for the ith firm, n_i is the number of items expected for the ith firm, where $n \leq 21$, and X_{ij} is 1 if the jth items are disclosed for firm i and 0 otherwise.

BSIZE refers to board size, represented by the natural log of the total number of directors on the board. BIND represents board independence and is measured by the proportion of independent directors on a board. DOWN refers to directors' ownership and is measured based on the proportion of shares owned by directors. INSOWN represents institutional ownership and is measured using the proportion of shares owned by institutional shareholders. MULDIRECT refers to the proportion of directors having multiple directorships. ROA refers to the return on total assets and is calculated by dividing profits by total assets.

3.2. *Data and sample*

Data on the corporate governance factors, such as board size, board independence, institutional ownership, directors' ownership, multiple directorships, and profitability factors, such as ROA, were collected from the banks' annual reports. Regarding the extent of GBDs in annual reports, data were again collected using the banks' annual reports. The annual reports are available on the banks' websites.

3.3. *Panel data regression (random effect model)*

To account for the heterogeneity of the banks' characteristics in our sample, the study applies a panel data framework accordingly. The Hausman test favors a random effect model (Prob > Chi(2)1:0.789), and to take into account the possible issues of heteroskedasticity and autocorrelation, the robust random effects are subsequently estimated.

4. Findings and Analysis

4.1. *Correlation matrix*

Table 1 shows the correlation results of the study as a preliminary analysis. It presents the strength of the association between the variables. It shows that board size, board independence, directors' ownership, institutional ownership, and ROA are positively correlated with the dependent variable (GBDI). This finding is in line with past studies (Bose *et al.*, 2018). However, it can be observed from the table that multiple directorships are negatively correlated with the dependent variable.

Table 1. Correlation matrix (Pearson correlation).

Variables	GBDI	BSIZE	BIND	DOWN	INSOWN	MULDIRECT	ROA
GBDI	1.000						
BSIZE	0.679	1.000					
BIND	0.542	0.619	1.000				
DOWN	0.193	0.171	0.170	1.000			
INSOWN	0.397	0.467	0.362	0.059	1.000		
MULDIRECT	−0.063	−0.093	−0.082	−0.015	−0.051	1.000	
ROA	0.215	0.173	0.158	0.046	0.165	0.023	1.000

The limitations of the pairwise correction coefficient are known, as it tends to give the associations in isolation and not disclose the direction of causality. Subsequently, we analyze the hypothesized relationships through a multiple regression model, specifically the random effect panel data approach.

4.2. *Random effect estimates*

The robust panel data estimates of the multivariate regression model specified and discussed earlier are summarized in Table 2 and are subsequently discussed thereafter.

4.2.1. *Analysis of results*

H1: Board Size and Green Banking Disclosures

Our results show that board size has a significant and positive influence on GBDs. H1 is therefore supported. This positive relationship is in accord with several studies (De Villiers *et al.*, 2011; Bose *et al.*, 2018; Hermawan & Gunardi, 2019). Chan *et al.* (2014) claim that the board has the responsibility to ensure that the firm complies with regulations, thereby disclosing information. Moreover, a large board size implies the representation of different stakeholders. The board's benefits are somehow linked with stakeholders' interests, which means that when stakeholders' interests are accounted for, the level of green disclosures will increase. Stakeholder theory posits that more green disclosures enhance the firms' ties with their creditors, suppliers, and shareholders. From an agency theory perspective, the

Table 2. Regression results (robust random estimates).

Variables	**Model 1**
Constant	−0.005
BSIZE	**0.065*****
	(2.243)
BIND	015**
	(2.103)
DOWN	0.022
	(1.12)
INSOWN	**0.226***
	(0.004)
MULDIRECT	0.124
	(1.24)
ROA	0.163*
	(2.588)***
N	160
Adjusted R_2	0.532
F value	21.34

Note: *, **, and *** denote the significance levels at 10, 5, and 1 percent, respectively.

board has the responsibility to perform actions that protect the interests of shareholders, and this can be done by providing more green disclosures.

H2: Board Independence and Green Banking Disclosures

Our findings support H2, as a positive and significant relationship is found between board independence and GBDs. This result is consistent with other studies, such as those by Rupley *et al.* (2012) and Hermawan and Gunardi, (2019). Our results are also in line with agency and stakeholder theories, which claim that independent directors are more conscientious and pay greater attention to stakeholders' interests when making board decisions (Zahra & Stanton, 1988; Chen & Roberts, 2010). As such, independent directors have the power to encourage the quality of disclosures of green banking and force managers to disclose green banking information, which is consistent with the finding by Rupley *et al.* (2012).

H3: Institutional Ownership and Green Banking Disclosures

Our findings show a positive and significant relationship between institutional ownership and GBDs. H3 is therefore supported. Our findings concur with Jiang and Habib (2009) and Rao *et al.* (2012). Institutional shareholders focus on the long-term performance of organizations. They will support the green practices of their investees (Mahoney & Roberts, 2007).

H4: Director Ownership and Green Banking Disclosures

We hypothesized a negative relationship between director ownership and GBD. However, our results show a positive and insignificant relationship between the two, consistent with past studies (Oh *et al.*, 2011; Bae *et al.*, 2018). The positive relationship is probably because of special requirements by the regulator to be transparent and disclose more information. The insignificant relationship is possibly due to the negligible ownership by directors in their respective banks. Owner-directors may favor making more disclosure if that builds their reputation as global citizens (Barnea & Rubin, 2010).

H5: Multiple Directorships and Green Banking Disclosures

Our findings show a positive but insignificant relationship between multiple directorships and GBDs. This result is consistent with the finding by Mooneeapen *et al.* (2021), who argue that the Mauritian context is quite distinct from other countries regarding multiple directorships. Directors come from a close-knit group and are nominated to boards due to personal connections and family relationships (Mahadeo *et al.*, 2012) and also hold long tenures. Directors thus adopt a groupthink behavior, and due to their high number of board commitments, these directors cannot contribute effectively to board discussions and promote GBDs.

H6: Profitability and Green Banking Disclosures

As per our results, ROA has a positive and significant relationship with the extent of GBDs and is in line with studies such as those by Tagesson *et al.* (2009) and Cormier *et al.* (1999). The result implies that an increase in profitability increases green disclosures. When firms are profitable, they can devote more resources toward green initiatives, and consequently, they will try to influence public opinion by disclosing more information (legitimacy theory). Similarly, from a stakeholder theory standpoint, banks will try to demonstrate to their primary stakeholders that profitability and green initiatives can be achieved simultaneously and thus disclose more green information.

5. Conclusion

Banking activities are not known to be harmful to the environment. However, banks hold a position of trust in society, and their actions can inspire corporates and individuals to adopt environment-friendly initiatives that contribute toward a sustainable world. The board's primary role is to reduce information asymmetry between management and stakeholders/shareholders. Information disclosure is one of the ways to bridge this gap.

We investigated how corporate governance practices via board characteristics and ownership structures affect GBDs. Our findings showed that board size, board independence, institutional ownership, and profitability positively and significantly influence GBD. We found no evidence of the influence of director ownership and multiple directorship on GBDs.

Our findings present implications for regulators, academics, and practitioners. Board size is positively associated with GBDs. The management of banks can use this finding to plan their board size to meet the needs of stakeholders effectively. Similarly, board independence is also positively associated with GBDs. Regulators can use this finding to issue guidelines or regulations about board independence. The current Code of Corporate Governance for Mauritius (2016) only states that there must be a balance between executive and independent directors. In light of our findings, regulators may opt for a greater proportion of independent directors to guarantee greater information disclosure to stakeholders. We also found evidence of the busyness hypotheses in the Mauritian context. Directors holding multiple directorships cannot effectively promote green practices through the interorganizational exchange of knowledge and resources. Regulators can consider limiting the number of directorships for meaningful contributions by board members. Mooneeapen *et al.* (2021) report that, on average, 72 percent of board members hold multiple directorships in Mauritian companies. The outcomes of this study also have theoretical implications that support basic arguments of legitimacy and stakeholder theories that explain the factors that influence green disclosures.

This study is not without limitations, and there are opportunities to further expand this research. Our study uses content analysis to measure the extent of GBD, which is prone to human measurement errors. The same applies to the measurement of variables. However, steps were taken to minimize the chance of these errors occurring. The measurement of GBDs focused on quantity, thus neglecting disclosure quality. Nonetheless, the findings of this study provide interesting insights into GBDs in a developing country context, especially at a time when climate change and sustainable practices are high on the agendas of governments and corporates. Future research can consider extending the sample of companies, such as conducting cross-country research in Africa, where there is a shortage of studies. The number of independent variables can also be extended to include more ownership structure and country variables. Researchers can also investigate the quality of GBDs and assess the similarities and differences between the determinants of the quantity of GBDs.

Appendix 1

Green banking activities			
1.	Banks' policies to protect the environment.	12.	Banks awarded for their eco-friendly activities and reporting practices.
2.	To finance client projects, such as eco-friendly projects.	13.	Banks' clients awarded for protecting the environment.
3.	Reduction of paper waste through emails, using double side and recycled papers.	14.	Preserving heritage buildings and protecting the environment by tree plantation.
4.	Policies to reduce wastage of water and gas in operations.	15.	Implementation of a climate change fund.
5.	Use of eco-friendly materials, such as recycled paper.	16.	Building green branches.
6.	Conservation of energy in operations.	17.	Green marketing in banks' letterheads and other communications.
7.	Measures for climate change and reducing employees' business travels.	18.	Banks training their employees to engage in green operations.
8.	Introduction of new green initiatives, such as online banking, ATMs, and mobile banking.	19.	Amount of money allocated annually to green banking.
9.	Banks' relation with green bodies.	20.	Actual amount spent on green banking.
10.	Banks analyzing the impacts their clients' businesses have on the environment before financing them.	21.	Use of separate pages to report green banking activities in annual reports.
11.	Seminars and workshops organized by the banks to increase awareness in the country.		

Appendix 2

List of banks considered in the study:

ABC Banking Corporation
AfrAsia Bank
Bank of Baroda
Bank One
Banyan Tree Bank Limited
BCP Bank Mauritius Ltd.
Century Banking Corporation Limited
Development Bank of Mauritius
HSBC Limited PLC
Investec Bank
MauBank Ltd.
SBI Bank Mauritius Ltd.
SBM Bank Mauritius Ltd.
Standard Bank Mauritius Limited
Standard Chartered Bank Mauritius Limited
The Mauritius Commercial Bank Ltd.

References

Ahmed, A. A. A. (2021). Corporate attributes and disclosure of accounting information: Evidence from the big five banks of China. *Journal of Public Affairs*, *21*(3), e2244.

Ahmed Haji, A. (2013). Corporate social responsibility disclosures over time: Evidence from Malaysia. *Managerial Auditing Journal*, *28*(7), 647–676.

Ali, W., Sandhu, M. A., Iqbal, J., & Tufail, M. S. (2016). Corporate governance and CSR disclosure: Evidence from a developing country. *Pakistan Journal of Social Sciences*, *36*(1), 225–238.

Bae, S. M., Masud, M., Kaium, A., *et al.* (2018). A cross-country investigation of corporate governance and corporate sustainability disclosure: A signaling theory perspective. *Sustainability*, *10*(8), 2611.

Barnea, A. & Rubin, A. (2010). Corporate social responsibility as a conflict between shareholders. *Journal of Business Ethics*, *97*(1), 71–86.

Ben-Amar, W., McIlkenny, P., & Mhedhbi, K. (2018). What explains voluntary corporate carbon disclosures in emerging markets? Research Handbook of Finance and Sustainability, 319.

Birindelli, G., Dell'Atti, S., Iannuzzi, A. P., & Savioli, M. (2018). Composition and activity of the board of directors: Impact on ESG performance in the banking system. *Sustainability, 10*(12), 4699.

Bose, S., Khan, H. Z., Rashid, A., *et al.* (2018). What drives green banking disclosure? An institutional and corporate governance perspective. *Asia Pacific Journal of Management, 35*(2), 501–527.

Brac Bank (2017). Disclosure on green banking [online]. Retrieved from https://www.bracbank.com [Accessed on 29 December 2020].

Brammer, S. & Pavelin, S. (2008). Factors influencing the quality of corporate environmental disclosure. *Business Strategy and the Environment, 17*(2), 120–136.

Branco, M. C. & Rodrigues, L. L. (2008). Social responsibility disclosure: A study of proxies for the public visibility of Portuguese banks. *The British Accounting Review, 40*(2), 161–181.

Brown, N. & Deegan, C. (1998). The public disclosure of environmental performance information — A dual test of media agenda setting theory and legitimacy theory. *Accounting and Business Research, 29*(1), 21–41.

Chan, M. C., Watson, J., & Woodliff, D. (2014). Corporate governance quality and CSR disclosures. *Journal of Business Ethics, 125*(1), 59–73.

Chen, J. C. & Roberts, R. W. (2010). Toward a more coherent understanding of the organization–society relationship: A theoretical consideration for social and environmental accounting research. *Journal of Business Ethics, 97*, 651–665.

Cooke, T. E. (1989). Disclosure in the corporate annual reports of Swedish companies. *Accounting and Business Research, 19*(74), 113–124.

Cormier, D., Aerts, W., Ledoux, M. J., *et al.* (2009). Attributes of social and human capital disclosure and information asymmetry between managers and investors. *Canadian Journal of Administrative Sciences/ Revue Canadienne des Sciences de l'Administration, 26*(1), 71–88.

Coulson, A. B. (2009). How should banks govern the environment? Challenging the construction of action versus veto. *Business Strategy and the Environment, 18*(3), 149–161.

Courtois, S., Gombart, C., Pignatel, I., *et al.* (2011). Multiple directorships and CAC-40 natural environmental disclosures. *Journal of the Asia Pacific Centre for Environmental Accountability, 17*(1), 28–50.

Day, R. & Woodward, T. (2009). CSR reporting and the UK financial services sector. *Journal of Applied Accounting Research, 10*(3), 159–175.

De Villiers, C., Naiker, V., & Van Staden, C. J. (2011). The effect of board characteristics on firm environmental performance. *Journal of Management, 37*(6), 1636–1663.

Deegan, C. & Rankin, M. (1996). Do Australian companies report environmental news objectively? An analysis of environmental disclosures by firms prosecuted successfully by the Environmental Protection Authority. *Accounting, Auditing & Accountability Journal*, *9*(2), 50–67.

Elsakit, O. M. & Worthington, A. C. (2014). The impact of corporate characteristics and corporate governance on corporate social and environmental disclosure: A literature review. *International Journal of Business and Management*, *9*(9), 1.

Elshabasy, Y. N. (2018). The impact of corporate characteristics on environmental information disclosure: An empirical study on the listed firms in Egypt. *Journal of Business and Retail Management Research*, *12*(2), 232–241.

Forgione, A. F. & Migliardo, C. (2020). CSR engagement and market structure: Evidence from listed banks. *Finance Research Letters*, *35*, 101592.

Freeman, R. E., Wicks, A. C., & Parmar, B. (2004). Stakeholder theory and the corporate objective revisited. *Organisation Science*, *15*(3), 364–369.

Ghabayen, M. A., Mohamad, N. R., & Ahmad, N. (2016). Board characteristics and corporate social responsibility disclosure in the Jordanian banks. *Corporate Board: Role, Duties and Composition*, *12*(1), 84–99.

Ghazali, N. A. M. (2007). Ownership structure and corporate social responsibility disclosure: some Malaysian evidence. *Corporate Governance: The International Journal of Business in Society*, *7*(3), 251–266.

Grassa, R., Moumen, N., & Hussainey, K. (2021). What drives risk disclosure in Islamic and conventional banks? An international comparison. *International Journal of Finance & Economics*, *26*(4), 6338–6361.

Habbash, M. (2016). Corporate governance and corporate social responsibility disclosure: Evidence from Saudi Arabia. *Journal of Economic and Social Development*, *3*(1), 87.

Hackston, D. & Milne, M. J. (1996). Some determinants of social and environmental disclosures in New Zealand companies. *Accounting, Auditing & Accountability Journal*, *9*(1), 77–108.

Haniffa, R. M. & Cooke, T. E. (2005). The impact of culture and governance on corporate social reporting. *Journal of Accounting and Public Policy*, *24*(5), 391–430.

Hermawan, A. & Gunardi, A. (2019). Motivation for disclosure of corporate social responsibility: Evidence from banking industry in Indonesia. *Entrepreneurship and Sustainability Issues*, *6*(3), 1097–1106.

Hill, C. W. & Jones, T. M. (1992). Stakeholder-agency theory. *Journal of Management Studies*, *29*(2), 131–154.

Hossain, D. M., Bir, A., Sadiq, A. T., *et al.* (2016). Disclosure of green banking issues in the annual reports: A study on Bangladeshi banks. *Middle East Journal of Business*, *55*(3034), 1–12.

Htay, S. N. N., Rashid, H. M. A., Adnan, M. A., *et al.* (2012). Impact of corporate governance on social and environmental information disclosure of Malaysian listed banks: Panel data analysis. *Asian Journal of Finance & Accounting, 4*(1), 1–24.

Islam, M. S. & Das, P. C. (2013). Green banking practices in Bangladesh. *IOSR Journal of Business and Management, 8*(3), 39–44.

Jackling, B. & Johl, S. (2009). Board structure and firm performance: Evidence from India's top companies. *Corporate Governance: An International Review, 17*(4), 492–509.

Jiang, H. & Habib, A. (2009). The impact of different types of ownership concentration on annual report voluntary disclosures in New Zealand. *Accounting Research Journal, 22*(3), 275–304.

Johnson, R. A. & Greening, D. W. (1999). The effects of corporate governance and institutional ownership types on corporate social performance. *Academy of Management Journal, 42*(5), 564–576.

Kathy Rao, K., Tilt, C. A., & Lester, L. H. (2012). Corporate governance and environmental reporting: An Australian study. *Corporate Governance: The International Journal of Business in Society, 12*(2), 143–163.

Khan, A., Muttakin, M. B., & Siddiqui, J. (2013). Corporate governance and corporate social responsibility disclosures: Evidence from an emerging economy. *Journal of Business Ethics, 114*(2), 207–223.

Kiliç, M., Kuzey, C., & Uyar, A. (2015). The impact of ownership and board structure on Corporate Social Responsibility (CSR) reporting in the Turkish banking industry. *Corporate Governance, 15*(3), 357–374.

Lexpress (2009). Initiative 175: la MCB lance des actions en faveur du développement durable. Retrieved from https://www.lexpress.mu/article/initiative-175-la-mcb-lance-des-actions-en-faveur-du-d%C3%A9veloppement-durable [Accessed on 22 March 2022].

Lopez Iturriaga, F. J. & Morros Rodriguez, I. (2014). Boards of directors and firm performance: The effect of multiple directorships. *Spanish Journal of Finance and Accounting/Revista Espanola de Financiacion y Contabilidad, 43*(2), 177–192.

Mahadeo, J. D., Soobaroyen, T., & Hanuman, V. O. (2012). Board composition and financial performance: Uncovering the effects of diversity in an emerging economy. *Journal of Business Ethics, 105*(3), 375–388.

Mahoney, L. & Roberts, R. W. (2007, September). Corporate social performance, financial performance and institutional ownership in Canadian firms. *Accounting Forum, 31*(3), 233–253.

Masud, M., Hossain, M., & Kim, J. (2018a). Is green regulation effective or a failure: Comparative analysis between Bangladesh Bank (BB) green guidelines and global reporting initiative guidelines. *Sustainability, 10*(4), 1267.

Masud, M. A. K., Nurunnabi, M., & Bae, S. M. (2018b). The effects of corporate governance on environmental sustainability reporting: Empirical evidence from South Asian countries. *Asian Journal of Sustainability and Social Responsibility, 3*(1), 3.

Matten, D. & Moon, J. (2008). "Implicit" and "explicit" CSR: A conceptual framework for a comparative understanding of corporate social responsibility. *Academy of management Review, 33*(2), 404–424.

McKendall, M., Sánchez, C., & Sicilian, P. (1999). Corporate governance and corporate illegality: The effects of board structure on environmental violations. *The International Journal of Organizational Analysis, 7*(3), 201–223.

McKendall, M., Sánchez, C., & Sicilian, P. (1999). Corporate governance and corporate illegality: The effects of board structure on environmental violations. *The International Journal of Organizational Analysis.*

Mehedi, S. & Kuddus, M. A. (2017). Green banking: A case study on Dutch-Bangla bank Ltd. *Academy of Accounting and Financial Studies Journal, 21*(2), 1–20.

Michelon, G. & Parbonetti, A. (2012). The effect of corporate governance on sustainability disclosure. *Journal of Management & Governance, 16*(3), 477–509.

Mo Ibrahim Foundation (2020). Latest news. Retrieved from https://mo.ibrahim.foundation/news/2020/2020-ibrahim-index-african-governance-key-findings [Accessed on 27 March 2022].

Mooneeapen, O., Abhayawansa, S., Ramdhony, D., & Atchia, Z. (2022). New insights into the nexus between board characteristics and intellectual capital disclosure: The case of the emerging economy of Mauritius. *Journal of Accounting in Emerging Economies, 12*(1), 29–51.

Mousa, G. & Hassan, N. T. (2015). Legitimacy theory and environmental practices: Short notes. *International Journal of Business and Statistical Analysis, 2*(1), 42–53.

Nawaiseh, M. E. (2015). Do firm size and financial performance affect corporate social responsibility disclosure: Employees' and environmental dimensions? *American Journal of Applied Sciences, 12*(12), 967.

Ntim, C. G. & Soobaroyen, T. (2013). Corporate governance and performance in socially responsible corporations: New empirical insights from a neo-institutional framework. *Corporate Governance: An International Review, 21*(5), 468–494.

Oh, W. Y., Chang, Y. K., & Martynov, A. (2011). The effect of ownership structure on corporate social responsibility: Empirical evidence from Korea. *Journal of Business Ethics, 104*(2), 283–297.

Ramdhony, D., Rashid, A., Gow, J., & Soobaroyen, T. (2022). The influence of corporate governance and corporate foundations on corporate social responsibility (CSR) reporting practices. *Journal of African Business*, *23*(3), 816–832.

Rupley, K. H., Brown, D., & Marshall, R. S. (2012). Governance, media and the quality of environmental disclosure. *Journal of Accounting and Public Policy*, *31*(6), 610–640.

Shamil, M., M. Shaikh, J., Ho, P. L., *et al.* (2014). The influence of board characteristics on sustainability reporting: Empirical evidence from Sri Lankan firms. *Asian Review of Accounting*, *22*(2), 78–97.

Tagesson, T., Blank, V., Broberg, P., *et al.* (2009). What explains the extent and content of social and environmental disclosures on corporate websites: A study of social and environmental reporting in Swedish listed corporations. *Corporate Social Responsibility and Environmental Management*, *16*(6), 352–364.

Tara, K. & Singh, S. (2014). Green banking: An approach towards environmental management. *Prabandhan: Indian Journal of Management*, *7*(11), 7–20.

Tran, Q. T., Vo, T. D., *et al.* (2021). Relationship between profitability and corporate social responsibility disclosure: Evidence from Vietnamese listed banks. *The Journal of Asian Finance, Economics and Business*, *8*(3), 875–883.

Waddock, S. A. & Graves, S. B. (1997). The corporate social performance–financial performance link. *Strategic Management Journal*, *18*(4), 303–319.

Zahra, S. A. & Stanton, W. W. (1988). The implications of board of directors composition for corporate strategy and performance. *International Journal of Management*, *5*(2), 229–236.

Part II
Environmental Disclosure, Standards and Relevance

https://doi.org/10.1142/9781800614482_0006

Chapter 6

How Should Sustainable Finance Standards Be Designed for Developing Countries?

Kathrin Berensmann

German Institute of Development and Sustainability (IDOS), Bonn, Germany

kathrin.berensmann@idos-research.de

Abstract

Sustainable finance took on a crucial role in supporting a sustainable recovery over the course of the COVID-19 crisis. An appropriate global framework for sustainable financial management is essential for mobilizing sufficient financial resources to achieve the Sustainable Development Goals (SDGs). Sustainable finance regulations and standards elaborated for developed countries with fairly mature financial markets and strong institutions may not be appropriate for developing countries with less-developed financial markets and weaker institutions. Experience gained from comparable regulatory processes being applied to developing countries, for example financial standards such as the Basel capital and liquidity standards, has shown that adopting a single set of financial standards to developed and developing countries will not work. For these reasons, the principle of proportionality should be applied. Simplified sustainable finance standards that take into account institutional and regulatory capacities should be elaborated and enacted in developing countries because less-complex financial regulations can be more effective and easier to implement, supervise, and monitor. Global policy-making institutions and forums should better engage developing countries as active participants in designing a global sustainable financial governance. International institutions and development cooperations should provide targeted capacity building and training.

1. Introduction

Sustainable finance[1] has taken on a crucial role in supporting a sustainable recovery following the COVID-19 crisis. An appropriate global framework for sustainable financial management, including sustainable finance standards, is essential for mobilizing sufficient financial resources to achieve the Sustainable Development Goals (SDGs). Regulations for sustainable finance, including standards for defining, implementing, and monitoring sustainable finance instruments, assume an important role in further developing the market for sustainable finance, thereby mobilizing financial resources for attaining the SDGs.

While there are some papers on sustainable finance regulations, including standards with a focus on green bond standards and green taxonomies (Azhgaliyeva *et al.*, 2020; Berensmann, 2017; Deschryver *et al.*, 2020; EC, 2018, 2021a, 2021b; Ehlers & Packer, 2017; Ehlers *et al.*, 2021; EIB & CGFC, 2017; EU, 2019, 2020; G20 SFWG, 2021; ICMA, 2020a, 2020b; Maragopoulos, 2022; OECD, 2020; SBN, 2018; Tripathy *et al.*, 2020; World Bank, 2020c; Zhang, 2020), there are no academic publications on how to design sustainable finance standards in developing countries. There are some policy papers making proposals on how to design and implement sustainable finance standards in developing countries, including the proposal of the International Platform on Sustainable Finance (IPSF) for a Common Ground Taxonomy (IPSF, 2021a, 2021b), one policy paper related to this proposal published by the UN-DESA and the IPSF (2021), as well as a paper provided by the Bank for International Settlements (BIS) (Ehlers *et al.*, 2021). Only one policy paper by the Organization for Economic Co-operation and Development (OECD) United Nations

[1]Sustainable finance means that private and governmental players on the market consider aspects of sustainability in their decisions. In line with the environment, social, and governance (ESG) approach, this includes climate and environmental protection (green finance) as well as economic and social aspects. In addition, it includes the long-term economic viability of the supported institutions and actors and the stability of the entire financial system in which they work (BMF, 2021; ICMA, 2020a). Sustainable finance has two important goals: First, it aims to provide financial resources for the implementation of the 2030 Agenda, and second, it contributes to preserving the long-term value of assets by ensuring that the financial sector does no harm, reduces financial risks, and increases the resilience of the national and global financial systems.

Development Program (UNDP) addresses in more detail the role of development cooperation in implementing sustainable finance standards in developing countries (OECD & UNDP, 2020).

This chapter addresses this research gap by exploring the two main questions: (i) How should sustainable finance standards be designed for developing countries? and (ii) How can international institutions and development cooperation support the implementation of sustainable finance standards in developing countries? To the author's knowledge, there is no research paper available that deals with the specific design of sustainable finance standards for developing countries, adopts the principle of proportionality, and compares the implementation of the Basel standards in developing countries with the adoption of sustainable finance standards in developing countries.

Designing a global sustainable financial governance framework that works in all settings — in industrialized countries, emerging markets, and developing countries — is challenging. First, country-specific circumstances, such as the development and capacity of a country's financial system, have to be taken into account. A "one size fits all" approach will not work. A flexible approach according to the principle of proportionality that takes into account the development of a country's financial market, the quality of its institutions, and its human resource capacity is needed. Second, it is difficult to include all private and public actors in the design of a global sustainable financial governance framework because this framework has been elaborated by different public and private actors, institutions, and authorities over a long period of time. Developing countries have rarely been included in designing and deciding on sustainable finance regulations, such as standards, unlike emerging markets, which have even established their own regulations.

This chapter is structured as follows. Section 2 provides a brief overview of the current architecture of sustainable finance standards and its proliferation. Section 3 discusses the benefits and challenges of sustainable finance standards in developing countries. In Section 4, the lessons learnt from the adoption of the Basel standards in developing countries for implementing sustainable finance standards are discussed. Section 5 concludes and outlines the role of the international community to support sustainable finance standards in developing countries. It deals with the questions of how international institutions and development cooperations could support the implementation of sustainable finance standards in developing countries and how public or private actors in developing countries can be better involved in setting these standards.

2. Proliferation of Sustainable Finance Standards

A large number of institutions or forums have shaped sustainable finance strategies and standards, leading to a proliferation of sustainable finance regulations, including standards. Various standards have been put in place for sustainable finance instruments at different levels — international, regional, national, and even subnational. In the same vein, there are different standards for sustainable finance and its subcategories, such as green finance. These standards have been designed and set by various public actors, including governments and international institutions, and by private actors, including private financial actors or private institutions, such as the International Capital Market Association, the Institute of International Finance, and stock exchanges.

Examples of general sustainable finance standards established by public entities comprise the multilateral development banks' (MDBs) Common Principles for Climate Change Mitigation Finance Tracking, the Taskforce on Climate Related Financial Disclosures (TCFD), the European sustainable finance strategy, including the green finance taxonomy and the European Green Bond Standard, and the Association of South east Asian Nations (ASEAN) Green Social and Sustainability Bond standards.[2] Further institutions that contribute to designing and setting sustainable finance standards comprise foremost the G20 Sustainable Finance Working Group, reestablished under the Italian G20 Presidency; the Network of Central Banks and Supervisors for Greening the Financial System (NGFS); the Coalition of Finance Ministers for Climate Action (CMFCA); and the Financial Stability Board (FSB). In addition, many countries have established sustainable finance standards, including China, Japan, Malaysia, Thailand, New Zealand, Argentina, Egypt, Nigeria, Kenya,

[2]Other examples include the UN Global Compact, the UN Principles for Responsible Investing, the United Nations Environment Programme Finance Initiative Principles for Positive Impact Finance and the UN Sustainable Stock Exchanges initiative standard.

Morocco, South Africa, Norway, and the United Kingdom (EC, 2021a, 2021b; OECD & UNDP, 2020).

Box 1: Sustainable Finance Strategy of the European Union

Within the framework of the EU's Sustainable Finance Strategy, the EU is setting important standards for sustainable finance that will serve as a model for other regions and countries and thus, to some extent, will also be exported to them. In order to mobilize substantial private capital for the transition to a sustainable economy, the EU has started to establish a framework for a sustainable financial system in the EU with the 2018 "Sustainable Growth Financing Action Plan" and, building on this, with the 2021 "Strategy for Financing the Transition to a Sustainable Economy." The 2018 Action Plan has three main elements: (i) taxonomy with a classification system for sustainable activities (ii) standards and benchmarks for sustainable finance instruments and (iii) disclosure requirements for companies on the effects of companies' activities on the environment and sustainability risks. Based on the 2018 Action Plan, the EU 2021 has developed a new strategy that comprises four building blocks: (i) tools and measures for the transition to sustainability (ii) making a sustainable financial system inclusive (iii) increasing the resilience and contribution of the financial sector and (iv) supporting an international strategy for a sustainable financial system. Overall, the EU has put together a comprehensive package for the design of a sustainable financial system and launched a strategy that is unique (EC, 2021a, 2021b; Berensmann, 2022).

There has been a proliferation of sustainable finance standards put in place by private institutions or alliances, including the Global Impact Investing Network, the Global Investors for Sustainable Development Alliance, the Global Reporting Initiative, the Global Sustainable Investment Alliance, the Impact Management Project, the Sustainability Accounting Standards Board, and the World Benchmarking Alliance (OECD & UNDP, 2020). This proliferation of standards is different from the financial standards set up in the past. The Basel standards have been designed and established by the FSB and the Basel Committee on Banking Supervision (BCBS), which received their mandate from the G20.

Box 2: Proliferation of green bond standards

One illustrative example of a proliferation of standards on various levels are the green bond standards (Berensmann, 2017; Ehlers & Packer, 2017; EIB, 2017). The Green Bond Principles (GBP) represent the most important international standard and have been used as a guideline for other standards (ICMA, 2020b). Another important international standard is the climate bond standard established by the Climate Bonds Initiative (CBI, 2019). Diverse green bond standards at the regional and national levels have also been established, such as the EU Green Bond Standard (EU, 2019; EC, 2021a) and the ASEAN Green Bond Standards (ACMF, 2017). At the national level, several countries have implemented their national green bond standards. For example, China established the Green Bond Catalogue in 2017. But even at the national level, there are diverse green bond standards, as in China, where different standards have been established for sovereign and corporate green bonds (Berensmann, 2017).

2.1. *Challenges of market fragmentation*

The fragmentation of frameworks and instruments for sustainable finance, including taxonomies, standards, and labeling schemes, has led to increased complexity, which poses a number of problems not only for market actors, such as investors and companies, but also for governments and the public. Fragmentation leads to non-transparency of the regulations because it is difficult for market participants to be informed on different regulations.

Investors and companies/issuers have to adapt to different standards, which leads to high transaction costs, such as higher information costs associated with different regulations. It must be taken into account that many companies operate across countries because they are increasingly integrated via value chains. Inconsistent regulations for sustainable financing could lead to companies not applying new green technologies and sustainable business models. In addition, it is difficult for companies to integrate sustainability goals into their business models and measure their sustainability performance if there are different regulations. It would also be more difficult for companies to demonstrate that their investments comply with sustainable finance regulations. This could increase the risk of green- or SDG-washing.

Similarly, fragmentation also affects investors' ability to assess the risks and opportunities of sustainable investments and to identify sustainability performance. It also makes it difficult for investors to compare ratings and incorporate long-term material sustainability risks into credit ratings. In general, without harmonized standards and metrics, it is difficult to assess the financial sector's contribution to the SDG targets and the Paris Agreement.

For governments, harmonized regulations have the advantage that they can be based on existing ones, which would increase market acceptance because these regulations would be known to market participants. In addition, the development of a new regulatory framework by a country and its jurisdiction is sometimes associated with high costs and also requires sufficient expertise in this area. These costs can be reduced by aligning with existing regulations (UNDESA & IPSF, 2020, pp. 27–28).

A stronger global harmonization of regulations is thus associated with a number of advantages, but the specific features of the individual countries, regions, and jurisdictions should nevertheless be taken into account.

3. The Benefits and Challenges of Sustainable Finance Standards in Developing Countries

Often, financial regulations, including standards, from industrialized countries are transmitted to emerging and developing countries. Regulations for sustainable financial instruments, such as taxonomies and quality labels, are often developed and implemented in industrialized countries and regulated by their legal systems. However, as many of these investors have global investment mandates, these regulations also affect developing countries, such as the regulations of the Sustainable Finance Strategy of the EU, which also apply to the markets of developing countries. In addition, many regulations in developing countries are based on those in the EU, such as the South African green finance taxonomy, which is based on the one of the EU.

3.1. *Benefits of sustainable finance standards in developing countries*

Since standards enhance the market integrity for sustainable finance instruments and thereby support their development they can increase the development impact of private sustainable finance in developing countries.

Standards for sustainable finance instruments, including criteria regarding the definition and classification of sustainable activities, eligibility, disclosure, and impact reporting, are crucial. Standards push market integrity because they provide clarity for investors, companies, and banks on what constitutes sustainable financial instruments (G20 GFSG, 2018). Standards for definitions and taxonomies support investors in distinguishing between sustainable and non-sustainable financial instruments and thereby preventing SDG-washing. In this way, standards enhance confidence between issuers and investors (Berensmann, 2017; OECD & UNDP, 2020; SBN, 2018). In the same vein, a suitable definition is essential for internal budgeting, accounting, and measurement of the performance of financial institutions and for appropriate environmental risk management (G20 GFSG, 2016).

3.2. *Challenges of sustainable finance standards in developing countries*

Despite these advantages, there are some challenges associated with the implementation of sustainable finance standards in developing countries. It is difficult to develop universal instruments for all types of countries. Sustainable finance standards elaborated for developed countries and/or emerging economies with fairly mature financial markets may not be appropriate for developing countries with less-developed financial markets.

Sustainable investments are only possible when capital markets have reached a certain level of development. For example, it is difficult to issue sustainable bonds if the capital market is not well developed and is too narrow due to limited participation. Since government bonds often have a benchmark function, it is important for the development of sustainable bond markets so that they become deep and liquid markets that provide the basic infrastructure and benchmark yield curves necessary for domestic bond issuance and pricing. Furthermore, stock exchanges in these countries should also be sufficiently developed to allow sustainable investment funds to include companies from developing countries. For this, sufficient number of companies must be listed on the stock exchange (UNDESA & IPSF 2021, p. 31).

In addition, there is often a lack of available and verifiable data in developing countries. As a result, investors may not be able to assess the sustainability of these investments as well as that of investments in developed countries. It might be difficult, for example, for investors to assess the degree of alignment of the taxonomy for investments in developing countries (UNDESA & IPSF 2021, p. 32).

4. The Example of Basel Standards: Lessons Learnt for Sustainable Finance Standards

Experience gained from comparable processes being applied to financial standards for developing countries, especially the adoption of the Basel capital and liquidity standards, has shown that applying a single set of financial standards to developed countries, emerging markets, and developing countries will not work (Anginer *et al.*, 2019; Jones, 2014; Jones & Zeitz, 2017; Hohl *et al.*, 2018; FSB, 2012; World Bank, 2020b).

4.1. *Implementation of Basel standards in developing countries*

The Basel standards should contribute to a more stable international financial system by tightening banking standards worldwide, but the financial markets of developing countries are much less mature than those of the industrialized countries and emerging markets. Regulatory and institutional weaknesses and less supervisory capacity make it more difficult to implement the Basel standards in developing countries, in particular the implementation of the more advanced approaches to risk assessment in Basel II and the macro-prudential approach of Basel III (Jones, 2014).

The basic regulatory and supervisory measures contained in Basel III are important for the stabilization of banking systems in developed countries. They include well-capitalized banks that can cope with different market conditions and thus also with crises and a coherent market-based institutional and legal framework. In addition, strong, timely, and forward-looking supervisory measures should be introduced and implemented. However, not all of the regulations of Basel III are directly transferable to individual developing countries because regulatory measures and supervisory approaches work in different ways in diverse country contexts.

Box 3: Basel III regulation in response to the global financial crisis

The global financial crisis revealed that banking regulation and supervision have not been designed and implemented appropriately to prevent and deal with financial crises. The main reasons for the crisis were imperfect information and short-term funding for many assets in combination with high leverage ratios. The role of banking regulation and supervision is to provide the rules for the banking systems and their enforcement. While bank regulation comprises rules addressing the foundation and operations of banks supervision, focusing on overseeing the application of these regulations, one main task of banks is liquidity creation because they transform short-term liquid deposits into long-term illiquid assets (World Bank, 2020b, p. 2).

The G20 mandated the FSB to develop and promote effective regulatory, prudential, and other measures for the financial sector. The BCBS drew up the third Basel framework agreement, Basel III. These are part of this regulatory reform agenda and essentially contain new capital and liquidity requirements for banks. The aims of the Basel III framework and capital regulations have been to enhance the quantity and quality of capital (World Bank, 2020b, p. 4; Hohl *et al.*, 2018, p. 3).

For these reasons, the principle of proportionality should be applied (World Bank, 2020b, pp. 23–25). According to this principle, bank regulation and supervision in developing countries should be adequate to the supervisory capacity, institutional environment, and specific roles of banks in those countries. Basel II and III were developed for more complex banking sectors in developed countries, and the regulations suggested might be too complex for numerous banking systems in developing countries and could even adversely affect banking systems with a less-developed financial system and weaker institutions (Jones & Zeitz, 2017, pp. 90–91; Restoy, 2018; World Bank, 2020b, p. 23).

Indeed, many developing countries have been selective and have avoided some of the more complicated elements, such as the use of internal models to assess bank risk. The capacity of supervisors in developing countries has not improved sufficiently, and it has therefore not been possible to apply the more complex banking regulations (World Bank, 2020b, p. 93).

Empirical evidence on the reforms implemented in developing countries, their effect on the stability of the financial system, and the lending behavior of local banking sectors is rare. In addition to Jones and Zeitz (2017), Castro Carvalho *et al.* (2017), and Hohl *et al.* (2018), the World Bank has partly closed this gap with its Global Financial Development Report 2019/2020 on bank regulation and supervision.

Many developing countries that do not belong to the BCBS and have therefore not been formally required to put Basel standards in place have implemented at least part of them (Jones & Zeitz, 2017; Hohl *et al.*, 2018; World Bank, 2020b). According to the World Bank report, almost 40 percent of developing countries have adopted some elements of Basel III (World Bank, 2020b, p. 5). But while 96 upper-middle-, middle-, and low-income countries were assessed in this World Bank report,[3] only 25 were low-income countries (LICs), and only five of these had applied part of the Basel III regulations (World Bank, 2020b, p. 5).

Jones and Zeitz (2017) have found that developing countries have put in place the simpler Basel II standard regulation for credit, market, and operational risks and have hardly adopted more complex components addressing internal risks. In the same vein, simple elements of Basel III, including a new definition of capital and the leverage ratio, have been implemented, rather than the more complex approaches, including liquidity ratios or the countercyclical buffer.

For this reason, simplified prudential, financial regulations that take into consideration the institutional and regulatory capacities

[3]According to the World Bank, developing countries comprise upper-middle-, middle-, and low-income countries, as defined in the World Bank's Word Development Indicators database. In this report, this definition is adopted, and the countries classified as offshore financial centers have been excluded (World Bank, 2020b, p. 50).

of countries should be adopted. In particular, less-complex financial regulations can mean more effective implementation by supervisors and better monitoring. Applied to the banking sector, proportionality would imply adopting simplified prudential rules for small or non-complex financial institutions in order to lower implementation costs. For example, regulators in developing countries should concentrate on simpler capital ratios and prioritize establishing supervisory capacity that promotes the implementation of simplified regulations and facilitates monitoring of their local financial systems (World Bank, 2020b, p. 23). Anginer *et al.* (2019) have shown that more developed countries with stronger regulatory, supervisory capacities and more developed institutions have adopted more advanced regulations.

4.2. *Lessons learnt for sustainable finance standards*

In the same vein, developing countries often lack the necessary capacity, institutions, data, and financial resources to implement sustainable finance standards (EC, 2022; World Bank, 2020a). However, there could be a trade-off between high standards and developing countries' interests in the development of feasible standards. Too stringent standards could also impede the development of sustainable finance markets, in particular in developing countries. For example, the introduction of standards to increase transparency and accountability could result in decreasing financial flows to developing countries, even though these countries are most likely to need the funds to achieve the SDGs. A compromise needs to be found between, on the one hand, high qualitative standards that can only be achieved in developed financial markets with good institutions and appropriately trained actors, and, on the other hand, feasibility in developing countries with less-developed financial markets. It is crucial to take country-specific circumstances into account, in which the quality and/or quantity of standards for sustainable finance are lowered in exchange for gains in the feasibility of implementing corresponding standards.

Here, it would also be appropriate to adopt the "principle of proportionality." Sustainable financial regulation, such as sustainable finance standards for developing countries, should be designed in a different way from those for more developed countries.

Simplified sustainable finance standards that take institutional and regulatory capacities into account should be elaborated and enacted in developing countries because less-complex financial regulations can be more effective and easier to implement, supervise, and monitor.

Against this background, we need a common ground in terms of regulations and standards, and on the other hand, we need to be flexible enough to adapt the sustainable finance framework, including regulations and standards, to the country-specific circumstances. There are several possible solutions to implementing such a strategy.

One option would be to elaborate on core sustainable financial regulations and standards, such as sustainable financial standards, for all countries. Based on these core regulations, countries could differentiate the degree of complexity for diverse country types by (i) reducing the degree of granularity of their regulations, (ii) focusing on one or a few goals, and (iii) taking into account improvement rates rather than non-static thresholds.

First, developing countries could adopt the same language and standards as the developed-country taxonomies and tools, but these should be adapted with a lower level of detail. For example, developing countries could adjust the degree of granularity of their taxonomies compared to the taxonomies of developed countries, such as in terms of key performance indicators. This would have the advantage of applying a common language and standards across developed and developing countries, thereby increasing coherence between the taxonomies as well as increasing transparency for global investors. However, the adjustment of granularity should not compromise the achievement of the internationally agreed sustainability goals (UNDESA & IPSF, 2021, p. 32).

Second, references to local taxonomies developed according to similar principles and objectives could be allowed (UNDESA & IPSF, 2020, p. 32). Another suggestion is that taxonomies in developing countries should focus on one or a few goals in the first step and add more goals over time to cover all sustainability topics defined in the SDGs. For example, some countries prefer to focus their sustainability classifications and labels or standards on only one goal, such as reducing greenhouse gases, while others will aim to achieve multiple goals (UNDESA & IPSF, 2021, p. 28).

Third, as the carbon intensity of companies in developing countries will often be higher initially, they could still show the same rate of improvement to be considered sustainable. An improvement rate could be applied as a universal measure and non-static threshold. For example, a reduction in emissions by a certain percentage could be applied (UNDESA & IPSF, 2021, p. 32).

4.3. *EU taxonomy: European standard for financing into sustainability or the Common Ground Taxonomy*

Using the example of taxonomies, it will be shown how taxonomies can be standardized for different country contexts and how the concept of proportionality can be applied. With a green taxonomy, standards for environmentally sustainable investments are set. Taxonomies are systems for classifying sustainable economic activities and are intended to increase transparency about sustainable investments and thus strengthen confidence in these investments. So far, green taxonomies are standards for classifying green activities. On the one hand, they are intended to support investors and issuers in the implementation of their sustainable activities. In this respect, taxonomies provide issuers with principles or requirements that they must fulfill in order for their activities to be classified as sustainable and thus demonstrate that their activities make a significant contribution to sustainability goals. On the other hand, taxonomies are intended to offer investors a transparent and credible list of potential sustainable investments. Taxonomies thus form the basis for further political measures in the field of sustainable finance and are thus an essential prerequisite, for example, for the application of regulations in the field of sustainable finance (IPSF, 2021b).

Taxonomies for green investments are suitable for the application of the concept of proportionality because green taxonomies are currently being developed more than 25 countries (Cabrera *et al.*, 2022), and the IPSF currently elaborates a green Common Ground Taxonomy — a uniform basic taxonomy. The EU and China established a working group on taxonomies in 2020, which is co-chaired by both countries and open to all IPSF members and observers. In the framework of the Common Ground Taxonomy, the similarities between the taxonomies of the EU and China are presented. Only areas that appear in both taxonomies are analyzed in terms of objectives, eligibility criteria, activities, and thresholds. By January 2022, the

IPSF presented a comparison table with technical assessment criteria for up to 80 economic activities in six sectors (agriculture/forestry and fisheries, manufacturing, electricity/gas, water supply and waste management/waste, construction, and transport and storage), focusing on activities significantly contributing to climate change mitigation. No other environmental objectives or requirements are included at this stage, such as "do no significant harm" and "minimum social safeguards." A significant value of this work is the methodology used in the Common Ground Taxonomy. Taxonomies may initially concentrate on one or more objectives of an environmental and/or social nature. Later on, these goals could be expanded to integrate all sustainability themes outlined in the SDGs.

The Common Ground Taxonomy is intended to enhance comparability and interoperability of taxonomies for green, sustainable investments and thereby avoid fragmentation in the market. The aim is to work out the commonalities and differences between their different approaches, outcomes, and criteria and to develop a comparative method for taxonomies that can be used as a template for global harmonization in the future. The ultimate goal is to establish a common language for all taxonomies that would help improve the comparison and interoperability of sustainable finance definitions at the international level and promote cross-border green economy investments. In so far, it improves transparency for investors and companies by providing a common reference point for defining investments that are deemed environmentally sustainable in different jurisdictions.

This comparative table is not legally binding, but merely represents the technical state of the art. Similarly, the Common Ground Taxonomy is not an overarching taxonomy that brings about changes in the taxonomies of the EU, China, or any country in the world. Hence, the Common Ground Taxonomy does not constitute a proposal for international standards or even a legal document that sets a global standard for other jurisdictions. In this respect, the Common Ground Taxonomy is an analytical tool or reference for other jurisdictions, which can assist in the development their own taxonomies in a supportive manner. Different countries — market participants and regulators — could build on these frameworks and adapt this framework to local contexts, for example by adding additional building blocks (e.g., more detailed criteria or other sectors) (IPSF, 2021a).

Overall, the Common Ground Taxonomy represents a significant step toward the harmonization of sustainable finance standards and is in accordance with other international forums and their roadmaps, including the Roadmap of the G20 Sustainable Finance Working Group. It is the first comprehensive comparison of the EU and Chinese taxonomies for each activity and the relevant technical screening criteria. The Common Ground Taxonomy provides a methodology for comparing taxonomies in various jurisdictions. This methodology will be further developed in the coming years to include new sectors and activities as well as additional environmental targets, such as DNSH or minimum guarantees.

5. Conclusion and the Role of the International Community in Supporting Sustainable Finance Standards in Developing Countries

Sustainable finance took on a crucial role in supporting a sustainable recovery following the COVID-19 crisis. An appropriate global framework for sustainable financial management, including sustainable finance regulations and standards, is essential for mobilizing sufficient financial resources to achieve the SDGs. Sustainable finance regulations, including standards elaborated for developed countries with fairly mature financial markets and strong institutions, may not be appropriate for developing countries with less-developed financial markets and weaker institutions. Experience gained from comparable regulatory processes being applied to developing countries, including financial standards such as the Basel capital and liquidity standards, has shown that adopting a single set of financial standards to developed and developing countries will not work. For these reasons, the principle of proportionality should be applied. According to this principle, bank regulation and supervision in developing countries should be adequate for the supervisory capacity, institutional environment, and specific roles of banks in those countries. Simplified sustainable finance standards that take institutional and regulatory capacities into account should be elaborated and enacted in developing countries because less-complex financial regulations can be more effective and easier to implement, supervise, and monitor. There are at least three ways to reduce the complexity, as follows: (i) lowering the degree of granularity of their regulations, (ii) concentrating on one or a few goals, and (iii) considering improvement rates rather than non-static thresholds.

Core sustainable financial regulations, such as the Common Ground Taxonomy, for all countries could be worked out. A further differentiation could take place with regard to the degree of complexity for diverse country types. In view of today's interconnected global financial system, it will be a challenge to implement diverse regulations for different categories of countries. Nevertheless, differences in regulation might be appropriate as long as these differences are transparent to all financial market participants.

5.1. *The role of the international institutions and development cooperation*

Since developing countries often lack the capacity and financial resources to implement sustainable finance standards, international institutions and development cooperations assume the role of strengthening the capacities of developing countries. Bilateral and multilateral donors should therefore provide national and local government officials and national development banks with targeted capacity building and training.

Specific multilateral facilities established at international financial institutions, including the MDBs, could provide capacity building and training in the area of sustainable finance standards. The Debt Management Facility of the IMF and World Bank, for example, conducts capacity building and training in the field of debt management, financed by bilateral donors.

In order to implement appropriate standards in developing countries, it is necessary to take into account country-specific circumstances with regard to the development and capacities of the financial system and to adapt sustainable finance standards to these specific needs in developing countries. From the outset, sustainable investment approaches should be accounted for in capital market development plans (UNDESA & IPSF, 2021).

International institutions and development cooperations should promote the adoption of the "principle of proportionality," according to which sustainable financial regulation should be designed to be suitable for its purpose. In addition, international institutions and development cooperations should encourage simplified sustainable finance standards that take into consideration the institutional and regulatory capacities in developing countries because less-complex financial regulations can be more effective and are easier to implement, supervise, and monitor.

5.2. *Involvement of actors from developing countries in setting sustainable finance standards*

To design adequate sustainable finance standards, public (private) actors of developing countries should be involved in setting sustainable finance standards. While public (private) actors of emerging economies have often been included in elaborating and/or establishing sustainable finance standards, LICs, in particular, have hardly ever been included in decisions on the design of such standards. However, in view of the proliferation of sustainable finance standards, it is more difficult to provide solutions on how to involve developing countries in setting them up.

Developing countries are either not formally represented or have little voting power in central institutions that decide on sustainable finance, namely the international financial institutions, including the MDBs, the NGFS, the CMFCA, and the FSB. In addition, the private sector designing sustainable finance standards is dominated by private actors, including institutions and alliances dominated by industrialized countries and/or emerging markets, such as in the International Capital Market Association or the Institute of International Finance. A further forum for discussing sustainable finance standards is the so-called "International Platform on Sustainable Finance," established by the EU to promote global exchange and thus create an appropriate and inclusive dialogue forum with the participation of various countries, including some developing countries (India, Indonesia, Kenya, and Senegal), for sustainable finance.

Against this background, global policy-making institutions and forums should better engage developing countries as active participants in designing a global sustainable financial governance, including sustainable finance standards. Moreover, to enhance the participation of developing countries, it will be crucial to support and incentivize developing countries' membership in various institutions, including the NGFS, the CMFCA, and the FSB. In addition, developing countries should receive higher voting powers in international financial institutions, including the MDBs. In the same vein, developing countries should be better enabled to bring their ideas to the different working groups of the G20, including the Development Working Group and the G20 Sustainable Finance Study Group. Similarly, discussions on sustainable finance standards should also be carried out more intensively in universal forums, including the Financing for Development and Development Cooperation Forums held at the UN.

As sustainable finance and, in particular, the implementation of sustainable finance strategies, including sustainable finance regulations and standards, are only in the planning stage or have just been implemented, little empirical evidence is available. For this reason, research on sustainable finance strategies is often associated with the initial research stage.

Abbreviations

ACMF	Asian Capital Markets Forum
ASEAN	Association of Southeast Asian Nations
BIS	Bank for International Settlements
CBI	Climate Bonds Initiative
CMFCA	Coalition of Finance Ministers for Climate Action
EC	European Commission
EIB	European Investment Bank
ESG	Environmental, Social, and Governance
EU	European Union
EU-GBS	European Union Green Bond Standards
FSB	Financial Stability Board
GBP	Green Bond Principles
GFSG	Green Finance Study Group
IATF	Inter-agency Task Force on Financing for Development
ICMA	International Capital Markets Association
IMF	International Monetary Fund
IPSF	International Platform on Sustainable Finance

LIC	Low Income Country
MDBs	Multilateral Development Banks
NGFS	Network of Central Banks and Supervisors for Greening the Financial System
OECD	Organization for Economic Co-operation and Development
SBN	Sustainable Banking Network
SDGs	Sustainable Development Goals
TCDF	Taskforce on Climate Related Financial Disclosures
TEG	Technical Expert Group
WB	World Bank
UNDP	United Nations Development Program
UNEP	United Nations Environment Program

References

Asian Capital Markets Forum (ACMF) (2017, November). ASEAN (Association of Southeast Asian Nations) green bond standards. Retrieved from http://www.theacmf.org/ACMF/upload/ASEAN_Green_Bond_Standards.pdf.

Anginer, D., Bertay, A. C., Cull, R. J., *et al.* (2019). Bank regulation and supervision ten years after the global financial crisis (Policy Research Working Paper WPS9044). Washington, DC: World Bank.

Azhgaliyeva, D., Kapoor, A., & Liu, Y. (2020). Green bonds for financing renewable energy and energy efficiency in Southeast Asia: A review of policies. ADBI Working Paper Series, No. 1073, Asian Development Bank Institute (ADBI), Tokyo.

Beck, T., Jones, E., & Knaack, P. (2018). Basel standards and developing countries: A difficult relationship. Vox, CEPR Policy Portal. Retrieved from https://voxeu.org/article/basel-standards-and-developing-countries.

Berensmann, K. (2017). Upscaling sustainable bond markets: The need for harmonised green bond standards (Briefing Paper 10/2017). Bonn: German Development Institute/Deutsches Institut für Entwicklungspolitik (DIE). Retrieved from https://www.idos-research.de/en/briefing-paper/article/upscaling-green-bond-markets-the-need-for-harmonised-green-bond-standards/.

Berensmann, K. (2022). Finanzierung der Transformation zur Nachhaltigkeit: Eine Herkulesaufgabe für die EU? In *Zeitschrift für die gesamte Kredtiwirtschaft* (Vol. 1, pp. 33–38).

Bundesministerium der Finanzen (BMF) (2021). *Sustainable Finance. Deutsche Sustainable Finance Strategie.* Berlin: Author.

Cabrera, M. M., Youngeun Shin, S., & Hinojosa, J. (2022). *Towards a common pathway across sustainable finance taxonomies.* Retrieved from https://www.ccap.org/post/ccap-and-giz-publish-towards-a-common-pathway-across-sustainable-finance-taxonomies.

Castro Carvalho, A. P., Hohl, S., Raskopf, R., *et al.* (2017). Proportionality in banking regulation: A cross-country comparison. Financial Stability Institute Insights on policy implementation No. 1, August 2017, Bank for International Settlements (BIS), Basel.

Climate Bonds Initiative (CBI) (2019, March). Climate resilience principles. A framework for assessing climate resilience investments. Retrieved from https://www.climatebonds.net/files/page/files/climate-resilience-principles-climate-bonds-initiative-20190917-.pdf.

Deschryver, P. & de Mariz, F. R. (2020). What future for the green bond market? How can policymakers, companies, and investors unlock the potential of the green bond market? *Journal of Risk and Financial Management, 13*(3), 1–26.

European Commission (EC) (2018). Action plan: Financing sustainable growth, Brussel. Retrieved from https://eur-lex.europa.eu/legal-content/DE/TXT/PDF/?uri=CELEX:52018DC0097&from=EN.

European Commission (EC) (2021a). Proposal for a regulation of the European parliament and of the council on European green bonds. Strasbourg. https://eur-lex.europa.eu/resource.html?uri=cellar:e7721 2e8-df07-11eb-895a-01aa75ed71a1.0001.02/DOC_1&format=PDF.

European Commission (EC) (2021b). Strategy for financing the transition to a sustainable economy, Strasbourg. Retrieved from https://eur-lex.europa.eu/resource.html?uri=cellar:9f5e7e95-df06-11eb-895a-01aa75ed 71a1.0001.02/DOC_1&format=PDF.

European Commission (EC) (2022, October 12). Platform usability report. Platform recommendations on data and usability as part of taxonomy reporting. Retrieved from https://finance.ec.europa.eu/system/files/2022-10/221011-sustainable-finance-platform-finance-report-usability_en_1.pdf.

Ehlers, T. & Packer, F. (2017, September). Green bond finance and certification. Bank for International Settlements (BIS) Quarterly Review, pp. 89–104. Retrieved from https://www.bis.org/publ/qtrpdf/r_qt1709h.pdf .

Ehlers, T., Gao, D. N., & Packer, F. (2021). A taxonomy of sustainable finance taxonomies, No. 118 in BIS Papers from Bank for International Settlements, Basel. Retrieved from https://www.bis.org/publ/bppdf/bispap118.pdf.

European Investment Bank (EIB) & China's Green Finance Committee (GFC) (2017). The need for a common language in green finance. Towards a standard-neutral taxonomy of the environmental use of proceeds. Phase I Report. Retrieved from https://www.eib.org/attachments/press/white-paper-green-finance-common-language-eib-and-green-finance-committee.pdf.

European Union (EU) (2019). Report on the EU green bond standard. Financing a sustainable European economy. Technical Expert Group (TEG) Report. Retrieved from https://ec.europa.eu/info/sites/info/files/business_economy_euro/banking_and_finance/documents/190618-sustainable-finance-teg-report-green-bond-standard_en.pdf.

European Union (EU) (2020, March). Taxonomy: Final report of the technical expert group on sustainable finance. Technical Expert Group (TEG) Report. Retrieved from https://ec.europa.eu/info/sites/default/files/business_economy_euro/banking_and_finance/documents/200309-sustainable-finance-teg-final-report-taxonomy_en.pdf.

Financial Stability Board (FSB) (2012). *Identifying the Effects of Regulatory Reforms on Emerging Market and Developing Economies: A Review of Potential Unintended Consequences.* Basel: Author.

G20 GFSG (Green Finance Study Group) (2018). G20 sustainable finance synthesis report 2017. Retrieved from http://unepinquiry.org/wp-content/uploads/2018/11/G20_Sustainable_Finance_Synthesis_Report_2018.pdf.

G20 GFSG (Green Finance Study Group) (2016). G20 green finance synthesis report 2016. Retrieved from http://unepinquiry.org/wp-content/uploads/2016/09/Synthesis_Report_Full_ EN.pdf; https://g20sfwg.org/wp-content/uploads/2021/10/G20-Sustainable-Finance-Roadmap.pdf.

G20 SFWG (Sustainable Finance Working Group) (2021). 2021 Synthesis report, G20 Italian Presidency, Rome, Retrieved from https://g20sfwg.org/wp-content/uploads/2021/11/Synth_G20_Final.pdf.

Gortsos, C. (2020, December 6). The Taxonomy Regulation: More Important Than Just as an Element of the Capital Markets Union. European Banking Institute Working Paper Series, 2020/80. Available at SSRN: https://ssrn.com/abstract=3750039 or http://dx.doi.org/10.2139/ssrn.3750039.

Hohl, S., Sison, M. C., Stastny, T., *et al.* (2018). The Basel framework in 100 jurisdictions: Implementation status and proportionality practices (Financial Stability Institute Insights on Policy Implementation, 11). Bank for International Settlements. Retrieved from https://www.bis.org/fsi/publ/insights11.pdf.

International Capital Markets Association (ICMA) (2020a). Sustainable finance high level definitions, Zurich. Retrieved from https://www.icmagroup.org/assets/documents/Regulatory/Green-Bonds/Sustainable-Finance-High-Level-Definitions-May-2020-110520v4.pdf.

International Capital Markets Association (ICMA) (2020b). *Green Bond Principles. Voluntary Process Guidelines for Issuing Green Bonds.* Paris: Author. Retrieved from https://www.icmagroup.org/green-social-and-sustainability-bonds/.

International Platform on Sustainable Finance (IPSF) (2020, October). International platform on sustainable finance. Annual Report 2020. Retrieved from https://ec.europa.eu/info/sites/default/files/business_economy_euro/banking_and_finance/documents/international-platform-sustainable-finance-annual-report-2020_en.pdf.

International Platform on Sustainable Finance (IPSF) (2021a). Common ground taxonomy — Climate change mitigation. Instruction Report, Bruxelles. Retrieved from https://ec.europa.eu/info/sites/default/files/business_economy_euro/banking_and_finance/documents/211104-ipsf-common-ground-taxonomy-instruction-report-2021_en.pdf.

International Platform on Sustainable Finance (IPSF) (2021b, November). International platform on sustainable finance. Annual Report. Retrieved from https://ec.europa.eu/info/files/international-platform-sustainable-finance-annual-report-2021-en.

Jones, E. (2014). Global banking standards and low income countries: Helping or hindering effective regulation? (Global Economic Governance (GEG) Working Paper, 2014/91). Oxford: University of Oxford.

Jones, E. & Zeitz, A. O. (2017). The limits of globalizing Basel banking standards. *Journal of Financial Regulation*, *3*(1): 89–124.

Maragopoulos, N. (2022). Towards a European Green Bond: A Commission's Proposal to Promote Sustainable Finance. European Banking Institute Working Paper Series, 2022/103. Available at SSRN: https://ssrn.com/abstract=3933766 or http://dx.doi.org/10.2139/ssrn.3933766.

Organisation for Economic Co-operation and Development (OECD) (2017). *Mobilising Bond Markets for a Low-Carbon Transition.* Paris: Author.

Organisation for Economic Co-operation and Development (OECD) (2020). Developing sustainable finance definitions and taxonomies. https://doi.org/10.1787/134a2dbe-en.

Organisation for Economic Co-operation and Development/United Nations Development Program (OECD & UNDP) (2020). Framework for SDG aligned finance. Retrieved from https://www.oecd.org/development/financing-sustainable-development/Framework-for-SDG-Aligned-Finance-OECD-UNDP.pdf.

Restoy, F. (2018). Proportionality in financial regulation. Speech Presented to Financial Stability Institute and IMF Meeting on Proportionality in Financial Regulation and Supervision, 2019, 8 May, Basel, Switzerland.

Sustainable Banking Network (SBN) (2018). Global progress report 2018. Washington, DC. Retrieved from https://www.ifc.org/wps/wcm/connect/71e6f2f5-8fb5-40a1-bc17-e04a85037980/SBN-GlobalProgress Report.pdf?MOD=AJPERES.

Tripathy, A., Mok, L., & House, K. (2020, September 2). Defining climate-aligned investment: An analysis of sustainable finance taxonomy development. *The Journal of Environmental Investing, 10*(1). Available at http://www.thejei.com/journal/ or SSRN: https://ssrn.com/abstract=3684926.

United Nations-Department of Economic and Social Affairs and International Platform on Sustainable Finance (UN-DESA & IPSF) (2021). Improving compatibility of approaches to identify, verify and align investments to sustainability goals. Input paper for the G20 Sustainable Finance Working Group. Retrieved from https://g20sfwg.org/ wp-content/uploads/2021/09/G20-SFWG-DESA-and-IPSF-input-paper.pdf.

World Bank (2020a). Capital markets development: A primer for policymakers. Retrieved from https://openknowledge.worldbank.org/bit stream/handle/10986/36058/Capital-Markets-Development-A-Primer-for-Policymakers.pdf?sequence=1&isAllowed=y.

World Bank (2020b). Global financial development report 2019/2020: Bank regulation and supervision a decade after the global financial crisis. Retrieved from https://openknowledge.worldbank.org/handle/10986/32595.

World Bank (2020c, June). Developing a national green taxonomy: A World Bank guide. Retrieved from https://documents1.worldbank.org/curated/en/953011593410423487/pdf/Developing-a-National-Green-Taxonomy-A-World-Bank-Guide.pdf.

Zhang, H. (2020). Regulating green bonds in the People's Republic of China: Definitional divergence and implications for policy making. ADBI Working Paper Series, No. 1072, Asian Development Bank Institute (ADBI), Tokyo.

https://doi.org/10.1142/9781800614482_0007

Chapter 7

Environmental Disclosure in Financial Institutions: A Critical Review of the Literature

Eleonora Broccardo[†,§], Graziano Coller[†,¶], and Maria Mazzuca[*,‡,||]

[†]*University of Trento, Trento, Italy*
[‡]*University of Calabria, Arcavacata, Italy*
[§]*eleonora.broccardo@unitn.it*
[¶]*graziano.coller@unitn.it*
[||]*maria.mazzuca@unical.it*

Abstract

We map academic studies on climate-related risks and environmental disclosures focusing on financial institutions. The bibliometric analysis highlights and discusses the relevant contributions and influential research streams of the main studies. Our analysis may help both policymakers, in terms of outlining their actions to meet disclosure requirements and standards, and academics, to provide focus for their future research. We argue that more empirical research is needed to understand whether further disclosure requirements could add value to reporting institutions.

Further research investigating which market and/or financial institutions' specific characteristics enhance such disclosure could help fully understand the interconnections between disclosure of environmental risks and firms' values. More attention should be paid to the insurance sector. Finally, disclosure of information about specific areas of

[*]Corresponding author.

the financial institutions' businesses that have not yet been sufficiently considered, such as lending and underwriting, should be emphasized to increase disclosure effectiveness.

1. Introduction

The existing literature on corporate social responsibility (CSR) disclosure is huge. In particular, attention reserved for sustainability (especially the environmental component of sustainability) is progressively increasing after the 2015 Paris Agreement on Climate Change.

The financial sector (including banks and insurers) has traditionally been considered less affected by environmental issues than other sectors. Undoubtedly, the scenario has changed profoundly in recent years, and this sector deserves more attention from regulators. Compared to other elements of sustainability, that is, governance and social components, regulators seem to be primarily focused on the climate risks and their disclosure.

In 2017, the Task Force on Climate-related Financial Disclosures (TCFD) (established by the G20's Financial Stability Board) published recommendations to encourage companies to disclose climate-related risks and opportunities. The European Commission (EC) urged companies to implement these recommendations, and many governments and financial regulators worldwide integrated them into their guidance and policy frameworks. Examples include Australia, Canada, Hong Kong, Japan, Singapore, South Africa, and some EU member states (EC, 2019).

The attention of the European Parliament and the European Commission on environmental and sustainability issues is expressed through directives, regulations, and guidelines. The "non-financial reporting directive" (NFRD) (Directive 2014/95/Eu of the European Parliament and of the Council) introduced some new disclosure requirements for large firms, which are public-interest entities that include banks and insurers. Specifically, in their management report, these firms shall include a statement containing information on non-financial matters (environmental, social, and employee matters, human rights, bribery, and corruption). The objective of the NFRD is to improve the quality and quantity of corporate non-financial information reporting. In April 2021, the EC adopted a corporate sustainability reporting directive (CSRD) proposal, which would amend the NFRD. The proposal extends the scope of reporting requirements to all large and listed companies (except listed micro-enterprises). It requires an audit of reported data and machine-readable data to feed into the European single-access point envisioned in the capital markets union action plan. The proposal introduces more detailed reporting requirements and mandatory EU sustainability reporting standards. The European Financial Reporting Advisory Group (EFRAG) would develop the standards, and the first set of standards would be adopted by October 2022.

In 2019, the so-called Sustainable Finance Disclosure Regulation[1] on sustainability-related disclosures in the financial services sector introduced certain standards to harmonize pre-contractual and ongoing disclosures to be offered to end investors. This regulation needs to be read in conjunction with the following two supplemental regulations: (i) Regulation 2020/852 of the European Parliament and of the Council containing the EU taxonomy of environmentally sustainable investments; and (ii) the climate benchmarks Regulation 2019/2089.

In 2017, the EC published non-mandatory guidelines to help companies disclose environmental and social information. In March 2018, the EC published the Action Plan on Financing Sustainable Growth with a focus on finance and its role. In June 2019, the EC published guidelines on reporting climate-related information, consisting of a new supplement to the existing guidelines on non-financial reporting, which remain applicable. These 2019 non-binding guidelines are part of the action plan proposed for disclosures for all the companies that fall under the scope of the NFRD, regardless of their sector of activity. In Annex I, further guidance for banks and insurance companies is offered for their unique business activities.

Overall, regulators are moving in two directions. The first involves enhancing the disclosure requirements focused on environmental issues. The second encompasses the increasing attention to finance and financial institutions, such as banks and insurance companies.

As discussed above, further disclosure requirements (and standards) on environmental issues will be introduced in the future. The introduction of these requirements is generally motivated

[1]SFDR-Regulation (Eu) 2019/2088 of the European Parliament and of the Council.

by the benefits commonly associated with disclosure, both for market participants and reporting companies. The EU regulators also declare that they aim to achieve some of the goals that are aimed at the possibility of reducing information asymmetries in the principal–agent relationship. Focusing on the climate-related information, the EC (2019) states that better disclosure can have benefits for the reporting company itself, leading to:

- improvement in management and strategic planning due to the increased awareness and understanding of climate-related risks and opportunities within the company;
- a more diverse investor base and a potentially lower cost of capital due to several reasons, such as the inclusion in sustainability-focused indices or the improved credit ratings;
- a more constructive dialogue with stakeholders (in particular, investors and shareholders); and
- an improvement in reputation and maintenance of the social license to operate.

Despite such presumed benefits, the literature on CSR and environmental disclosure is fragmented, both from theoretical and empirical perspectives. Two competing arguments appear to justify the link between CSR activities and environmental disclosure in firms. The first argument, commonly referred to as voluntary disclosure theory, suggests that companies have incentives to disclose "good news" to better compete with companies with "bad news" by avoiding the adverse selection problem (Dye, 1985; Verrecchia, 1983). This perspective predicts a positive relationship between environmental performance and environmental disclosure. From a sociopolitical perspective, the second argument justifies the CSR activities and disclosure according to a multi-theoretical framework (Cormier *et al.*, 2005). Frameworks for this argument include the political economy theory, the legitimacy theory, and the stakeholder theory. Sociopolitical theories assume a firm as an economic entity that cannot be separated from the social context in which it operates and lives and is shaped and influenced. To survive, the company must obtain the support and approval of both its primary (e.g., shareholders, employees, customers) and secondary (e.g., media, special interest groups) stakeholders (Clarkson, 1995). CSR activity and CSR disclosure are part of the communication process necessary to create and maintain such support. Based on stakeholder and legitimacy theories, several authors have advanced theoretical arguments on CSR activity and disclosure (e.g., Gray *et al.*, 1995; Campbell, 2007; Hooghiemstra, 2000; Maignan & Ralston, 2002). Sociopolitical theories predict a negative association between environmental performance and the level of discretionary environmental disclosures.

From an empirical perspective, the results are mixed too. The increased level of disclosure does not necessarily determine the increase in soundness of the financial institutions and the system in general. The reasons may be found in the potential negative relationship between the disclosure and the environmental performance and the specific costs associated with the disclosure. There are direct costs related to the production of the information and indirect costs, such as proprietary costs (Verrecchia, 1983). Proprietary costs may pertain to the manager revealing information to environmental regulators and other environmental activist groups that increase the probability of criticism, sanction, or attack (see Li *et al.*, 1997).

Our analysis aims to contribute to this fragmented literature using the lens of who is interested in the financial intermediaries, and limiting our focus to climate-related risks disclosure. Our interest in financial institutions matches that shown by regulators over the past few years. Similarly, our focus on climate issues and their disclosure reflects the importance that the environment has recently gained compared to the other pillars of CSR and ESG (governance and social).

This chapter aims to map the academic studies on climate-related risks and environmental disclosures that focus on financial institutions. First, we develop a bibliometric analysis to highlight the most relevant contributions and influential research streams and trends. This analysis is based on a keyword search analysis in the ISI Web of Science and Scopus databases. Second, we review and discuss the main contributions of each study to understand the state of the field and address the research agenda. Our analysis may help both policymakers, to outline their actions in terms of requirements and standards, and academics, to better focus their future empirical research.

Our findings suggest that more empirical research is needed to understand whether further disclosure requirements could add value to the reporting institutions. This chapter underlines that further research investigating which market and/or financial institutions' specific characteristics enhance such disclosure could provide a better understanding of the interconnections between disclosure of environmental risks and firms' value. Importantly, our analysis shows that attention should be paid to the insurance sector, it being an almost completely ignored sector that is becoming relevant for climate issues, as demonstrated by the increased attention it is receiving from regulators. Finally, the disclosure of information about areas of business not yet considered, such as lending and asset underwriting, should be emphasized to increase disclosure effectiveness.

The chapter is organized as follows. Section 2 defines the methodology and presents the data. Section 3 reports the bibliometric analysis results. Section 4 presents the results of the analysis of the contributions. Section 5 concludes.

2. Methodology and Data

To select high-quality academic contributions to financial institutions' climate-related risks and environmental disclosures, we searched two leading databases of the world's scientific research output across all disciplines: (a) the Web of Science and (b) Scopus. Both sources extensively cover publishers in this field of study.

Table 1 summarizes the selection process we followed to identify the relevant publications. As the first step, we adopted the following search strategy in the title, abstract, and keywords search fields: ("environment*" OR "climate*") AND ("financial institution*" OR "bank*" OR "insur*") AND ("disclosure*"). The queries were conducted on February 15, 2022, and resulted in 658 studies. In the second step, editorials, conference proceedings, abstracts, and working papers were removed to select documents that had passed a regular and high-standard peer-review process. We selected only documents written in English, eliminated duplicates, and reduced the sample to 505 studies. In the third step, two authors, experts in the sustainable finance and disclosure field, checked the title, keywords, and abstract to eliminate studies that do not address the topic under consideration and further reduced the sample to 45 studies. Each author individually judged the relevance of each paper first, and after a discussion on divergent cases, a shared decision was made. This process led to the exclusion of papers not exclusively focused on financial institutions or CSR, ESG, or climate risks but not on their

Table 1. Identification of publications.

1. Search in databases of scholarly publications	$N = 658$
• Search strategy: ("environment*" OR "climate*") AND ("financial institution*" OR "bank*" OR "insur*") AND ("disclosure*")	
• Search fields: title, abstract, and keywords	
• N (the Web of Science) = 395	
• N (Scopus) = 263	
2. Check for duplicates, language, and type of document	$N = 505$
• Elimination of editorials, conference proceedings, abstracts, and working papers	
• Elimination of documents not in English language	
• Elimination of duplicates	
3. Broad pertinence check	$N = 45$
• By reading title, keywords, and abstract, elimination of studies that do not address climate-related risk and environmental disclosure	
4. Specific pertinence check	$N = 35$
• By reading the full text, elimination of studies that do not address climate-related risk and environmental disclosure	
5. Expert validation of final dataset	$N = 35$

⇓

Extension of data per record
Matching with SCImago
(journals only)

⇓	⇓
Bibliometric analysis	**Analysis of contributions**

disclosure. In addition, papers focused on ESG or CSR disclosure but not on climate or environmental disclosure were excluded. Some of these papers also study integrated reporting or sustainable reporting. These papers are relevant in general terms as they fit into the general topic of CSR or ESG disclosure and non-financial reporting. Even though they could be relevant for our analysis and they could add some insights to our study, we excluded them mainly for two reasons: (i) From a contents point of view, they are not sufficiently directed to the observation of climate and environmental information; (ii) from a methodological perspective, these papers represent only a tiny piece of the most comprehensive literature on the CSR and non-financial disclosure (as we limit the research on the Scopus and Web of Science databases using the selected keyword and not including, for instance, the words "CSR" and "ESG"). In the fourth step, the same two authors analyzed the full text of each publication to exclude documents that do not focus on the disclosure of environmental risk by financial institutions. After this screening step, 10 papers were excluded from the sample. Following the completion of these four steps, a total of 35 papers were included in the analysis.

This set of papers was analyzed using a twofold approach comprising a bibliometric analysis and an analysis of the contributions of each paper. This allowed the inclusion of both quantitative and qualitative analyses to provide a map of the academic studies on climate-related risks and environmental disclosures and to highlight the most influential research streams and trends.

For the bibliometric analysis, the date, source name, type of publication, the total number of citations, keywords, the abstract of each reference, and information about the authors were collected. We also matched the research area categories provided by the SCImago Journal Rank website to each journal. To analyze the content, the authors followed an iterative process of reading, framing, and revising their understanding of the papers individually and collectively for each reference.

3. Bibliometric Analysis Results

Table 2 summarizes information about the final sample, consisting of 35 studies (34 papers and one review) published from 2004 to 2022 in 26 different journals. Only five papers are single-authored; there are 82 authors in our sample, and the average number of authors per paper is 2.34. Only seven authors authored two publications, namely Amrana, Bimha, Bose, Caby, Kanz, Lamarque, and Ziane. Caby, Lamarque, and Ziane coauthored two publications (Caby *et al.*, 2020, 2022). With 4.97 average years from publication, the average number of citations per document is 17.11, with an average number of citations per year per document equal to 2.04.

Table 3 summarizes the number of total citations (TC) and the number of average citations per year (TCY) collected by each paper: 11 papers collected at least 10 citations, and eight papers collected

Table 2. Main information about the sample.

Description	Results
MAIN INFORMATION ABOUT DATA	
Timespan	2004–2022
Sources (journals, books, etc.)	26
Documents	35
Average years from publication	4.97
Average citations per document	17.11
Average citations per year per document	2.04
References	2313
DOCUMENT TYPES	
Article	34
Review	1
DOCUMENT CONTENTS	
Author's keywords (DE)	123
AUTHORS	
Authors	82
Author appearances	89
Authors of single-authored documents	5
Authors of multi-authored documents	77
AUTHOR COLLABORATION	
Single-authored documents	5
Documents per author	0.427
Authors per document	2.34
Co-authors per document	2.54
Collaboration index	2.57

zero citations. The most cited paper in the sample, with 203 citations, is the one by Thompson and Cowton (2004), the first paper published in our sample. The number of citations may depend on the papers' publication date: Early published papers will collect more citations. The average number of citations per year better reflects the impact of each paper on the research stream about environmental disclosure in financial institutions. In our sample, six papers collected at least five citations per year, nine collected between 1 and 5 citations per year, and 12 collected 0 or 1.

The 35 articles in the data set are dispersed among 26 journals, showing that the discourse on environmental disclosure in financial institutions is widespread and fragmented (Table 4). Only four journals published more than one article on this topic, with a record of four by *Business Strategy and the Environment*, three

Table 3. Article's total citations and total citations per year.

Paper	Total citations (TC)	TC per year (TCY)
(Thompson and Cowton, 2004)	203	10.68
(Bose *et al.*, 2018)	50	10.00
(Sobhani *et al.*, 2012)	89	8.09
(Taslima and Salina, 2020)	20	6.67
(Gallego-Álvarez and Pucheta-Martínez, 2020)	17	5.67
(Campbell and Slack, 2011)	65	5.42
(Macve and Chen, 2010)	52	4.00
(Kılıç and Kuzey, 2019)	11	2.75
(Haigh and Shapiro, 2011)	31	2.58
(Thistlethwaite and Wood, 2018)	11	2.20
(Dong *et al.*, 2021)	4	2.00
(Thomä *et al.*, 2021)	4	2.00
(Galletta *et al.*, 2021)	3	1.50
(Mora Rodríguez *et al.*, 2021)	4	1.33
(Stechemesser *et al.*, 2015)	10	1.25
(Al-Dhaimesh and Zobi, 2019)	3	0.75
(Caby *et al.*, 2020)	2	0.67
(Broeders and Schlooz, 2021)	1	0.50
(Bukhari *et al.*, 2021)	1	0.50
(Carè, 2017)	3	0.50
(Gunawan *et al.*, 2021)	1	0.50
(Hanić *et al.*, 2021)	1	0.50
(Khan *et al.*, 2021)	1	0.50
(Colquitt *et al.*, 2006)	6	0.35
(Nikolaou and Yannacopoulos, 2009)	3	0.21
(Bimha and Nhamo, 2013)	2	0.20
(Faulk, 2009)	1	0.07
(Bimha, 2015)	0	0.00
(Birindelli *et al.*, 2022)	0	0.00
(Burnett and Schellhorn, 2016)	0	0.00
(Caby *et al.*, 2022)	0	0.00
(Caldecott, 2020)	0	0.00
(Calderon, 2020)	0	0.00
(Cerchiaro *et al.*, 2021)	0	0.00
(Chiaramonte *et al.*, 2021)	0	0.00

by the *Journal of Sustainable Finance and Investment*, and two by *Accounting Auditing & Accountability Journal* and the *British Accounting Review*. This low concentration reflects the situation of a field that is growing but is still being legitimized. In Table 4, papers

Table 4. Classification of articles per SCImago Journal Ranking (SJR) and average citations per year.

SJR	Sources	No. of articles	Average citations per year (TCY)			
			TCY≥5	5 > TCY ≥1	1 > TCY > 0	TCY= 0
Q1	*Business Strategy and the Environment*	4	(Gallego-Álvarez and Pucheta-Martínez, 2020)	(Galletta *et al.*, 2021)	(Khan *et al.*, 2021)	(Birindelli *et al.*, 2022)
	Accounting Auditing & Accountability Journal	2		(Macve and Chen, 2010; Haigh and Shapiro, 2011)		
	British Accounting Review	2	(Thompson and Cowton, 2004; Campbell and Slack, 2011)			
	Asia Pacific Journal of Management	1	(Bose *et al.*, 2018			
	British Journal of Management	1		(Thistlethwaite and Wood, 2018)		
	Electricity Journal	1			(Faulk, 2009)	
	Journal of Business Research	1				(Caby *et al.*, 2022)
	Journal of Cleaner Production	1	(Sobhani *et al.*, 2012)			
	Sustainability Accounting Management and Policy Journal	1		(Dong *et al.*, 2021)		

(*Continued*)

Table 4. (*Continued*)

SJR	Sources	No. of articles	Average citations per year (TCY)			
			TCY≥5	5 > TCY ≥1	1 > TCY > 0	TCY= 0
	Technological Forecasting and Social Change	1			(Caby *et al.*, 2020)	
	The European Journal of Finance	1				(Chiaramonte *et al.*, 2021)
Q2	*Journal of Sustainable Finance and Investment*	3		(Thomä *et al.*, 2021)		(Caldecott, 2020; Calderon, 2020)
	Environment Development and Sustainability	1			(Gunawan *et al.*, 2021)	
	Geneva Papers on Risk and Insurance: Issues and Practice	1		(Stechemesser *et al.*, 2015)		
	International Journal of Bank Marketing	1		(Kılıç and Kuzey, 2019)		
	Journal of Financial Reporting and Accounting	1		(Mora Rodríguez *et al.*, 2021)		
	Journal of Islamic Marketing	1	(Taslima and Salina, 2020)			
	North American Actuarial Journal	1			(Colquitt *et al.*, 2006)	
	Technology Analysis and Strategic Management	1				(Cerchiaro *et al.*, 2021)

Q3	*International Journal of Green Economics*	1	(Bukhari *et al.*, 2021)	
	International Journal of Monetary Economics and Finance	1	(Nikolaou and Yannacopoulos, 2009)	
	Journal of Risk Management in Financial Institutions	1	(Broeders and Schlooz, 2021)	
Q4	*Banks and Bank Systems*	3	(Al-Dhaimesh and Zobi, 2019; Bimha and Nhamo, 2013)	(Burnett and Schellhorn, 2016)
	ACRN Journal of Finance and Risk Perspectives	1	(Carè, 2017)	
	Risk Governance and Control: Financial Markets and Institutions	1		(Bimha, 2015)
ND	*MANAGEMENT (CROATIA)*	1	(Hanić *et al.*, 2021)	

are grouped according to the quality of sources (SCImago quartile) and the average number of citations per year, as calculated in Table 3. We split the papers according to four classes of citations per year (TCY $\geq$ 5; 5 $>$ TCY $\geq$ 1; 1 $>$ TCY $>$ 0; TCY = 0).

Among the 26 journal outlets, 25 were listed in the SCImago Journal Ranking database. These journals were linked to the subject area and quartiles as provided in the SCImago database to overview the disciplinary areas and the influence of the outlets hosting each contribution (Tables 4 and 5). The articles spread across nine disciplinary areas that are also very distant in terms of knowledge base, such as "Business, Management, and Accounting," "Engineering," and "Psychology". From 2004 to 2022, most articles were published in journals associated with the "Business, Management, and Accounting" and the "Economics, Econometrics, and Finance" areas. Only from 2012 onward were some articles published in journals associated with the "Energy," "Engineering," and "Environmental Science" areas. This fact is probably due to the very peculiar nature of financial institutions, which rarely fits with research interests in those areas. The SCImago database classifies 11 journals over 26 (42.3 percent) in the first quartile (Q1), eight (30.8 percent) in the second quartile, three in the third quartile (Q3), and three in the fourth quartile (Q4). Figure 1 and Table 5 show that the number of papers published in Q1 outlets increases over time, indicating that the distribution of contributions on this topic is addressed in high-quality journals in a more significant percentage than a homogeneous distribution among quartiles. Overall, the bibliometric analysis shows that environmental disclosure in financial institutions is an emerging topic for research that may be addressed from many different perspectives.

To investigate if specific trends emerge in the literature on banks' environmental risk disclosure, we checked for the 10 most frequent words in the author-defined keywords. We excluded from the search the following terms: "bank," "banking," "banks," "banking industry," and "banking sector". Results (Figure 2) show that "climate change" (nine counts), "environmental disclosure" (four counts), and "carbon disclosure and emission" (six counts) are the most frequently used keywords. No industry-specific term stands out, thus suggesting

Table 5. Number of articles per year, SCImago subject area, and SCImago Journal Rank (SJR).

SCImago subject area																			
BMA	BMA					BMA	BMA	BMA	BMA	BMA		BMA	BMA	BMA	BMA	BMA	BMA	BMA	BMA
DS			DS											DS					
EEF			EEF			EEF	EEF	EEF		EEF		EEF	EEF	EEF	EEF	EEF	EEF	EEF	
E						E			E									E	
ENG									ENG										
ES									ES								ES	ES	ES
M			M															M	
P																	P		
SS						SS				SS			SS			SS	SS	SS	SS
SJR	2004	2005	2006	2007	2008	2009	2010	2011	2012	2013	2014	2015	2016	2017	2018	2019	2020	2021	2022
Q1	1					1	1	2	1						2		2	4	2
Q2			1									1				1	4	3	
Q3						1												2	
Q4										1		1	1	1		1			
Total no. of articles	1		1			2	1	2	1	1		2	1	1	2	2	6	9	2

Notes: BMA = Business, Management and Accounting; DS = Decision Sciences; EEF = Economics, Econometrics and Finance; E = Energy; ENG = Engineering; ES = Environmental Science; M = Mathematics; P = Psychology; SS = Social Sciences.

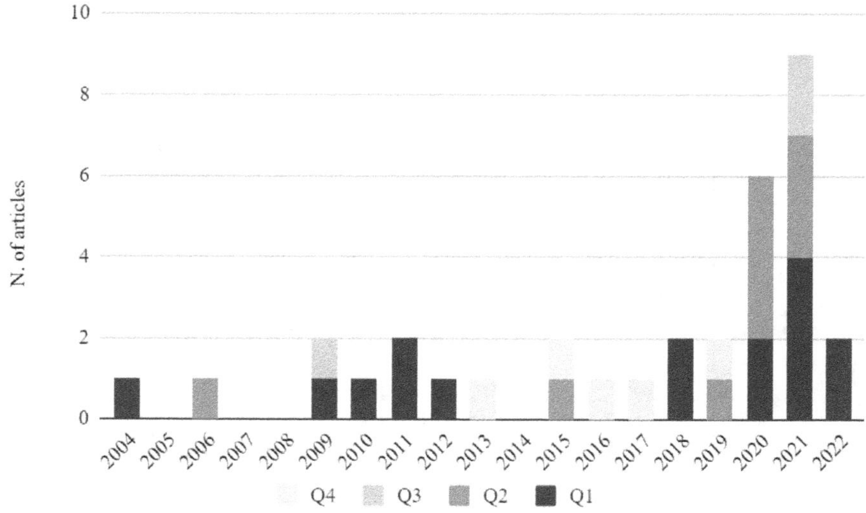

Figure 1. Number of articles per year and SCImago Journal Rank (SJR).

Figure 2. Ten most frequent keywords (excluding bank).

that environmental disclosure in banks, to date, does not highlight specific investigated issues, but generally refers to broad and common concerns (carbon emissions, climate change, and environment) affecting every firm in every sector.

4. Analysis of the Contributions

4.1. *Research approaches*

As a first step in analyzing the content, the contributions were classified according to their research approach, i.e., theoretical, empirical, or argumentative (Table 6).

Only two papers have a "pure" theoretical approach: Nikolaou and Yannacopoulos (2009), focusing on the insurance sector, and Cerchiaro *et al.* (2021), addressing banks' opportunities. Only one paper discusses a conceptual framework (Bukhari *et al.*, 2021). With a probabilistic approach that is deliberately kept as simple as possible, Nikolaou and Yannacopoulos (2009) aim to quantify the following statement: "an accurate picture of the state of the firms towards environmental issues will result in lower premia charged from an insurer to the firms." The authors present a model to investigate how environmental information disclosure through environmental reports could assist insurance companies in setting fair insurance premia and thus permit more efficient risk management of the firm by deciding the optimal insurance coverage of the firm. The main result shows that the probability of unexpected environmental risks can be eliminated when firms implement specific environmental strategies, namely by recording and disclosing environmental information through formal accounting systems. Focusing on financial intermediaries, Cerchiaro *et al.* (2021) show how the challenges of mandatory ESG reporting can be overcome by exploiting the opportunities of distributed ledger technologies (DLTs). A DLT network substantially reduces allocated resources for disclosure tasks while facilitating data sharing and communication across participants. However, the limitations of considerable investments in technology infrastructure, organizations' understanding, skills, and culture toward digital solutions have to be considered. Bukhari *et al.* (2021) propose a green banking adoption conceptual framework based on the theoretical foundation of the natural resource-based view (RBV) of the firm. Such a framework aims to provide a green banking adoption pathway for national regulatory authorities and individual banks.

Three papers offer an argumentative approach. Faulk (2009) discusses the implications of the National Association of Insurance Commissioners rule that mandated broad disclosures by insurance

Table 6. Number of articles per type of research.

Theoretical conceptual framework	Argumentative	Empirical
(Nikolaou and Yannacopoulos, 2009)	(Faulk, 2009)	(Thompson and Cowton, 2004)
(Cerchiaro *et al.*, 2021)	(Caldecott, 2018)	(Colquitt *et al.*, 2006)
(Bukhari *et al.*, 2021)	(Broeders and Schlooz, 2021)	(Macve and Chen, 2010)
		(Campbell and Slack, 2011)
		(Haigh and Shapiro, 2011)
		(Sobhani *et al.*, 2012)
		(Bimha, 2015)
		(Bimha and Nhamo, 2013)
		(Stechemesser *et al.*, 2015)
		(Burnett and Schellhorn, 2016)
		(Carè, 2017)
		(Bose *et al.*, 2018)
		(Thistlethwaite and Wood, 2018)
		(Al-Dhaimesh and Zobi, 2019)
		(Kılıç and Kuzey, 2019)
		(Caby *et al.*, 2020)
		(Calderon, 2020)
		(Gallego-Álvarez and Pucheta-Martínez, 2020)
		(Taslima and Salina, 2020)
		(Dong *et al.*, 2021)
		(Chiaramonte *et al.*, 2021)
		(Galletta *et al.*, 2021)
		(Gunawan *et al.*, 2021)
		(Hanić *et al.*, 2021)
		(Khan *et al.*, 2021)
		(Mora Rodríguez *et al.*, 2021)
		(Thomä *et al.*, 2021)
		(Birindelli *et al.*, 2022)
		(Caby *et al.*, 2022)
3 studies	3 studies	29 studies

companies regarding the impact of climate change on their financial stability.

Caldecott (2018) highlights how the challenge of aligning finance with climate change objectives needs to be addressed by implementing structural climate risk management initiatives, which need to be articulated, developed, and scaled across the financial system. Broeders and Schlooz (2021) focus on challenges and risks for central banks' environmental risk management, offering recommendations for identifying, assessing, mitigating, and disclosing climate change uncertainty.

Most of the papers (29) addressed the financial institutions' environmental disclosure through various empirical approaches and deserved a more in-depth examination, as presented in the following Section 4.2.

4.2. *Empirical contribution: Research questions, methodology, and sample*

Given the relatively new interest in academia and the small sample of papers, it is not straightforward to identify a synthesis and interpretation of these contributions. To offer a complete picture of the empirical research, we first classify the papers by country, thus dividing the sample into single-country (Table 7) and cross-country studies (Table 8). Data on the research question, methodology, sample size, and observed period were collected for each subsample. Papers are grouped by country/countries and ordered according to the date of publication of the first paper focusing on that country or countries. Second, we highlight the main streams emerging from this classification.

As reported in Tables 7 and 8, most of the studies (18) focus on a single country, with the UK, the US, and Bangladesh being the most analyzed countries. While studies considering financial intermediaries' environmental disclosure in the UK and the US date back earlier, with the work of Thompson and Cowton (2004) being the seminal one, far more recent are the studies about developing countries, such as Bangladesh and South Africa. Several single-country papers focus on countries where the climate risks are more severe, such as developing countries or transition economies, such as China, Indonesia, Serbia, and Turkey. Cross-country studies, consisting of 11 papers, are more recent: Half of the contributions consider a sample of worldwide banks, and most have been published very recently, starting from 2020. With regard to the nature of the analyzed institutions, only four studies address the insurance sector (Colquitt *et al.*, 2006; Thistlethwaite & Wood, 2018; Thomä *et al.*, 2021; Stechemesser

Table 7. Single-country studies.

Country	Author	Research question	Methodology	Sample	Period
UK	(Thompson and Cowton, 2004)	To explore the interface between bank lending and the demand for environmental information	**Survey:** Postal questionnaire survey 12 semi-structured interviews with senior officers of banks	All institutions within the UK monetary sector: 141 banks	1994
UK	(Macve and Chen, 2010)	To investigate both the nature of the success and shortcomings of equator principles reporting	**Interview:** Semi-structured interviews with a senior representative of Barclays, HBSC, and KPMG environmental consultants	Two banks (Barclays and HSBC)	2008
UK	(Campbell and Slack, 2011)	To gain detailed evidence from sell-side bank analysts on their views of bank environmental disclosures	**Interview content analysis:** Interview and analysis of the narratives contained in banks' annual reports	19 bank analysts	2004–2006
USA	(Colquitt *et al.*, 2006)	To estimate and document the market's reaction to the reserves increase announcements for the purpose of recognizing expected asbestos and environmental (A&E) liability	**Econometric:** Ordinary least squares (OLS) regression analysis	28 "potentially exposed" insurers	1992–2001
USA	(Burnett and Schellhorn, 2016)	To rank the overall climate change action performance of US financial firms across multiple dimensions of this effort and identify the climate change action metrics for which success was most difficult to achieve	**Econometric:** Dichotomous Rasch model	32 financial firms	2013

USA	(Thistlethwaite and Wood, 2018)	To assess the degree to which insurance companies are "rescaling" risk management practices to accommodate the temporal and spatial uncertainties associated with climate change	**Content analysis:** A content analysis of the NAIC Climate Risk Disclosure Survey	178/183 insurers	2012–2015
Bangladesh	(Sobhani *et al.*, 2012)	To describe the status of disclosure practices of corporate sustainability in the banking industry in Bangladesh	**Content analysis:** Content analysis of the annual reports and corporate websites	29 banks listed on the Dhaka and Chittagong Stock Exchanges	2009
Bangladesh	(Bose *et al.*, 2018)	To investigate the influence of regulatory guidance and several corporate governance factors on the green banking disclosure practices of Bangladeshi commercial banks	**Econometric:** Ordinary Least Squares (OLS)	All banking firms (ranging from 38 to 47)	2007–2014
Bangladesh	(Taslima and Salina, 2020)	To examine the financial performance of selected commercial banks that offered green financing in Bangladesh	**Interview report analysis:** Quantitative (report on green data) and qualitative (interview responses) thematic analysis approach	Five conventional private commercial banks and five *Shariah*-based private commercial banks	2012–2014

(*Continued*)

Table 7. (*Continued*)

Country	Author	Research question	Methodology	Sample	Period
Bangladesh	(Khan *et al.*, 2021)	To analyze if green banking disclosure affect firm value of banks and if the green banking disclosure and firm value relationship is conditional on a contextual factor, namely, the NPLs of banks	**Econometric:** Multiple regression	30 banks	2008–2014
South Africa	(Bimha and Nhamo, 2013)	How banks in South Africa quantify and benchmark carbon emissions	**Content analysis:** Content analysis of sustainability and annual reports (website publication)	Banks with the largest asset values (nine banking institutions representing 76.84 percent of assets of the South African banking sector)	2013
South Africa	(Bimha, 2015)	To establish the implications of loans made by banks on a short- and long-term basis to the JSE 100 companies in view of the carbon emissions they report	**Econometric:** Calculation of carbon risk embedded in long-term and short loans of the JSE100 companies	The Johannesburg Stock Exchange top 100 companies that participate in the Carbon Disclosure Project	2010–2014

Jordan	(Al-Dhaimesh and Zobi, 2019)	To examine the impact of sustainability accounting disclosures on financial performance	**Econometric:** Ordinary Least Squares (OLS)	11 banks selected based on sustainability data availability	2013–2017
Turkey	(Kılıç and Kuzey, 2019)	To test the impact of size, profitability, age, listing status, and foreign ownership on the disclosure score	**Content analysis/ Econometric:** Quantitative content analysis of annual and sustainability reports (multiple regression and fractional regression analysis)	24 banks	2010–2016
China	(Dong *et al.*, 2021)	To provide a longitudinal analysis of influences on China's financial sector's sustainability reporting practices and to examine "green finance" disclosures and to undertake subsector comparisons	**Content analysis/ Survival analysis:** Content analysis to examine the volumes, frequency, and content of sustainability disclosures. Survival analysis to identify factors significant in firms' initiation of these disclosures	Financial institutions (ranging from 39 to 55)	2007–2016

(*Continued*)

Table 7. (*Continued*)

Country	Author	Research question	Methodology	Sample	Period
Indonesia	(Gunawan *et al.*, 2021)	To explore the sustainability performance and green banking practices by examining disclosures in sustainability reports using GRI standards and the Shaumya and Arulrajah (2016) framework	**Content analysis:** Content analysis to analyze the sustainability reports issued in the Indonesian banking sector	21 banks	2009–2017
Serbia	(Hanić *et al.*, 2021)	To analyze the environmental disclosure practice in the Serbian banking sector, to highlight the degree of disclosure in systemically important banks, and to examine if there is a positive relationship between the banks' CSR practice and their financial performance	**Content analysis:** Content analysis of the annual and sustainability reports	10 banks, five of which were classified as systemically important banks	2015–2019
Swiss	(Thomä *et al.*, 2021)	To analyze whether the 2017 Swiss pilot study evidence measurement improved the management of transition risks	**Survey analysis:** Survey feedback from a 2017 pilot study conducted with Swiss pension funds and insurance companies	79 Swiss pension funds and insurance companies	2017

Table 8. Cross-country studies.

Countries	Author	Research question	Methodology	Sample	Period
USA–EU–AUS	(Haigh and Shapiro, 2011)	To identify the significance of carbon emissions reporting for investment banking	**Interview/Content analysis:** Interview to functionaries at selected financial institutions	32 professionals working in financial institutions	2010
USA–EU–ASIA	(Stechemesser *et al.*, 2015)	To analyze how insurers adapt to climate change impacts and how adaptation relates to corporate financial performance	**Content analysis/ Econometric:** Content analysis of insurers' adaptation efforts as reported to the Carbon Disclosure Project. Regression analysis to investigate positive relationships between climate knowledge absorption and performance measures	59 available responses of insurance companies to the CDP	2010
EU	(Carè, 2017)	To provide better knowledge of the relationship between credit risk management process and environmental risk and to offer several suggestions to banks and regulators with regard to the ways of disclosing information about environmental risks	**Case studies:** Multiple case studies	Eight European banks included among the global systemically important banks	2011–2015

(Continued)

Table 8. (*Continued*)

Countries	Author	Research question	Methodology	Sample	Period
EU	(Chiaramonte *et al.*, 2021)	To investigate the joint and separate effects of environmental, social, and governance (ESG) scores on bank stability for the European banking sector	**Econometric:** Differences-in-differences (DID) analysis	84 banks	2005–2017
EU	(Mora Rodríguez *et al.*, 2021)	To explore how both stock prices and "online popularity" can register the impact of environmental reports being made public under the premise of a key global actor, the CDP	**Econometric:** Nonlinear statistical methodology (i.e., the autoregressive fractionally integrated moving average estimation model)	15 listed banks	2004–2015
Worldwide	(Caby *et al.*, 2020)	To identify the determinants of banks' voluntary climate change disclosure and the quality of that disclosure	**Econometric:** Least-square regression and multivariate logit analysis	117 banks	2018

Worldwide	(Calderon, 2020)	To investigate what governance mechanisms have been created to support the implementation of sustainable lending	**Content analysis:** Content analysis of website	62 members of the Global Alliance for Banking on Values	2013
Worldwide	(Gallego-Álvarez and Pucheta-Martínez, 2020)	To analyze environmental disclosure in the banking industry considering the framework of the varieties of capitalism (coordinated market economies (CMEs) versus liberal market economies (LMEs)). To assess if gender diversity and board-specific skills play a moderating role in the reporting of environmental information, within both CME and LME contexts	**Econometric:** Generalized method of moments	3,517 international financial entities-years observations	2005–2016

(*Continued*)

Table 8. (*Continued*)

Countries	Author	Research question	Methodology	Sample	Period
Worldwide	(Galletta *et al.*, 2021)	To establish whether the actual management and governance effectiveness toward sustainability generates tangible effects on environmental disclosure performance	**Econometric:** Ordered logit estimation techniques	330 bank-year observations	2011–2015
Worldwide	(Birindelli *et al.*, 2022)	To test if a stronger commitment to climate change has a positive impact on the quality of bank loans, reducing overall credit risk	**Econometric:** Fixed-effects model for panel data	143 banks	2011–2019
Worldwide	(Caby *et al.*, 2022)	To analyze the impact of climate-change-related managerial practices and managerial quality on banks' financial performance	**Econometric:** Panel data model, generalized method of moments	137 banks	2011–2019

et al., 2015), while the majority assess banks or financial institutions in general. With regard to the adopted empirical methodology, the following approaches emerge: content analysis (performed on the firm's disclosure report and/or website), survey, interview, and econometric analysis. Content analysis and survey are the most common research methodologies applied to the single-country analysis, while the econometric approach is far more predominant in the cross-country analysis, where wider data availability allows for this type of study. With regard to the observed period, a group of papers, using mainly survey and content analysis approaches, perform cross-sectional data analysis; most of the econometric studies consist of time series analysis, with the most recent ones considering more than 10 years of data (Mora Rodríguez *et al.*, 2021; Gallego-Álvarez & Pucheta-Martínez, 2020; Chiaramonte *et al.*, 2021). With regard to the sample size, the most recent cross-country econometric papers offer the largest number of observed financial institutions, with Caby *et al.* (2020, 2022) and Birindelli *et al.* (2022) being the papers observing more than one hundred banks, and Gallego-Álvarez and Pucheta-Martínez (2020) assessing more than 3,500 observations. Non-econometric approach-based papers show a high variance in terms of the size of the observed financial institutions, ranging from two interviewed banks (Barclays and HSBC) in the paper by Macve and Chen (2010) to around 180 survey responses analyzed in the paper by Thistlethwaite and Wood (2018).

With regard to the second level of the contributions' analysis, the main streams described in the following emerged.

4.2.1. *The relationship between banks' environmental risk disclosure and lending activities*

Some papers focus on the usefulness of environmental disclosure in banks' lending decisions. The relevance of environmental disclosure is questioned: The emerging picture confirms the concerns that social and environmental implications are not part of banks' risk and lending processes' valuation models. Interestingly, this is the view of papers published further back in time, between 2004 and 2011.

The seminal paper is by Thompson and Cowton (2004), who identified the following three levels of risk that banks may face associated with environmental exposure through lending: indirect, direct, and reputational risks. The research questions addressed in the survey are the following: How do banks incorporate the environment into lending decisions; which sources of information are used by banks when making corporate lending decisions that involve environmental considerations; and what are the lending bankers' views on developments in environmental reporting. The main results show that bankers consider annual reports a relevant source to disclose information on corporate environmental impact and express some desire for extensions to environmental disclosure. However, such desired developments are relatively narrow in scope. Protection of loans is considered much more important than developing a more comprehensive disclosure in a separate form of a corporate environmental report.

Campbell and Slack (2011), explicitly referring to the decision-usefulness questions raised by Thompson and Cowton (2004), highlight detailed evidence from 19 UK sell-side bank analysts on their views of bank environmental disclosures. Specifically, the authors investigate the current use of environmental disclosure and its decision-usefulness to the analysts; analysts' views on the potential future materiality of environmental disclosure; and analysts' attitude to environmental risk, its recognition, and the link between bank lending and both environmental risk and disclosure relevance. The main results show that bank analysts view annual report environmental disclosures as irrelevant and immaterial. There is no evidence that they concern themselves with the environmental risks associated with loan decisions. This is associated with the sell-side perspective frame of reference (short- to medium-term and overtly financial). Pressure for environmental information further along the supply chain (e.g., from fund managers) and/or a major environmental incident may be the only drivers of a significant change in the analysts' attitudes to environmental issues.

Macve and Chen (2011) collected information through semi-structured interviews with relevant parties and decision-makers within Barclays, HSBC, and KPMG environmental consultants to illuminate the effectiveness of a voluntary code, such as the Equator Principles, developed by banks to encourage consideration of environmental and social issues in project financing. The main evidence suggests that there is scope for further improvement in the provision of detail at the operational level, the standardization of presentation, and assurance standards. The flexibility in such a voluntary code is consistent with the enlightened shareholder theory explanation of how banks respond to CSR and sustainability concerns. At the same time, such a code as "soft law" provides, among others, the advantage of assisting banks in building a shared social construction in responding to stakeholder pressures and concerns.

Haigh and Shapiro (2011) identified carbon emissions reports and interviewed officials at selected financial institutions in the US, Europe, and Australia to assess the significance of carbon emissions reporting for investment banking. Through a semiotic lens interpretation approach to data and with a functional perspective of decision-usefulness, the authors highlight that environmental investing for well-diversified investors constitutes a discourse of the imaginary. While reported variations in industrial carbon emissions levels have been ignored in asset allocation decisions, financialized constructs have been used to represent heavier polluters as superior "carbon performers." The main implication is that risk assessment is likely to be erroneous if it refers to measures that deflate carbon emissions by firms' revenues.

4.2.2. *The relationship between banks' environmental risk disclosure and bank economic/financial characteristics*

A group of relevant and recent papers investigates how banks' environmental risk disclosure impacts economic and/or financial indicators.

Khan *et al.* (2021) analyze green banking disclosure in listed banks in Bangladesh. The authors first aim to explore the direct relationship between green disclosure and firm value and investigate which key contextual conditions (e.g., NPLs) affect green disclosure and therefore affect (increase or decrease) firms' value. Their main findings indicate that, while green disclosure has a positive effect on the overall firm value of banks, this positive effect is negatively moderated by the banks' non-performing loans. The authors suggest that green disclosure alone is insufficient for creating market value for banks. Other contextual matters need attention to understand the relationship between green disclosure and banks' market value.

Chiaramonte *et al.* (2021) focus on bank stability. Specifically, the authors aim to investigate the joint and separate effects of environmental, social, and governance (ESG) scores on bank stability using a sample of European banks operating in 21 countries covering the financial crisis (2005–2017). The results show that the total ESG score and its sub-pillars reduce bank fragility during periods of financial distress. In times of financial turmoil, the integration of ESG practices into banks' internal processes seems beneficial in reducing bank fragility: The longer the duration of ESG disclosures, the greater the benefits on stability.

However, bank stability is also related to other bank- or country-specific factors, such as bank capital, asset quality, income diversification, and the ECB's unconventional liquidity injections. The research supports both stakeholder theory and the idea that moral capital creates value and resilience for firms.

Birindelli *et al.* (2022) aim to test whether a stronger commitment to climate change, proxied by the climate change score from the Carbon Disclosure Project (CDP), positively impacts bank loans' quality, reducing overall credit risk. Moreover, they assess the moderating effect of the country's environmental performance, where the bank is located. The main finding suggests that the commitment to climate issues lowers the risk level of bank loans when banks have a medium–high level of attention to these issues. In other words, the relationship between a bank's climate change commitment and its credit risk shows an inverted-U-shaped function. To obtain a lower credit risk — and better loan quality — banks should reach medium–high levels of commitment to climate change issues. Additionally, the country location of the bank does play a key role. In countries with better environmental performance, credit risk reduction emerges at lower levels of climate change commitment.

Caby *et al.* (2022) focus on the influence of climate change management. They empirically aim to measure the impact of climate-change-related managerial practices and managerial quality on traditional banks' financial performance measures. By studying a sample of banks from both emerging and developed countries, empirical evidence shows that, although banks seem to be aware of the consequences of climate change on their businesses, they are far from the point of making it a strategic topic and remain very timid in terms of operational implementation. Results confirm the influence of the traditional bank- and country-specific variables. Interestingly, banks' exposure to climate-related loss events appears neutral concerning their profitability. In contrast, the impact on banks' profitability of the CDP score and the board-level interest are significant and positive. Conversely, all the other "management" variables have no significant influence, which is a signal that implementing sound climate change management is neither detrimental nor positive to profitability. The authors conclude that climate change management is still awaiting concrete implementation in the banking industry.

4.2.3. *The relationship between banks' environmental risk disclosure and governance*

A group of papers takes a corporate governance perspective by explaining the relationship between corporate governance and banks' strategies to enhance their environmental disclosure and/or environmental performance. These papers aim to test whether corporate governance processes and factors are correlated with financial institutions' environmental disclosure.

Bose *et al.* (2018) analyze the influence of regulatory guidance and several corporate governance factors on Bangladeshi commercial banks' green banking disclosure practices. The main results show that the issuance of green banking regulatory guidance by the Central Bank of Bangladesh in 2011 positively influenced the level of green banking disclosure. Over time, disclosure practices in the banking sector have converged and become a routine process. Moreover, while some corporate governance characteristics, such as board size and institutional ownership, positively affect green banking disclosure, others, such as the presence of independent directors on the board, seem to play no role.

Gallego-Álvarez and Pucheta-Martínez (2020) analyze the banks' environmental disclosure considering the framework of the varieties of capitalism, thus comparing coordinated market economies (CMEs) versus liberal market economies (LMEs). Furthermore, the authors aim to assess whether gender diversity and board-specific skills play a moderating role in reporting environmental information within CME and LME contexts. Their principal findings show that banks are more likely to disclose environmental matters in CME cultures. Moreover, their results support predictions on the positive moderating role women directors on the boards of banks in CME cultures have in reporting environmental issues. However, contrary to predictions, specific skills of the board of directors do not result in higher environmental disclosure in CMEs than in LMEs.

Galletta *et al.* (2021) aim to establish whether the actual management and governance effectiveness toward sustainability impacts environmental disclosure performance. The study focuses on the carbon disclosure of worldwide banks, particularly on specific governance strategies, i.e., board of director monitoring and managerial incentives. Their results show an increase in environmental performance by implementing managerial incentives related to climate change, associated with the highest level of responsibility of the board of directors. Moreover, when the highest level of direct responsibility for climate-related issues is entrusted to the board or senior managers, banks' environmental performance increases.

4.2.4. *The analysis of the insurance sector*

Very few papers, namely those by Colquitt *et al.* (2006), Thistlethwaite and Wood (2018), Thomä *et al.* (2021), and Stechemesser *et al.* (2015), focus on the insurance sector. Colquitt *et al.* (2006) are the first to apply econometric analysis to quantify the market's reaction to the reserves increase announcements made between 1992 and 2001 in the US to cover expected asbestos and environmental (A&E) liability. The purpose of the study was to highlight the role played by the introduction of Footnote 24 by the NAIC in 1995, which required insurers to provide a five-year history of environmental reserves and claim payments. The authors find that the announcement of A&E reserves increases after 1995 had no statistically significant effect on the market value of the announcing insurers, thus confirming that any additional accounting disclosure provides valuable information on insurers' exposure. Thistlethwaite and Wood (2018) and Thomä *et al.* (2021) analyze how environmental risk challenges the insurers' risk management practices by performing a content analysis of a survey conducted by the US National Association of Insurance Commissioners and of Swiss pension funds and insurance companies, respectively. Stechemesser *et al.* (2015), the only cross-country analysis, aims to empirically measure how insurers' adaptation to climate change affects corporate financial performance. Although adaptation is likely to involve costs, the principal results show that it may also bring financial benefits that outweigh both adaptation costs and possible negative financial effects arising from climate change.

4.2.5. *Papers referring to a specific theory*

A few papers clearly identify the exact theory their empirical analysis refers to or aims to test. Among the papers analyzing the insurance sector, we found the following theories: the enlightened shareholder theory, within the broader motivations for CSR (Macve & Chen, 2010); the vertical conceptualization of scale (Thistlethwaite & Wood, 2018); and the dynamic capability view (Stechemesser *et al.*, 2015). Among the remaining contributions, we found the following theories: institutional theory (Bose *et al.*, 2018; Dong *et al.*, 2021); stakeholder theory (Galletta *et al.*, 2021; Chiaramonte *et al.*, 2021); RBV; signaling theory and institutional theory (Birindelli *et al.*, 2022); varieties of capitalism framework (Gallego-Álvarez & Pucheta-Martínez, 2020).

5. Concluding Remarks

This chapter systematically maps the literature on environmental disclosure in banks and insurance companies using the Web of Science and Scopus databases. The bibliometric analysis of a sample of 35 (academic) studies published from 2004 to 2022 in 26 different journals yields interesting results. Only five papers are single-authored, with an average author per paper of 2.34 (of a total of 82 authors). The authors' concentration level is quite limited (only seven authors authored two publications). The average number of citations per document is 17.11, and the average number per year is 2.04. The discourse on environmental disclosure in financial institutions is widespread and fragmented in terms of journals' concentration (the 35 articles are dispersed among 26 journals) and disciplinary areas (nine areas are covered). The distribution of contributions is addressed in high-quality journals in a more significant percentage than a homogeneous distribution among quartiles. Overall, the bibliometric analysis shows that environmental disclosure in financial institutions is an emerging topic for research, which may be addressed from many different perspectives. The analysis of the main specific trends reveals that, to date, environmental disclosure in banks does not highlight specific investigated issues and generally refers to broad and common concerns (carbon emission, climate change, and environment) affecting every firm in every sector.

The papers are then classified according to their research approach: theoretical/conceptual (three papers), argumentative (three papers), and empirical (29 papers). Empirical papers address the topic using a variety of empirical methodologies.

A few papers refer to a specifically identified theory that their empirical analysis is related to or aims to test. Emerging theories are the enlightened shareholder theory, the dynamic capability view, the institutional theory, the stakeholder theory, the resource-based view, the signaling theory, and the varieties of capitalism framework. We classify the empirical articles on the banking sector into three groups focused on the relationship between banks' environmental-risk disclosure and lending activity, their economic/financial characteristics, and their governance. The separate analysis of the insurance sector considers four papers and shows mixed results.

Our analysis may help both policymakers, in terms of outlining their actions to meet disclosure requirements and standards, and academics to provide focus for their future research. The findings suggest that more empirical research is needed to understand whether further disclosure requirements could add value to the reporting institutions. Our results indicate that further research investigating which market and/or financial institutions' specific characteristics enhance such disclosure could help fully understand the interconnections between disclosure of environmental risks and firms' value. More attention should be paid to the insurance sector. Finally, disclosure of information about areas of business not yet fully considered, such as lending and asset underwriting activities, should be emphasized to increase disclosure effectiveness.

The very narrow focus of this chapter, i.e., the strict selection of contributions analyzing only financial institutions, limits its ability to capture relevant conclusions arising from the literature on environmental disclosure issues. The relatively new interest in climate issues in financial institutions has not yet produced a complete and consolidated framework on this topic. Consequently, our findings will be necessarily amended in a few years when more studies will address this issue. The specific nature of banks and insurance companies lets them play a crucial role as intermediaries. The environmental risk of a financial institution is strictly connected to the environmental risk of each financed or insured firm in its held portfolio. In the future, we argue that how the climate disclosure provided by banks and insurance companies' customers affects lending, investment, and underwriting decisions will become particularly relevant. The most recent trends in climate disclosure standards (i.e., the EU guidelines and the task force mentioned above) stress this point by explicitly taking into account specific disclosure on the ability of banks and insurance companies to incorporate climatic aspects into their lending/underwriting policies. Consequently, environmental disclosure of financial institutions (the focus of this chapter), the issue of customers'/insured firms' disclosure, and its relevance in lending/underwriting policies must be evaluated for their potential interconnections. Further research is needed to synthesize and discuss a broader perspective on this issue.

References

Bimha, A. & Nhamo, G. (2013). Conceptual framework for carbon footprinting in the South African banking sector. *Banks and Bank Systems*, *8*(4), 19–33.

Bimha, A. (2015). Carbon risk analysis of the South African Banks' lending to the JSE100 CDP companies. *Risk Governance and Control: Financial Markets and Institutions*, *5*(4), 123–137.

Birindelli, G., Bonanno, G., Dell'Atti, S., *et al.* (2022). Climate change commitment, credit risk and the country's environmental performance: Empirical evidence from a sample of international banks. *Business Strategy and the Environment*, *31*(4), 1641–1655.

Bose, S., Khan, H. Z., Rashid, A., *et al.* (2018). What drives green banking disclosure? An institutional and corporate governance perspective. *Asia Pacific Journal of Management*, *35*(2), 501–527.

Broeders, D. & Schlooz, M. (2021). Climate change uncertainty and central bank risk management. *Journal of Risk Management in Financial Institutions*, *14*(2) 121–130.

Bukhari, S. A. A., Hashim, F., & Amran, A. (2021). Green banking: A conceptual framework. *International Journal of Green Economics*, *15*(1), 59–74.

Burnett, A. & Schellhorn, C. (2016). Leadership performance of financial firms on climate change action. *Banks and Bank Systems*, *11*(2), 103–109.

Caby, J., Ziane, Y., & Lamarque, E. (2020). The determinants of voluntary climate change disclosure commitment and quality in the banking industry. *Technological Forecasting and Social Change*, *161*, 120282.

Caby, J., Ziane, Y., & Lamarque, E. (2022). The impact of climate change management on banks profitability. *Journal of Business Research, 142*, 412–422.

Campbell, J. L. (2007). Why would corporations behave in socially responsible ways? An institutional theory of corporate social responsibility. *Academy of Management Review, 32*(3), 946–967.

Carè, R. (2017). Exploring environmental disclosure in banks. Evidence from the Euro area. *ACRN Oxford Journal of Finance and Risk Perspectives 6*(2), 18–40.

Caldecott, B. (2020). Climate risk management (CRM) and how it relates to achieving alignment with climate outcomes (ACO). *Journal of Sustainable Finance & Investment, 12*(4), 1167–1170.

Calderon, F. (2022). Governance mechanisms for sustainable lending: An exploratory study of existing practices. *Journal of Sustainable Finance & Investment, 12*(4), 1146–1166.

Campbell, D. & Slack, R. (2011). Environmental disclosure and environmental risk: Sceptical attitudes of UK sell-side bank analysts. *The British Accounting Review, 43*(1), 54–64.

Cerchiaro, D., Leo, S., Landriault, E., *et al.* (2021). DLT to boost efficiency for financial intermediaries. An application in ESG reporting activities. *Technology Analysis and Strategic Management*, 1–14.

Chiaramonte, L., Dreassi, A., Girardone, C., & Piserà, S. (2022). Do ESG strategies enhance bank stability during financial turmoil? *Evidence from Europe. The European Journal of Finance, 28*(12), 1173–1211.

Clarkson, M. B. E. (1995). A stakeholder framework for analyzing and evaluating corporate social performance. *Academy of Management Review, 20*(1), 92–117.

Colquitt, L. L., Hoyt, R. E., & McCullough, K. A. (2006). The impact of asbestos and environmental reserves increases on shareholder wealth. *North American Actuarial Journal, 10*(3), 17–31.

Commissione Europea (2019). Orientamenti Sulla Comunicazione Di Informazioni Di Carattere Non Finanziario: Integrazione Concernente La Comunicazione Di Informazioni Relative Al Clima (2019/C 209/01).

Cormier, D., Magnan, M., & Van Velthoven, B. (2005). Environmental disclosure quality in large German companies: Economic incentives, public pressures or institutional conditions? *European Accounting Review, 14*(1), 3–39.

Dong, S., Xu, L., & McIver, R. (2021). China's financial sector sustainability and "green finance" disclosures. *Sustainability Accounting, Management and Policy Journal, 12*(2), 353–384.

Dye, R. A. (1985). Disclosure of Nonproprietary Information. *Journal of Accounting Research*, *23*(1), 123–145.

Faulk, R. O. (2009). Lifting the veil: Pressures mount for climate change disclosures. *The Electricity Journal*, *22*(6), 59–67.

Gallego-Álvarez, I. & Pucheta-Martínez, M. C. (2020). Environmental strategy in the global banking industry within the varieties of capitalism approach: The moderating role of gender diversity and board members with specific skills. *Business Strategy and the Environment*, *29*(2), 347–360.

Galletta, S., Mazzù, S., & Naciti, V. (2021). Banks' business strategy and environmental effectiveness: The monitoring role of the board of directors and the managerial incentives. *Business Strategy and the Environment*, *30*(5), 2656–2670.

Gray, R., Kouhy, R., & Lavers, S. (1995). Corporate social and environmental reporting. A review of the literature and a longitudinal study of UK disclosure. *Accounting, Auditing and Accountability Journal*, *8*(2), 47–77.

Gunawan, J., Permatasari, P., & Sharma, U. (2022). Exploring sustainability and green banking disclosures: A study of banking sector. *Environment, Development and Sustainability*, *24*(9), 11153–11194.

Haigh, M. & Shapiro, M. A. (2011). Carbon reporting: Does it matter? *Accounting, Auditing and Accountability Journal*, *25*(1), 105–125.

Hanić, A., Jovanović, O., & Stevanović, S. (2021). Environmental disclosure practice in the Serbian banking sector. *Management*, *26*(2), 115–144.

Hel Al-Dhaimesh, O. & Kamel Al Zobi, M. (2019). The effect of sustainability accounting disclosures on financial performance: An empirical study on the Jordanian banking sector. *Banks and Bank Systems*, *14*(2), 1–8.

Hooghiemstra, R. (2000). Corporate communication and impression management — New perspectives why companies engage in corporate social reporting. *Journal of Business Ethics*, *27*(1–2), 55–68.

Khan, H. Z., Bose, S., Sheehy, B., *et al.* (2021). Green banking disclosure, firm value and the moderating role of a contextual factor: Evidence from a distinctive regulatory setting. *Business Strategy and the Environment*, *30*(8), 3651–3670.

Kılıç, M. & Kuzey, C. (2019). Determinants of climate change disclosures in the Turkish banking industry. *International Journal of Bank Marketing*, *37*(3), 901–926.

Li, Y., Richardson, G. D., & Thornton, D. (1997). Corporate disclosure of environmental information: Theory and evidence. *Contemporary Accounting Research*, *14*(3), 435–474.

Macve, R. & Chen, X. (2010). The "equator principles": A success for voluntary codes? (R. L. Burritt, Ed.). *Accounting, Auditing and Accountability Journal, 23*(7), 890–919.

Maignan, I. & Ralston, D. A. (2002). Corporate social responsibility in Europe and the U.S.: Insights from businesses' self-presentations. *Journal of International Business Studies, 33*(3), 497–514.

Mora Rodríguez, M., Flores Muñoz, F., & Valentinetti, D. (2020). Corporate impact of carbon disclosures: A nonlinear empirical approach. *Journal of Financial Reporting and Accounting, 19*(1), 4–27.

Nikolaou, I. E. & Yannacopoulos, A. N. (2009). The effect of environmental accounting on financial risk management of firms via insurance. *International Journal of Monetary Economics and Finance, 2*(1), 1–15.

Sobhani, F. A., Amran, A., & Zainuddin, Y. (2012). Sustainability disclosure in annual reports and websites: A study of the banking industry in Bangladesh. *Journal of Cleaner Production, 23*(1), 75–85.

Stechemesser, K., Endrikat, J., Grasshoff, N., *et al.* (2015). Insurance companies' responses to climate change: Adaptation, dynamic capabilities and competitive advantage. *The Geneva Papers on Risk and Insurance — Issues and Practice, 40*(4), 557–584.

Taslima, J. & Salima, K. (2020). Exploring green banking performance of Islamic banks vs. conventional banks in Bangladesh based on *Maqasid Shariah* framework. *Journal of Islamic Marketing, 11*(3), 729–744.

Thistlethwaite, J. & Wood, M. O. (2018). Insurance and climate change risk management: Rescaling to look beyond the horizon: Insurance and climate change risk management. *British Journal of Management, 29*(2), 279–298.

Thomä, J., Murray, C., Jerosch-Herold, V., *et al.* (2021). Do you manage what you measure? Investor views on the question of climate actions with empirical results from the Swiss pension fund and insurance sector. *Journal of Sustainable Finance and Investment, 11*(1), 47–61.

Thompson, P. & Cowton, C. J. (2004). Bringing the environment into bank lending: Implications for environmental reporting. *The British Accounting Review, 36*(2), 197–218.

Verrecchia R. E. (1983). Discretionary disclosure. *Journal of Accounting and Economics, 5*, 179–194.

https://doi.org/10.1142/9781800614482_0008

Chapter 8

Disclosure on Climate-Related Risks in the Insurance Sector: The State of the Art in Europe

Maria Mazzuca[*,†], Damiana Giuseppina Costanzo[‡], and Angela Coscarelli[§]

University of Calabria, Arcavacata, Italy
[†]*maria.mazzuca@unical.it*
[‡]*dm.costanzo@unical.it*
[§]*angela.coscarelli@unical.it*

Abstract

In this chapter, we study climate-related risk disclosure in the European insurance sector by reviewing the literature to frame the analysis. Subsequently, we discuss climate-related risks and their disclosure in the insurance sector, and we analyze the regulatory framework, focusing on the European context. Finally, we develop an empirical analysis of 43 European insurance companies during 2016–2020. The analysis is developed in three stages. First, a new disclosure index is constructed based on the key performance indicators contained in the European Commission guidelines provided in 2019. Second, the disclosure index is used to assess the level of climate-related risk disclosure in the sample insurance companies. Finally, a rating index is constructed (using principal component analysis) to summarize the most important information content. This synthetic index possesses a greater information power as it extracts new (informative) components. Overall, the results suggest that the level of disclosure differs among European countries, and it tends to increase over time. However, the situation appears jeopardized with reference to four information areas investigated.

[*]Corresponding author.

1. Introduction

Sustainability, and especially the environmental component of sustainability, has been progressively receiving increasing attention since the 2015 Paris Agreement on climate change. The financial sector (including banks and insurers) is typically considered less interested in environmental problems compared to other sectors. However, during the past few years, the scenario has changed as regulators have reserved more attention for financial institutions (FIs). The regulators seem to be especially focused on climate risks and their disclosure, compared to the governance and social components, which are the other pillars of sustainability. Overall, we argue that the main directions followed by the regulators are: to define mandatory minimum standards of non-financial disclosure, specifically focusing on environmental issues; and to increase attention on the disclosure offered by FIs, such as banks and insurance companies.

In 2017, the Task Force on Climate-related Financial Disclosures (TCFD, 2017) (established by the G20's Financial Stability Board) published recommendations to encourage companies to disclose information on climate-related risks and opportunities. The European Commission (EC) encourages companies to implement these recommendations. Several governments and financial regulators around the world are integrating them into their guidance and policy frameworks. Examples include Australia, Canada, Hong Kong, Japan, Singapore, and South Africa, as well as some EU member states (EC, 2019).

The attention of the European Parliament and the European Commission on environmental and sustainability issues is expressed through directives, regulations, and guidelines. The "non-financial reporting directive" (NFRD) (Directive 2014/95/EU of the European Parliament and of the Council) (NFRD, 2014) can be considered a milestone of the European legal framework, as it introduces some new disclosure requirements for large firms, which are public-interest entities (therefore including banks and insurers). These requirements stipulate that a firm's management report should include a non-financial statement (NFS) containing information on non-financial matters. In 2021, the EC adopted a proposal for a corporate sustainability reporting directive (CSRD) that extends the scope and requirements of the NFRD. It aims at introducing more detailed reporting requirements and a mandate to report according to EU sustainability reporting standards to be developed by the European Financial Reporting Advisory Group (EFRAG, 2021). The first set of standards have been entered into force at the end of 2022.

In 2017, the EC (2017) published non-binding guidelines to help companies disclose environmental and social information. On June 2019, the EC (2019) supplemented the 2017 guidelines with new non-binding guidelines, which are part of the Action Plan on Financing Sustainable Growth adopted by the EC in March 2018. The 2019 guidelines proposed disclosures for all the companies that fall under the scope of the NFRD. In Annex I of this directive, further guidance for banks and insurance companies is provided, given their special business activities. In this chapter, we use these guidelines to develop an empirical analysis, which can be considered a reference framework for all companies wishing to develop an effective disclosure on climate risks.

In the near future, further disclosure requirements (and standards) on environmental issues will be introduced. The motivations underlying this choice stem from the various benefits commonly associated with disclosure, both for market participants and for the reporting companies. The EU regulators also aim to achieve some declared goals, all consistent with the possibility of reducing information asymmetries in principal–agent relationships (EC, 2019). However, we argue that the introduction of disclosure requirements is a critical and controversial choice. This is especially true for the financial sector, where FIs risk becoming a sounding board for (climate) issues due to the complex relationships that bind them to their depositors and underwriters. This chapter aims to further develop the discussion on environmental disclosure and contribute to the open debate focusing on the European insurance sector that currently appears to be almost completely ignored by the academic literature.

This chapter is structured as follows. In Section 2, we briefly review the literature to frame our analysis. In Section 3, we discuss climate-related risks and disclosures in the insurance sector. In Section 4, we analyze the regulatory framework, focusing on the European context. In Section 5, we discuss an empirical strategy.

In Sections 6 and 7, we develop an empirical analysis and discuss the findings. In the final section, we conclude.

2. Theories of Corporate Social Responsibility and Environmental Disclosure

In this section, we briefly discuss the theoretical and empirical literature on corporate social responsibility (CSR) and environmental disclosure. This brief discussion is useful to frame the context in which the analysis reported in this chapter is developed. For a review of the literature specifically focused on climate disclosure in FIs, see Chapter 7.

Climate disclosure is a type of non-financial disclosure to be included in the broader framework of CSR disclosure. The literature on CSR and environmental disclosure is fragmented, both from theoretical and empirical perspectives. To justify CSR/environmental disclosure, two competing arguments are generally recognized. The first perspective, commonly referred to as voluntary disclosure theory, suggests that companies have incentives to disclose "good news" to better compete with companies with "bad news" by avoiding the adverse selection problem (Dye, 1985; Verrecchia, 1983). This perspective predicts a positive relation between environmental performance and environmental disclosure.

From a sociopolitical perspective, several theories justifying CSR activities and disclosure describe a multi-theoretical framework (Cormier *et al.*, 2005). These theories include political economy theory, legitimacy theory, and stakeholder theory. Sociopolitical theories start from the idea that a firm is an economic entity that cannot be separated from the social context in which it operates and lives and by which it is shaped and influenced. To survive, the company must obtain the support and approval of both its primary stakeholders (e.g., shareholders, employees, and customers) and secondary ones (e.g., media and special interest groups) (Clarkson, 1995). CSR activity and CSR disclosure are part of the communication process necessary to create and maintain this support. Starting from this assumption and based on stakeholder and legitimacy theories, several authors have advanced various theoretical arguments on CSR activity and disclosure (e.g., Gray *et al.*, 1995; Campbell, 2000; Hooghiemstra, 2000; Maignan & Ralston, 2002). Sociopolitical theories predict a negative association between environmental performance and the level of discretionary environmental disclosures.

From an empirical perspective, the results are also mixed. This is because the increased level of disclosure does not necessarily determine the increase in the soundness of firms, FIs, and the system in general. The reasons should be sought in the potential negative relationship between disclosure and environmental performance and in the presence of costs specifically associated with the disclosure. The costs include direct costs related to the production of information and indirect costs, such as proprietary costs (Verrecchia, 1983). Proprietary costs can pertain to the manager revealing information to environmental regulators and other environmental activist groups that increase the probability of criticism, sanction, or attack (see Li *et al.*, 1997).

If we consider the literature on climate-related disclosure and specifically on disclosure by FIs, we find that very few studies have been conducted so far. For a review of this literature, see Chapter 7.

To conclude, given the multi-theoretical framework on CSR disclosure, considering the mixed results of the empirical literature on CSR and climate disclosure, and taking into account the very few studies specifically focused on environmental disclosure and FIs, we argue that additional (empirical) studies are needed to understand better whether further (non-financial) climate disclosure requirements could actually add value to the reporting institutions and to the system. The focus on insurance companies permits the evaluation of a sector almost ignored by the literature, which, however, is becoming important for climate issues, as demonstrated by the progressively increased attention from the regulators.

Starting from the research opportunity given by both the publication of the new EC guidelines in 2019 and the introduction in the near future of new requirements and standards for climate disclosure, we investigate the following research questions: What is the level of disclosure in the European insurance sector? What type of information is provided? What are the main gaps evidenced in this disclosure?

3. Climate-Related Risks Disclosure in Insurance Companies

3.1. *Types of climate-related risks and transmission channels to financial risks*

Typically, environmental- and climate-related risks are grouped into two broad categories (Table 1).[1] The first includes physical risks, referring to the effects of global warming, such as a higher occurrence of extreme weather events or a rise in the sea level; these effects can have an impact on the occurrence of health, property, or catastrophe insurance events (NGFS, 2020).

The second category of climate-related risks includes transition risks. They arise from human efforts to address environmental and climate challenges, including changes in public policies, technological breakthroughs, shifts in investors' or the public's sentiments, and disruptive business model innovations (NGFS, 2020).

Physical and transition risks can affect all companies directly or indirectly through their supply chains. Impacts include reduced revenues, increased costs, higher costs of capital, and the non-availability of insurance. These risks are further classified by the TCFD (2017).

Table 1. The matrix of climate risks.

Physical risks	Acute risks Event-driven risks related to weather events Chronic risks Referred to long-term shifts in climate patterns (such as those related to the increase in temperatures)
Transition risks	Policy and legal risks Technological risks Market risks Reputation risks

Source: Authors' elaboration on TCFD (2017).

[1] In this chapter, we use the terms environmental and climate risks as synonyms, even though climate risks are a subset of environmental risks (NGFS, 2020a).

To complete the discussion on the risks studied in this chapter, we need to focus on emissions. The Greenhouse Gas (GHG) Protocol[2] sets out three "scopes" of emissions, the reporting of which is included in the guidelines of the TCFD (2017) discussed in the following section. The concept of scopes helps delineate direct and indirect emission sources, improve transparency, and provide utility for different types of organizations and different types of climate policies and business goals. The three "scopes" are defined for GHG accounting and reporting purposes:

(1) Scope 1 refers to all direct GHG emissions;
(2) Scope 2 refers to electricity and indirect GHG emissions;
(3) Scope 3 refers to other indirect GHG emissions. It is an optional reporting category that allows for the treatment of all other indirect emissions. Scope 3 emissions are a consequence of the activities of a company but occur from sources not owned or controlled by it. Some examples of Scope 3 activities are the extraction and production of purchased materials, the transportation of purchased fuels, and the use of sold products and services. (World Resources Institute and World Business Council for Sustainable Development, 2004).

The impact of climate risks on banks and insurers is related to the effects that they produce on financial risks, those typically affecting FIs. The understanding of these transmission channels helps capture the link between the insurers and the environmental risks and why there is a need to consider these risks in their global strategy. NGFS (2020, 2020b) focused on these transmission channels (Figure 1), as we discuss in the following section.

[2]"The Greenhouse Gas Protocol Initiative is a multi-stakeholder partnership of businesses, non-governmental organizations (NGOs), governments, and others convened by the World Resources Institute (WRI), a U.S.-based environmental NGO, and the World Business Council for Sustainable Development (WBCSD), a Geneva-based coalition of 170 international companies. Launched in 1998, the Initiative's mission is to develop internationally accepted greenhouse gas (GHG) accounting and reporting standards for business and to promote their broad adoption." (World Resources Institute and World Business Council for Sustainable Development, 2004).

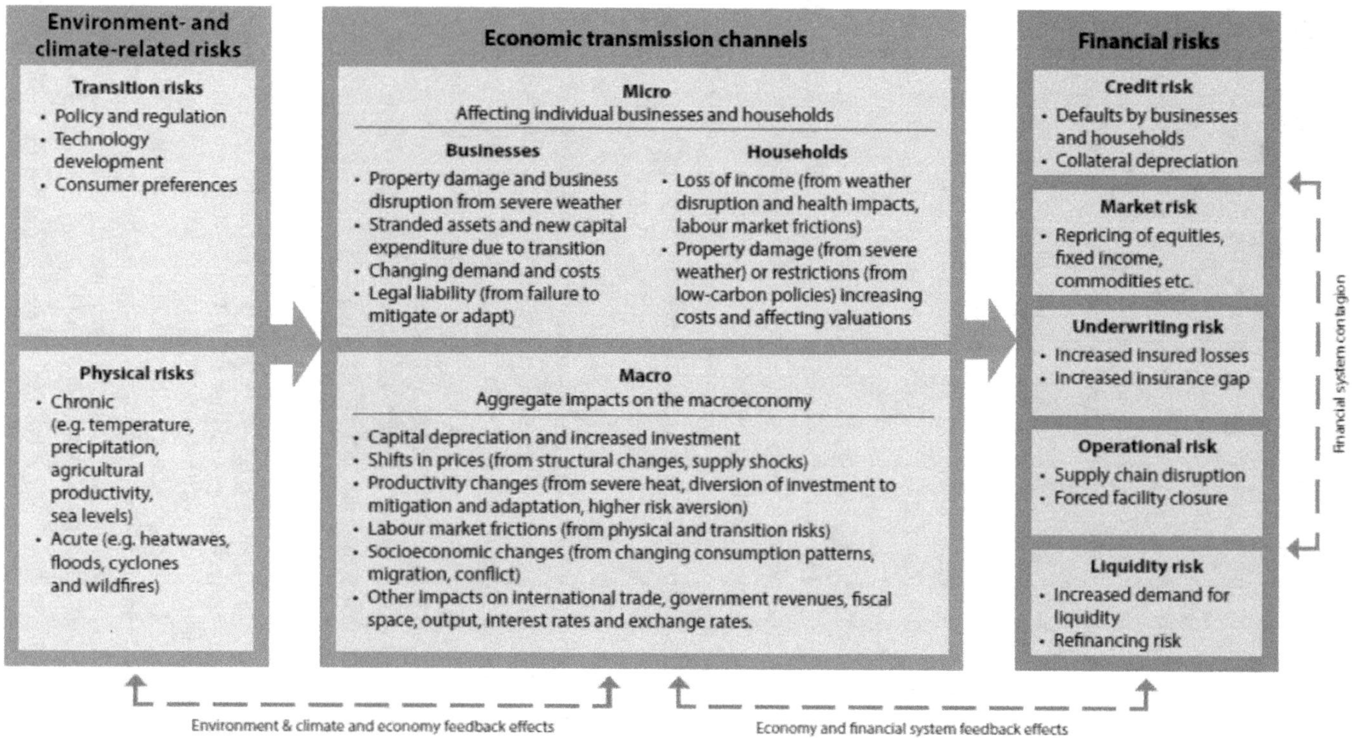

Figure 1. From environmental to financial risks.
Source: NGFS (2020, 2020b).

If we focus on transition risks, we note that they impact both micro (businesses and households) and macro levels. This creates financial risks for lenders and investors. It is possible to imagine a contagion from the environmental to the financial system that results in a kind of ecosystem.

When we turn our attention to physical risks, we note that they affect the economy in two ways. Acute impacts, related to extreme weather events, can lead to damage to businesses and properties. These events can increase underwriting risks for insurers and impair asset values. Chronic impacts can affect labor, capital, and agricultural productivity. These changes will require a significant level of investment and adaptation by companies, households, and governments.

The most typical impact on the insurers is recognized in the underwriting risk, directly deriving from physical risks. However, other financial risks also affect the insurance companies when they act as investment companies and operate as asset managers.

3.2. *Impact of climate-related risks on the insurance companies and the importance of their disclosure*

Climate change and its related risks have very significant implications for insurers' underwriting, investing, and even operating businesses. Examples of the impact of climate risks on insurance companies could be imagined as follows. Extreme weather events could lead to damage to physical assets, including real estate, productive capital and infrastructure, and loss of life, with consequent property and casualty insurance losses, adverse effects on the balance sheets of households and firms, increases in defaults, and potential financial sector distress. Moreover, given that the real estate and agriculture sectors are both more immediately exposed to the physical impact of climate change and considering that insurers are typically exposed to these sectors, major impacts could affect both the asset and liability sides of their balance sheets. Moreover, the rise of these risks could cause an increase in premiums or a decrease in coverage that could lead to further uninsured losses: the so-called protection gap.

As evidenced by the TCFD (2017), better disclosure of the financial impacts of climate-related risks and opportunities is important to make more informed financial decisions by the investors, lenders, and insurance underwriters. In detail, this effect could have a negative or positive impact (opportunities). The negative effect could be perceived on the balance sheet, income statement, and cash flow statement.

If we focus on the motivations for disclosure, we argue that they could have specific importance for insurance companies. In general terms, this importance is related to the special fiduciary nature of the relationship between the insurers and their stakeholders, including their customers. While we note that both practitioners and academics reserve low attention to climate risks and their disclosure by insurance companies, we argue that these issues are especially important in this sector for several reasons.

First, the FIs are important to achieve the sustainability goals at a global system level because they contribute to resource allocation. In the case of banks, this allocation is attained mainly through loans, and in the case of insurers, they act as investment companies. Without sufficient, reliable, and comparable sustainability-related information disclosed by investment companies, the financial sector cannot efficiently allocate capital to investments able to drive solutions for sustainability.

Second, unlike most non-financial firms, banks and insurance companies are both providers and users of climate-related information. As such, they can exacerbate climate-related risks if their investments and insurance underwriting policies support economic activities that contribute to climate change via actions that are harmful the environment (such as GHG emissions, deforestation, and forest degradation). Conversely, they can promote the transition to a low-carbon and climate-resilient economy and increase awareness of the transition by integrating into their policies and procedures an evaluation of the potential impact of their investments, loans, and insurance contracts on climate change.

Third, most of the exposure of a FI to climate-related risks is likely to stem from the financial activities it undertakes. According to the GHG Protocol, financial firms should fall under Scope 3. However, an examination of the disclosures by large euro area banks and insurers suggests that, even though Scope 3 emissions are often reported, these institutions typically (explicitly) exclude emissions related to financial assets from that measure. Scarce and inconsistent information on climate-related risks embedded in assets makes the pricing of climate risks difficult for investors and authorities. Market data providers (such as Bloomberg and Refinitiv) have developed environmental scores that, however, suffer from significant discretion in environmental scoring. While several recent studies have also found that environmental disclosures can affect the market valuation of non-financial businesses, the impact is less clear for FIs (e.g., Jakubik & Uguz, 2021). Specifically, environmental disclosures appear to have no impact on stock market valuations for banks, but some impact for insurers, perhaps due to a greater investor scrutiny of insurers owing to their higher exposure to physical climate-change risks, given insurance liabilities (Carbone *et al.*, 2019). However, disclosures by the financial sector could contribute to fostering an early assessment of climate-related risks and opportunities, improve the pricing of climate-related risks, and lead to more informed capital allocation decisions (TFCD, 2017).

Fourth, the presence of effective disclosure and transparency is strictly related to market discipline. This is so true and important that both the Solvency and Basel frameworks include a third pillar that is focused on the disclosure requirements needed for the market discipline to function. A subsequent interesting and important question is about the role of climate-related disclosure in market discipline.

The increasing importance of ESG disclosure in the financial sector is signaled by several initiatives developed at the industry level too. In 2019, the United Nations Principles for Responsible Investing (PRI) had more than 2,500 signatories (representing over $80 trillion in assets under management) that agreed to implement six voluntary principles, three of which related to the ESG issues, as follows: incorporating ESG issues into investment analysis and decision-making processes; being active owners and incorporating ESG issues into our ownership policies and practices; and seeking appropriate disclosure on ESG issues by the entities in which we invest (RepRisk, 2020).

While it is evident that the ESG disclosure is an integrated pillar of the PRI, the concrete importance and the level of this disclosure are not sufficiently studied. Instead, there is little consensus among rating agencies and public entities on the type of information that needs to be disclosed. "ESG rating agencies and data providers offer a wide range of products. However, each agency has developed its own research scope, scoring methodology, and sources of raw data to assess a company's corporate sustainability and ESG factors" (RepRisk, 2020). Moreover, while several studies focus on the ESG rating, only a few are focused on the ratings of ESG disclosure.

4. Regulatory Framework

4.1. *Recommendations of the Task Force on climate-related financial disclosures*

The Task Force (TCFD, 2017) recommendations are grouped into four thematic areas: governance, strategy, risk management, and metrics and targets. For each area, some key climate-related financial disclosures are recommended, and all together, they constitute the disclosure framework, helping investors and other stakeholders understand how reporting organizations think about and assess climate-related risks and opportunities (TCFD, 2017). While some disclosures are recommended for all firms, some special and supplemental guidance is provided for the financial sector. Figures 2 and 3 report all the disclosures provided by the Task Force and those supplementally provided for the financial sector, respectively.

The Task Force also highlights the fundamental principles of implementing an effective disclosure:

(1) They should present relevant information.
(2) They should be specific and complete.
(3) They should be clear, balanced, and understandable.
(4) They should be consistent over time.
(5) They should be comparable among organizations within a sector, industry, or portfolio.
(6) They should be reliable, verifiable, and objective.
(7) They should be provided on a timely basis.

4.2. *The European framework and the Commission guidelines*

The European regulatory framework in which we are interested includes both non-financial disclosure *tout court* and non-financial disclosure focused on climate and environmental issues. The

Governance	Strategy	Risk Management	Metrics and Targets
Disclose the organization's governance around climate-related risks and opportunities.	Disclose the actual and potential impacts of climate-related risks and opportunities on the organization's businesses, strategy, and financial planning where such information is material.	Disclose how the organization identifies, assesses, and manages climate-related risks.	Disclose the metrics and targets used to assess and manage relevant climate-related risks and opportunities where such information is material.
Recommended Disclosures	**Recommended Disclosures**	**Recommended Disclosures**	**Recommended Disclosures**
a) Describe the board's oversight of climate-related risks and opportunities.	a) Describe the climate-related risks and opportunities the organization has identified over the short, medium, and long term.	a) Describe the organization's processes for identifying and assessing climate-related risks.	a) Disclose the metrics used by the organization to assess climate-related risks and opportunities in line with its strategy and risk management process.
b) Describe management's role in assessing and managing climate-related risks and opportunities.	b) Describe the impact of climate-related risks and opportunities on the organization's businesses, strategy, and financial planning.	b) Describe the organization's processes for managing climate-related risks.	b) Disclose Scope 1, Scope 2, and, if appropriate, Scope 3 greenhouse gas (GHG) emissions, and the related risks.
	c) Describe the resilience of the organization's strategy, taking into consideration different climate-related scenarios, including a 2°C or lower scenario.	c) Describe how processes for identifying, assessing, and managing climate-related risks are integrated into the organization's overall risk management.	c) Describe the targets used by the organization to manage climate-related risks and opportunities and performance against targets.

Figure 2. Task force on climate-related financial disclosures (2017): Recommended disclosures.
Source: TCFD (2017).

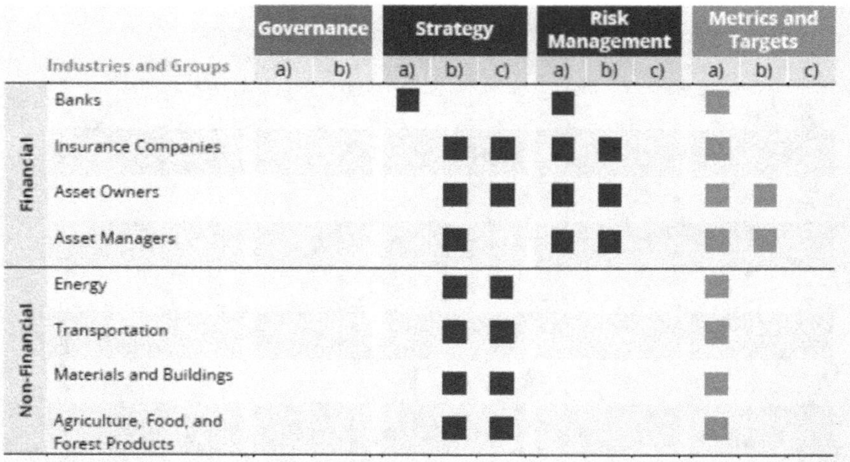

Figure 3. Task Force on climate-related financial disclosures (2017): Recommended disclosures supplementally provided for the financial sector.
Source: TCFD (2017).

attention of the European Parliament and the European Commission on environmental and sustainability issues is expressed through their legislative activities, transposed into directives and regulations. Also, the guidelines are an important piece of the European institutions' activity. Table 2 reports the main regulations in Europe.

The starting point is the NFRD DIR 2014/95 (NFDR, 2014), the most important legislation at the European level. The directive is transposed into the national legislations, and has been applicable since the fiscal year 2017. The NFRD introduced new disclosure requirements for large firms, which are public-interest entities (including banks and insurance companies). Specifically, in their management report, these firms should include an NFS containing information on non-financial matters (environmental, social, and employee matters, human rights, bribery, and corruption). The objective of the NFRD is to improve the quality and quantity of corporate non-financial information reporting. In April 2021, the EC

Table 2. Regulatory framework on non-financial disclosure in Europe.

Year	Regulation	Description
2014	Non-financial Reporting Directive (Directive 2014/95) (NFRD, 2014)	Large undertakings which are public-interest entities exceeding on their balance sheet dates the criterion of the average number of 500 employees during the financial year shall include in the management report a non-financial statement containing information to the extent necessary for an understanding of the undertaking's development, performance, position, and impact of its activity, relating to, as a minimum, environmental, social and employee matters, respect for human rights, anti-corruption, and bribery matters.
2019	Sustainable Finance Disclosure Regulation (SFDR) (Regulation 2019/2088) (EP, 2019a)	Regulation (EU) 2019/2088 of The European Parliament and of The Council on sustainability-related disclosures in the financial services sector. Harmonized rules for financial market participants and financial advisers on transparency with regard to the integration of sustainability risks and the consideration of adverse sustainability impacts in their processes and the provision of sustainability-related information with respect to financial products.*
2019	Climate Benchmarks Regulation (Regulation 2019/2089) (EP, 2019b)	Regulation (EU) 2019/2089 of The European Parliament and of The Council amending Regulation (EU) 2016/1011 as regards EU Climate Transition Benchmarks, EU Paris-aligned Benchmarks and sustainability-related disclosures for benchmarks.
2020	Taxonomy regulation (Regulation 2020/852) (EP, 2020)	Regulation (EU) 2020/852 of The European Parliament and of The Council. Establishment of a framework to facilitate sustainable investment, and amending Regulation (EU) 2019/2088.
2021	Proposal for a Corporate Sustainability Reporting Directive (CSRD) (EC, 2021)	Proposal for a Directive amending Directive 2013/34/EU, Directive 2004/109/EC, Directive 2006/43/EC, and Regulation (EU) No 537/2014, as regards corporate sustainability reporting.

Notes: *Regulation 2019/2088 requires financial market participants and financial advisers who provide investment advice or insurance advice to provide sustainability-related disclosures to end investors. This regulation aims to reduce information asymmetries in principal–agent relationships with regard to the integration of sustainability risks, the consideration of adverse sustainability impacts, the promotion of environmental or social characteristics, and sustainable investment by requiring financial market participants and financial advisers to make pre-contractual and ongoing disclosures to end investors when they act as agents of those end investors (principals) (EP, 2019a). Two disclosures are required: a pre-contractual and an ongoing disclosure (on websites and in periodic reports).

(2021) adopted a proposal for the CSRD, which would amend the NFRD. The proposal extends the scope to all large and listed companies (except listed micro-enterprises), requires the audit of reported information, and requires companies to "tag" the reported information digitally so that it is machine readable and feeds into the European single-access point envisaged in the capital markets union action plan. The proposal introduces more detailed reporting requirements and a mandate to report according to EU sustainability reporting standards. The draft standards would be developed by the EFRAG (2021). The first set of standards would be adopted by October 2022. (https://ec.europa.eu/info/business-economy-euro/company-reporting-and-auditing/company-reporting/corporate-sustainability-reporting_en).

In 2019, the so-called sustainable finance disclosure regulation, or SFDR (Regulation 2019/2088), on sustainability-related disclosures in the financial services, required financial market participants and financial advisers that provide investment or insurance advice to provide sustainability-related disclosures to end investors (EP, 2019). This regulation aims to reduce information asymmetries in principal–agent relationships with regard to the integration of sustainability risks, the consideration of adverse sustainability impacts, the promotion of environmental or social characteristics, and sustainable investment by requiring financial market participants and financial advisers to make pre-contractual and ongoing disclosures to end investors when they act as agents of those end investors (principals) (EP, 2019a). Two disclosures are required: a pre-contractual and an ongoing disclosure (on websites and in periodic reports). To understand the more general framework, this regulation needs to be read together with the following two supplemental regulations: the taxonomy of environmentally sustainable investments (Regulation 2020/852) (EP, 2020) and the climate benchmarks (Regulation 2019/2089) (EP, 2019b).

In 2017, the EC published the guidelines on non-financial reporting (methodology for reporting non-financial information) (2017/C 215/01) (EC, 2017) to help companies that fall under the scope of the NFRD disclose environmental and social information. The EC suggested that they could represent best practices for all companies that disclose non-financial information.[3] Companies are encouraged and guided to disclose high-quality, important, useful, consistent, and more comparable non-financial (environmental, social, and governance-related) information in a way that fosters resilient and sustainable growth and employment and provides transparency to stakeholders. Moreover, the information is provided to avoid undue administrative burden, boilerplate disclosures, or a mere box-ticking exercise.

In March 2018, the EC published the Action Plan on Financing Sustainable Growth (EC, 2018), moving the focus to finance and its role. In June 2019, the EC provided guidelines on reporting climate-related information (EC, 2019), which supplemented the 2017 guidelines. These non-binding guidelines are part of the action plan. The same guidelines highlight the importance of climate-related risk disclosures related to the possibility of reducing information asymmetries in principal–agent relationships. Focusing on climate-related information, the EC (2019) stated that better disclosure can have the following benefits for the reporting company itself: improvement in management and strategic planning due to the increased awareness and understanding of climate-related risks and opportunities within the company; a more diverse investor base and a potentially lower cost of capital due to several reasons, such as inclusion in sustainability-focused indices or improved credit ratings; a more constructive dialogue with stakeholders (in particular, investors and shareholders); an improvement in reputation and maintenance of a social license to operate.

In Annex I, further guidance for banks and insurance companies is provided, given their special business activities. These guidelines are used to develop our empirical analysis. We argue that they represent best practices and can be considered a reference framework for all companies wishing to develop effective disclosure on climate risks.

[3]Article 2 of the NFRD refers to "guidance on reporting" and sets out that "the Commission shall prepare non-binding guidelines on methodology for reporting non-financial information, including non-financial KPIs, general and sectoral, with a view to facilitating relevant, useful, and comparable disclosure of non-financial information by undertakings".

We use them to construct the disclosure index (DI) employed in the current analysis aimed at assessing the level of environmental disclosure in European insurance companies.

5. Empirical Strategy

To date, little empirical analysis has been directed specifically at the insurance sector. Therefore, this chapter is intended as an explorative study aimed at understanding the level and quality of environmental disclosure in insurance companies. We argue that the description of the state of the art of climate disclosure in this sector is the basis for a better interpretation of the insurers' attitudes regarding climate issues and for the design of the strategy to be adopted by the regulators in terms of potential disclosure requirements.

The empirical strategy develops according to the following steps:

(1) *Sample selection*: We use the Insurance Focus Database to select a sample of insurance companies according to two criteria: (i) the location, that is, Europe 14 plus the United Kingdom (until 2020); (ii) the availability of public documents containing information on climate-related risks.

(2) *Construction of a DI on climate-related risks*: This index is developed using the disclosure framework provided by the EC guidelines on reporting climate-related information (EC, 2019). The guidelines constitute a complex document that contains a specific section providing the key performance indicators (KPIs) to be disclosed. Several KPIs are suggested and grouped into four information areas: GHG emissions, energy, physical risks, and green finance. The provision of these indicators is recommended to companies with the aim of increasing the comparability of the non-financial information they communicate. In detail, we employ the KPIs included in Annex I "Further guidance for banks and insurance companies" of the guidelines (EC, 2019). Taken as a whole, these KPIs contribute to outlining a (minimum) standard framework, toward which the perspectives of the companies should move. In this chapter, these indicators are the items/information used to construct the DI.

(3) *Disclosure assessment*: For each insurance company included in the sample, we assess the level of disclosure using a manual content analysis and by measuring the degree of compliance with our DI. The data on the level of disclosure are collected either from the NFSs included in the management report (thus, in the annual report) or from a separate report (such as sustainability reports, CSR reports, or similar). These two types of documents are taken into consideration (if written in English or Italian) for 2016–2020. The measurement of the disclosure takes place in a binary way: If the information/item envisaged by the index is contained in the document, the value 1 is attributed; if the KPIs are not provided, the value 0 is attributed.

(4) *Rating index (RI) on the disclosure of climate-related risks*: An overall RI is proposed by using a statistical multivariate analysis strategy. Specifically, we employ principal component analysis (PCA), performed on our disclosure sub-indices — those derived from the four information areas in which the KPIs are grouped — by considering only 2020.

6. Disclosure Assessment: A Climate-Related Disclosure Index

Before discussing the RI obtained using the statistical multivariate analysis strategy, in this section, we offer a descriptive statistical analysis of climate-related disclosure provided by the sample companies. The initial sample includes 329 European insurers, that is, all the active insurance companies from 2016 to 2020. Subsequently, the screening of the sample firms is conducted based on the data availability. The companies for which public documents/reports containing climate information could not be found or those provided in a language other than Italian or English are excluded. The final sample is composed of 43 companies (see Appendix A). The countries analyzed are: the UK, France, the Netherlands, Luxembourg, Sweden, Denmark, Finland, Germany, and Spain. Of the companies, 46.5 percent come from the UK and 11.6 percent come from Germany (Figure 4).

To meet the expectations of the EU guidelines, the companies should communicate the indicators and targets used to assess

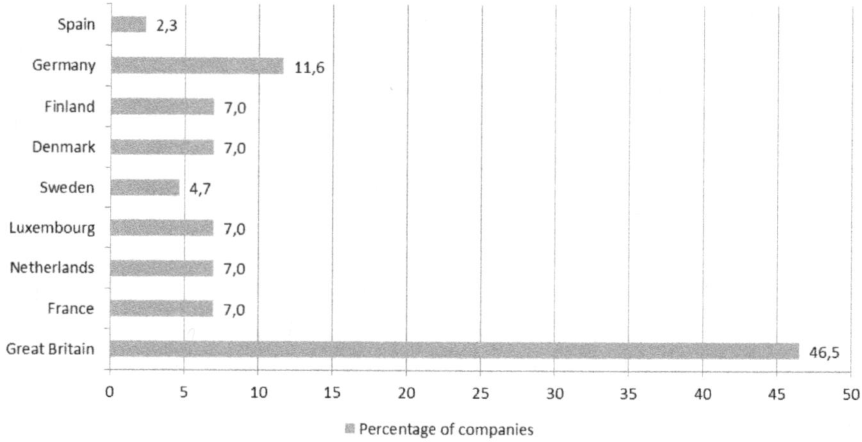

Figure 4. Percentage of companies by countries.

climate-related risks and opportunities in accordance with the company strategy and its risk management processes. Therefore, insurance companies should communicate the KPIs grouped into the following information areas: GHG emissions, energy, insurance underwriting activity, and green finance (Table 3).

For each company and for each information area, we calculate the proportion of positive answers on the total of items (sum of 1 on the total) 2016–2020.

In 2016, we observe that several companies present a low value of DI in all four areas (Figure 5). This is important because several companies do not disclose the information at all. We also note the absence of data for some companies.

After four years (Figure 6), the situation changes: There is a greater propensity to disclose information relating to all four information areas of the DI.

Figure 7 shows the results of the DI by country in 2020. Several companies in the UK did not disclose information in the green finance area. On the contrary, in Sweden, a greater propensity to disclose is registered, even though only two companies are included in the sample.

The analysis carried out so far has some obvious limitations, mainly linked to the limited availability of data. Another criticality derives from the way in which the information was collected and

Table 3. Key performance indicators (KPIs) grouped into four information areas.

Greenhouse gas emissions	Direct GHG emissions; indirect GHG emissions from the production of acquired and consumed electricity, steam, heat or cold; all other indirect GHG emissions generated in the company's value chain which carries out the communication; and objectives in terms of absolute GHG emissions.
Energy	Consumption and/or production total energy from sources renewable and non-renewable; relative objective to efficiency energy; target of consumption and/or production of renewable energy.
Insurance underwriting activity	Breakdown of the exposure insurance toward the economic sectors by line of business; percentage of products they include climate-related risks in the process insurance relating to contracts individual; number and value of products climate-related insurance offered; maximum expected loss due to natural disasters caused by climate change; total losses attributable to insurance claims for expected natural disasters and unexpected natural disasters by type of event and geographical segment.
Green finance	Green bond ratio; green debt ratio.

is therefore linked to the construction of the DI. It is, therefore, an index obtained from the combination of four sub-indices, which, however, express qualitatively very different types of information. It is thus a question of being able to obtain synthetic information, that is, an information index with a better information capacity from a qualitative point of view. This must find a solution from a technical and quantitative point of view. There are many variables in our dataset — the four sub-indices — that could be related to each other. Our problem consists in creating a synthetic index capable of expressing a more relevant information power. A simple solution could be to create an index obtained from the average of the four sub-indices for each firm in the sample. However, an average would not make economic sense. The PCA used in the following section is a statistical technique that lends itself to solving the above problem as it allows the number of variables to be reduced, thereby losing the least amount of information possible.

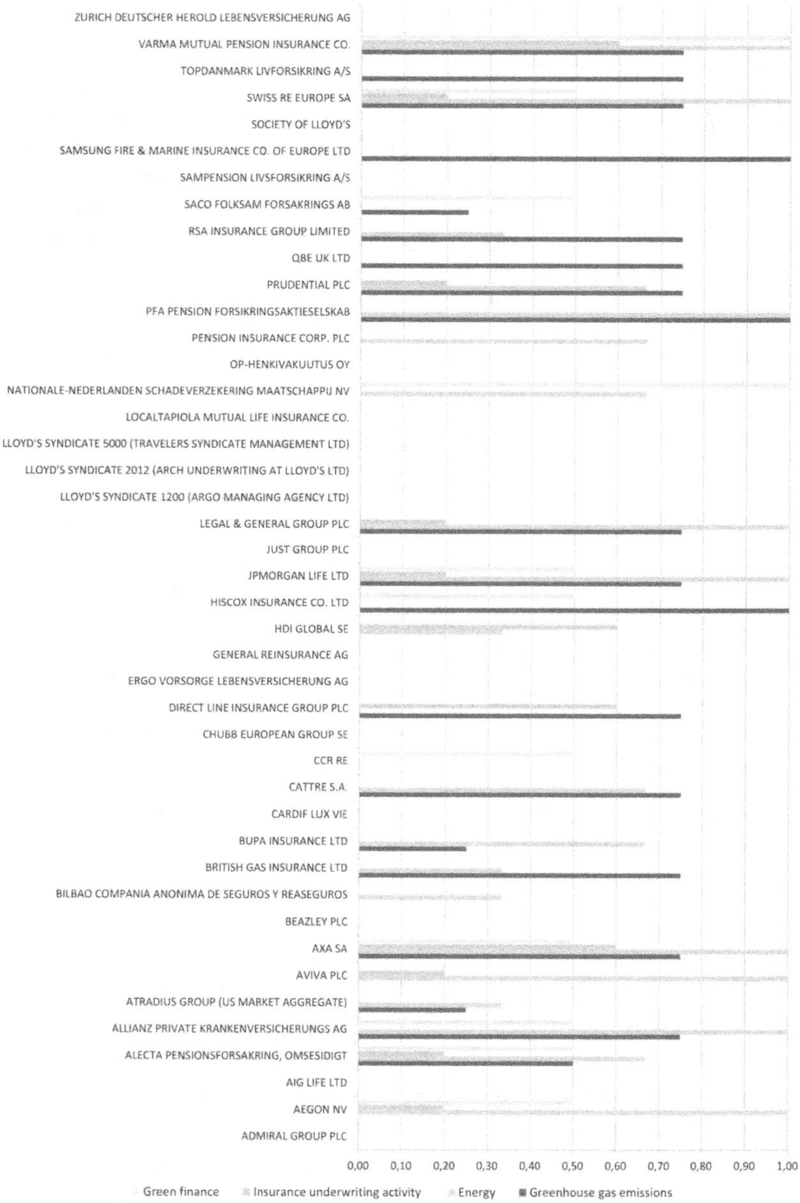

Figure 5. Disclosure index of four information areas: Greenhouse gas emissions, energy, insurance underwriting activity, and green finance, 2016.

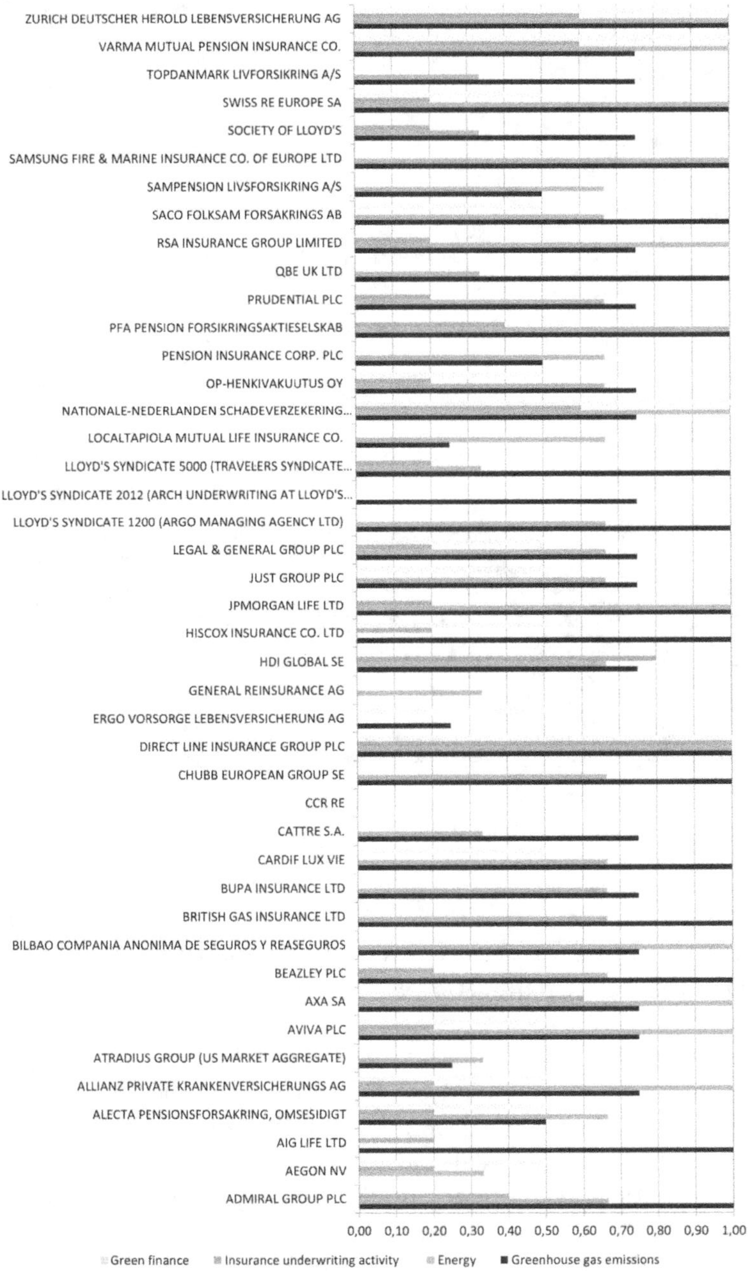

Figure 6. Disclosure index of four information areas: Greenhouse gas emissions, energy, insurance underwriting activity, and green finance, 2020.

Countries	Companies	Greenhouse gas emissions	Energy	Insurance underwriting activity	Green finance
Great Britain	ADMIRAL GROUP PLC	1,00	0,67	0,40	0,00
	AIG LIFE LTD	1,00	0,00	0,20	0,00
	AVIVA PLC	0,75	1,00	0,20	0,50
	BEAZLEY PLC	1,00	0,67	0,20	0,00
	BRITISH GAS INSURANCE LTD	1,00	0,67	0,00	0,00
	BUPA INSURANCE LTD	0,75	0,67	0,00	0,00
	DIRECT LINE INSURANCE GROUP PLC	1,00	1,00	1,00	1,00
	HISCOX INSURANCE CO. LTD	1,00	0,00	0,20	0,50
	JPMORGAN LIFE LTD	1,00	1,00	0,20	0,00
	JUST GROUP PLC	0,75	0,67	0,00	0,50
	LEGAL & GENERAL GROUP PLC	0,75	0,67	0,20	0,50
	LLOYD'S SYNDICATE 1200 (ARGO MANAGING AGENCY LTD)	1,00	0,67	0,00	0,00
	LLOYD'S SYNDICATE 2012 (ARCH UNDERWRITING AT LLOYD'S LTD)	0,75	0,00	0,00	0,00
	LLOYD'S SYNDICATE 5000 (TRAVELERS SYNDICATE MANAGEMENT LTD)	1,00	0,33	0,20	0,00
	PENSION INSURANCE CORP. PLC	0,50	0,67	0,00	0,00
	PRUDENTIAL PLC	0,75	0,67	0,20	0,00
	QBE UK LTD	1,00	0,33	0,00	0,00
	RSA INSURANCE GROUP LIMITED	0,75	1,00	0,20	0,00
	SAMSUNG FIRE & MARINE INSURANCE CO. OF EUROPE LTD	1,00	1,00	0,00	0,00
	SOCIETY OF LLOYD'S	0,75	0,33	0,20	0,00
France	AXA SA	0,75	1,00	0,60	0,50
	CHUBB EUROPEAN GROUP SE	1,00	0,67	0,00	0,00
	CCR RE	0,00	0,00	0,00	0,00
Netherlands	AEGON NV	0,00	0,33	0,20	0,50
	ATRADIUS GROUP (US MARKET AGGREGATE)	0,25	0,33	0,00	0,00
	NATIONALE-NEDERLANDEN SCHADEVERZEKERING MAATSCHAPPIJ NV	0,75	1,00	0,60	1,00
Luxembourg	CARDIF LUX VIE	1,00	0,67	0,00	0,50
	CATTRE S.A	0,75	0,33	0,00	0,00
	SWISS RE EUROPE SA	1,00	1,00	0,20	0,50
Sweden	ALECTA PENSIONSFORSAKRING, OMSESIDIGT	0,50	0,67	0,20	0,50
	SACO FOLKSAM FORSAKRINGS AB	1,00	0,67	0,00	0,50
Denmark	PFA PENSION FORSIKRINGSAKTIESELSKAB	1,00	1,00	0,40	0,00
	SAMPENSION LIVSFORSIKRING A/S	0,50	0,67	0,00	0,00
	TOPDANMARK LIVFORSIKRING A/S	0,75	0,33	0,00	0,00
Finland	LOCALTAPIOLA MUTUAL LIFE INSURANCE CO.	0,25	0,67	0,00	0,00
	OP-HENKIVAKUUTUS OY	0,75	0,67	0,20	0,50
	VARMA MUTUAL PENSION INSURANCE CO.	0,75	1,00	0,60	1,00
Germany	ALLIANZ PRIVATE KRANKENVERSICHERUNGS AG	0,75	1,00	0,20	0,50
	ERGO VORSORGE LEBENSVERSICHERUNG AG	0,25	0,00	0,00	0,50
	GENERAL REINSURANCE AG	0,00	0,33	0,00	0,00
	HDI GLOBAL SE	0,75	0,67	0,80	0,00
	ZURICH DEUTSCHER HEROLD LEBENSVERSICHERUNG AG	1,00	1,00	0,60	1,00
Spain	BILBAO COMPANIA ANONIMA DE SEGUROS Y REASEGUROS	0,75	1,00	0,00	0,00

Figure 7. Disclosure index of four information areas: Greenhouse gas emissions, energy, insurance underwriting activity, and green finance by countries, 2020.

7. Synthesis of Information: A Composite Disclosure Rating Index

The descriptive analysis allows some characteristics of the four information areas to be highlighted according to which the KPIs are grouped, while also focusing on the different countries. In this section, we obtain an overall disclosure RI by using PCA. This multivariate statistical technique (Jolliffe, 1986) permits the analysis of a database in which the observations are described by several inter-correlated quantitative dependent variables. Its goal is to extract the important information from the database to represent it as a set of new orthogonal variables, called principal components (PCs), and to display the pattern of similarity between the observations and variables as points on maps. The multivariate statistical technique permits the most important information content (variance) to be summarized in a database by means of a smaller set of summary indices called PCs, which can be more easily visualized and analyzed.

In our study, PCA is performed on four disclosure index data by considering 2020 only. The choice of year was constrained by the availability of data during the observation period of the phenomenon. First, we observe the correlation matrix and the explained variance (Table 4).

The correlation between the disclosure insurance underwriting activity index and the disclosure green finance index is quite high (about 0.6).

The PCA shows the existence of four factors, and in particular, the first two components explain about 74 percent of the total variability (Table 5).

Furthermore, Table 6 explains the weights of each DI, which allows us to define each component extracted.

Table 4. Correlation matrix.

	Discl._GES	**Discl._E**	**Discl._IUA**	**Disc._GF**
Discl._GES	1.00	0.21	0.19	0.07
Discl._E		1.00	0.40	0.38
Discl._IUA			1.00	0.58
Disc._GF				1.00

Table 5. Explained variance table.

Components	**Total**	**Percentage of variance**	**Percentage cumulative**
1	1.99	49.82	49.82
2	0.96	24.06	73.88
3	0.64	16.05	89.93
4	0.40	10.06	100

Table 6. Weight's principal components.

Disclosure index	Components 1	2	3	4
Discl._GES	0.37	0.90	0.20	0.09
Discl._E	0.72	0.09	−0.68	−0.01
Discl._IUA	0.83	−0.14	0.29	−0.44
Disc._GF	0.79	−0.34	0.22	0.43

The first two components explain 74 percent (cumulative variance) of information, and we observe that the first is mostly dominated by the disclosure insurance underwriting activity index, green finance, and energy index. The second, in contrast, is heavily and positively dominated by the DI GES.

Figure 8 presents the first two PCs of our sample. Positive scores on both PCs characterize firms that make disclosures on all four dimensions. Positive scores on the first PC and negative scores on the second PC characterize firms that do not make disclosure on the GES dimension, while the reverse order (negative score on the first PC and positive score on the second PC) characterizes firms that make disclosure on the GES dimension but not the other indicators. We can see from Figure 8 that in our sample, firms that do not make disclosure on all four dimensions are also present.

Figure 9 shows in detail which companies are characterized by the first PC: with a negative score, that is, they do not disclose about insurance activity, energy, and green finance, and with a positive score, that is, they disclose the same indicators. In Figure 10, we explain the companies characterized by the second PC: with a negative score, that is, they do not disclose GES, and with a positive score, that is, they disclose the same indicator.

Finally, through a statistical multivariate analysis, we construct an overall RI of climate-related risks for the sample insurers. We observe the profile of the companies using this index to classify them in order to disclose about climate. This is an interesting result that helps confirm the (right) effort of the regulators whose attention toward the information offered by financial institutions (such as banks and insurance companies) has grown over the years.

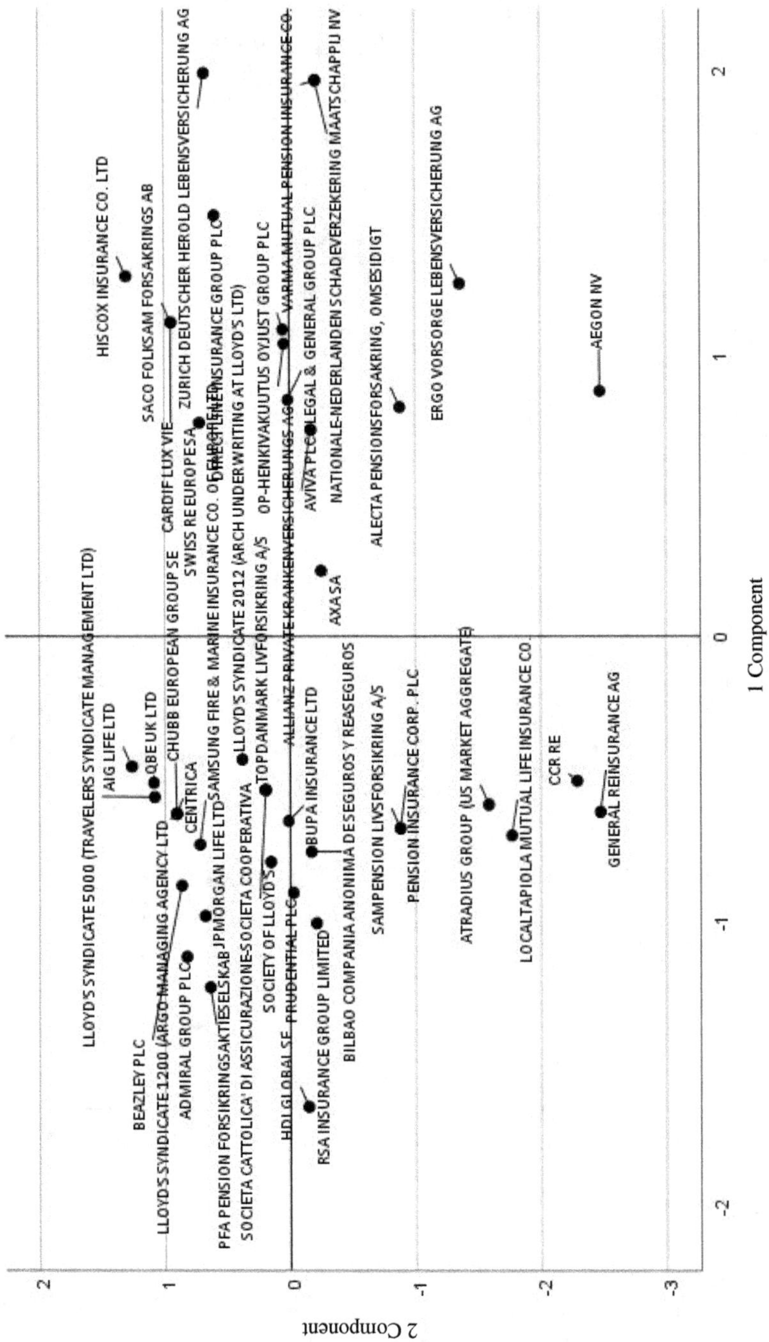

Figure 8. The two principal components by disclosure index.

Insurance activity & Energy & Green finance	
Companies don't disclose	*Companies disclose*
ADMIRAL GROUP PLC	AEGON NV
AIG LIFE LTD	ALECTA PENSIONSFORSAKRING, OMSESIDIGT
ATRADIUS GROUP (US MARKET AGGREGATE)	ALLIANZ PRIVATE KRANKENVERSICHERUNGS AG
BEAZLEY PLC	AVIVA PLC
BILBAO COMPANIA ANONIMA DE SEGUROS Y REASEGUROS	AXA SA
BUPA INSURANCE LTD	CARDIF LUX VIE
CCR RE	DIRECT LINE INSURANCE GROUP PLC
CENTRICA	ERGO VORSORGE LEBENSVERSICHERUNG AG
CHUBB EUROPEAN GROUP SE	HISCOX INSURANCE CO. LTD
GENERAL REINSURANCE AG	JUST GROUP PLC
HDI GLOBAL SE	LEGAL & GENERAL GROUP PLC
JPMORGAN LIFE LTD	NATIONALE-NEDERLANDEN SCHADEVERZEKERING MAATSCHAPPIJ NV
LLOYD'S SYNDICATE 1200 (ARGO MANAGING AGENCY LTD)	OP-HENKIVAKUUTUS OY
LLOYD'S SYNDICATE 2012 (ARCH UNDERWRITING AT LLOYD'S LTD)	SACO FOLKSAM FORSAKRINGS AB
LLOYD'S SYNDICATE 5000 (TRAVELERS SYNDICATE MANAGEMENT LTD)	SWISS RE EUROPE SA
LOCALTAPIOLA MUTUAL LIFE INSURANCE CO.	VARMA MUTUAL PENSION INSURANCE CO.
PENSION INSURANCE CORP. PLC	ZURICH DEUTSCHER HEROLD LEBENSVERSICHERUNG AG
PFA PENSION FORSIKRINGSAKTIESELSKAB	
PRUDENTIAL PLC	
QBE UK LTD	
RSA INSURANCE GROUP LIMITED	
SAMPENSION LIVSFORSIKRING A/S	
SAMSUNG FIRE & MARINE INSURANCE CO. OF EUROPE LTD	
SOCIETA CATTOLICA' DI ASSICURAZIONE-SOCIETA COOPERATIVA	
SOCIETY OF LLOYD'S	
TOPDANMARK LIVFORSIKRING A/S	

Figure 9. Companies by first component with negative and positive scores.

GES disclosure index	
Companies don't disclose	*Companies disclose*
AEGON NV	ADMIRAL GROUP PLC
ALECTA PENSIONSFORSAKRING, OMSESIDIGT	AIG LIFE LTD
ALLIANZ PRIVATE KRANKENVERSICHERUNGS AG	BEAZLEY PLC
ATRADIUS GROUP (US MARKET AGGREGATE)	BUPA INSURANCE LTD
AVIVA PLC	CARDIF LUX VIE
AXA SA	CENTRICA
BILBAO COMPANIA ANONIMA DE SEGUROSY REASEGUROS	CHUBB EUROPEAN GROUP SE
CCR RE	DIRECT LINE INSURANCE GROUP PLC
ERGO VORSORGE LEBENSVERSICHERUNG AG	HISCOX INSURANCE CO. LTD
GENERAL REINSURANCE AG	JPMORGAN LIFE LTD
HDI GLOBAL SE	JUST GROUP PLC
LOCALTAPIOLA MUTUAL LIFE INSURANCE CO.	LEGAL & GENERAL GROUP PLC
NATIONALE-NEDERLANDEN SCHADEVERZEKERING MAATSCHAPPIJ NV	LLOYD'S SYNDICATE 1200 (ARGO MANAGING AGENCY LTD)
PENSION INSURANCE CORP. PLC	LLOYD'S SYNDICATE 2012 (ARCH UNDERWRITING AT LLOYD'S LTD)
PRUDENTIAL PLC	LLOYD'S SYNDICATE 5000 (TRAVELERS SYNDICATE MANAGEMENT LTD)
RSA INSURANCE GROUP LIMITED	OP-HENKIVAKUUTUS OY
SAMPENSION LIVSFORSIKRING A/S	PFA PENSION FORSIKRINGSAKTIESELSKAB
VARMA MUTUAL PENSION INSURANCE CO.	QBE UK LTD
	SACO FOLKSAM FORSAKRINGS AB
	SAMSUNG FIRE & MARINE INSURANCE CO. OF EUROPE LTD
	SOCIETA CATTOLICA' DI ASSICURAZIONE-SOCIETA COOPERATIVA
	SOCIETY OF LLOYD'S
	SWISS RE EUROPE SA
	TOPDANMARK LIVFORSIKRING A/S
	ZURICH DEUTSCHER HEROLD LEBENSVERSICHERUNG AG

Figure 10. Companies by second component with negative and positive scores.

8. Conclusion

In this chapter, we studied climate-related risk disclosures in the European insurance sector. The research opportunity arises both from the publication of the guidelines on the disclosure of climate issues and environmental risks in 2019 and from the introduction in the near future of new standard requirements for non-financial disclosure. We investigate the level of disclosure in the European insurance sector and the type of information provided.

An original strategy is employed, according to which the analysis is developed in three stages. First, a new DI is constructed based on the KPIs provided by the EU guidelines. These KPIs are grouped into four information areas (each constituting a kind of subindex): greenhouse gas emissions, energy, insurance underwriting activity, and green finance. Second, the DI is used to assess the level of climate-related risks disclosure in the sample insurance companies. Finally, an RI is constructed (using PCA) to summarize the most important information content. This synthetic index possess a greater information power as it extracts new (informative) components. The RI adds value to the analysis because it permits the classification of the insurance companies, while also considering the type of information disclosed.

Forty-three insurance companies (mainly from the UK and Germany) are explored over the 2016–2020 period. Overall, at the beginning of the analysis period (2016), the sample companies present a very low value of DI. After four years (2020), the propensity to disclose information relating to all the four information areas in which the KPIs are grouped increases.

Finally, PCA for the year 2020 shows that the first two components explain 74 percent (cumulative variance) of information: The first is mostly dominated by the disclosure insurance underwriting activity index, green finance, and energy index. The second, in contrast, is heavily and positively dominated by the disclosure index GES.

Overall, the results suggest that the level of disclosure differs among European countries, and it tends to increase over time. However, the situation appears jeopardized with reference to the four information areas investigated.

Appendix A: Sample of Insurance Companies

Admiral Group Plc
Aegon Nv
Aig Life Ltd
Alecta Pensionsforsakring, Omsesidigt
Allianz Private Krankenversicherungs Ag
Atradius Group (Us Market Aggregate)
Aviva Plc
Axa Sa
Beazley Plc
Bilbao Compania Anonima De Seguros Y Reaseguros
Bupa Insurance Ltd
Cardif Lux Vie
Ccr Re
Centrica
Chubb European Group Se
Direct Line Insurance Group Plc
Ergo Vorsorge Lebensversicherung Ag
General Reinsurance Ag
Hdi Global Se
Hiscox Insurance Co. Ltd
Jpmorgan Life Ltd
Just Group Plc
Legal & General Group Plc
Lloyd's Syndicate 1200 (Argo Managing Agency Ltd)
Lloyd's Syndicate 2012 (Arch Underwriting At Lloyd's Ltd)
Lloyd's Syndicate 5000 (Travelers Syndicate Management Ltd)
Localtapiola Mutual Life Insurance Co.
Nationale-Nederlanden Schadeverzekering Maatschappij Nv

Op-Henkivakuutus Oy
Pension Insurance Corp. Plc
Pfa Pension Forsikringsaktieselskab
Prudential Plc
Qbe Uk Ltd
Rsa Insurance Group Limited
Saco Folksam Forsakrings Ab
Sampension Livsforsikring A/S
Samsung Fire & Marine Insurance Co. of Europe Ltd
Società Cattolica di Assicurazione-Società Cooperativa
Society of Lloyd's
Swiss Re Europe Sa
Topdanmark Livforsikring A/S
Varma Mutual Pension Insurance Co.
Zurich Deutscher Herold Lebensversicherung Ag

References

Campbell, J. L. (2007). Why would corporations behave in socially responsible ways? An institutional theory of corporate social responsibility. *Academy of Management Review*, *32*(3), 946–967.

Carbone S., Giuzio, M., & Mikkonen, K. (2019). Climate risk-related disclosures of banks and insurers and their market impact. *Financial Stability Review*, ECB, November 2019, pp. 64–67.

Clarkson, M. B. E. (1995). A stakeholder framework for analyzing and evaluating corporate social performance. *Academy of Management Review*, *20*(1), 92–117.

Cormier, D., Magnan, M., & Van Velthoven, B. (2005). Environmental disclosure quality in large German companies: Economic incentives, public pressures or institutional conditions? *European Accounting Review*, *14*(1), 3–39.

Dye, R. A. (1985). Disclosure of non-proprietary information. *Journal of Accounting Research*, *23*(1), 123–145, Spring.

EC-European Commission (2017). Guidelines on non-financial reporting (methodology for reporting non-financial information), Information from European Union Institutions, Bodies, Offices and Agencies, Communication from the Commission (2017/C 215/01).

EC-European Commission (2018). Action Plan: Financing Sustainable Growth, Communication from the Commission to the European Parliament, the European Council, the Council, the European Central Bank, the European Economic and Social Committee and the Committee of the Regions, Com(2018) 97 Final, Brussels, 8.3.2018

EC-European Commission (2019). Guidelines on reporting climate-related information Information from European Union Institutions, Bodies, Offices and Agencies, Communication from the Commission, (2019/C 209/01) EC-European Commission (2021). Proposal for a Directive of the European Parliament and of the Council Amending Directive 2013/34/EU, Directive 2004/109/EC, Directive 2006/43/EC and Regulation (EU) No 537/2014, as regards corporate sustainability reporting, Brussels, 21.4.2021 Com(2021), 189 final, 2021/0104 (COD).

EC-European Commission (2021). Proposal for a directive amending Directive 2013/34/EU, Directive 2004/109/EC, Directive 2006/43/EC and regulation (EU) No. 537/2014, as regards corporate sustainability reporting.

EFRAG-European Financial Reporting Advisory Group (2021). Proposals for a Relevant and Dynamic Eu Sustainability Reporting Standard setting, *Final Report*, February, pp. 1–228.

EP-European Parliament (2019a). Regulation (Eu) 2019/2088 of the European Parliament and of the Council of 27 November 2019 on Sustainability-related Disclosures in the Financial Services Sector.

EP-European Parliament (2019b). Regulation (EU) 2019/2089 of the European Parliament and of the Council of 27 November 2019 Amending Regulation (EU) 2016/1011 as Regards EU Climate Transition Benchmarks, EU Paris-aligned Benchmarks and sustainability-related disclosures for benchmarks.

EP-European Parliament (2020). Regulation (EU) 2020/852 of the European Parliament and of the Council of 18 June 2020 on the Establishment of a Framework to Facilitate Sustainable Investment, and Amending Regulation (EU) 2019/2088.

Gray, R., Kouhy, R., & Lavers, S. (1995). Corporate social and environmental reporting. A review of the literature and a longitudinal study of UK disclosure. *Accounting, Auditing and Accountability Journal, 8*(2), 47–77.

Hooghiemstra, R. (2000). Corporate communication and impression management — New perspectives why companies engage in corporate social reporting. *Journal of Business Ethics, 27*(1–2), 55–68.

Jakubik, P. & Uguz, S. (2021). Impact of green bond policies on insurers: Evidence from the European equity market. *Journal of Economics and Finance*, *45*, 381–393.

Jolliffe, I. T. (1986). *Principal Component Analysis.* New York: Springer-Verlag.

Li, Y., Richardson, G. D., & Thornton, D. (1997). Corporate disclosure of environmental information: Theory and evidence. *Contemporary Accounting Research*, *14*(3), 435–474.

Maignan, I. and Ralston, D. A. (2002). Corporate social responsibility in Europe and the U.S.: Insights from businesses' self-presentations. *Journal of International Business Studies*, *33*(3), 497–514.

Non-Financial Reporting Directive (NFRD) (2014). Directive 2014/95/Eu of The European Parliament and of the Council of 22 October 2014 (amending Directive 2013/34/EU as regards disclosure of non-financial and diversity information by certain large undertakings and groups).

Network for Greening Financial System (NGFS) (2020a, September). *Overview of Environmental Risk Analysis by Financial Institutions.* Technical document (available at https://www.ngfs.net/sites/default/files/medias/documents/overview_of_environmental_risk_analysis_by_financial_institutions.pdf).

Network for Greening the Financial System (NGFS) (2020b, May). Guide for Supervisors — Integrating climate-related and environmental risks into prudential supervision. Technical document (available at https://www.ngfs.net/sites/default/files/medias/documents/ngfs_guide_for_supervisors.pdf).

RepRisk (2020). Overview of ESG rating, data providers and applications in NGFS — Network for greening the financial system. Case Studies of Environmental Risk Analysis Methodologies, Occasional Paper.

Task Force on Climate-related Financial Disclosure (TCFD) (2017). Recommendations of the Task Force on Climate-related Financial Disclosure, Final Report.

Verrecchia, R. E. (1983). Discretionary disclosure. *Journal of Accounting and Economics*, *5*, 179–194.

World Resources Institute and World Business Council for Sustainable Development (2004, March). The greenhouse gas protocol: A corporate accounting and reporting standard, (Revised Edition). Retrieved from www.ghgprotocol.org/standards/corporate-standard.

https://doi.org/10.1142/9781800614482_0009

Chapter 9

The Relevance of Environmental, Social, and Governance Issues in Corporate Valuation: Concepts and Reflections

Murad Harasheh[*,†] **and Giovanni Cardillo**[‡]
Department of Management, University of Bologna, Italy
[†]*murad.harasheh@unibo.it*
[‡]*giovanni.cardillo2@unibo.it*

Abstract

In this chapter, we present the theoretical value relevance of sustainability and ESG[1] performance from a finance and investment point of view. The central concept is to figure out how ESG performance could be used as value-relevant information for financial markets, and through what channels ESG could create value for companies and financial market investors. We also show the interaction between the real economy and financial markets through a preferences shift. We discuss the idiosyncratic and systematic channels through which the ESG effect could be transmitted to value. Furthermore, we show the ESG cash flow drivers that potentially impact value and the systematic risk drivers through financial markets that affect the cost of capital and value. Finally, we establish a framework for discounted cash flow, incorporating the real and financial sides of the economy, influencing the potential value effects from ESG.

*Corresponding author.

[1]ESG stands for environmental, social, and governance. The terms ESG and sustainability are used interchageably in this context.

1. Introduction

There has been mounting interest in ESG issues and their implications on businesses, markets, finance, and investment activities. It is not uncommon, at this stage, that empirical studies provide no conclusive (or even confusing) evidence on the implications of integrating ESG and sustainability issues into the finance and investment world. Theoretically, business sustainability performance is mirrored by the adequacy of corporate reporting. However, there is still no standard framework for corporate sustainability reporting (integrated or non-financial reporting), which makes it challenging to verify the accuracy of such reporting, thus compromising the assurances provided by third parties. In this regard, stakeholders, including financial industry insiders, have expressed concern of "greenwashing" which is related to suspicious ESG disclosures that leads to ESG scandals employing deceptive marketing practices. Misleading information creates confusion, especially among retail/uninformed investors, and markets cannot distinguish between good and bad ESG performers. On the other hand, traditional financial reporting is well established, and assurance is guaranteed by internal (audit committee) and external (external auditors, financial analysts, and public authorities) parties. Furthermore, corporate reporting aims to provide adequate disclosure that improves the informational efficiency among market players, thus reducing speculative actions and confusion.

1.1. *Related literature*

Several academic studies and practitioners' reports highlight that the implementation of ESG policies is associated with better corporate financial performance, measured with backward- and forward-looking variables (Albuquerque *et al.*, 2020; Buchanan & Marques, 2018; Servaes & Tamayo, 2013; Yadav *et al.*, 2017). Several theories support this positive relationship (Tensie *et al.*, 2021):

- *Stakeholder theory*: Firms with better performance can manage a wide range of social stakeholders more effectively through advanced and efficient risk management.
- *Shared value theory*: Well-performing firms create value for internal and external stakeholders, where external stakeholders are

those agents who are not directly involved in the principal firm's operations.

- *Conflict-resolution theory*: Firms' sustainability processes help firms augment the corporate financial performance through innovation and differentiation processes.
- *Legitimacy theory*: Firms, while existing, must comply with the values and norms of the society in which they are embedded.
- *Resource-based view*: Internal resources (e.g., employees and intangible assets) help firms gain a competitive advantage.

Although most papers postulate a positive correlation between ESG policy implementation and financial performance, the literature also provides mixed evidence. For instance, Brammer *et al.* (2006) find a negative relationship between a firm's ESG risk inclusion and performance, while Tensie *et al.* (2021) suggest that the relationship mentioned above might depend on the kind of firms investigated, for example, financial and non-financial firms. Finally, Bauer *et al.* (2005) and Renneboog *et al.* (2008) found no statistically significant relationship between firm sustainability and financial performance. In this context, the main argument in support of these pieces of evidence is the overinvestment theory (Barnea & Rubin, 2010), according to which corporate managers and large block holders might overinvest in CSR activities to extrapolate private benefits and improve their reputation as good global citizens (the warm-glow effect).

Based on these arguments, the relationship between firm sustainability performance is not clear *a priori*. It remains an empirical question since scholars have focused on specific constituent pillars of a firm's ESG performance (Koçak *et al.*, 2022), different empirical strategies, the agents and contexts of analysis, and sample periods. In this context, the COVID-19 pandemic severely affected financial markets, and the real economy brought about a new emphasis on the debate about the role of sustainability for the firm's performance considerations. Implementing ESG policies is often considered one of the main drivers of a firm's resilience to unexpected social and economic shocks (Albuquerque *et al.*, 2020). For instance, Ding *et al.* (2021) and Lee *et al.* (2022) find that firms with higher ESG scores fared better during the pandemic than firms with lower scores, experiencing milder drops in their stock prices. This might be evidence that ESG investing might provide downside protection during bad states of the economy (Tensie *et al.*, 2021), which is coherent with recent asset managers' practices prioritizing ESG risks in investment decisions (Wu & Juvyns, 2020).

Therefore, in this chapter, we present the theoretical value relevance of sustainability and ESG performance from a finance and investment point of view, referring to basic concepts and reflections. The central idea is to figure out how ESG performance could be value-relevant information to financial markets and through what channels ESG could create value for companies and financial market investors. In this regard, we discuss the idiosyncratic and systematic channels through which the ESG effect could be transmitted to value: the cash flow channel through enhanced reputation in the product (real) market and compliant strategy, and the risk channel through financial markets that affects the cost of capital and value. We establish a framework of discounted cash flow (DCF), incorporating the real and financial sides of the economy, influencing the potential value created from ESG.

Then, we discuss the financial markets and investment considerations regarding the emerging financial instruments and investment funds supporting the sustainability transition, e.g., responsible investments, green and social bonds, investment portfolios, and other ESG-related financial instruments. In this sense, financial markets could be creating new asset classes related to the sustainability transition. Now, from a classical financial and investment perspective, different asset classes are allocated on the capital market line (CML) according to their risks and returns (risk–return trade-off principle). Regarding the new sustainability-related asset classes, where can they be allocated on the CML? If they are riskier than the market average, they should be allocated on the upper right, but on the lower left if they are less risky. However, in this period of sustainability transition, it is still immature to judge this asset class in terms of the risk–return trade-off.

Subsequently, we introduce the concept of changing preferences, i.e., in the transition period, we witness a structural change in the preferences of consumers, producers (the real side of the economy), and investors (the financial side of the economy). Consumers are more responsible in their consumption, preferring more sustainable products; producers also change preferences by producing sustainably. Such changes are reflected on the financial side, where investors prefer to include more sustainable financial assets in their portfolios. This means that consumer preference curves and production frontiers are shifting inward and that the CML is rotating, making investors more risk-averse, i.e., consumers, producers, and investors are becoming more inclined to sustainable products regardless of their economic conditions.

Finally, we introduce the concept of environmental emergency, where we need to act urgently regardless of value creation (cost–benefit analysis) to achieve the determined sustainable goals.

The rest of the chapter is organized as follows. Section 2 introduces preliminary concepts and the evolution of sustainability and ESG concepts and reporting. Sections 3–6 deal with value relevance rationale, ESG financial instruments, transition and preferences shift, and valuation implications, respectively. Section 7 presents the conclusions.

2. Preliminary Concepts

We agree that there is no solid definition for "sustainability" — a term that has been used by scholars, regulators, policymakers, and market players, leading to confusion, different taxonomies, and inconsistent representations and frameworks. Perhaps, interested parties agree on the constituent pillars of sustainability: economic, social, and environmental aspects. However, there are no clear guidelines for evaluating the three pillars and whether they are equally important. In the same regard, the development and the integration of the sustainability concept into the business and financial worlds have passed through parallel pathways. Such pathways are chronologically related, but they are not the same. Figure 1 shows a flowchart demonstrating the concept.

Pure economic growth and pure profit maximization were the dominant economic and business models until the 1960s, when the Western countries needed reconstruction after the Second World War. Later on, the economic model adapted to include not only pure economic aspects but also the social dimension (economic development), which also coincided with the emergence of a new business model that incorporated the social aspect into the business activity (CSR stakeholders' focus). Then emerged the circular economy model

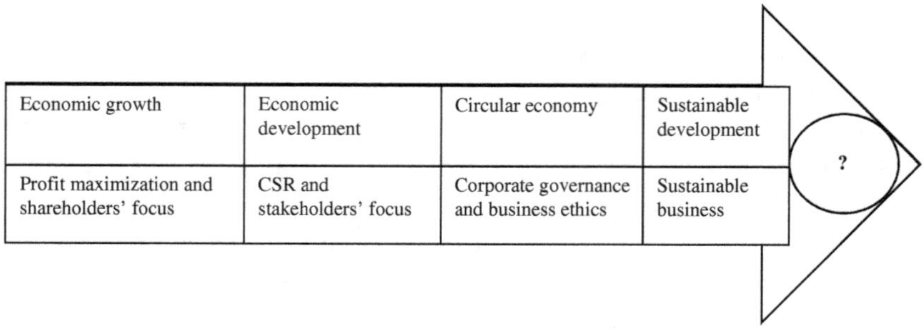

Figure 1. Concept evolution.

that was mainly technical and process-oriented; the same period also emphasized business ethics, which implicitly includes environmental responsibility, but was not a diffused business model. In the past 10 years, economic and business models have been changing, trying to adapt to the new paradigm by focusing explicitly on the sustainability aspect by explicitly integrating climate risks (such as greenhouse gases (GHGs)) to achieve the long-term climate objectives coordinated at the global, regional, and national levels. However, regardless of the definition of sustainability and all terminology related to it, we should admit that climate change is a scientific fact, not a belief, irrespective of the causes and drivers. Second, a change is already underway, and the sustainability transition has begun to mitigate climate risks.

Before discussing implications and opportunities in financial markets, the starting point should always be the real economy, which comprises production, supply chains, and demand that incorporate our production–consumption behaviors and are responsible for climate change. Then, the financial side of the economy should adapt to the new reality for the sustainability transition through designing and offering ESG financial products that reflect the change. Multiple factors induce such a drastic change:

- *Demand side*: Consumers demand more sustainable products, and investors require more sustainable financial investments.
- *Supply side*: Producers are more aware of sustainable issues and attempt to incorporate ESG into their business models. Adopting responsible and sustainable models benefits the private entities (enhanced public image and reputation, and innovation) and the public (climate change mitigation and innovation).

- *Regulations*: Regulators and policymakers are also interested in sustainability issues, and recently, politicians have included climate issues on their election agendas.

Moreover, the stakeholder-oriented approach does not alter any business's classical value-maximization principle. Value maximization calls for responsible business actions today to achieve strategic value maximization in the long run without compromising the interests of other stakeholders, which, in effect, corresponds to the old/new concepts of good corporate governance. Now, the question is: Are we dealing with the same classical governance concept just with new terminology and a stronger determination to reach our long-term objectives? In this regard, big companies sometimes escape from taking necessary actions, indulging instead in luxurious pretenses, which means they commit tax evasions but promote themselves as sustainability leaders. This brings us to the vital question on the role of a firm in the economy and society: What do business sustainability practices really mean when combined with tax evasion? Remember how Milton Friedman defined socially responsible business: "there is one and only one social responsibility of business — to use its resources and engage in activities designed to increase its profits so long as it stays within the rules of the game, which is to say, engages in open and free competition without deception or fraud" (Friedman, 1970). Companies are trying to get their sustainability rating and gain a reputation as a sustainable brand; however, fundamentally, we know more about unsustainable practices than sustainable ones. Many talk about sustainability, but we still don't really know what a sustainable practice is. That's why it is easier to judge an unsustainable practice than a sustainable one, and rejecting the unsustainability assumption does not guarantee that the business is sustainable. This is like testing the null hypothesis; rejecting the null does not mean accepting the alternative hypothesis. Many are discussing sustainability and granting sustainability certificates without recognizing this issue.

Furthermore, it is essential to distinguish between ESG performance (impact) and ESG reporting quality. Unlike financial performance reporting, it is still challenging from technical and regulatory standpoints to assess and judge ESG performance. Financial performance is evaluated through the quality of financial reporting that has been well established for almost a century; financial reports are analyzed and assessed by internal and external finance and accounting experts; in this sense, financial reports are more informative than ESG reports. ESG-related reports require financial and economic expertise and technical disciplines to evaluate the climate-related risks in a business activity. They are primarily prepared internally by the same accounting personnel and evaluated and analyzed by the same entities used to assess classical financial reports.

Additionally, the lack of standard ESG and climate risk reporting makes it more challenging for third parties to evaluate the quality of such information. Many ESG and sustainability rating agencies issue ESG ratings using personalized procedures, making the ratings less credible. Therefore, the lack of ESG corporate disclosure and rating fundamentals adds confusion, resulting in biased investment and financial decisions. The value of information is derived from its adequacy (right quantity, quality, and timing), and too little information stimulates speculation, especially among informed or sophisticated investors. At the same time, too much information (especially unassured) creates confusion, particularly among uninformed or retail investors who tend to make biased investment decisions. Finally, we are in the initial phases of the sustainability transition (a long-term structural change in the production and consumption sides) through voluntary and mandatory commitments. Many companies are trying to impress the markets and stakeholders by being ESG responsible or pretending to be ESG responsible by decorating their reports, and that's why it is still early to judge the quality of non-financial reporting, especially of that related to climate mitigation.

3. Value

Before analyzing whether ESG information is relevant to the financial market and corporate valuation, it is essential to demonstrate why there should and should not be a relevance by considering the following issues:

(1) *ESG reporting and ESG performance*: If we assume that the financial environment, including financial markets, is informationally efficient, we should expect that ESG reporting reflects ESG's true performance. However, the financial environment is not perfect, and asymmetries arise among the market players

that affect the degree of relevance of ESG information, especially in the transition period.

(2) From a law and economics (regulatory) point of view, the design of rules and regulations contributes to ESG information's relevance. The rule design establishes to whom the regulator allocates or assigns the rights and obligations; thus, we should distinguish between voluntary and mandatory ESG disclosures and performance. Specific climate objectives should be reached by 2030 and 2050. Climate conventions (COP21 in Paris and its subsequent summits) led to national climate plans, whereby signing countries pledged to achieve the specified climate goals. The national goals are achieved through businesses and individuals, which implicitly establishes an obligation to be climate responsible. In the same way, some regulators are obligating firms to disclose ESG information and climate risks and the ways to mitigate them, such as the European Union (EU) directive on non-financial reporting (NFRD[2]) and the EU Regulation 2019/2088[3] on sustainability-related disclosures in the financial services sector. The point is that since there is an obligation to perform responsibly and disclose adequately, why should ESG information be relevant? The idea is that like paying taxes, which is a must, such disclosures should not generate any reward for the firm.

(3) If the rule is the obligation to comply with the regulations to achieve the climate goals, the compliant firm should not be rewarded, but the non-compliant one should be penalized.

(4) On the contrary, if the regulation establishes voluntary ESG performance and disclosure, we expect firms that voluntarily comply to be rewarded, while the firms doing nothing are not penalized.

---

[2]Directive 2014/95/EU — also called the non-financial reporting directive (NFRD) — lays down the rules on disclosure of non-financial and diversity information by certain large companies. This directive amends the Accounting Directive 2013/34/EU

[3]Regulation (EU) 2019/2088 of the European Parliament and of the Council of 27 November 2019 on sustainability-related disclosures in the financial services sector. This regulation requires financial market participants and financial advisers to publish written policies on the integration of sustainability risks and ensure the transparency of such integration.

The latter is the case of the South African King report[4] on corporate disclosure. The third version of the report established mandatory integrated reporting for all publicly traded companies.

(5) However, differences could be observed within the same groups (compliant and non-compliant) according to their ESG performance and reporting (reflected in the different ESG ratings).

Moreover, *ex ante* and *ex post* regulations are political tools to manage negative externalities when the market mechanism alone cannot solve them effectively and efficiently. Optimally designed (efficient-level) regulations and enforcement should be able to deal with externalities without creating distortions. However, an overregulated environment might also hinder the transition to achieve climate goals through stringent regulations, increasing the cost of compliance and impeding innovations and growth. The EU is a context characterized by many and strict climate and ESG regulations, creating a tight business environment, leading EU companies to relocate to less-stringent regions, causing a carbon leakage, not a carbon reduction.

4. ESG Financial Instruments

Classical financial instruments create incentives for trading and investment through risk–return trade-offs that reflect the heterogeneous risk profiles of investors. Conservative investors prefer low-risk assets, requiring low returns, whereas aggressive investors tend to invest in risky securities, requiring higher remuneration. Liquidity could be another dimension for creating investment motives, in which investors prefer liquid assets regardless of their risk–return composition.

When it comes to ESG securities, are they considered new asset classes that meet investors' liquidity needs and risk tolerance?

[4]The first King Report (1994) heralded a new departure in stakeholder accountability. King II (2002) suggested further integration of sustainability into governance and reporting, but in 2009, King III insisted on integrated reporting for companies listed on the JSE, and through the JSE listing requirements, companies are therefore obliged to produce an integrated report.

Investors and investment funds are increasingly considering ESG securities and adjusting their portfolios using inclusion or exclusion strategies for various reasons:

(1) *Risk–return considerations*: ESG financial assets should lie on the security market line (SML) for the risk–return relation. If they are riskier, investors require higher returns, while investors require lower returns if they are less risky.
(2) *Liquidity considerations*: The ease of buying and selling the asset without losing value (low spreads) might also be an investor's consideration besides the risk–return trade-off.
(3) *Diversification considerations*: When ESG assets' performance is weakly or negatively correlated with other classical financial assets, including ESG, securities could benefit by reducing the overall portfolio risk.

As shown in Figure 2, if markets tend to be informationally efficient, ESG securities should comply with risk–return considerations; their over/underperformance with respect to a benchmark should be justified according to the classical finance theory (risk–return) at least in the long run.

However, the penetration of ESG investments in the finance world is relatively new. The challenges in the verifiability and assurance of ESG information — at least in the transitory period — make the relevance of ESG to financial markets ambiguous, which creates anomalies in ESG securities' trading by making unjustifiable profits and losses.

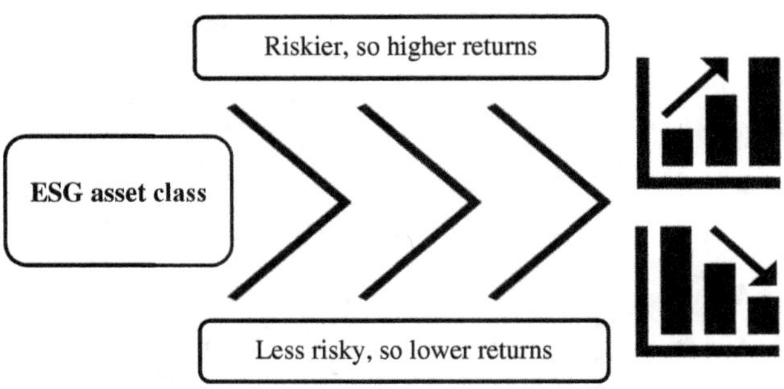

Figure 2. Risk-return considerations.

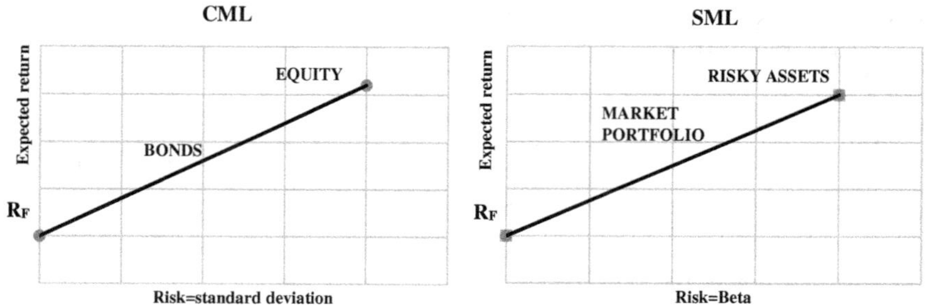

Figure 3. CML and SML.

Furthermore, ESG investments (funds or portfolios) should lie on the CML, and an individual ESG security should stay on the SML. But where should they be allocated? On the upper right (riskier) or the lower left (safer)? Figure 3 shows the individual security and portfolio approaches to investments:

- If ESG investments are allocated on the lower-left side of both lines, it means that they are safer and underperform compared to the market benchmark.
- Instead, if they are allocated on the upper-right side of both lines, they outperform and are considered risky investments.
- If they outperform (underperform) while they are less risky (riskier), it could indicate:
  - a market anomaly that wouldn't last for a long time;
  - that investors overreact to sustainability issues, which means "sentiment" controls the market;
  - that markets should adjust as new and more quality sustainability information is disclosed.

So far, we have assumed that the ESG performance is related to the systematic risks. However, before analyzing the risk–return trade-off, it is worth examining what kind of risk ESG performance is more related to, leading to different implications on investment and firm valuation:

(1) Systematic risk is part of the total risk caused by factors beyond the control of an individual company and is related to factors that are exogenous to firms. All investments or securities are subject

to systematic risk; therefore, it is a non-diversifiable risk. It cannot be diversified away by holding many securities. Systematic risk includes prevalent market risk, interest rate risk, inflation risk, and exchange rate risk. If the ESG performance is more related to the systematic risk, then ESG investments could be considered another asset class depending on how investors perceive it (preference and aversion).

(2) Idiosyncratic (specific) risk is a type of investment risk that is related to an individual asset (firm), a group of assets (sector), or, in some cases, a particular asset class. Idiosyncratic risk is also referred to as a specific risk or unsystematic risk. Therefore, after considering the systematic component, idiosyncratic risk is the residual part of the total risk. Specific risk can generally be mitigated in an investment portfolio with diversification. It includes a firm's business, financial, operational, and strategic risks. In this case, if the ESG performance is mainly related to a specific risk, then ESG securities are not considered new asset classes; they are just another security emission (offering) reflecting the issuer's risk characteristics.

(3) The total risk comprises all risks related to an investment or security; it includes the systematic and idiosyncratic components of risk.

Furthermore, finance and investment theory states that any assumed risk should be compensated with an additional rate of return. However, only the systematic risk component should be remunerated, requiring a premium on risky investments according to their connectedness to market factors. Perhaps, the capital asset pricing model (CAPM) is a prominent model of risk pricing; it states that investors require a premium for risk over the risk-free rate as compensation for risky assets:

$$E(R_i) = R_f + \beta_i(E(R_m) - R_f)$$

where $E(R_i)$ = capital asset expected return,
R_f = risk-free rate of interest,
B_i = beta coefficient that indicates sensitivity of the market (systematic risk measure),
$E(R_m)$ = expected return of the market, and
$B_i(E(R_m) - R_f)$ = asset risk premium.

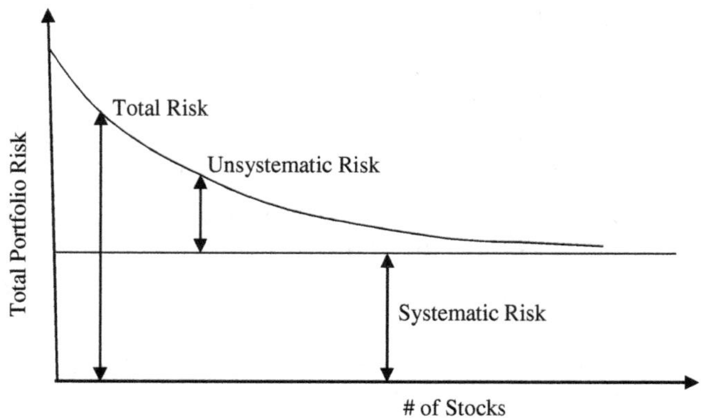

Figure 4. Impact of diversification.

Now, let's discuss investment considerations and diversification (Figure 4):

- If ESG is related to systematic risk, the firm's performance should stay on the SML, and the beta coefficient justifies the over- or underperformance.
- Suppose that ESG is firm-specific (idiosyncratic). In that case, the systematic risk component (beta) should not be affected. No premium or discount is required for investing in firms with good or bad ESG performance. Such specific risk is eliminated through portfolio diversification, unless a strategic investor seeks the firm's control (and assumes the firm's entire risk).

5. Transition and Preferences Shift

It is undeniable that we live in a period of socioeconomic and ecological transformation on both sides of the economy: the real economy, including production and consumption, and the financial economy, including finance, investment, and systems. Referring to the demand and supply sides in inducing the sustainability transition, it appears that the players on both the real and financial sides of the economy are demanding more sustainable products. Given the mounting awareness of sustainability issues, investors and consumers (demand side) as well as producers (supply side), accompanied by regulations and political intent, are changing their preferences toward sustainable production, consumption, and investment. It is a self-fulfilling prophecy; when the herd (consumers, producers, and investors) asks for more emphasis on ESG and sustainability issues, ESG products and sustainable companies might outperform.

It is worth noting that economic activities generate externalities (here, we refer to them as negative externalities) associated with costs (externality costs). Sometimes, the supply chain of the economic activity (production) does not incorporate such costs, making the final price unreflective of the total price, including the private and external costs. Private costs do not always correspond to the full social cost of a product, service, or activity. The difference between private and total social costs is the cost of externality; pollution and gas emissions are external costs related to production. External costs are directly associated with producing or delivering a good or service but are not assumed directly by the producer. External costs arise when environmental costs are not paid, causing market failures and economic inefficiencies at the local, state, national, and even international levels. Figure 5 demonstrates the interaction between the financial and real economies regarding ESG integration:

(1) On the financial side of the economy, we are facing a change in investors' aversion (preferences for ESG investments). For the same level of risk, investors are asking for different levels of return and risk premiums. Therefore, it is a matter of preference rather than the risk profile of the ESG products. The collective awareness and regulations induce such a change.
(2) Consumers are more aware of sustainability issues at the consumption level, and consumption behavior is changing accordingly; thus, consumers are no longer indifferent to the consumption of certain goods. Indifference curves are used in contemporary microeconomics to demonstrate consumer preference and the limitations of a budget. Economists have adopted the principles of indifference curves in the study of welfare economics. Standard economics suggests that the optimal consumption bundle is where a consumer's indifference curve is tangent to their budget line. In this regard, welfare would be affected (reduced) when the system incorporates the cost of negative externalities in the final price. Hence, a loss of welfare is due to preference changes; given

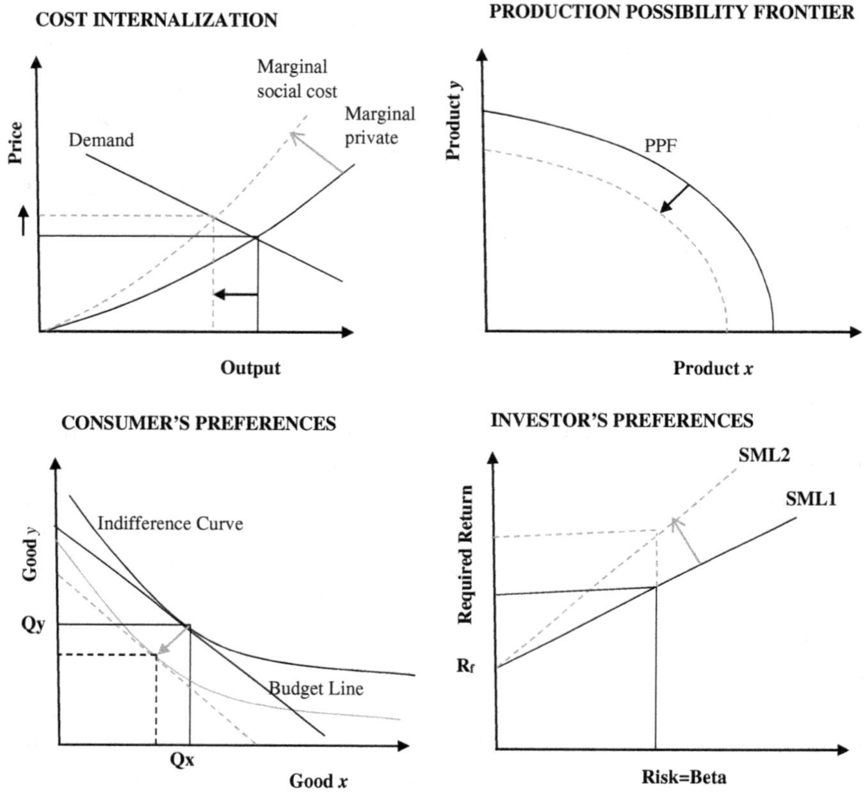

Figure 5. Preferences and interaction between real and financial markets.

a fixed income, conscious consumers buy fewer (but more sustainable) products, allocating them on a lower indifference curve.

(3) On the production side, producers also face a constant production budget but, at the same time, adopt more sustainable and responsible production, which adds to the production cost — the same amount of output at a higher cost or the same cost but a lower production quantity. Accordingly, the production possibility frontier (PPF) will shift inward as the production side of the economy incorporates a part of the externality cost. The PPF is the set of points at which the producer (or the economy) most efficiently allocates the available resources to produce as many goods as possible. If producers are unable to pass through the additional costs related to sustainability and compliance, they will assume

the total cost, which affects the final quantity produced; hence, an inward shift in the PPF might be noted. When it shifts inward, the economy shrinks due to a failure to allocate resources and optimal production capability. A shrinking economy could result from a decrease in supplies or a deficiency in technology. At the end of the day, somebody has to assume the extra costs from internalizing external costs, raising socioeconomic implications related to distributional issues:

$$Social\ cost = Private\ production\ cost + Externality\ cost$$

(4) However, if utilized well, technology and innovations might help maintain the same level of utility and welfare or even improve it without affecting the consumers' budget lines or the producers' cost of internalizing the externality.

The discussion mentioned above highlights the importance of a holistic multidisciplinary approach in dealing with sustainability issues and how to integrate ESG factors into the financial world. The real and financial worlds are connected, and they should reflect each other. In this regard, the financial side of the economy sometimes leads the real side. It stimulates it by creating a financial system capable of designing innovative ESG financial products to finance the sustainability transition in the real economy, enhancing awareness on sustainability issues and enforcing the assurance of the ESG information quality.

We should also emphasize the distributional implications of internalizing the cost of climate externalities in the real economy. Who will pay for such costs? A question that raises critical issues on the distributional effect. If producers have enough power to pass on the extra cost to final clients, consumers will pay the externality cost. For example, in a competitive market, the European carbon allowance (EUA) cost could be borne entirely by the producers, shrinking their profit margins, or could be added (totally or partially) to the final price, allowing consumers to bear the external cost. In the end, allocating the external cost depends on various factors, such as market microstructure (market power and concentration), regulations, and consumer activism. On the other hand, if the cost is borne by public funds, the taxpayers pay at the end of the day, reducing welfare.

6. Valuation Implications

The presented discussions have direct implications for portfolio construction and adjustment on the one hand and financial valuation on the other:

- *Portfolio considerations*: If ESG performance is more related to idiosyncratic risk, investors shouldn't require higher premiums on such investments since diversification can eliminate specific risks. According to the CAPM, only systematic risk is compensated by requiring higher premiums. In this case, ESG assets can be used as a risk hedge in a well-diversified portfolio when the correlation between ESG asset performance and classical assets is low or negative.
- *Valuation considerations*: Assuming that ESG performance is related to systematic risk and if investors perceive ESG firms as safer, they require lower returns and hence a lower firm's cost of capital and a higher value. On the other hand, if investors perceive ESG performance to have a higher risk profile due to the additional cost of integrating ESG factors, the firm's cost of capital would be higher, which decreases the firm's value. In this regard, there are two channels through which ESG performance would impact a firm's value, depending on the relationship between ESG performance and risk categories (systematic or specific). Accordingly, we build a valuation framework showing the channels, value drivers, and connections to risk categories. The two channels are the product or real market channel and the financial market channel that affect future cash flows and/or the discount rate (cost of capital).

***Real (product) market channel*:** The product market channel would affect the future cash flows, positively or negatively, according to specific regulations, consumers' preferences, and climate cost internalization. The product market would impact cash flows through the following value drivers:

(1) *Reputation*: When customers value the firm's responsibility toward the environment and other social aspects, demand for the firm's product will increase, driving up cash flows and enhancing the firm's value. Such a driver is mainly considered an idiosyncratic factor for socially and environmentally responsible firms.

(2) *Innovation*: Well-designed ESG-related regulations stimulate private innovations that help achieve public benefits (climate risk mitigation) and private benefits (reputation and cash flow from innovative solutions). Thoughtful innovations could be a way to mitigate climate risks without compromising welfare.

(3) *Climate compliance*: There is a growing trend for mandatory business practices that consider ESG factors in business models and corporate reporting. Firms must comply with such regulations by changing their business models, production technologies, and reporting processes. Such compliance would add to the total business cost, negatively affecting future cash flows and decreasing the firm's value. The question is whether to expense or capitalize ESG-related costs. The answer depends on the obligatory nature of the directives, the accounting practices, and whether sustainable business models would be able to create goodwill thanks to being socially and environmentally responsible. Compliance costs are also related to firm-specific factors.

(4) *Variability of cash flows*: For specific businesses and sectors, climate events affect value by contributing to the variability of cash flows. Global commodity companies that deal with the production, transportation, and consumption of agricultural, energy, and metallic commodities would be negatively influenced when the frequency of natural disasters due to climate change increases. Such risks and dangers should be mitigated through risk management techniques. This driver could be a firm-specific or a systematic factor.

(5) *Litigation*: Firms not complying with ESG integration directives might save some compliance costs in the short run. However, they would be subject to litigation and lawsuits by stakeholders, which drains their future cash flows and reduce the firm's value. This driver is generally a firm-specific factor.

Financial market channel: For standalone valuation purposes, if the ESG performance is more related to firm-specific risk, it affects valuation through cash flows, but such risk can be eliminated with diversification. However, the consideration would be different when valuing firms for strategic purposes, such as mergers and acquisitions, strategic investors, and other business deals aiming to capture the firm's control; in this case, the deal also incorporates the firm-specific factors by considering a premium or discount.

Regarding the systematic channel, in a standalone valuation, the value drivers for firms become systematic through the cost of capital. If market investors perceive firms with higher ESG performance as safer, they should require lower rates of return, lowering the cost of capital and thus enhancing the firm's value. Assuming that the CAPM still holds in the transition period, we expect firms with higher ESG performance to have lower market betas, lower risk premiums, and thus a lower cost of capital. The financial market is an entirely systematic channel through which ESG performance could be relevant to a firm's valuation from a standalone perspective (financial investors, not strategic investors). We developed the following valuation diagram (Figure 6) showing how ESG performance could be a value relevant to firms through different channels and value drivers.

Furthermore, real and financial market channels that affect firms' future cash flows and the perceived risk through various value drivers are not mutually exclusive. A firm might simultaneously deal with multiple value drivers that might cancel out the value effect or magnify it.

Finally, we propose this value-relevance framework, but the effects of ESG performance and information are yet to be discovered. We are still at the beginning of the socioeconomic and environmental transformation, in which: societies are becoming different in terms of consumption choices, the drivers of the economic growth are not the same as one or two decades ago, and businesses are also adapting by changing their business models by integrating new value drivers. The financial side of the economy has to reflect such changes by facilitating or hindering them. The capital needed for the transition to reach the long-term climate goals is channeled through the financial system. Efficient financial systems enhance ESG informational adequacy by enforcing the assurance, transferring the needed funds at a lower cost (eliminating market frictions) and improving investors' confidence in financial markets and ESG-related products. Given the ambiguity and lack of standardization and assurance regarding the relevance of ESG factors to the business and finance world, firms try to capitalize on ESG issues by decorating their reports (greenwashing), showing unrealistic performance to influence the cash flow drivers or

Real (product) market channel effect through value drivers and mainly capture the *idiosyncratic risk*:

1. Reputation: increase (decrease) FFCFs through good (bad) corporate reputation regarding ESG factors.
2. Innovation: regulations stimulate innovations to achieve public and private benefits.
3. Compliance cost: the cost of environmental compliance might reduce cash flows, at least in the short-run.
4. Operating risk: the variability of cash flows due to climate-related disasters could cause huge losses.
5. Litigation: bad performing firms are subject to litigation causing FFCFs to reduce.

$$Value = \sum_{t=1}^{t=n} \frac{FFCF_t}{(1+i)^n}$$

Value: Enterprise value using asset-side valuation

FFCFs: Future free cash flows

i: the discount rate that reflects the weighted average cost of capital (*WACC*)

Financial market channel effect through the cost of capital as a value driver that captures the *systematic risk*:

1. When investors perceive good ESG performers as lower systematic risk.
2. Lower systematic risk translates into a lower firms cost of capital and discount factor.

Thus, the firm's value is maximized.

Figure 6. Financial valuation framework.

the cost of capital. Investment managers also sell, market, and package ESG products as prospering products to fulfill specific market needs. Financial market authorities should be aware of such behaviors, aiming to prevent the occurrences of what we refer to "green or ESG scandals/crises." Some market players started to ring the bell on moral hazard issues and the ESG investment's ability to outperform as claimed by investment managers, creating false hope, overselling outperformance, and contributing to the delay of regulatory intervention.

7. Conclusion

In this chapter, we provided a holistic approach to the relevance of ESG information on a firm's value, illustrating the evolution of the sustainability concept, the rationale for value relevance from a regulatory (law and economics) point of view, and finally the implications to real and financial markets.

At the policy and regulatory levels, regulations should be efficiently designed to create incentives for market players to comply with regulations and innovate at the same time; otherwise, a loss of welfare could be observed. Furthermore, in the transition period, regulations and markets should move hand-in-hand in creating incentives and channeling (allocating) funds to reach the long-term climate goals.

Studies draw divergent conclusions on the impact of ESG performance and assets on investment and firm valuation. The results depend on the context, time period, and proxies for the ESG performance. Such divergent findings are not strange (or even unexpected), given the following attributes:

a. We are in a period of ecological and socioeconomic transition, which entails changing preferences and might compromise welfare unless intelligent solutions are provided.
b. A lot of less-assured information creates confusion, and markets are still not fully digesting ESG-related information. The confusion is not only limited to retail (uninformed) investors but also to financial analysts who act as informational agents (intermediaries) to guarantee the quality of corporate information.
c. There is yet no standard proxy for ESG performance, making assurance more challenging.
d. ESG performing firms and ESG products could not be exclusively explained by the risk–return trade-off, but liquidity and portfolio diversification concerns could play a role in explaining their behavior.

Finally, if we want to successfully make the sustainability transition to achieve long-term climate objectives, cost–benefit analysis and financial return should be less relevant since some stakeholders and environmental activists refer to the current situation as a climate emergency. Therefore, we should be open to compromising part of our welfare — at least in the short and medium terms — to smooth the transition and achieve climate objectives by creating a better environment for future generations because there is *only* one planet for us to live on.

References

Albuquerque, R., Koskinen, Y., Yang, S., *et al.* (2020). Resiliency of environmental and social stocks: An analysis of the exogenous COVID-19 market crash. *The Review of Corporate Finance Studies*, *9*(3), 593–621. https://doi.org/10.1093/RCFS/CFAA011.

Barnea, A. & Rubin, A. (2010). Corporate social responsibility as a conflict between shareholders. *Journal of Business Ethics*, *97*(1), 71–86. https://doi.org/10.1007/S10551-010-0496-Z.

Bauer, R., Koedijk, K., & Otten, R. (2005). International evidence on ethical mutual fund performance and investment style. *Journal of Banking & Finance*, *29*(7), 1751–1767. https://doi.org/10.1016/J.JBANKFIN.2004.06.035.

Brammer, S., Brooks, C., & Pavelin, S. (2006). Corporate social performance and stock returns: UK evidence from disaggregate measures. *Financial Management*, *35*(3), 97–116. https://doi.org/10.1111/J.1755-1755-053X.2006.TB00149.X.

Buchanan, S. & Marques, J. C. (2018). How home country industry associations influence MNE international CSR practices: Evidence from the Canadian mining industry. *Journal of World Business*, *53*(1), 63–74. https://doi.org/10.1016/J.JWB.2017.07.005.

Ding, W., Levine, R., Lin, C., *et al.* (2021). Corporate immunity to the COVID-19 pandemic. *Journal of Financial Economics*, *141*(2), 802–830. https://doi.org/10.1016/J.JFINECO.2021.03.005.

Friedman, M. (1970). A Friedman doctrine — The social responsibility of business is to increase its profits. *The New York Times*, September 13. Retrieved from https://www.nytimes.com/1970/09/13/archives/a-friedman-doctrine-the-social-responsibility-of-business-is-to.html.

Koçak, E., Bulut, U., & Menegaki, A. N. (2022). The resilience of green firms in the twirl of COVID-19: Evidence from S&P500 carbon efficiency index with a Fourier approach. *Business Strategy and the Environment*, *31*(1), 32–45. https://doi.org/10.1002/BSE.2872.

Lee, S., Lee, D., Hong, C., *et al.* (2022). Performance of socially responsible firms during the COVID-19 crisis and trading behavior by investor type: Evidence from the Korean stock market. *Finance Research Letters*, *45*, 102660. https://doi.org/10.1016/J.FRL.2021. 102660.

Renneboog, L., Ter Horst, J., & Zhang, C. (2008). Socially responsible investments: Institutional aspects, performance, and investor behavior. *Journal of Banking & Finance*, *32*(9), 1723–1742. https://doi.org/10.1016/J.JBANKFIN.2007.12.039.

Servaes, H. & Tamayo, A. (2013). The impact of corporate social responsibility on firm value: The role of customer awareness. *Management Science*, *59*(5), 1045–1061. https://doi.org/10.1287/MNSC.1120.1630.

Tensie, W., Ulrich, A., Tracy, V. H., *et al.* (2021). ESG and financial performance. Uncovering the relationship by aggregating evidence from 1,000 plus studies published between 2015 and 2020. Retrieved from chrome-extension://efaidnbmnnnibpcajpcglclefindmkaj/viewer.html?pdfurl=https%3A%2F%2Fwww.stern.nyu.edu%2Fsites%2Fdefault%2Ffiles%2Fassets%2Fdocuments%2FNYU-RAM_ESG-Paper_2021%2520Rev_0.pdf&clen=1796205&chunk=true.

Wu, J. & Juvyns, V. (2020). COVID-19 shows ESG matters more than ever. J. P. Morgan asset management. Retrieved from https://am.jpmorgan.com/sg/en/asset-management/per/insights/market-insights/on-the-minds-of-investors/covid-19-esg-matters/.

Yadav, P. L., Han, S. H., & Kim, H. (2017). Sustaining competitive advantage through corporate environmental performance. *Business Strategy and the Environment*, *26*(3), 345–357. https://doi.org/10.1002/BSE.1921.

Part III

Green Finance & Sustainable Development Goals

https://doi.org/10.1142/9781800614482_0010

Chapter 10

Financing Renewable Energy Transition Toward Sustainable Development Goals: Policies and Economic Implications in the Era of Climate Change

Diem Thi Hong Vo[†,§] **and Hai Hong Trinh**[*,‡,¶,||]

[†]*Department of Economics and Finance, University of Canterbury, Christchurch, New Zealand*

[‡]*School of Economics and Finance, Massey Business School, Massey University, Palmerston North, New Zealand*

[§]*diemthihong.vo@gmail.com*

[¶]*h.h.trinh@massey.ac.nz*

[||]*hai.hong.trinh.econfin@gmail.com*

Abstract

Since the Sustainable Development Goals (SDGs) were established by the United Nations in 2015, a sustainable energy transition (SET) has played a crucial role as the seventh SDG for sustainable development, climate change adaptation, and mitigation. To provide sufficient access to affordable, reliable, and modern energy services, as well as to increase the overall energy efficiency and the portion of renewable energy in the world's energy mix, countries across the globe need appropriate policies for boosting the consumption of sustainable energy. Policies might differ for each country or region depending on its specific economic

[*]Corresponding author.

development; however, they all play a crucial role in the world's energy transition, energy efficiency, and SDGs. This chapter provides an up-to-date framework of the determinants of financing the SET and a newly developed framework of capital mobilization for financing the SET, highlighting the roles of green finance worldwide. Given the newly developed theoretical framework and financial development in general, we find the critical functionality of sustainable capital markets and instruments for global capital mobilization, where policy incentives play an undeniable role in the SET. This chapter provides important implications for policymakers, non-governmental organizations, and governments in financing energy transition in the era of climate change toward the SDGs.

1. Introduction

Industrial development leads to increased fossil fuel demand, which is a tremendous threat to climate change mitigation (Bhutta *et al.*, 2022; Güney, 2019; Lin & Ren, 2020). The growing demand for traditional energy resources has prompted authorities worldwide to seek alternative solutions, such as developing green energy technologies. Renewable and sustainable energy sources play key roles in reducing fossil fuel carbon dioxide emissions and mitigating climate change impacts toward the Sustainable Development Goals (SDGs). However, fossil fuels still account for roughly 80 percent of the share of global energy consumption (Johnsson *et al.*, 2019). Across different sectors, the use of energy for residential purposes accounts for more than 40 percent of global energy usage. This causes a range of adverse effects on health and climate. This would become a bigger problem for our current systems, as the United Nations (UN) projects that the global population will reach approximately 9.7 billion by 2050. Promisingly, the ongoing developments in electric vehicle technologies have brought the transportation sector's energy usage to a sustainable level (Johnsson *et al.*, 2019). Furthermore, to deal with the limitation of fossil fuels as the main cause of environmentally harmful carbon emissions, a number of actions have been proposed and executed throughout the world, for instance, the agreement on recovering the ozone layer, namely the 1987 Montreal Protocol. The Paris Agreement, adopted at COP21 in 2015, is another effort toward this trend. Subsequently, several energy policies and plans have been formed globally.

It is hard to refuse the benefits of new green energy technologies, such as solar, wind, and biomass. These sustainable renewable energy

(RE) sources offer more choices for energy consumption. This offer, ultimately, strengthens national positions to achieve energy security. Moreover, RE can provide easy access to energy, significantly boosting social and economic development. Last but not least, the most obvious advantage of RE is that it helps reduce the negative impacts of economic growth on climate change and human health (Khan *et al.*, 2020).

Although the benefits of using RE far outweigh the convenience and rewards of using fossil fuels in terms of economic and environmental impacts, the transition from the traditional use of energy to the new forms of energy usage to achieve a cleaner future is still facing obstacles. Also, it seems clear that RE policies have not been sufficient to accelerate investments in alternatives to fossil fuels, such as low-carbon energy (Johnsson *et al.*, 2019). To achieve a smooth transition, policymakers should match the critical need for energy with efforts to address the inefficiencies in traditional energy usage (Alasseri *et al.*, 2020; Pitelis *et al.*, 2020; ul Abideen *et al.*, 2019).

There are many obstacles to the process of moving from fossil-fuel-based energy sources to RE sources, such as the limitations of currently available technologies in producing RE or a low acceptance rate in changing the existing systems to adaptive RE systems. However, financial investment is the most challenging barrier to the transition process. To achieve an effective and desirable renewable energy transition (RET), a tremendous amount of capital will be required (Hall *et al.*, 2017; Steffen, 2020). Despite the fact that the costs associated with RE production have reduced in recent years due to new technological innovations (IRENA, 2019), there is still a slow upward trend in investment for RE projects. A lack of appropriate policies could be the main reason for this paradox. Investors in the RE sector are less likely to take risks, as they see the commitment from their governments as not strong enough. This hesitation is the biggest problem for financing the RET.

This chapter aims to provide a review of financing renewable and green energy policies for sustainable energy transitions (SETs) and achieving the SDGs. We elaborate on determinants, financial roles and challenges, incentives, policies, and solutions for accelerating the RET by reviewing sustainable policies, which are presented in Tables 1–3. Particularly, the chapter highlights the main barriers hindering the establishment of RE projects and investments in clean energy production. This work discusses crucial incentives, financial instruments, and necessary strategies commonly used worldwide to overcome these obstacles and speed up investment processes and the SET. A few studies investigating the financing of the RET focus only on a specific region or country or a separate policy. Hence, based on empirical review findings, this work provides a comprehensive picture of the financial RET landscape. Then, the chapter provides critical suggestions and financial and economic implications to policymakers, scholars, and experts from public and private agencies. Finally, we provide an up-to-date framework of determinants in SET and a newly developed framework of capital mobilization for financing SETs.

The rest of the chapter is organized as follows: Section 2 reviews the literature on the policies of RET. Section 3 presents rarely discussed strategies to speed up the implementation of RET and the current gaps in the existing literature. Section 4 is the conclusion.

2. Literature on Policies of Renewable Energy Transitions

The literature review revealed that the transition from the traditional use of energy toward the use of RE started at the end of the 20th century. This process occurred slowly at the beginning but has achieved several milestones owing to the enhancement of technologies, greater energy use efficiency, and the efforts of governments across various countries. This section covers key factors determining the RET, the roles of financial policies, and what trends and challenges a country or region might face in the process toward the RET.

2.1. *Determinants of SETs*

The SET depends on various determinants, including specific policies for specific regions or countries, types of funding for RE investments, and the level of advancement of technologies in the RE field (Figure 1). For the policies, it should be noted that the policy designs and their effects across regions or countries vary because of the different levels of resource availability. In Germany, for instance, the strategy to achieve the RET involves focusing on investments in RE of new entrants, such as small power enterprises. Schiffer & Trüby

Table 1. Determinants of the SET according to the literature.

Factor	Brief description	Country/Region	References
Low-carbon/clean technologies, technological innovation, and technology transfer	For transforming a country's energy systems toward a low-carbon economy with policies needed for technology transfer from developed to developing countries	Worldwide	IEA (2017a, 2020b), Ockwell *et al.* (2008), and Schiffer & Trüby (2018)
Energy demand	A challenge faced by countries with lower income levels requires typically rapid growth in energy demand	Lower-income countries or regions, such as Central and South America, Africa, India, South East Asia, China, Eurasia, and Middle East/North Africa	IEA (2017b)
Energy supply	The entire world depends on countries rich in fossil fuels for their energy needs. Oil and gas companies are unwilling to diversify their portfolios and investing less in the renewables sectors	The EU, North and South America	Hartmann *et al.* (2021) and Pickl (2019)
Alternative low-carbon energy sources	The high cost of low-carbon/clean energy increases pressure on RET policies for investment and acceleration of the low-carbon transition. Capital costs for biomass and installing solar and wind farms are the biggest obstacles to a RET	Southern Europe, Greece, Croatia, Hungary, Slovakia, and the Czech Republic	Zhang *et al.* (2021), Punda *et al.* (2017), and Ćetković & Buzogány (2016)

(*Continued*)

Table 1. (*Continued*)

Factor	Brief description	Country/Region	References
Economic growth	Although economic growth causes energy consumption, high economic growth enables investment in RE, biomass energy infrastructure, and biomass supply. In contrast, low-economic growth is less likely to increase RE consumption	*Countries*: Austria, Belgium, Bulgaria, Croatia, the Republic of Cyprus, the Czech Republic, Denmark, Estonia, Finland, France, Germany, Greece, Hungary, Ireland, Italy, Latvia, Lithuania, Luxembourg, Malta, the Netherlands, Poland, Portugal, Romania, Slovakia, Slovenia, Spain, Sweden, and China *Regions*: Asia-Pacific, OECD, BRIC, NAFTA, East Asia, East Europe, and EU15	Fang & Chang (2016), Fang & Chen (2017), Le *et al.* (2021), Pablo-Romero & Sánchez-Braza (2015), Shahbaz *et al.* (2022), and Sharma *et al.* (2021)
Human capital	Human capital adopts new environment-friendly technologies and enhances energy efficiency in production processes and economic performance, which in turn reduces CO_2 and increases RE generation	The US, China, India, OECD, Asia Pacific, BRIC, NAFTA, East Asia, East Europe, and EU15	Fang & Chen (2017), Pablo-Romero & Sánchez-Braza (2015), Rafi *et al.* (2021), Salim *et al.* (2017), Shahbaz *et al.* (2019), Shahbaz *et al.* (2022), and Yao *et al.* (2019)
Research and development	Technology development lowers RE costs, which leads to increased investment in the RE sectors due to anticipated higher returns. Furthermore, exploiting RE relies	China, Europe, OECD	Shahbaz *et al.* (2022), Bointner *et al.* (2016), and Carbajo & Cabeza (2018)

	heavily on the capability of harvesting and storage resources, such as biomass, solar, wind, and ocean thermal energy		
Smart energy systems and infrastructure financing	RE potential assessment, infrastructure development, and successful integration into the system to achieve the reduction of GHG emissions	Australia	Trinh (2021) and Li *et al.* (2020)
Financial development	Financial development mitigates carbon risk and increases RE consumption around the world. Financial support is essential for constructing RE infrastructures and developing and applying appropriate technologies. Lack of funding for R&D in RE causes delays in generating and implementing updated RE technologies	180 countries worldwide	Trinh *et al.* (2022), Le *et al.* (2020), and Adenle (2020)
Carbon finance	Finance supports the reduction of unavoidable carbon emissions by funding other compensatory projects that contribute to carbon emissions reduction	Global evidence	Khan *et al.* (2021)

(*Continued*)

Table 1. (*Continued*)

Factor	Brief description	Country/Region	References
Energy storage technologies	Energy storage technologies provide a feasible solution for the intermittent nature of RE. Energy storage has many potential applications in RE generation, power transmission, distribution, and utilization, which is necessary for the effective implementation of the RET	China, the US, Japan, and the EU	Yao *et al.* (2016), Parra *et al.* (2017), Gallo *et al.* (2016), Mahmoud *et al.* (2020), and Zsiborács *et al.* (2019)
Social conditions of society	Social-economic conditions of society impact RE awareness and usage behavior. While wealthy users can afford and are willing to pay for extra capital needed to consume clean energy, such as solar energy, poor households prefer cheaper alternatives, typically non-sustainable energy sources, such as coal. Therefore, the more the inequality in socio-economic conditions, the slower the process of the RET	Bangladesh and China	Khan *et al.* (2019) and IRENA (2019)

Note: Reviewed by the authors, with the most recent studies on the SET and its determinants.

Table 2. Policy instruments for the SET by country.

Period	Brief description	Country/Region	References
Since 1970s	Energiewende as Germany's energy transition program for a nuclear-free and low-carbon economy	Germany	Carbon Brief (2016), CLEW (2019), Jacobs (2012), Schiffer & Trüby (2018), and Ćetković & Buzogány (2016)
Since 1970s	Brazil's sugarcane-based ethanol program is a way to substitute imported petroleum fuels and reduce greenhouse gas emissions	Brazil	Hira & De Oliveira (2009), Gee & McMeekin (2011), and Solomon and & (2011)
Since 1970s	France successfully developed commercial nuclear power for electricity creation, transitioning away from petroleum fuels	France	Solomon & Krishna (2011)
Since 1970s	US Project Independence was designed to increase domestic supply from all sources, including RE, energy conservation, and effective and new technologies, to reduce imported oils and fossil fuels	The US	Solomon & Krishna (2011)
Since 1990s	Using a market-based approach through tax incentives, high emission taxes, and low-interest rate credit for RE investment to encourage customers to use electricity and alternative RE	Middle East, North Africa, and the UK	Benasla *et al.* (2019)
Since 1990s	Subsidize oil enterprises investing in oil technologies to reduce their oil usage and move toward RE	Europe and Latin America	Bersalli *et al.* (2020)

(*Continued*)

Table 2. (*Continued*)

Period	Brief description	Country/Region	References
Since 1970s	Technology-push policy instruments, such as financing R&D for RE, government-sponsored R&D, and tax credits for R&D investments are applied in Europe to deal with energy security issues and environment and climate objectives	The EU, Norway, Turkey, and the UK	Gökgöz & Güvercin (2018), De Negri *et al.* (2020), and Ćetković & Buzogány (2016)
Since 1980s	China uses a policy mix, including CO_2 emission reduction from conventional energy, promoting clean and RE technologies, and encouraging an increase in non-fossil-fuel consumption share	China	Li & Taeihagh (2020)
Since 2000s	Feed-in tariff is a RET policy designed to accelerate and promote RE and low-carbon electricity generation, which aims to achieve the target of GHG emission reduction	Europe and Latin America, the UK, Algeria, Australia, Canada, China, the Czech Republic, France, Germany, Greece, India, Indonesia, Iran, Ireland, Israel, Italy, Japan, the Netherlands, South Africa, Spain, Switzerland, Thailand, Uganda, Ukraine, the US, and Puerto Rico	Council (2016), KPMG (2013), Li *et al.* (2020), Bersalli *et al.* (2020), Ćetković & Buzogány (2016), and Sawin *et al.* (2013)

Table 3. Financing instruments/incentives for the SET.

Instrument	Brief description	Country/Region	References
Green finance, such as green bonds, green banks, and financial technologies	RE projects are often high risk, uncertain, and have lower returns. Boosting up green finance, such as providing loans at a minimum rate for RE investments, is essential to accelerate the RET and achieve the SDGs	South-East Asia, Pacific, the US, Bangladesh, India, China, Mongolia, the EU, Central Asia, Middle East, Latin America	Yoshino *et al.* (2019), Sachs *et al.* (2019), IRENA (2020a), IEA (2020a), and Bhattacharyya (2022)
Public finance and financial subsidy	Government and public financial support improve emission-intensive infrastructure, new equipment, and RE technologies, which facilitate and accelerate R&D and the RET	Sub-Saharan Africa, Europe, and Central Asia, East Asia and Pacific, Latin America and the Caribbean, Middle East and North Africa, South East Asia	De Negri *et al.* (2020) and Zhang *et al.* (2021)
Carbon finance includes tax credits, carbon taxes, or reducing tariffs on green projects	Carbon financing policies encourage green projects by reducing taxes on low-carbon projects and importing clean technologies. Also, generating and increasing a carbon taxing system, taxing fossil fuels, and imposing carbon penalties for emissions	The UK, Australia, Canada, Chile, Switzerland, Norway, Sweden, New Zealand, China, the EU, the US, India, Russia, Brazil, and Japan	Curtin *et al.* (2017), Zhao *et al.* (2016), and Bhattacharyya (2022)

(Continued)

Table 3. (*Continued*)

Instrument	Brief description	Country/Region	References
Rural community-based funds and village funds	These funds are for small- and medium-sized low-carbon energy projects, RE infrastructure, community energy development, and help low-income households access clean energy	Worldwide, especially in developing countries	IRENA (2020b)
Climate bonds initiative	An international organization that aims to promote investments in projects for a low-carbon transition and climate action by the stimulation of sustainable debt markets, including green, social, sustainability, sustainability-linked, and transition (GSS+)-labeled bonds	International	https://www.climatebonds.net

Note: Prepared by the authors to highlight the roles of sustainable capital markets and commonly used instruments for financing the SET.

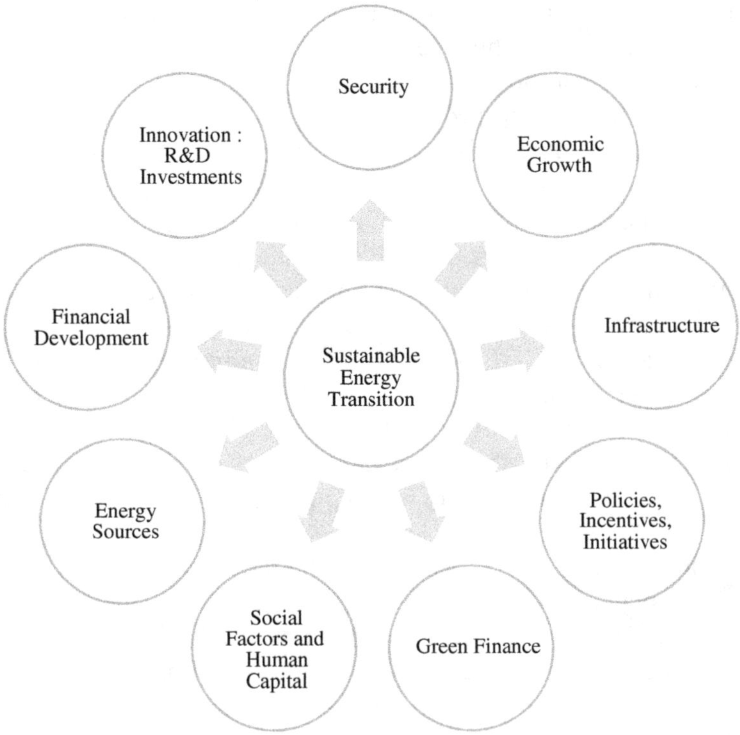

Figure 1. Determinants of the SET: A conceptualized framework proposed by the authors based on the literature.

(2018) examine the German policy framework and point out that while the government puts significant efforts into reducing greenhouse gas (GHG) emissions to 80 percent by 2050, it seems to fail in its two main sectors, industry and transport. Conversely, the policies of the RET in the Middle East and North African countries and the UK take advantage of market-based approaches to achieve their targets (Benasla *et al.*, 2019). By imposing high taxes on emissions and providing low-interest-rate credits for RE projects, the governments try to make the price of renewable electricity affordable to customers. Policymakers in China pursue a state-controlled approach to sort out its problem of heavy pollution (Sheng *et al.*, 2018). This RET policy framework might not be an excellent example for other countries to follow since the RET, in this process, needs the collaboration of all stakeholders to ensure a smooth transition. The policymaking process should account for the availability of resources. For example, due to the availability of more solar radiation, African countries need less support for solar energy projects than European countries, such as Slovenia. More importantly, most governments agree on the point that financing mechanisms need to be properly designed along with the RET to boost the process (Punda *et al.*, 2017).

The second factor for the RET is the role of traditional and international large oil corporations. As recorded by the International Energy Agency (IEA, 2018), these oil companies are responsible for nearly 50 percent of GHG emissions globally. Therefore, a slight change in their business model would be a huge step in the RET. Indeed, major oil companies in Europe have received subsidies for their investments in oil technologies to reduce oil consumption while increasing the consumption of clean products as alternatives to oil (Bersalli *et al.*, 2020).

Another important determinant of the RET is funding from public and private sectors. Public funding plays a significant role in financing RE research and development (R&D). Obviously, the main obstacle to the RET is the high cost of implementing RE projects. New practical technologies can solve this problem by reducing the cost of RE. Eventually, lower costs of RE projects would encourage all stakeholders to invest in RE due to anticipated higher returns. To boost this process, governments should play a central role in financing the R&D of RE. Evidence from Gökgöz & Güvercin (2018) has shown that the success of the RET in Europe is a result of government investments in the R&D of RE. In the same vein, De Negri *et al.* (2020) report that public funding from governments, non-governmental organizations (NGOs), or other institutions is insufficient to guarantee the RET process. In this transition, private financing seems to fill the gaps that public financing cannot cover. Curtin *et al.* (2017) emphasize that feed-in tariffs, subsidies, and allowances for RE usage can get citizens involved in the RET.

Last but not least, energy storage technologies are a crucial factor for an effective RET due to the intermittent nature of RE (Mahmoud *et al.*, 2020; Zsiborács *et al.*, 2019) and the fact that, unlike traditional energy, RE is non-dispatchable without an energy storage system. There has been a need for changes in financial policies to develop more effective technologies for storing RE, which can promote the involvement of all stakeholders in developing private or community RE storage technologies.

2.2. *Financing policies for a SET*

2.2.1. *Green finance*

Since 2017, the global investment in RE has gone down by 3 percent (Sachs *et al.*, 2019). This negative trend is going to continue due to the low cost and availability of conventional energy sources, such as fossil fuels. As a result, the expansion of green energy is limited, and it reduces energy security. This trend, consequently, counteracts the significant efforts made by many governments and international organizations to mitigate climate change. Generally, financial providers are more interested in conventional energy projects than clean energy ones, mostly because of the high risk and uncertainty associated with RE projects and their lower rates of return (Yoshino *et al.*, 2019). Therefore, if a country wants to achieve the SDGs, it should establish a new green finance strategy to boost the financing of RE investments that bring about environmental benefits. The new financial instruments and policies can be in the form of green bonds, green banks, green financial technologies, community-based green funds, etc. (Sachs *et al.*, 2019).

Recently, there have been several promising methods to finance green projects. Green banks and bonds have some potential to foster green energy development. Their loan services can offer better credit conditions for investors in green energy projects. Also, through the dissemination of information about the benefits of RE, green bonds appear to bring long-term, reasonably priced capital to reassess an RE project (Sartzetakis, 2021; Tolliver *et al.*, 2019). However, fossil fuels still dominate energy investment because of the risky and long-term nature of financing low-carbon energy projects. One possible solution is to make use of non-bank credits, such as insurance and pension funds, to finance green projects (Gianfrate & Lorenzato, 2018). These funds can hold long-term financial resources and meet the requirements of RE projects. Another method of speeding up the RET is the establishment of green central banking. Central banks not only take responsibility for stabilizing their financial systems, but they are also in charge of protecting the environment. Thus, it is a promising idea for governments around the world to take part in the RET by addressing climate-related and other environmental risks at a system level. Their appropriate regulations and power can promote sustainable development in the finance and energy sectors (Dikau & Volz, 2018). Community-based and village funds are an optimistic method of funding small- and medium-sized low-carbon energy projects. The major objective of these funds is to connect investors with green projects in their own areas. As local environmental benefit recipients, the investors have more incentives to take actions that directly affect their standard of living.

2.2.2. *Public and private finance*

Public finance is a fundamental catalyst for the clean energy transition (Ragosa & Warren, 2019). It invests in emission-intensive infrastructure, new equipment, and clean technologies to accelerate the energy transition. Development finance institutions provide capital to attract private investment in clean energy technologies and low-carbon energy projects. Most RE projects only attract private investment, depending on state financial subsidies (Jolink & Niesten, 2021). Public finance costs are also sufficiently low to accelerate the energy transition while keeping it affordable. Public finance also offers long-term debt for RE projects and supports new technologies from household to community levels.

Private financing could play an essential role in the RET. To promote the investment of private funds in green projects, authorities should employ fiscal policies to increase the rate of return for RE projects. Particularly, governments can apply tax credits or tax relief to encourage the implementation of green projects. It is worth noting that private investors tend to avoid very early seed investments and often target particular areas, such as IT and biotech. Recently, with the development of green technologies, low-carbon projects are attracting more interest from this type of funding. Public policies and investment also play a vital role in mobilizing finance in private sectors and technologies (Mazzucato & Semieniuk, 2018).

3. Discussion

3.1. *Challenges for accelerating renewable energy transitions*

To achieve a smooth RET, authorities and key stakeholders should foresee the major economic, social, and technological challenges and form effective policies to overcome these barriers. The economic challenges refer to the lack of financing for green energy projects or the impacts of low-priced fossil fuels. Governments around the world tend to subsidize the conventional energy sector to develop new industrial zones and eventually boost economic growth (Al-Badi & AlMubarak, 2019). However, these fossil fuel subsidies need to be removed since they accelerate the demand for non-sustainable energy and slow down the RET (Qadir *et al.*, 2021; Zeppini & Van Den Bergh, 2020). The subsidies can be identified in three forms: direct financial support, special tax treatments, and trade policies. In the past decades, most countries have provided some form of support for the conventional energy sector. These policies vary across regions and have different effects on the movement toward sustainable development. Recently, there has been an upward trend in supporting green energy consumption due to the rise in oil prices and an increase in public awareness of environmental issues.

Social barriers include incorrect or biased awareness about RE. The transition requires an appropriate understanding of clean energy sources. However, traditional energy providers tend to argue that RE is costly and unstable (Safari *et al.*, 2019). They make the public believe that fossil fuels are reliable, stable, and secure. Most RE forms are more expensive than non-renewable energy. Also, several studies point out the scarcity of RE in meeting the world's energy demand (Harjanne & Korhonen, 2019). Furthermore, some research papers highlight that RE projects are expensive and cannot guarantee positive financial benefits (Zakaria *et al.*, 2019). This social barrier becomes more severe if there is no public support for RE projects. Individuals and institutions tend to target projects if they can envision rewards from their investments. Without any support from governments, RE projects could become less attractive to investors. Cost unawareness is also a challenge if project assessors lack updated knowledge about the RE market. Eventually, investors or governments tend to underestimate the present value of RE projects. They decide based on past prices in the RE market (Sgouridis *et al.*, 2016). As a result, they might choose conventional energy projects without accounting for the changes in prices of RE projects. The transition toward clean energy usage also depends on the socio-economic conditions of society. While wealthy users can afford and are willing to pay for the extra capital needed to consume clean energy, such as solar energy, poor households tend to prefer cheaper alternatives, which are normally non-sustainable energy sources, such as coal. Therefore, the greater the inequality in socio-economic conditions, the slower the process of RET.

Last but not least, technology is a significant force in the RET. New innovations in the RE sector can help reduce the cost of implementing RE projects. With reasonable costs, key stakeholders are more attracted to RE investments due to higher returns. The investments in the R&D of the RET can be supported by private and public equities. However, investors tend to favor mature technologies with low risks to secure their investments. As a result, lack of funding for R&D in the RE sector leads to delays in creating and implementing newer RE technologies (Adenle, 2020). In this case, authorities could choose the option of approaching venture capitalists to accelerate the RET due to the high-risk, high-return attributes of RE research projects.

3.2. *Suggestions for a successful RET*

Energy is important for the development of a modern economy. Increasing traditional energy demand causes environmental pollution, which is a threat to society's development. RE is promoted as a vital alternative resource. Various financial supports and incentives have been discussed extensively in the literature. However, academic research on the RET mainly focuses on technological development. To promote the share of RE in the energy sector and achieve a successful RET, a wider area needs to be analyzed, including analyzing the effect of financial methodologies on potential RET or examining affecting management strategies.

Policy design plays an important role in achieving a clean energy future. However, policy design has only been discussed based on demand-pull or supply-push policies, such as only focusing on financial benefits to increase RE usage or intending to develop a business environment in which RE is encouraged to use. These include R&D investment and tax reductions for green projects. Studies investigating hybrid policies incorporating demand-pull and supply-push policies are limited in the literature. There is a need to generate a stream of literature on hybrid policy design for the RET.

RE projects require high start-up costs and long payback periods. These disadvantages hinder the competition of RE with traditional energy. Therefore, in the primary stage of development, financial support by governments and other public authorities, such as green credit, green bonds, and RE subsidies, is crucial to constructing RE infrastructures and intellectual properties. A developed financial system generates appropriate investment in advanced technologies and boosts the RE sector (Adom *et al.*, 2020; Brunnschweiler, 2010). In addition, low interest rates and soft loans for RE enterprises could increase RE consumption and reduce energy intensity (Al Mamun *et al.*, 2018). Loans with low interest rates help RE firms reduce their production costs.

On the other hand, a carbon tax is an important tool to reduce the consumption of fossil fuels and carbon emissions. A carbon tax leads to an increase in production costs when using traditional energy and may cause the capital to flow into RE projects (Yang *et al.*, 2019). The market becomes more competitive for RE and the RET. For example, in Chile, the imposed carbon tax causes an increase of 3.4 percent in the marginal cost, which leads to reduced carbon emissions (Vera & Sauma, 2015). Furthermore, a carbon tax could stimulate the development of clean energy and highly efficient enterprises with low carbon emissions. In the long term, a carbon tax can increase government revenue, which can then be invested in green energy resources as low-interest loans, accelerating the energy transition.

Last but not least, there is a lack of examination of private financing for RE projects in the literature. Private financing refers to commercial banks, financial companies, investment organizations, and other private financial providers lending money with low or interest free loans or flexible payment durations. This encourages a community to be involved in the RET by crowdfunding for energy projects. There is a need to have a policy that encourages households to participate procedures for the RET. Typically, households are not interested in using clean energy because of its high cost.

In developing countries, the practice of green credit policy faces many difficulties, such as insufficient environmental awareness in society and inadequate technologies or talent. Hence, a suitable green financial policy should be built and developed.

4. Conclusion

With climate change posing the ultimate challenge to the world's economy (Nordhaus, 2019) owing to its rising economic costs due to the increase in carbon emissions risks worldwide for economic growth, the role of the SET is crucial to the UN's 2030 Agenda for Sustainable Development for targeting carbon neutrality. Through a thorough examination of previous studies on financing the SET, this chapter first provides a conceptualized theoretical framework of determinants in the SET, with the trajectories of economic growth (EG), financial development (FD), and the SET toward the SDGs, as presented in Figure 1. Besides the three main drivers for mitigating climate change impacts, other critical determinants have been highlighted in the recent studies on the SET, for instance, the roles of sustainable infrastructure investments (Trinh, 2021; Trinh *et al.*, 2021), human capital (Shahbaz *et al.*, 2019, 2022; Yao *et al.*, 2019), R&D (Shahbaz *et al.*, 2022; Carbajo & Cabeza, 2018), and clean energy technologies (IEA, 2017a, 2020b).

For financing the SET, prior studies have documented the functionality of FD (Adenle, 2020; Le *et al.*, 2020). However, since the heterogeneous impacts of FD have been detected worldwide (Trinh *et al.*, 2022), the role of FD is considered multidimensional, including that of financial markets (FM) and financial institutions (FI), with their accessibility, depth, and efficiency (FMA, FMD, FME and FIA, FID, FIE),[1] see Svirydzenka (2016). Leaning to the broader fields of green finance, and financing the SET, in particular, we highlight the

[1]FMA stands for financial markets development-access, FMD for financial markets development depth, FME for financial market development efficiency, FIA for financial institutions development access, FID for financial institutions development depth, and FIE for financial institutions development efficiency.

roles of sustainable capital markets (SCMs) that need more studies in the stream of literature on energy economics/finance. Besides FD, policymakers may further investigate the development of SCMs in capital mobilization for financing environmental-oriented projects where infrastructure and RE projects require a bulk of up-front investments, see reports by Climate Bond Initiatives.[2] Since recent studies on SCMs, such as green bond markets, lean toward asset pricing and corporate behaviors, the roles of SCMs along with FD, policies, and incentives are critical to policymakers, NGOs, and governments for a thorough consideration in financing the SET.

We provide a conceptual framework of capital mobilization for financing the SET in the era of climate change toward SDGs, as represented in Figure 2. This is particularly critical to emerging markets, where their FD and SCMs are still in the early stages compared to advanced markets, such as the US, Japan, and European countries. Since the importance of green finance in transferring capital flows to finance the SET is indisputable, along with FD and a stream of determinants presented in the extant literature, we propose a thorough review of the SET with a conceptualized framework for financing the SET, where green finance through SCMs needs further research for

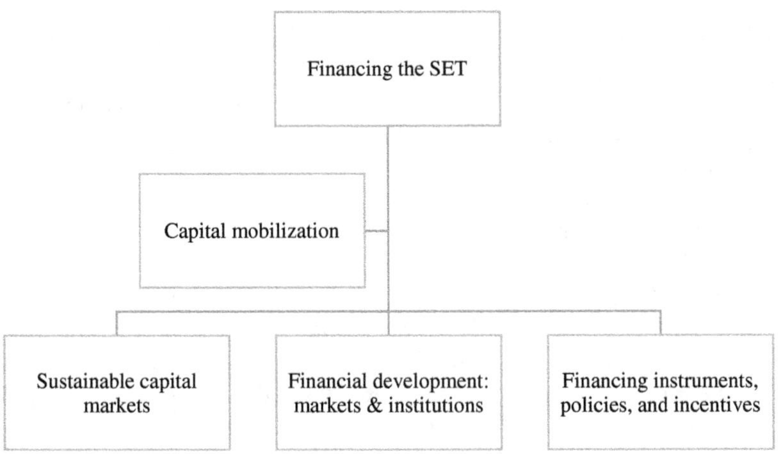

Figure 2. Framework of capital mobilization for financing the SET in the era of climate change.

[2]https://www.climatebonds.net/resources/reports.

an in-depth examination. This chapter is an up-to-date reference for policymakers and related organizations focusing on the role of the RET in the world's carbon neutrality target.

References

Adenle, A. A. (2020). Assessment of solar energy technologies in Africa-opportunities and challenges in meeting the 2030 agenda and sustainable development goals. *Energy Policy, 137*, 111180.

Adom, P. K., Appiah, M. O., & Agradi, M. P. (2020). Does financial development lower energy intensity? *Frontiers in Energy, 14*(3), 620–634.

Al Mamun, M., Sohag, K., Shahbaz, M., *et al.* (2018). Financial markets, innovations and cleaner energy production in OECD countries. *Energy Economics, 72*, 236–254.

Al-Badi, A. & AlMubarak, I. (2019). Growing energy demand in the GCC countries. *Arab Journal of Basic and Applied Sciences, 26*(1), 488–496.

Alasseri, R., Rao, T. J., & Sreekanth, K. (2020). Institution of incentive-based demand response programs and prospective policy assessments for a subsidized electricity market. *Renewable and Sustainable Energy Reviews, 117*, 109490.

Benasla, M., Hess, D., Allaoui, T., *et al.* (2019). The transition towards a sustainable energy system in Europe: What role can North Africa's solar resources play? *Energy Strategy Reviews, 24*, 1–13.

Bersalli, G., Menanteau, P., & El-Methni, J. (2020). Renewable energy policy effectiveness: A panel data analysis across Europe and Latin America. *Renewable and Sustainable Energy Reviews, 133*, 110351.

Bhattacharyya, R. (2022). Green finance for energy transition, climate action and sustainable development: Overview of concepts, applications, implementation and challenges. *Green Finance, 4*(1), 1–35. 10.3934/GF.2022001.

Bhutta, U. S., Tariq, A., Farrukh, M., *et al.* (2022). Green bonds for sustainable development: Review of literature on development and impact of green bonds. *Technological Forecasting and Social Change, 175*, 121378.

Bointner, R., Pezzutto, S., Grilli, G., *et al.* (2016). Financing innovations for the renewable energy transition in Europe. *Energies, 9*(12), 990. Retrieved from https://www.mdpi.com/1996-1073/9/12/ 990.

Brunnschweiler, C. N. (2010). Finance for renewable energy: An empirical analysis of developing and transition economies. *Environment and Development Economics, 15*(3), 241–274.

Carbajo, R. & Cabeza, L. F. (2018). Renewable energy research and technologies through responsible research and innovation looking glass: Reflexions, theoretical approaches and contemporary discourses. *Applied Energy*, *211*, 792–808.

Carbon Brief (2016). Timeline: The past, present and future of Germany's Energiewende. Retrieved from https://www.carbonbrief.org/timeline-past-present-future-germany-energiewende.

Ćetković, S. & Buzogány, A. (2016). Varieties of capitalism and clean energy transitions in the European Union: When renewable energy hits different economic logics. *Climate Policy*, *16*(5), 642–657. 10.1080/14693062.2015.1135778.

CLEW (2019). The main stories of Germany's Energiewende. Retrieved from https://www.cleanenergywire.org/factsheets/main-stories-germanys-energiewende.

Council, C. E. (2016). Progress and Status of the Renewable Energy Target.

Curtin, J., McInerney, C., & Gallachóir, B. Ó. (2017). Financial incentives to mobilise local citizens as investors in low-carbon technologies: A systematic literature review. *Renewable and Sustainable Energy Reviews*, *75*, 534–547.

De Negri, J. F., Pezzutto, S., Gantioler, S., *et al.* (2020). A comprehensive analysis of public and private funding for photovoltaics research and development in the European Union, Norway, and Turkey. *Energies*, *13*(11), 2743.

Dikau, S. & Volz, U. (2018). Central banking, climate change and green finance. Retrieved from https://eprints.soas.ac.uk/26445/.

Fang, Z. & Chang, Y. (2016). Energy, human capital and economic growth in Asia Pacific countries — Evidence from a panel cointegration and causality analysis. *Energy Economics*, *56*, 177–184. https://doi.org/10.1016/j.eneco.2016.03.020.

Fang, Z. & Chen, Y. (2017). Human capital and energy in economic growth — Evidence from Chinese provincial data. *Energy Economics*, *68*, 340–358. https://doi.org/10.1016/j.eneco.2017.10.007.

Gallo, A. B., Simões-Moreira, J. R., Costa, H. K. M., *et al.* (2016). Energy storage in the energy transition context: A technology review. *Renewable and Sustainable Energy Reviews*, *65*, 800–822. https://doi.org/10.1016/j.rser.2016.07.028.

Gee, S. & McMeekin, A. (2011). Eco-innovation systems and problem sequences: The contrasting cases of US and Brazilian biofuels. *Industry and Innovation*, *18*(3), 301–315.

Gianfrate, G. & Lorenzato, G. (2018). Stimulating Non-bank Financial Institutions' Participation in Green Investments. Retrieved from https://www.econstor.eu/bitstream/10419/190281/1/adbi-wp860.pdf.

Gökgöz, F. & Güvercin, M. T. (2018). Energy security and renewable energy efficiency in EU. *Renewable and Sustainable Energy Reviews, 96*, 226–239.

Güney, T. (2019). Renewable energy, non-renewable energy and sustainable development. *International Journal of Sustainable Development & World Ecology, 26*(5), 389–397.

Hall, S., Foxon, T. J., & Bolton, R. (2017). Investing in low-carbon transitions: Energy finance as an adaptive market. *Climate Policy, 17*(3), 280–298. 10.1080/14693062.2015.1094731.

Harjanne, A. & Korhonen, J. M. (2019). Abandoning the concept of renewable energy. *Energy Policy, 127*, 330–340.

Hartmann, J., Inkpen, A. C., & Ramaswamy, K. (2021). Different shades of green: Global oil and gas companies and renewable energy. *Journal of International Business Studies, 52*(5), 879–903.

Hira, A. & De Oliveira, L. G. (2009). No substitute for oil? How Brazil developed its ethanol industry. *Energy Policy, 37*(6), 2450–2456.

IEA (2017a). Energy Technology Perspectives 2017, IEA, Paris. Retrieved from https://www.iea.org/reports/energy-technology-perspectives-2017.

IEA (2017b). *World Energy Outlook 2017.* Paris: IEA. Retrieved from https://www.iea.org/reports/world-energy-outlook-2017.

IEA (2018). World Energy Outlook 2018: Electricity.

IEA (2020a). China's Emissions Trading Designing Efficient Allowance Allocation. Retrieved from https://iea.blob.core.windows.net/assets/d21bfabc-ac8a-4c41-bba7-e792cf29945c/China_Emissions_Trading_Scheme.pdf.

IEA (2020b). *Energy Technology Perspectives 2020.* Paris: IEA. Retrieved from https://www.iea.org/reports/energy-technology-perspectives-2020.

IRENA (2019). Renewable Power Generation Costs in 2019. Retrieved from https://www.irena.org/-/media/Files/IRENA/Agency/Publication/2020/Jun/IRENA_Power_Generation_Costs_2019.pdf.

IRENA (2020a). Renewable Energy Finance: Green Bonds. Retrieved from https://committee.iso.org/sites/tc322/home/projects/ongoing/ongoing-1.html.

IRENA (2020b). Stimulating Investment in Community Energy: Broardening the Ownweship of Renewable. Retrieved from https://coalition.irena.org/-/media/Files/IRENA/Coalition-for-Action/IRENA_Coalition_Stimulating_Investment_in_Community_Energy_2020.pdf.

Jacobs, D. (2012). The German Energiewende — History, targets, policies and challenges. *Renewable Energy Law and Policy Review, 3*(4), 223–233. Retrieved from http://www.jstor.org/stable/24324660.

Johnsson, F., Kjärstad, J., & Rootzén, J. (2019). The threat to climate change mitigation posed by the abundance of fossil fuels. *Climate Policy, 19*(2), 258–274.

Jolink, A. & Niesten, E. (2021). Chapter 12 — Financing the energy transition: The role of public funding, collaboration and private equity. In A. Rubino, A. Sapio, & M. La Scala (Eds.) *Handbook of Energy Economics and Policy* (pp. 521–547). Academic Press. https://doi-org.ezproxy.massey.ad.nz/10.1016/B978-0-12-814712-2.00012-9.

Khan, T., Khanam, S. N., Rahman, M. H., *et al.* (2019). Determinants of microfinance facility for installing solar home system (SHS) in rural Bangladesh. *Energy Policy, 132*, 299–308. https://doi.org/10.1016/j.enpol.2019.05.047.

Khan, S. A. R., Zhang, Y., Kumar, A., *et al.* (2020). Measuring the impact of renewable energy, public health expenditure, logistics, and environmental performance on sustainable economic growth. *Sustainable Development, 28*(4), 833–843.

Khan, M. K., Trinh, H. H., Khan, I. U., *et al.* (2021). Sustainable economic activities, climate change, and carbon risk: An international evidence. *Environment, Development and Sustainability.* doi:10.1007/s10668-021-01842-x.

KPMG (2013). *Taxes and Incentives for Renewable Energy.* Amsterdam, Netherlands: KPMG International.

Le, T.-H., Nguyen, C. P., & Park, D. (2020). Financing renewable energy development: Insights from 55 countries. *Energy Research & Social Science, 68*, 101537.

Le, T.-H., Boubaker, S., & Nguyen, C. P. (2021). The energy-growth nexus revisited: An analysis of different types of energy. *Journal of Environmental Management, 297*, 113351. https://doi.org/10.1016/j.jenvman.2021.113351.

Li, L. & Taeihagh, A. (2020). An in-depth analysis of the evolution of the policy mix for the sustainable energy transition in China from 1981 to 2020. *Applied Energy, 263*, 114611. https://doi.org/10.1016/j.apenergy.2020.114611.

Li, H. X., Edwards, D. J., Hosseini, M. R., *et al.* (2020). A review on renewable energy transition in Australia: An updated depiction. *Journal of Cleaner Production, 242*, 118475. https://doi.org/10.1016/j.jclepro.2019.118475.

Lin, R. & Ren, J. (2020). Renewable energy and sustainable development. *Journal of Renewable Energy and Sustainable Development, 6*(1), 3–7.

Mahmoud, M., Ramadan, M., Olabi, A.-G., *et al.* (2020). A review of mechanical energy storage systems combined with wind and solar applications. *Energy Conversion and Management, 210*, 112670.

Mazzucato, M. & Semieniuk, G. (2018). Financing renewable energy: Who is financing what and why it matters. *Technological Forecasting and Social Change*, *127*, 8–22. https://doi.org/10.1016/j.techfore.2017.05.021.

Nordhaus, W. (2019). Climate Change — The Ultimate Challenge for Economics. *American Economic Review*, *109*(6), 1991–2014. DOI: 10.1257/aer.109.6.1991.

Ockwell, D. G., Watson, J., MacKerron, G., *et al.* (2008). Key policy considerations for facilitating low carbon technology transfer to developing countries. *Energy Policy*, *36*(11), 4104–4115. https://doi.org/10.1016/j.enpol.2008.06.019.

Pablo-Romero, M. D. P. & Sánchez-Braza, A. (2015). Productive energy use and economic growth: Energy, physical and human capital relationships. *Energy Economics*, *49*, 420–429. https://doi.org/10.1016/j.eneco.2015.03.010.

Parra, D., Swierczynski, M., Stroe, D. I., *et al.* (2017). An interdisciplinary review of energy storage for communities: Challenges and perspectives. *Renewable and Sustainable Energy Reviews*, *79*, 730–749. https://doi.org/10.1016/j. rser.2017.05.003.

Pickl, M. J. (2019). The renewable energy strategies of oil majors — From oil to energy? *Energy Strategy Reviews*, *26*, 100370. https://doi.org/10.1016/j.esr.2019.100370.

Pitelis, A., Vasilakos, N., & Chalvatzis, K. (2020). Fostering innovation in renewable energy technologies: Choice of policy instruments and effectiveness. *Renewable Energy*, *151*, 1163–1172. https://doi.org/10.1016/j.renene.2019.11.100.

Punda, L., Capuder, T., Pandžić, H., *et al.* (2017). Integration of renewable energy sources in southeast Europe: A review of incentive mechanisms and feasibility of investments. *Renewable and Sustainable Energy Reviews*, *71*, 77–88. https://doi.org/10.1016/j.rser.2017.01.008.

Qadir, S. A., Al-Motairi, H., Tahir, F., *et al.* (2021). Incentives and strategies for financing the renewable energy transition: A review. *Energy Reports*, *7*, 3590–3606.

Rafi, M., Naseef, M., & Prasad, S. (2021). Multidimensional energy poverty and human capital development: Empirical evidence from India. *Energy Economics*, *101*, 105427. https://doi.org/10.1016/j.eneco.2021.105427.

Ragosa, G. & Warren, P. (2019). Unpacking the determinants of cross-border private investment in renewable energy in developing countries. *Journal of Cleaner Production*, *235*, 854–865.

Sachs, J. D., Woo, W. T., Yoshino, N., *et al.* (2019). Importance of green finance for achieving sustainable development goals and energy security. In *Handbook of Green Finance* (pp. 3–12). Springer.

Safari, A., Das, N., Langhelle, O., *et al.* (2019). Natural gas: A transition fuel for sustainable energy system transformation? *Energy Science & Engineering*, *7*(4), 1075–1094.

Salim, R., Yao, Y., & Chen, G. S. (2017). Does human capital matter for energy consumption in China? *Energy Economics*, *67*, 49–59. https://doi.org/10.1016/j.eneco.2017.05.016.

Sartzetakis, E. S. (2021). Green bonds as an instrument to finance low carbon transition. *Economic Change and Restructuring*, *54*(3), 755–779.

Sawin, J. L., Martinot, E., Barnes, D., *et al.* (2013). Renewables. *Global Status Report*, 46(38).

Schiffer, H.-W. & Trüby, J. (2018). A review of the German energy transition: Taking stock, looking ahead, and drawing conclusions for the Middle East and North Africa. *Energy Transitions*, *2*(1), 1–14. https://doi.org/10.1007/s41825-018-0010-2.

Sgouridis, S., Abdullah, A., Griffiths, S., *et al.* (2016). RE-mapping the UAE's energy transition: An economy-wide assessment of renewable energy options and their policy implications. *Renewable and Sustainable Energy Reviews*, *55*, 1166–1180.

Shahbaz, M., Gozgor, G., & Hammoudeh, S. (2019). Human capital and export diversification as new determinants of energy demand in the United States. *Energy Economics*, *78*, 335–349. https://doi.org/10.1016/j.eneco.2018.11.016.

Shahbaz, M., Song, M., Ahmad, S., *et al.* (2022). Does economic growth stimulate energy consumption? The role of human capital and R&D expenditures in China. *Energy Economics*, *105*, 105662. https://doi.org/10.1016/j.eneco.2021.105662.

Sharma, G. D., Tiwari, A. K., Erkut, B., *et al.* (2021). Exploring the nexus between non-renewable and renewable energy consumptions and economic development: Evidence from panel estimations. *Renewable and Sustainable Energy Reviews*, *146*, 111152. https://doi.org/10.1016/j.rser.2021.111152.

Sheng, C., Cao, Y., & Xue, B. (2018). Residential energy sustainability in China and Germany: The impact of national energy policy system. *Sustainability*, *10*(12), 4535. Retrieved from https://www.mdpi.com/2071-1050/10/12/4535.

Solomon, B. D. & Krishna, K. (2011). The coming sustainable energy transition: History, strategies, and outlook. *Energy Policy*, *39*(11), 7422–7431. https://doi.org/10.1016/j.enpol.2011.09.009.

Steffen, B. (2020). Estimating the cost of capital for renewable energy projects. *Energy Economics*, *88*, 104783.

Svirydzenka, K. (2016). Introducing a new broad-based index of financial development. International Monetary Fund. Retrieved from https://www.imf.org/en/Publications/WP/Issues/2016/12/31/Introducing-a-New-Broad-based-index-of-Financial-Development-43621.

Tolliver, C., Keeley, A. R., & Managi, S. (2019). Green bonds for the Paris agreement and sustainable development goals. *Environmental Research Letters*, *14*(6), 064009.

Trinh, H. H. (2021). Smart energy systems, infrastructure financing, and the wider economy. In M. Fathi, E. Zio, & P. M. Pardalos (Eds.). *Handbook of Smart Energy Systems* (pp. 1–23). Cham: Springer International Publishing.

Trinh, H. H., Sharma, G. D., Tiwari, A. K., & Vo, D. T. H. (2022). Examining the heterogeneity of financial development in the energy-environment nexus in the era of climate change: Novel evidence around the world. *Energy Economics*, 116, 106415.

ul Abideen, M. Z., Ellabban, O., Refaat, S. S., *et al.* (2019). A novel methodology to determine the maximum PV penetration in distribution networks. In *Paper Presented at the 2019 2nd International Conference on Smart Grid and Renewable Energy (SGRE).*

Vera, S. & Sauma, E. (2015). Does a carbon tax make sense in countries with still a high potential for energy efficiency? Comparison between the reducing-emissions effects of carbon tax and energy efficiency measures in the Chilean case. *Energy*, *88*, 478–488.

Yang, D.-X., Chen, Z.-Y., Yang, Y.-C., *et al.* (2019). Green financial policies and capital flows. *Physica A: Statistical Mechanics and Its Applications*, *522*, 135–146. https://doi.org/10.1016/j.physa.2019. 01.126.

Yao, L., Yang, B., Cui, H., *et al.* (2016). Challenges and progresses of energy storage technology and its application in power systems. *Journal of Modern Power Systems and Clean Energy*, *4*(4), 519–528. 10.1007/s40565-016-0248-x.

Yao, Y., Ivanovski, K., Inekwe, J., *et al.* (2019). Human capital and energy consumption: Evidence from OECD countries. *Energy Economics*, *84*, 104534. https://doi.org/10.1016/j.eneco.2019.104534.

Yoshino, N., Taghizadeh–Hesary, F., & Nakahigashi, M. (2019). Modelling the social funding and spill-over tax for addressing the green energy financing gap. *Economic Modelling*, *77*, 34–41.

Zakaria, S. U., Basri, S., Kamarudin, S. K., & Majid, N. A. A. (2019, June). Public awareness analysis on renewable energy in Malaysia. In *IOP Conference Series: Earth and Environmental Science*, *268*(1), p. 012105. IOP Publishing.

Zeppini, P. & Van Den Bergh, J. C. (2020). Global competition dynamics of fossil fuels and renewable energy under climate policies and peak oil: A behavioural model. *Energy Policy*, *136*, 110907.

Zhang, D., Mohsin, M., Rasheed, A. K., *et al.* (2021). Public spending and green economic growth in BRI region: Mediating role of green finance. *Energy Policy*, *153*, 112256. https://doi.org/10.1016/j.enpol.2021.112256.

Zhao, Z.-Y., Chen, Y.-L., & Chang, R.-D. (2016). How to stimulate renewable energy power generation effectively? — China's incentive approaches and lessons. *Renewable Energy*, *92*, 147–156. https://doi.org/10.1016/j.renene.2016.02.001.

Zsiborács, H., Baranyai, N. H., Vincze, A., *et al.* (2019). Intermittent renewable energy sources: The role of energy storage in the European power system of 2040. *Electronics*, *8*(7), 729.

https://doi.org/10.1142/9781800614482_0011

Chapter 11

The Role of Financing in Achieving Sustainable Development Goals: Economic and Legal Implications

Muhammad Azam[†,‖], **Ahmed Imran Hunjra**[*,‡,¶], and **Mohammad Kabir Hassan**[§,**]

[†]*Ghazi University, Dera Ghazi Khan, Pakistan*
[‡]*Rabat Business School, International University of Rabat, Morocco*
[§]*University of New Orleans, New Orleans, USA*
[‖]*muazam@gudgk.edu.pk*
[¶]*ahmedhunjra@gmail.com*
[**]*mhassan@uno.edu*

Abstract

This chapter describes the role of financing in achieving the Sustainable Development Goals (SDGs). The achievement of SDGs is an ongoing concern for the Millennium Development Goals, although the financial structure and sustainable investment projects are closely aligned with the SDGs. Our research provides useful insights into the fact that the dynamics of finance can be leveraged to close gaps and address the SDG challenges. Despite financial laws, financial structural difficulties have persisted in several countries from diverse regions over the years. These problems became more adverse during the COVID-19 pandemic, requiring greater attention toward resolution. This chapter contributes to the existing literature by shedding light on global economies through theoretical and practical analysis. We believe that such significant insights would guide the financial sector and regulators to achieve the SDGs, particularly in emerging economies.

[*]Corresponding author.

1. Introduction

As the Millennium Development Goals (MDGs) expired in 2015, the international community has been actively engaged in developing a new global development agenda. The SDGs are more important and comprehensive, and significant financing will be required for their implementation. Thus, a conventional approach to finance is inadequate, and a paradigm shift is required in development finance. Finance can play a revolutionary role in assisting the implementation of the post-2015 agenda. The MDGs were developed out of the Millennium Declaration signed by 189 countries in September 2000. The eight goals, each with a specific target, aimed to bring an end to poverty, eliminate disparities between men and women in terms of education and health, and promote long-term growth. After their adoption, the MDGs were debated at a variety of international forums. Developing nations accelerated reforms to stimulate growth and enhance the MDGs. Therefore, there was an urgent need for countries to investigate all available possibilities for financing their development.

It is estimated that annual investments of $1.5 trillion are required to achieve the targets of the Paris Agreement (Parkinson *et al.*, 2019). Signed by most countries worldwide in 2015, it commits governments to lead the financing of projects to combat climate change targets. There is a requirement at the government level that such kinds of macroeconomic and financial policies are adopted to ensure the financing of green technologies. Financial difficulties constitute a significant potential source of development financing, which is frequently ignored. There is a requirement to investigate the relationship between the SDGs' objectives and financial policy. The context of the relationship between the financial policies and the SDGs requires discussion, including key insights into the underlying concepts. This chapter discusses the relationship between the SDGs and the financial system and provides some critical observations on the existing role of the financial system, which are essential to understanding this argument.

In the current paradigm, it is essential to discuss the debate at the nexus of financial strategies and the SDGs (WHO, 2019). The literature has recently focused on the relationship between financial strategies to achieve the SDGs (Asongu & De Moor, 2015;

Asongu & Vo, 2020; Cirolia, 2020; Midgley, 2019; Zhou & Du, 2021). Some conventional views on the linkages between financial policies and SDG aims must be investigated further to incorporate policy coordination components into the discussion. Diverse themes, such as financial inclusion, the significance of the financial sector, and green financial derivatives, have arisen in the financial system, which has been given major weightage by the United Nations climate change finance conferences on SDG objectives (Arkhipova, 2017; Bracking, 2019; Wang & Dong, 2019). Under the current regime of COVID-19 pandemic issues around the world, the consideration of finances is receiving a great deal of attention and gaining popularity (Deloitte, 2020; Goodell, 2020; Wójcik & Ioannou, 2020). The impacts of lockdowns and other COVID-19 measures have influenced the loss of jobs and financial investments in various projects. It is observed that businesses and financial losses of the corporate sector are due to poor loan performance and the financial risk of the SDGs' target projects. Alternative financial measures are crucial for the financial development and the achievement of SDGs in the majority of economies to deal with the crisis after COVID-19.

This chapter begins with a discussion on the emergence of the notion of the SDGs to set the stage for an evaluation of the potential role of finance. The underlying principles and recent obstacles of finance are then examined, thus contributing to the sustainable finance literature. However, the primary focus of this chapter is on the discussion of financial system issues and their relationship with the SDGs, which can provide positive outcomes for financial–economic institutions in different parts of the world, particularly in developing economies, to support financial stabilization that contributes to the SDGs. The purpose of this chapter is to contribute to the literature through a comprehensive study of the role of finance in the multifaceted SDGs, with an emphasis on developing nations. This chapter also contributes to the literature by examining the effects of financial development on the SDGs.

2. History of the Sustainable Development Goals

The debate on long-term development goals begins with the UN SDGs. As part of the SDGs, all development decisions must incorporate environmental, social, and economic considerations (Harvey, 2021). Expanding on the MDGs, the United Nations introduced 17 SDGs targeting new areas of development. All of these goals are practically intertwined, meaning that fulfilling one has an impact on the others. All of the goals are expected to be completed by 2030, with some individual targets having earlier deadlines. Other UN and allied development organizations are undertaking supportive measures to help accelerate the achievement of the SDGs. The most important activities are presently underway to help achieve the SDGs. The following major objectives have been targeted by 2030: ending hunger, increasing food security and nutrition, and supporting sustainable agriculture, ensuring accessible and equitable quality education, encouraging possibilities for lifelong learning and achieving gender equality (Ejemeyovwi *et al.*, 2021). Further, these objectives include ensuring water, sanitation, supply and long-term management access to affordable, dependable, sustainable, and modern energy (Kataki *et al.*, 2017), thus encouraging inclusive and long-term growth in the economy and also sustainable employment and good working conditions. Equal access to justice should be offered for all until 2030 to build inclusive, responsible, and successful organizations at all levels for long-term growth (Kravchenko *et al.*, 2021). Investments should be made in basic infrastructure for an inclusive and sustainable economy and the development of innovations to improve equality both within and among countries, create cities and human settlements that are secure, resilient, and sustainable for everyone (UN Human Settlement Programme, 2018), and ensure that consumption and production patterns are sustainable. Action must be taken immediately to combat climate change and its implications. By 2030, the oceans, sea and marine resources should be protected and used responsibly for sustainable development. Terrestrial ecosystems and forest ecosystems should be conserved and restored by stopping desertification, reversing land degradation, and making efforts to conserve biodiversity as part of a holistic approach. The global collaboration for sustainable development should be reinvigorated and strengthened by putting the 2030 strategies into action.

To date, the pace of development in order to achieve the SDGs has been somewhat slow and uneven among countries owing to fundamental economic, social and political differences between them

(Liu *et al.*, 2021). When comparing wealthy nations with emerging nations, the disparity is considerably bigger. However, the fact that all countries are actively engaged in the SDGs' agendas and are making progress, albeit to varying degrees, is a noteworthy development. It is hard to keep track of and account for developments in any country when viewed from a global perspective. The United Nations compiles the most accurate information regarding the SDGs' progress. Organizing the required financial resources, especially in the developing world, is the main hurdle to achieving exceptional progress toward the SDGs (Swain, 2018). Unlike industrialized nations, which are mostly capable of self-financing, developing nations rely heavily on foreign aid. The United Nations and other international development organizations agree that developments on many of the goals are modest and in their initial stages at this point. Consequently, if countries continue to progress at their current rates, it will be impossible to achieve the SDGs by 2030. The risk is far bigger for poor nations, as they have too many problems to handle the SDGs as well. Consequently, the management of financial resources remains a significant obstacle to achieving the SDGs, particularly in developing nations (Mendez & Houghton, 2020).

The targets of the SDGs have increased the dependence of developing nations on donors and foreign governments. The majority of developing nations continue to rely heavily on funding from international development agencies and foreign donors such as the United Nations and other international, industrialized governments to organize and obtain financing for the SDGs. National governments finance a portion of the funding, while the private sector remains much less involved, thus underlining the fact that the current level of financing is much less than what is required to achieve the SDGs.

3. The Role of Finance in Achieving the Sustainable Development Goals

For sustainable development to succeed, a wide range of resources will have to be drawn from many different locations. Various parties, such as governments, enterprises, financial institutions, civil society organizations, and non-profits play a vital role in effective financing. The financial sector's ability to contribute to long-term development will be determined by how much money is made. Many people now realize that private enterprises should address environmental, social, and governance issues whilst making decisions and contributing to the achievement of objectives in their daily operations. Environmental and social risks are assessed by the International Finance Corporation (IFC) as part of its funding criterion for international projects. These hazards can be mitigated by implementing performance standards. Environmental and social risks are increasingly being considered by financial institutions as part of their risk assessment and management processes. According to the nature of a financial institution's culture, it can participate in social and environmental initiatives.

The IFC evolved from a value-protection to a value-creation perspective on corporate social responsibility (CSR). When investing in the financial sector, one has a wide range of possibilities available. There is now an emphasis on the societal impact of investment choices by businesses, as part of as the multifaceted decision on risk and profit. Such initiatives include investing in renewable energy and green technology companies, which are called "sustainability-focused investments" (Oliva & Rodrigues, 2010). Community investing, in which investments are made in impoverished communities or companies with a socially responsible purpose, can also have an impact, as it focuses on alleviating social and environmental problems. For companies to be involved in SDG-related investments, they need to be able to communicate their ideas and preferences about these issues (Zhou *et al.*, 2021).

Recently, there has been a huge increase in global sustainable investments, which provides evidence of the rise in awareness about the SDGs and associated measures. The demand for SDG financing is crucial. The SDG agenda, fulfilling the 17 objectives, requires yearly investments of \$5–7 trillion, and there is a \$2.5 trillion annual investment gap. This number represents only 7–10 percent of the world's GDP and 25–40 percent of the annual worldwide investments (Harrison, 2009).

The United Nations and states are attempting to reduce the investment gap through a variety of financial and investment channels that target the SDGs. Several variables lead to the failure of the tracking system. First, investments made privately do not have an authorized tag of SDGs. Second, international agencies, such as the World Bank and the United Nations, have only now recognized the relevance of tracking SDGs connected to national and cross-border financial transactions (Ritchie & Fisher, 2021). In addition, at the national scale, especially in the developing world, the concept of reporting and accountability for SDG-relevant international or domestic investment is still relatively new, and the majority of nations lack any framework for doing so. Thus, the primary difficulty in financing the SDGs continues to be a lack of awareness and comprehension of the current state of the world and the goals for SDG finance and investments. Climate-specific foreign direct investment (FDI), low-carbon investments, green loans by institutions and expenditures on renewable energy are the streams of investments that contribute to achieving the SDGs (Valdivia, 2016).

4. SDG Finance and Implementation Constraints

According to numerous scholars and practitioner reports, it is difficult to raise sufficient money for the SDGs since the remaining investment gap is so significant (ICSU, 2015; Hou *et al.*, 2020; Lawrence *et al.*, 2020; Rodić & Wilson, 2017; Zhang *et al.*, 2020). The extant SDG-related literature identifies several significant obstacles. First, the financing of the SDGs relies heavily on assistance and aid provided by developed nations to underdeveloped nations. However, when it comes to integrating the SDGs, affluent countries are commonly criticized for not being engaged or helpful with developing nations or donor agencies. This inclination toward non-cooperation and delays in prompt responses leads to insufficient financial transfers to developing nations for achieving the SDGs. Second, the developing nations and their financial sectors exhibit a lack of collaboration. The current state of investments demonstrates that the public sector is the most important source of SDG financing; as the private sector's contributions to SDG projects are negligible. Narrowing the investment gap requires increased private sector participation. Still, a lack of collaboration and desire prevails in both the advanced and developing worlds.

Due to the potential cost burdens and lack of appropriate incentive systems and public–private collaborations, private sector actors frequently require initiatives. However, within the formal financial markets and institutions, the non-participation of the private sector frequently places a greater emphasis on financial return than on social results. There is a lack of cooperation from the business sector that allows money to remain idle. It also explains the absence of a mature financial sector as a key impediment to channeling SDG-related funds.

Having explained the obstacles, we now illustrate some of the proposed resolutions. Before the adoption of the SDGs, governments and organizations were already working on the challenges linked to each of the 17 SDGs. Executing the SDGs in a cross-cutting or integrated way is a problem that necessitates cross-sector collaboration as well as participation from individual sectors (Risse, 2017). A cross-sectoral approach is usually required because funding is needed to fulfill goals in all sectors. Implementation of the SDGs requires revamping organizational or institutional structures to work across sectors, and it also prevents organizations or institutions from actively participating. When cross-sectoral approaches become overly complicated and impossible to put into practice, it becomes difficult to dedicate resources to the SDGs in the most efficient manner.

For some developing nations, the SDG agenda is challenging, and they lacked comprehension and readiness when the SDGs were first implemented, and many have lacked adequate planning for the SDGs up until this point. Consequently, even though the SDGs have been in existence for a number of years, many developing nations still struggle to conceptualize and plan the mobilization of funds and investments to address the SDGs. The problem is intensifying because the majority of developing nations do not incorporate SDG considerations into their national budgets and investment plans. A discussion is required to understand how strongly the success of the SDGs is dependent on the commitment of various national and international stakeholders. Understanding the involvement of governments, non-governmental organizations, corporations, and the research and technological communities is essential in this setting. SDG stakeholders' opinions and priorities on development frequently diverge due to varying and shifting agendas, which continuously leave an impact. As important as local and regional financing institutions are to the SDGs, their funding and investments are heavily restricted because of the concentration on their other goals and purposes. It is noted that incomplete information and a potentially deceptive view of the existing status and future requirements for SDG-related financing and investments have a devastating impact on SDG targets. Particularly in underdeveloped nations, where the majority lack robust, dependable, and high-quality data delivery networks, researchers have identified that the issue of a lack of appropriate, timely and high quality data is significantly more severe. The lack of such data continues to pose a significant obstacle to achieving the SDGs. Inequalities, capital constraints, and economic imbalance in the emerging world are to blame for the uneven and less inclusive nature of economic development in developed and developing nations. Certain nations have fluctuating growth rates, and others have a more steady but slower pace of growth, requiring them to concentrate on issues beyond the SDGs. Due to varying growth levels, all countries cannot follow the same goals as there will be varied results leading to the failure of SDG implementations (Atack, 2021).

There is a huge knowledge gap between industrialized and developing countries, which leads to inadequate growth potential due to considerable technological, economic, societal and knowledge disparities in the world economy. The huge disparity in development capabilities speeds up the process of formulating country-specific SDG investments and financial plans. Furthermore, in poor countries, a considerable percentage of the population still lacks adequate financial resources, rendering it hard to allocate SDG funds to those who are most in need. Many countries are plagued by weak governance, instability, and policy failure.

An extensive debate, highlighting the role of good governance in utilizing funds efficiently and effectively, is ongoing. At the practical, national level, however, many developing nations have weak governance, which is characterized by political instability, a lack of transparency, and corruption. It ultimately leads to the inability to obtain essential finance and ensure the efficient and effective use of available investments (Ball, 2020). For instance, many governments of developing countries are frequently accused of misusing financial support, primarily due to heavy bureaucracy, corruption, and a lack of accountability. In some developing nations, political instability and insecurity persist, putting at risk the systematic finance and investment initiatives for the SDGs. For instance, nations such as Syria and Iraq, which are experiencing widespread bloodshed or wars, are unable to finance and invest in the SDGs. Another dimension includes public policy and regulatory measures, with focus on how the public sector can contribute considerably more in the future. However, in developing nations, the government sector does not serve to its fullest extent. The assessment of real investment requirements in developing countries is hampered by the absence of proper strategic planning, management, and frameworks in the government sector. An inflexible tax structure in poor nations discourages the public sector from investing in the SDGs.

Due to differing government priorities, the budgetary process in developing nations has yet to take the SDGs into account to the greatest extent possible. In addition, regulatory systems for both the public and commercial sectors require significant attention to incorporate SDG principles. For instance, financial regulations and economic agents that comply with SDG objectives have environmental impacts. If the world wants to fulfill the SDGs by 2030, the financial obstacles must be resolved without delay. Based on the available SDG literature and discussions, it is possible to identify several techniques that could be useful in addressing the obstacles. Importantly, these mitigation measures are largely illustrative and not exhaustive. There is a requirement for increased collaboration within and between developing countries. Cross-country cooperation between advanced and developing nations can assist in the mobilization of a higher amount of financial resources for the latter, but collaboration between developing nations can also produce more successful international joint efforts. There should be more formal and informal conversations about SDG funding and investment difficulties via regional and international dialogues, workshops, and symposiums at the world, national, and regional levels to achieve SDGs. However, few such activities have been held in developing countries to date. The public and private sectors should work together more frequently. Corporate engagement is necessary since the SDGs are also relevant to private sector players' interests (Beyer *et al.*, 2018). The private sector's greater ability to fill funding and investment shortages makes effective public–private partnerships critical to achieving the SDGs. Additionally, international institutions, such as the UN, may adopt rules and incentivize private sector investment in the SDGs. IFC's direct collaboration with the business and public sectors in various developing countries is facilitating effective investments in SDG-related activities. Additionally, this necessitates lowering the foreign and domestic risks of SDG investments and raising the institutional capacity of private and public sector partners by increasing socio-economic opportunities with a monetary reward. There must be protocols in place to prevent the market from collapsing. It is possible to create an atmosphere that encourages new types of investments by providing clear principles and criteria for monitoring investment outcomes, with an aim to achieve a more equitable and inclusive economic development. Investing in the SDGs would be simpler and more efficient if countries experienced strong economic growth.

A higher degree of knowledge and awareness regarding the SDGs and their implementation would make the lives of ordinary people even better and could facilitate their implementation further. Such incentives have the potential to significantly expand stakeholder participation in the finance and investment agenda. In developing countries, identifying financial and investment needs necessitates careful planning at the government scale. With the help of the UN, government institutions may better plan and prepare for the SDGs by creating new planning and execution departments in conjunction with the national planning commission, the finance ministry, and other key financial agencies. Numerous governments and government agencies in poor countries lack adequate planning, preventing them from executing the SDG agenda successfully. At the state level, these SDG-adjusted policies might be extremely beneficial in getting the required public funds for the SDGs. Conventional financial markets may become more favorable to SDG activities if laws are changed to encourage or oblige all financial firms to finance social projects at a subsidized rate and to align their goods and services with the SDGs.

5. Legal Implications and Critical Discussion

An extensive discussion on the association between financing and development focuses on four fundamental pillars: domestic resource mobilization, better and smarter aid, domestic private finance, and overseas private finance. Finance has the potential to play a significant role in supporting all four of these pillars in this environment. Given the scale of the SDGs, finance can play a very important role in supporting their implementation and guaranteeing more robust and equitable growth, as discussed in the literature. Extensive discussion in the literature focuses on obstacles such as lack of stakeholder cooperation; lack of effective planning, governance, and regulatory framework; and inequity in international development. There is an impact on the true nature of SDG finance issues, especially in developing countries. The SDGs require a long-term approach and cannot be accomplished overnight. At the time of writing, it has been eight years since the SDGs were agreed, and there are only seven years left until the 2030 deadline The literature argues that SDGs cannot be attained within a specific timeframe unless significant and effective steps are made immediately to provide timely and sufficient financing. The role of the financial industry in achieving the SDGs will depend on the extent to which it may be influenced by stakeholders. Traditional financial policy thought critically considers finance and connects it more closely to the SDGs, particularly its unique qualities of finance, including backing financial transactions with real economic activities. Important demand-side reasons include the recent increase in demand for financial products from businesses. A more effective role for finance in the execution of the SDGs would include innovative product mix strategies, increased competence of financial intermediaries, and a conducive legal and regulatory framework. The MDGs and the requirements of financing instruments to improve the necessity for high-quality data cannot be overstated. In capitalist societies around the globe, finance can encourage actions that are socially inclusive, environmentally responsible, and development-promoting. Enhancing the contribution of the financial industry to the attainment of the SDGs requires the implementation of initiatives. Finance could help the fulfillment of the SDGs in many ways: providing financial stability, promoting financial inclusion, reducing vulnerability, increasing social and environmental activities, and improving infrastructure finance.

Due to its devastating impact on health, businesses, jobs, and livelihoods, the COVID-19 pandemic has recently prompted a focus on the discrepancy in social provision in numerous developing nations. As a result of the urgent need for socio-economic relief and recovery, the green bond market and environmental financing has been eclipsed by social and sustainable bonds. In addition, the global community has refocused its attention on the SDGs, with only 7 years remaining to achieve them, which may also have contributed to the recent increase in sustainability bonds and loans. Implementation of a recovery support system after COVID-19 will necessitate alignment with key analysis and planning processes, initiatives that endorse individual country actions, enhanced operational support for participating countries to accelerate SDG implementation, and monitoring countries progress to measure the SDG outcomes. The COVID-19 pandemic, the occurrence of zoonotic disease across the animal–human barrier, and its consequences on broader socioeconomic difficulties have emphasized the need for a renewed focus on biodiversity and natural capital and their connection to human development more obvious. Countries are looking at new ways to generate additional revenue and cultivate more sustainable practices as they create their funding plans using a combination of concessionary financing methods from traditional funding sources and other instruments. During the first half of 2020, $275 billion was raised in the capital markets through the issuance of sustainable bonds, syndicated loans, and equity capital, all of which were related to sustainable outcomes. This represents an increase of 47 percent over the first half of 2019.

Green bonds remained a prominent topic in 2020. Due to the pandemic, social and sustainability financing reached a peak in early 2020, with social financing increasing. Companies are increasingly incorporating SDG frameworks into their business models and perceiving SDG bonds as a financial instrument that might provide a flexible means of raising cash for SDG purposes, as opposed to a specific topic such as green or social bonds. In developing nations, the relative value of a social, sustainability, or green bond has been addressed frequently in terms of the additional expenses of issuing and monitoring sustainability indicators, including the increased financial incentives to an issuer in the form of lower capital costs. It is useful to distinguish SDG bonds from other sustainability instruments, despite the existence of numerous instruments. During the COVID-19 pandemic, the SDG framework's emphasis on inclusion assumed enormous importance, and it was crucial to find a strategy to improve inclusion while collecting funds for recovery. The majority of countries are guided by global development frameworks, and there have been difficulties in tying SDGs to project outcomes. The usefulness of the SDG framework resides in its interdisciplinarity which integrates different facets of development and promotes synergies. As far as the transaction process is concerned, green, social, sustainability and SDG bonds are identical to standard bonds. However, several significant strategic and operational challenges distinguish them from ordinary bonds. This must be taken into account during the issuance process.

This demonstrates the need for continued commitment to achieving the 17 SDGs established by the United Nations as the global blueprint to eradicate poverty, safeguard the environment, and assure prosperity. In addition to weak health systems, the pandemic has revealed several other obstacles, including lack of access to education, inability to meet clean water and sanitation standards, and insufficient food security. In the aftermath of COVID-19, every poor country will need to examine its progress in attaining the SDGs for equitable growth, protection of natural resources, and action to mitigate the effects of climate change. Even before the COVID-19 pandemic, achieving the SDGs was always difficult. Given the inherent risks, the lack of SDG projects meant that many developing nations were unable to mobilize the necessary resources from the private sector in the face of constrained public resources. The complexity of implementing SDG indicators and frameworks at the project level has been an additional issue impeding SDG achievement. COVID-19 has highlighted the urgent need for rapid planning and mobilization of resources toward the SDGs. The pandemic presents a new opportunity for governments to include the SDGs in their recovery plans to build resilience against future catastrophes.

6. Conclusion

Macroeconomic finances are essential for reducing impending world problems. The primary objective of this chapter is to investigate the role of financing in the achievement of SDGs. The unambiguous identification of key SDGs based on internationally agreed-upon commitments is significant. Concentration on just a few SDGs enhances focus, boosts investor confidence, and gives a solid reason for the deployment of funds. It is necessary to prioritize development target projects, for which financing work has already begun. Such activities are essential to increase collaboration between stakeholders and encourage government influencers to establish a robust project pipeline to achieve particular SDGs. Moreover, the incorporation of

SDG initiatives into a broader development plan can improve coordination and alignment across various stakeholders and economic sectors. It is essential to design such a financial mechanism to construct such bond-issuing institutions and adopt the SDG framework's broadly agreed principles. Changes to the policy and regulatory environment would be required to significantly increase the desire for investment.

This study assists policymakers, especially in developing nations, in a variety of ways by providing recommendations on how finance might be used to accomplish the SDGs, especially in emerging economies. This chapter is important because it explains the fundamental relationship between finance and SDGs. Comprehensive green financial derivatives report that includes bonds, loans, and conditional investment plans could be an option for policymakers. A more efficient strategy could boost the financial system's capacity to implement the green financial derivatives program smoothly and efficiently.

References

Arkhipova, V. (2017). "Green finance" as recipe for solving global problems. *HSE Economic Journal*, *21*(2), 312–332.

Asongu, S. A. & De Moor, L. (2015). Recent advances in finance for inclusive development: A survey. *SSRN Electronic Journal*. https://doi.org/10.2139/ssrn.2575667.

Asongu, S. A. & Vo, X. V. (2020). The effect of finance on inequality in Sub-Saharan Africa: Avoidable CO_2 emissions thresholds. *Environmental Science and Pollution Research*. https://doi.org/10.1007/s11356-020-09535-0.

Atack, L. (2021). A Proposal for Recalibrating SDG 4.7. Policy & Practice: *A Development Education Review*, *33*, 52–72. https://www.developmenteducationreview.com/sites/default/files/publications/Full%20Issue%2033%20PDF_0.pdf#page=55.

Ball, I. (2020). Reflections on public financial management in the Covid-19 pandemic. *Journal of Accounting and Organizational Change*. https://doi.org/10.1108/JAOC-10-2020-0160.

Bracking, S. (2019). Financialisation, climate finance, and the calculative challenges of managing environmental change. *Antipode*. https://doi.org/10.1111/anti.12510.

Cirolia, L. R. (2020). Fractured fiscal authority and fragmented infrastructures: Financing sustainable urban development in Sub-Saharan Africa. *Habitat International.* https://doi.org/10.1016/j.habitatint.2020.102233.

Deloitte (2020). Impact of COVID-19 on the finance and operations of China's retailing and the industry outlook. *China Chain Store & Franchise Association.*

Ejemeyovwi, J. O., Osabohien, R., Adeleye, B. N., *et al.* (2021). Household ICT utilization and food security nexus in Nigeria. *International Journal of Food Science.* https://doi.org/10.1155/2021/5551363.

Goodell, J. W. (2020). COVID-19 and finance: Agendas for future research. *Finance Research Letters.* https://doi.org/10.1016/j.frl.2020.101512.

Habitat, U. N. (2018). Tracking Progress Towards Inclusive, Safe, Resilient and Sustainable Cities and Human Settlements. SDG 11 Synthesis Report-High Level Political Forum 2018. https://discovery.ucl.ac.uk/id/eprint/10087018/1/SDG%2011%20Synthesis%20Report_web2.pdf.

Harrison, K. (2009). How "inconvenient" is Al Gore's climate message? *M/C Journal.* https://doi.org/10.5204/mcj.175.

Harvey, F. (2021). Mapping for a sustainable world. *International Journal of Cartography.* https://doi.org/10.1080/23729333.2021.1984071.

Hou, D., Bolan, N. S., Tsang, D. C. W., *et al.* (2020). Sustainable soil use and management: An interdisciplinary and systematic approach. In *Science of the Total Environment.* https://doi.org/10.1016/j.scitotenv.2020.138961.

ICSU (2015). Sustainable development goals and targets. International Council for Science. https://sdg.humanrights.dk/en/goals-and-targets.

Kataki, R., Bordoloi, N., Saikia, R., *et al.* (2017). An assessment on Indian government initiatives and policies for the promotion of biofuels implementation, and commercialization through private investments. In *Sustainable Biofuels Development in India.* https://doi.org/10.1007/978-3-319-50219-9_20.

Kravchenko, O., Reznichenko, I., Kucher, H., *et al.* (2021). Children's health and leisure institutions: Inclusive aspect. *Collection of Scientific Papers of Uman State Pedagogical University.* https://doi.org/10.31499/2307-4906.4.2021.250136.

Lawrence, A. W., Ihebuzor, N., & Lawrence, D. O. (2020). Some challenges militating against developing countries achieving SDG 4 on targets: Nigeria as case study. *Modern Economy.* https://doi.org/10.4236/me.2020.117093.

Liu, Y., Du, J., Wang, Y., *et al.* (2021). Evenness is important in assessing progress towards sustainable development goals. *National Science Review.* https://doi.org/10.1093/nsr/nwaa238.

Mendez, A. & Houghton, D. P. (2020). Sustainable banking: The role of multilateral development banks as norm entrepreneurs. *Sustainability (Switzerland)*. https://doi.org/10.3390/su12030972.

Midgley, J. (2019). Social policy and development: An overview. In *Handbook of Social Policy and Development*. https://doi.org/10.4337/9781785368431.00007.

Oliveira, E. R. De & Rodrigues, P. (2010). Measuring sustainability and sustainable knowledge management: Presenting a case for the tourism sector in Portugal. In *Proceedings of the European Conference on Knowledge Management, ECKM*.

Parkinson, S., Krey, V., Huppmann, D., *et al.* (2019). Balancing clean water-climate change mitigation trade-offs. *Environmental Research Letters*. https://doi.org/10.1088/1748-9326/aaf2a3.

Ritchie, H. & Fisher, D. (2021). COVID's lessons for climate from our world in data world view. *In Nature*, *598*, p. 9.

Rodić, L. & Wilson, D. C. (2017). Resolving governance issues to achieve priority sustainable development goals related to solid waste management in developing countries. *Sustainability (Switzerland)*. https://doi.org/10.3390/su9030404.

Sommariva, C., Nardon, E., Beyer, P., Hoelzl, M., Huijsmans, G. T. A., & Contributors, J. E. T. (2018). Electron acceleration in a JET disruption simulation. *Nuclear Fusion*, *58*(10), 106022. https://arxiv.org/pdf/1805.05655.pdf.

Swain, R. B. (2018). A critical analysis of the sustainable development goals. In *World Sustainability Series*. https://doi.org/10.1007/978-3-319-63007-6_20.

Valdivia, R. (2016). Is sustainable development of semi-subsistence mixed crop-livestock systems possible? An integrated assessment of Machakos, Kenya. In *PQDT — Global*.

Wang, C. & Dong, G. (2019). Research on Green Financial Ecology Construction Based on Low Carbon Economy. *Ekoloji Dergisi*, *107*.

WHO (2019). WHO Health Statistik 2019: Monitoring Health for the SDGs.

Wójcik, D. & Ioannou, S. (2020). COVID-19 and finance: Market developments so far and potential impacts on the financial sector and centres. *Tijdschrift Voor Economische En Sociale Geografie*. https://doi.org/10.1111/tesg.12434.

Zhang, Z., Cheng, H., & Yu, Y. (2020). Relationships among government funding, R&D model and innovation performance: A study on the chinese textile industry. *Sustainability (Switzerland)*. https://doi.org/10.3390/su12020644.

Zhou, D., Meinke, H., Wilson, M., *et al.* (2021). Towards delivering on the sustainable development goals in greenhouse production systems. *Resources, Conservation and Recycling*. https://doi.org/10.1016/j.resconrec.2020.105379.

Zhou, X. & Du, J. (2021). Does environmental regulation induce improved financial development for green technological innovation in China? *Journal of Environmental Management*. https://doi.org/10.1016/j.jenvman.2021.113685.

https://doi.org/10.1142/9781800614482_0012

Chapter 12

Is Green Finance a Myth or a Truth?

Mohamed Bechir Chenguel
Department of Finance and Accounting,
Higher Institute of Management and Computer,
University of Kairouan, Tunisia
bechir.chenguel@gmail.com

Abstract

The issue of addressing climate change aims to reduce greenhouse gas emissions. Green finance was created to reduce the negative impact of climate change. Green finance has used financial instruments like green bonds to finance projects for the good of the environment and the planet. After almost 10 years, with the persistence of global warming and climate change manifested by melting glaciers, droughts, and floods, all of these factors have called into question the efficiency of green finance. This chapter presents green finance and its instruments, and our contribution is to shed light on the aspects that may limit its effectiveness, such as the absence of incentives and, above all, the absence of green finance standards. In addition, we reveal that potential crises can arise in banks if they opt to finance green investments and abandon fossil fuel activities. All of these factors make the concept of green finance just an illusion.

1. Introduction

The notion of green finance has been around for 20 years, but it only became mainstream in 2015 with the adoption of the Paris Climate Agreement (Tolliver *et al.*, 2021). Its rise is due to the awareness of the existence of climate risks by financial institutions. Thus, authorities and regulators have urged financial institutions to recognize the climate risks borne by their asset portfolios and to make them public to investors (Caldecott *et al.*, 2021).

It started first in France, with Article 173 of the Law on Energy Transition of August 17, 2015, and then at the global level, with the recommendations of the "Task Force on Climate-Related Financial Disclosures" (TCFD) created by the Council of Financial Stability of the 26 major central banks and international institutions (Chenet, 2019). Green finance, therefore, brought together all the financial operations aimed at promoting energy transition and combating global warming (Boissinot *et al.*, 2016). This market has grown considerably and continues to grow. Thirteen years after the issuance of the first green bond by the World Bank in 2008, the green finance sector is booming, and its objective is to favor sustainable investments in order to support the ecological transition. This ambitious objective of green finance is based on its various players: large investment funds, banks, and even small savers (Berensmann & Lindenberg, 2019).

Our contribution in this chapter is the idea that despite the good intentions of green finance, global warming persists. Water scarcity, famine, and the proliferation of diseases are some of the consequences of global warming. In addition, more and more citizens want to act at their own level as consumers and savers.

Indeed, green finance is not only for large hedge funds (Simpson *et al.*, 2021); everyone, through the choice of his or her savings account, can favor a banking product geared toward sustainable development. Thus, the financial sector began to worry about the fight against global warming, and financial flows began to move toward renewable energies (Van Veelen, 2021).

However, the problem or limit that persists until now is the difficulty of measuring the carbon footprint and the risks associated with global warming. Driven by campaigns of non-governmental organizations and civil society associations, will the financial sector be able to play an active and positive role in the energy and ecological transition if public policies themselves do not evolve?

Through our research, we attempt to explain green finance, a relatively new concept, which has emerged in response to the climate-change-related negative effects of greenhouse gas emissions.

Second, we present the tools of green finance, which are green bonds issued to promote energy transition projects. Third, we focus on the aspects that caused the ineffectiveness of green finance and contributed to its low impact on the ecological transition process.

2. Green Finance

The first objective of green finance is to align financial flows with climate objectives by minimizing the negative impacts and maximizing the positive impacts of investments. To achieve this, there are several instruments available, such as specific financial products called green bonds, which are new ecological financial products accompanied by engagement policies with companies. The aim of these bonds is to exclude from their portfolios the assets of companies which are not ecological and harm the climate and biodiversity (González & Núñez, 2021). The second objective is to measure and mitigate the financial risks posed by climate change and the energy transition (Benedetti *et al.*, 2019). The first are physical risks (storms, forest fires, etc.), and the second are transition risks. In fact, the latter are caused by regulatory changes, intended to mitigate the magnitude and impact of climate change. For example, a coal-fired power station or a coal mine may become inoperable due to an excessively high carbon price or a change in consumer preferences. Green finance is part of an environmentally friendly approach, which is to say, an approach where investors will shift their funds to companies that develop products and services in favor of the energy transition in particular (Zhang *et al.*, 2021). The main tool of green finance is green bonds, issued with the aim of financing initiatives that fight against global warming and ensure the energy transition (Gianfrate & Peri, 2019). Investors can also select companies based on environmental criteria through green funds. To reduce their exposure to climate risks, and after having measured the carbon footprint of their portfolios, investors can disengage from companies emitting greenhouse gases or companies with risky environmental criteria (Apostolou & Papaioannou, 2021). Before arriving at this stage, some investors will ask for more information and more transparency from the companies in which they invest and will take a closer look at their climate strategies to adopt one in line with the two-degree-Celsius trajectory set by the

Paris Agreement (Strauch *et al.*, 2020). Green finance is a part of responsible investment whose purpose is to add respect for environmental, social, and governance criteria to the financial criteria. Green finance needs a structuring framework and qualifying criteria to move forward and disseminate the good practices it recommends (Debrah *et al.*, 2021). It calls for making low-carbon investments and tries to encourage and establish investments that resort to the decarbonization of all energy vectors. Green finance also invests in the growing electrification of sustainable energy uses and gradually abandons projects using fossil fuels. It encourages the development of compact and sustainable cities, including the renovation of buildings, toward energy savings (Bibri & Krogstie, 2021). Green finance ensures the decarbonization of the transport sector by encouraging and investing in the electric transport sector. It also invests in the reforestation and restoration of thousands of hectares of degraded land around the world, with the goal of increasing natural carbon (Di Sacco *et al.*, 2021). To achieve these ends and make these investments a reality, funds must be available and dedicated to these objectives in order to make the energy transition a success. Green finance needs investment tools, which are green bonds.

2.1. *Green bonds as a tool for green finance*

A green bond is a bond loan intended to finance an environmental or "green" project (Banga, 2019). Like classic bond loans, green bonds thus concern the markets of private companies and sovereigns. The issuance of green bonds must meet at least one of the following four criteria: fight against climate change; protection of biodiversity; reduction of water, air, and soil pollution; and adaptation to climate change (Flammer, 2020). It is essentially public authorities, the World Bank, and development banks that will play a leading role in the promotion of these green bonds, which represent a very important lever for financing new environmental projects. The responsibility of investors is to adopt this type of financial product to meet the expectations of savers wishing to make their savings more virtuous. The difference between a traditional bond issue and a green bond issue is the environmental impact expected by the investment (Liaw, 2020). Reporting directly to the general management and financial management of a company, the green bond constitutes a means of measuring the environmental performance of an investment project, such as the financing of a wind farm or the creation of wind farm sites — renewable energies and green infrastructure (Shideler & Hetzel, 2021). In addition, a green bond also makes it possible to direct the money raised toward specific activities, assess the environmental risk of a project, trace the flows from the central treasury, and benefit from frequent reporting on the use of funds. The interest also concerns the investor; in fact, the latter knows exactly in which project his savings are invested and can therefore judge the quality of issuers through the various environmental risk assessments of the green bond and of the issuer in general (Chiesa & Barua, 2019). For the issuers of green bonds, the interest lies above all in an approach to communication and legitimacy. They can thus prove their sustainable approach to the financing of projects, linking speeches and actions. It also allows for a more direct dialogue between investors and issuers, unlike equity financing (equity issues), which does not generally identify investment projects.

2.2. *Green bonds and the real environmental impact*

The heat waves that particularly affect northern countries, the lack of rain in some regions, and the floods in others have served as reminders of the urgency to step up the fight against global warming and reduce the impact of human activities on the environment. To this end, it will be necessary to mobilize considerable resources to direct these activities toward the appropriate projects. The tool that is capable of fulfilling this role is obviously the green bond. The originality of green bonds is that they are used to finance ecological projects (Gibon *et al.*, 2020). In fact, the green bond market has grown rapidly since its inception 10 years ago. In 2020, the volume of issues amounted to $155 billion, which is roughly double the amount in 2019. With the constant strengthening of standards for construction, recycling, or greenhouse gas emissions, the market can be expected to continue to grow (Liu *et al.*, 2020). Companies will also have to place their strategies in a sustainable development perspective, which will help extend the scope covered by green bonds (Bhutta *et al.*, 2022). Faced with the climate emergency, the immediate response from the financial sphere is to direct more investments

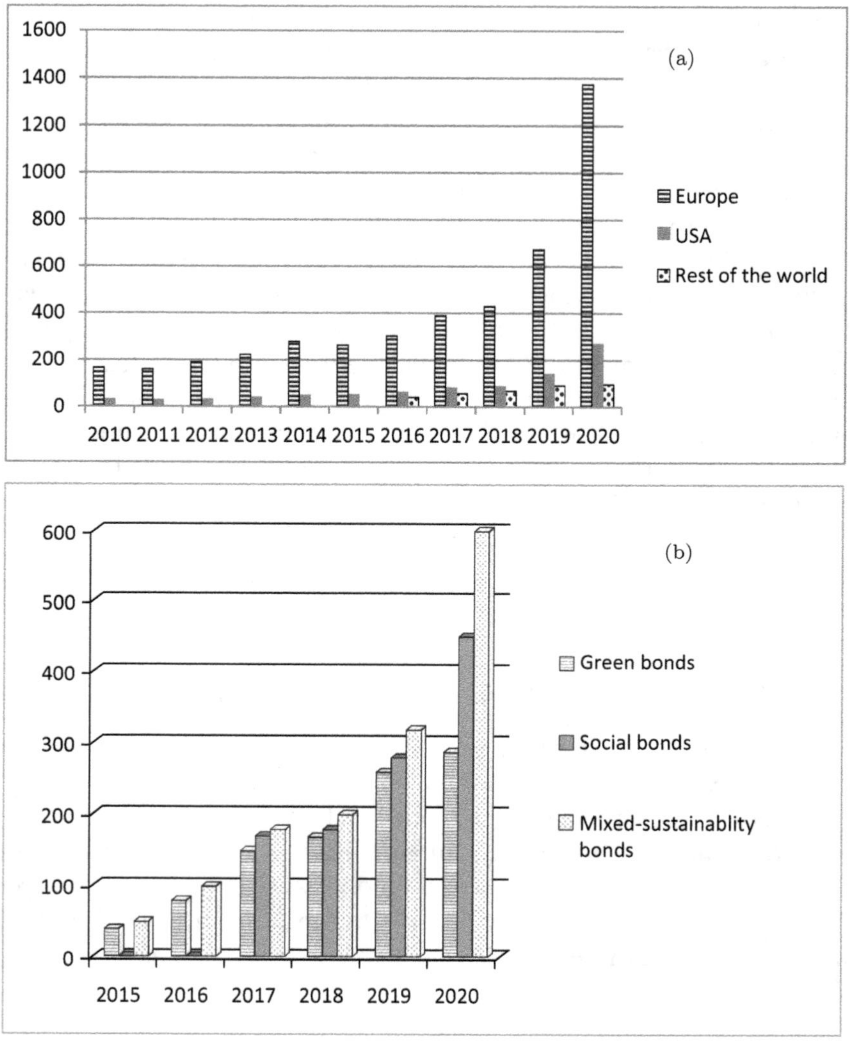

Figure 1. (a) Growth of the sustainable bond market, 2015–2020 (billions of dollars). UNCTAD, Bloomberg data. (b) Bonds Evolution, 2000–2021. UNCTAD, SSE database.

toward renewable energies, clean transport, etc. As a result, the number of products and assets under "sustainable" management, taking into account environmental, social, and governance performance, is unmistakably starting to grow. Figure 1 clearly illustrates the evolution of the curve denoting the funds allocated to green finance. The same goes for green bonds, a flagship product of sustainable market finance.

Other indicators illustrate the growing importance of the sustainability dimension in stock market activities. The companies that can benefit from these investments and these green bonds are:

- companies installing infrastructure to produce renewable energy, using green bonds to finance the construction of wind farms or photovoltaic plants;
- companies which set up production methods that are less polluting or more economical in natural resource usage;
- companies with technology invested in the recycling and recovery of components dangerous to the environment;
- companies developing technologies with the objective of eliminating dependence on fossil fuels;
- companies investing in innovative energy production and storage systems;
- companies' investments aimed at helping with thermal insulation or the development of transport vehicles of the future;
- companies in the real estate sector engaged in the construction of buildings with a low environmental footprint through the incorporation of solar panels and designs allowing a better natural ventilation;
- local communities seeking to set up more ecological modes of urban transport or installations, which allow for the recycling and recovery of waste.

All these different investors need green bonds to finance their ecological projects all over the world (Gianfrate & Peri, 2019). However, currently, the market seems to be stagnating. In fact, the issuers are mainly governments, companies in the energy sector, and financial institutions.

2.3. *The conditions needed for green finance success*

Companies have an interest in signaling their commitments to sustainable development by issuing green bonds. Those that fail to do so can cause concern among investors and their industrial partners.

The incentive is strong enough for a large number of companies to adopt these guidelines for the ecological transition (Biscione *et al.*, 2021). Investors must also participate in market development and let people know that they also contribute to the protection of the environment. Those who will take the first step will encourage the sector to give green bonds a larger share of their portfolios. The advantage of these bonds is therefore their simplicity since it is easy to distinguish what is ecological and what is not. Companies financed by green bonds will be required to honor their commitments since their credibility is at stake (Perkins, 2021). The funds will thus have to be directed to ecological projects and will have to be audited. If it is a question of respecting stricter environmental standards, the results will have to be demonstrated and compared with the standards. The development of the green trust market should be accompanied by a rise in the number of analysts specializing in environmental issues and determining the criteria and standards to be respected (Laborda & Sánchez-Guerra, 2021). Therefore, companies and investors will be assisted by experts who can guide their strategies.

3. Green Finance: Reality or Illusion?

After almost 10 years since the birth of this new concept, the question of measuring its impact still remains: How do we assess the environmental benefit of an investment project? (O'Mahony, 2021). The answer lies in creating and applying a standard tool that is capable of measuring the expected result of each project. The advantage lies in the fact that each green bond is different; therefore, the environmental impact measurement will certainly be done by the project, that is to say, between the expectations of the project, its implementation, and its results (Falsen & Johansson, 2015). Often, the effort to put in place a green bond involves the issuer asking for additional remuneration from the investor to offset the cost generated by this effort. Determining the cost and price is therefore complex, knowing that investors are not always ready to pay more for a project that could have been financed by a traditional bond. This can create an imbalance between supply and demand. Nevertheless, as is the case with responsible investment in equities, green investors in the bond market are often willing to pay more and do not prioritize price (Sharma *et al.*, 2021).

3.1. *Green finance and the persistent rise in CO_2 emissions*

The financial aspect of the economic, environmental, and societal transition aims to slow down projects, including long-term environmental damage (McCauley & Heffron, 2018). Green finance will act in such a way as to make decisions that no longer finance certain polluting projects and direct funding toward others that are ecological (Abbas *et al.*, 2021). This is the purpose of green finance and green bonds. Green finance must transform and encourage projects that promote transition, channel funding toward virtuous projects, and direct sources of funding for projects with a strong ecological impact. However, after all these years, the findings are not in line with expectations, and the effects of green financing have not been able to regress the curves of greenhouse gas emissions (Emenekwe *et al.*, 2021). According to the latest report from the International Energy Agency (IEA), the World Bank, and the World Economic Forum, the positive intentions are not reflected in the expected results (Wang *et al.*, 2022). Although the problem is not related to financing, $150 billion is invested in renewable energy projects every year; the financing of polluting activities persists, with a single oil exploration investing on average $500 billion per year (Niyazbekova *et al.*, 2021). According to the Climate Bonds Initiative, the green bond market crossed the threshold of $1 trillion in annual issuance in 2020 (Torvanger *et al.*, 2021). It may sound like a lot, but it is only 5 percent of the global investment and a small fraction of the global bond market, for a total of $128.3 trillion. Scientists warn about insufficient results.

In addition, at this rate, the decade leading up to 2030 will not achieve the goals of sustainable development. Moreover, it is probable that greenhouse gas emissions will continue to rise. Therefore, there is a problem that will challenge the credibility of green finance (Gilchrist *et al.*, 2021). After all these years, the expected results of green finance are disappointing, and the question is: Why is the financial world somehow refusing to take action? Three explanations can be put forward:

(1) The incentives to act remain weak.
(2) Finance is not yet structured to manage and measure the direct impacts in terms of prices and profits.

(3) The norms and standards are very imprecise and, consequently, not very restrictive.

3.1.1. *Lack of incentives*

Bankers, governments, and their financial market regulators have not acted adequately. All these authorities did not present the necessary incentives to encourage the use of these green finance instruments (Zhang *et al.*, 2021). Likewise, the pricing systems facing banks remain determined by markets, which are indifferent to the constraints and limits of CO_2 emissions. In addition, there is still no real carbon tax, tax systems remain biased in favor of emissive activities (such as subsidizing air and agricultural fuel), and insurance premiums remain largely indifferent to the risks of stranded assets (Dong *et al.*, 2022). In addition, there is currently no incentive or performance bonus on green financing and no penalty for returns on non-green investments. It is about appealing to a certain environmental ethics as part of due diligence, which is limited to the principles of social and environmental responsibility (Parker, 2021).

3.1.2. *Lack of a concept of climate cost*

Green funding generally focuses on labeling an end goal, such as funding an activity for the production of wind power or solar panels (Akomea-Frimpong *et al.*, 2021). However, in the absence of the concept of "climate cost," it is impossible to know the true emissive impact of a particular good or service on the environment. This lack of calculation or knowledge of the environmental and social price of a funded service is at the heart of a complexity that green funding has not been able to decipher until now (Huang & Zhang, 2021). There is also some confusion between the notions of social and environmental responsibility and the notion of transitioning to the 2030 agenda. Indeed, the difference between the concepts: "do no harm" and "do well" is not very clear.

3.1.3. *Lack of shared standards*

The concept of "green" concerns any investment aimed at reducing pollution. In fact, projects and innovations in the fields of electric urban transport, waste treatment, wastewater treatment, and renewable energies fall into this category of priority green funding.

However, the impact analysis shows that "green" financing is not always as green as might think (Dikau & Volz, 2021).

We can cite the example of electric urban transport, identified as "green," while the necessary electricity can come from polluting energy sources with high emissions. In the absence of universal standards defining "green," each organization will present a standard that suits it, and it is difficult to ensure that the criteria used by green bond issuers will really take into account all the intervening elements and not just prioritize the final object (Gilchrist *et al.*, 2021). Some authors say that we should focus on concrete indicators, such as the impact on biodiversity. An example is the "social and responsible investment" (SRI) label, which is supposed to guarantee proper consideration of ESG criteria (Fedele *et al.*, 2021). However, according to the non-governmental organization Reclaim Finance, 94 percent of "ISR funds" supply companies with highly doubtful environmental and social practices (Cuvelier *et al.*, 2021). There are even polluting companies (oil or gas) with a good ESG rating. This is explained by the fact that these companies devote even a small part of their financial resources to activities dedicated to renewable energies. Other labels on the market are unanimously recognized as more efficient. This is the case with the GreenFin label, which excludes players in fossil fuels and nuclear, or Finansol, the solidarity savings fund label, in which money is redirected to actors whose social and environmental utility is recognized by an independent committee drawn from civil society (Popescu *et al.*, 2021). Supporters of green finance see this new market for labeled funds as the first step toward self-regulation in the financial world (Akomea-Frimpong *et al.*, 2021). Today, responsible products exist. Even the SRI label, though criticized, has real potential if we continue to lobby for players to toughen the rules and be more transparent (Alda, 2021).

4. Green Finance and Banks

Banks in their annual reports always seem to encourage green finance, but in real terms, they have not yet given up on financing polluting activities and the fossil fuel industry (Khan *et al.*, 2021). The Rainforest Action Network report studied the case of two powerful banks: HSBC, known for having excellent extra-financial performance, and

JP Morgan, which has cut funding to the fossil fuel industry in recent years (Bhattacharyay, 2021). Despite their commitment to green finance, these banks were unable to offset their investments in fossil fuels. This is unfortunately the case with the majority of banks around the world. This doubts the ability of green finance to reorient the financial sector sustainably and effectively toward models that are more protective of the environment (Bai, 2011). Indeed, for the largest banks, the abandonment of investments in fossil fuels is likely to trigger a financial crisis within these banking establishments (Spasić *et al.*, 2021). Since the Paris Agreement was signed in 2015, there have been new commitments from banks or insurers to finance and fight against climate change. But according to Semieniuk *et al.* (2021), this ecological transition can be very expensive in terms of banking and financial crises. In fact, the reports drawn up by several banking and financial players adopting this green finance movement in 2021 have not been very satisfactory. Financial banking players cannot maximize the return on their investments and agree to reduce it on other investments to limit the climatic constraints (Ameli *et al.*, 2021). Several researchers explained that green investments leading to a reduction in greenhouse gas emissions could not meet the profitability criteria desired by the financial sector (Grundström & Miedel, 2021). In addition, if they want to achieve high returns, this requires very large investments, the financial benefits of which are not guaranteed. Grandjean *et al.* (2021) concluded from their research that if we invest a large amount of money in green projects, the expected profitability is not certain, which makes the concept of green finance opaque. We can therefore see that green finance works in the same way as traditional finance, but with more dominant environmental objectives than financial objectives. Couix and Giraud (2021) presented a pioneering analysis of fossil assets held by the 11 largest European banks. In fact, they estimated an amount of €532 billion to be invested in fossil fuel assets, or 95 percent of their equity. According to the authors, this constitutes a major risk because they adversely affect the climate and could experience a rapid and sharp devaluation. Indeed, if these fossil assets lost 80 percent of their value, the equity of Société Générale and Crédit Agricole would plunge into the red and those of the German banks, Deutsche Bank, and Commerz Bank would be exhausted. Couix and Giraud (2021) added that these fossil assets must be cut from the bank balance sheets before they jeopardize any financing capacity for ecological reconstruction. The French Banking and Insurance Supervisory Authority, in its first climate stress test, estimates that these banking establishments have a risk of financial losses linked to the forced transition that the fossil fuel sectors will have to make to comply with the Paris Agreement (Alogoskoufis *et al.*, 2021). Extractive industries, chemicals, metallurgy, and waste represented 9.7 percent of the banks' credit portfolio and 17 percent of the insurers' portfolio (ACPR Bank of France, 2021).

These warnings about the limits of green finance remind us that it is governments and businesses that can change the real economy first (Hedberg, 2021), and their actions must be urgently needed to remedy climate change and the accelerated destruction of biodiversity. Green finance has so far remained a marginal activity, and "sustainable" funds represent only 3.3 percent of the total assets in the world. For their part, durable bonds barely reach 1.3 percent of the global mandatory market.

5. Conclusion

The new concepts of ecological investments, responsible savings, and green bonds seek to make the world of finance give up its dependence on fossil fuels by giving it a greener and more sustainable image. Financing the energy transition means developing "green" or "sustainable" finance, whose objective is to bring capital to ecological and social projects. Many green finance products have recently appeared on the market, and they strive to distinguish themselves by taking into account other ecological data with financial profitability. These new products are based on the assessments established by the private rating agencies founded on the environmental, social, and governance criteria. The problems that have arisen in this green finance system are its opaque methodology and the lack of a common framework. The challenge now is to make people aware of the fundamental role they have to play and to communicate better across the entire industry. In fact, the demand for green finance depends on a few clients, and the ecological transition cannot be funded by the current arguments and guidelines.

Despite their growth, funds labeled by Greenfin and Finansol remain marginal compared to the overall savings amounts. If we want to finance the transition, the only solution is to redirect the existing financial flows intended for fossil fuels to new and greener investments. To meet this ambition, the financial world is promoting green bonds as a new mechanism. For government decision-makers, financial authorities, and the companies themselves, this involves going to the financial markets to issue debt. Unlike traditional bonds, debt is conditional on financing an ecological and social project. Nevertheless, according to Grandjean *et al.* (2021), currently, green finance is still only an illusion, and there is no evidence that green bonds can accelerate the energy and ecological transitions. Indeed, whatever the nature of the green or conventional bonds, a company will pay the same interest rates. Therefore, for the company, there is no financial incentive to encourage investment in green bonds. In other words, current green projects only exist by the will of the actors and entrepreneurs who create them. Finance, with its funding yield parameters, plays no role in encouraging the choice of green bonds, but it just creates the illusion of adding the term "green" to the bond. Indeed, if we want to encourage the ecological character, the public and financial authorities must get involved further in the financial sphere. Regarding the substance of the problem, several financial players and non-governmental organizations have raised the problem of the lack of a benchmark for what is a "green" project. In addition, each institution has the free choice to define green project according to its convictions. Another problem reinforcing this illusion of green finance is the heavy dependence on polluting sectors. In fact, the banks seem little encouraged to adopt the transition, and this is because of their extreme dependence on the polluting sectors in which they have been investing for several decades. The degree of dependence on the fossil fuel sector is strong enough to create a real risk of financial destabilization, especially when there is too rapid a devaluation of fossil assets. This is very serious, especially when we add the fact that banks and several organizations heavily finance projects and industries heavily dependent on fossil energy (aeronautics, automobiles, etc.). Thus, the entire stability of the financial and banking system is at stake, as a possible loss in the value of their fossil assets would weigh heavily on their balance sheets. In fact, as long as these polluting energy assets exist, banks will have no interest in investing in the transition. In actuality, despite the COP16, COP21, COP24, and COP26 meetings, nothing is going well, and the objectives are far from being achieved. Green finance's efforts to accelerate the decarbonization of industries remain ineffective.

To conclude, current regulators and green finance promoters must act in light of the factors cited above. The environmental disaster keeps accelerating, and more and more people are concerned about what is happening. It is therefore obvious that green finance alone will not save the planet, and the 2015 Paris Agreement is no longer enough. It is not only the finance sector that should be changed but also our entire life system, including our way of producing and consuming. For further insight, we hope that future studies can empirically explore and make the connection between carbon footprint and green bond financing to clarify the link between these two parameters of green finance.

References

Abbas, M. G., Wang, Z., Bashir, S., *et al.* (2021). Nexus between energy policy and environmental performance in China: The moderating role of green finance adopted firms. *Environmental Science and Pollution Research*, *28*, pp. 63263–63277.

ACPR Bank of France (2021). Euro système. https://acpr.banque-france.fr/sites/default/files/medias/documents/20210504_press_release_acpr_bdf_the_acpr_publishes_the_results_of_the_first_climate_pilot_exercisefv.pdf.

Akomea-Frimpong, I., Adeabah, D., Ofosu, D., *et al.* (2021). A review of studies on green finance of banks, research gaps and future directions. *Journal of Sustainable Finance & Investment*, *12*(4), 1241–1264.

Alda, M. (2021). The environmental, social, and governance (ESG) dimension of firms in which social responsible investment (SRI) and conventional pension funds invest: The mainstream SRI and the ESG inclusion. *Journal of Cleaner Production*, *298*, 126812.

Alogoskoufis, S., Dunz, N., Emambakhsh, T., Hennig, T., Kaijser, M., Kouratzoglou, C., & Salleo, C. (2021). ECB economy-wide climate stress test: Methodology and results (No. 281). ECB Occasional Chapter.

Ameli, N., Dessens, O., Winning, M., *et al.* (2021). Higher cost of finance exacerbates a climate investment trap in developing economies. *Nature Communications*, *12*(1), 1–12.

Apostolou, A. & Papaioannou, M. G. (2021). Integration of environmental factors into portfolio risk assessment. *The Journal of Impact and ESG Investing*, *4*(1).

Bai, Y. (2011). Financing a green future: An examination of China's banking sector for green finance. The International Institute for Industrial Environmental Economics. *Master Thesis*, IMEN56 20111.

Banga, J. (2019). The green bond market: A potential source of climate finance for developing countries. *Journal of Sustainable Finance & Investment*, *9*(1), 17–32.

Ben Caldecott, E. H., Cojoianu, T., Kok, I., & Pfeiffer, A. (2021). Stranded assets: A climate risk challenge Inter American development Bank ICB MG 481.

Benedetti, D., Biffis, E., Chatzimichalakis, F., *et al.* (2019). Climate change investment risk: Optimal portfolio construction ahead of the transition to a lower-carbon economy. *Annals of Operations Research*, *299*, 847–871.

Berensmann, K. & Lindenberg, N. (2019). Green finance: Across the universe. In *Corporate Social Responsibility, Ethics and Sustainable Prosperity*, Chapter 11 (pp. 305–332).

Bhattacharyay, B. N. (2021). Managing climate-related financial risk: Prospects and challenges. In *New Frontiers in Conflict Management and Peace Economics: With a Focus on Human Security*. Emerald Publishing Ltd.

Bhutta, U. S., Tariq, A., Farrukh, M., *et al.* (2022). Green bonds for sustainable development: Review of literature on development and impact of green bonds. *Technological Forecasting and Social Change*, *175*, 121378.

Bibri, S. E. & Krogstie, J. (2021). A novel model for data-driven smart sustainable cities of the future: A strategic roadmap to transformational change in the era of big data. *Future Cities and Environment*, *7*(1), 1–25.

Biscione, A., Caruso, R., & de Felice, A. (2021). Environmental innovation in European transition countries. *Applied Economics*, *53*(5), 521–535.

Boissinot, J., Huber, D., & Lame, G. (2016). Finance and climate: The transition to a low-carbon and climate-resilient economy from a financial sector perspective. *OECD Journal: Financial Market Trends*, *2015*(1), 7–23.

Chenet, H. (2019). Climate change and financial risk. Springer International Publishing, pp. 393–419.

Chiesa, M. & Barua, S. (2019). The surge of impact borrowing: the magnitude and determinants of green bond supply and its heterogeneity across markets. *Journal of Sustainable Finance & Investment*, *9*(2), 138–161.

Couix, Q. & Giraud, G. (2021). La difficile conversion à l'écologie de la recherche en économie. In *Annales des Mines-Responsabilite et environnement* (No. 1, pp. 21–24). Cairn/Softwin.

Cuvelier, L., Satow, A., Pinson, L., Harrell, C., Best, D., Kar, T., & Le Gal, G. (2021). Slow burn: The asset managers betting against the planet. The Inaugural 2021 Asset Managers' Coal Scorecard.

Debrah, C., Chan, A. P. C., & Darko, A. (2021). Green finance gap in green buildings: A scoping review and future research needs. *Building and Environment*, *207*, 108443.

Di Sacco, A., Hardwick, K. A., Blakesley, D., *et al.* (2021). Ten golden rules for reforestation to optimize carbon sequestration, biodiversity recovery and livelihood benefits. *Global Change Biology*, *27*(7), 1328–1348.

Dikau, S. & Volz, U. (2021). Central bank mandates, sustainability objectives and the promotion of green finance. *Ecological Economics*, *184*, 107022.

Dong, F., Li, Y., Gao, Y., *et al.* (2022). Energy transition and carbon neutrality: Exploring the non-linear impact of renewable energy development on carbon emission efficiency in developed countries. *Resources, Conservation and Recycling*, *177*, 106002.

Emenekwe, C. C., Onyeneke, R. U., & Nwajiuba, C. U. (2021). Financial development and carbon emissions in Sub-Saharan Africa. *Environmental Science and Pollution Research*, *29*(13), 19624–19641.

Falsen, C. & Johansson, P. (2015). Mobilizing the debt market for climate change mitigation. *Experiences from the Early Green Bonds Market.* Report No. 2015.04, Master's Thesis within the Industrial Ecology Programme University of Technology.

Fedele, G., Donatti, C. I., Bornacelly, I., *et al.* (2021). Nature-dependent people: Mapping human direct use of nature for basic needs across the tropics. *Global Environmental Change*, *21*, 102368.

Flammer, C. (2020). Green bonds: Effectiveness and implications for public policy. *Environmental and Energy Policy and the Economy*, *1*(1), 95–128.

Gianfrate, G. & Peri, M. (2019). The green advantage: Exploring the convenience of issuing green bonds. *Journal of Cleaner Production*, *219*, 127–135.

Gibon, T., Popescu, I. Ş., Hitaj, C., *et al.* (2020). Shades of green: Life cycle assessment of renewable energy projects financed through green bonds. *Environmental Research Letters*, *15*(10), 104045.

Gilchrist, D., Yu, J., & Zhong, R. (2021). The limits of green finance: A survey of literature in the context of green bonds and green loans. *Sustainability, 13*(2), 478.

González, C. I. & Núñez, S. (2021). Markets, financial institutions and central banks in the face of climate change: Challenges and opportunities. *Banco de Espana Occasional Chapter*, (2126).

Grandjean, A., Lefournier, J., & Giraud, G. (2021). *L'illusion de la finance verte*. Éditions de l'Atelier.

Grundström, G. & Miedel, I. (2021). Sustainable investing: On the relation between sustainability rating and greenhouse gas emissions. DIVA 2021, p. 69.

Hedberg, A. (2021). The European green deal: How to turn ambition into action. EPC Discussion Chapter 04 November 2021.

Huang, H. & Zhang, J. (2021). Research on the environmental effect of green finance policy based on the analysis of pilot zones for green finance reform and innovations. *Sustainability, 13*(7), 3754.

Khan, M. A., Riaz, H., Ahmed, M., *et al.* (2021). Does green finance really deliver what is expected? An empirical perspective. *Borsa Istanbul Review, 22*(3), 586–593.

Laborda, J. & Sánchez-Guerra, Á. (2021). Green Bond Finance in Europe and the Stock Market Reaction. *Estudios de economía aplicada, 39*(3), 5.

Liaw, K. T. (2020). Survey of Green Bond pricing and investment performance. *Journal of Risk and Financial Management, 13*(9), 193.

Liu, J., Liu, Y., & Wang, X. (2020). An environmental assessment model of construction and demolition waste based on system dynamics: A case study in Guangzhou. *Environmental Science and Pollution Research, 27*(30), 37237–37259.

McCauley, D. & Heffron, R. (2018). Just transition: Integrating climate, energy and environmental justice. *Energy Policy, 119*, 1–7.

Niyazbekova, S., Moldashbayeva, L., Kerimkhulle, S., Dzholdoshev, N., Dzholdosheva, T., & Serikova, M. (2021). "Green" bonds — A tool for financing "green" projects in countries. In *E3S Web of Conferences* (Vol. 244, p. 10060). EDP Sciences.

O'Mahony, T. (2021). Cost-Benefit Analysis and the environment: The time horizon is of the essence. *Environmental Impact Assessment Review, 89*, 106587.

Parker, C. (2021). Are banks responsible for animals? A critical review of animal welfare and climate disruption in banks' due diligence policies for agribusiness lending. A critical review of animal welfare and climate disruption in banks' due diligence policies for agribusiness lending (September 5, 2021).

Perkins, R. (2021). Governing for growth: Standards, emergent markets, and the lenient zone of qualification for green bonds. *Annals of the American Association of Geographers, 111*(7), 2044–2061.

Popescu, I. S., Hitaj, C., & Benetto, E. (2021). Measuring the sustainability of investment funds: A critical review of methods and frameworks in sustainable finance. *Journal of Cleaner Production, 314*, 128016.

Semieniuk, G., Campiglio, E., Mercure, J. F., *et al.* (2021). Low-carbon transition risks for finance. *Wiley Interdisciplinary Reviews: Climate Change, 12*(1), e678.

Sharma, G. D., Tiwari, A. K., Talan, G., *et al.* (2021). Revisiting the sustainable versus conventional investment dilemma in COVID-19 times. *Energy Policy, 156*, 112467.

Shideler, J. C. & Hetzel, J. (2021). Financing the transition. In *Introduction to Climate Change Management* (pp. 139–168). Cham: Springer.

Simpson, N. P., Mach, K. J., Constable, A., *et al.* (2021). A framework for complex climate change risk assessment. *One Earth, 4*(4), 489–501.

Spasić, D., Denčić-Mihajlov, K., & Poposki, K. (2021). A critical review of the climate-related reporting requirements in the financial service sector. In *International Scientific Conference Strategic Management and Decision Support Systems in Strategic Management 2021* (pp. 382–389).

Strauch, Y., Dordi, T., & Carter, A. (2020). Constraining fossil fuels based on 2 C carbon budgets: The rapid adoption of a transformative concept in politics and finance. *Climatic Change, 160*(2), 181–201.

Tolliver, C., Ryota Keeley, A., & Managi S. (2021). Green bonds for the Paris agreement and sustainable development goals. *Environmental Research Letters, 14*(2019), 064009. https://doi.org/10.1088/1748-9326/ab1118.

Torvanger, A., Maltais, A., & Marginean, I. (2021). Green bonds in Sweden and Norway: What are the success factors? *Journal of Cleaner Production, 324*, 129177.

van Veelen, B. (2021). Cash cows? Assembling low-carbon agriculture through green finance. *Geoforum, 118*, 130–139.

Wang, Q., Guo, J., & Li, R. (2022). Official development assistance and carbon emissions of recipient countries: A dynamic panel threshold analysis for low-and lower-middle-income countries. *Sustainable Production and Consumption, 29*, 158–170.

Zhang, D., Mohsin, M., Rasheed, A. K., *et al.* (2021). Public spending and green economic growth in BRI region: Mediating role of green finance. *Energy Policy, 153*, 112256.

https://doi.org/10.1142/9781800614482_0013

Chapter 13

Green Finance, Corporate Performance, and the Role of Financial Institutions

Fateh Saci[*,†,§] **and Boualem Aliouat**[‡,¶]

[†]*University of Nîmes (Chrome EA 7352), Nîmes, France*

[‡]*Group of Research in Management (GRM), University Côte d'Azur, Nice, France*

[§]*sacifateh@yahoo.fr*

[¶]*boualem.aliouat@univ-cotedazur.fr*

Abstract

This chapter mainly deals with the systemic relevance and paradoxes of green finance, both in terms of organizational performance and the contribution of conventional or unconventional financial institutions in achieving the objectives of a sustainable environmental economy. The objective of this chapter is to highlight the impact of climate risks on the financial performance of the company and to show to what extent the durability and competitiveness of companies are based on an adjustment toward a "sustainable" strategy. Our chapter focuses on the effect of CO_2 emissions on corporate performance. Using CDP data from a sample of the world's 500 largest companies, the results of our regression model show a negative correlation between CO_2 emissions and company performance scores. The results of our qualitative interviews with 14 interviewees attest to the progressive disengagement of banks toward polluting companies.

[*]Corresponding author.

1. Introduction

Green finance is undoubtedly the missing link in a responsible economy. Its development is a way of accelerating virtuous investments in accordance with new environmental mechanisms and ethical performance objectives. More specifically, the risk associated with climate change has raised questions for several decades, with regard to both the performance of companies and financial instruments adapted to sustainable investments. Stern (2007) presents, in his report on environmental issues, an alarming observation of the risks facing the world. His studies show that climate damage could represent 5–20 percent of the gross world product of states. Faced with this worrying observation and in an environment where competitiveness and performance have become keywords, it appears more and more urgent to integrate these climate risks as an essential variable in all strategic considerations.

Moreover, to identify and measure these risks, the Financial Stability Board has classified the risks linked to climate change into three main categories: physical risks, liability risks, and transition risks. First, physical risks result from the impacts of a weather event or weather conditions, such as floods and storms, on the value of financial assets. They particularly affect insurance liabilities. Second, liability risks are the consequences that could arise if actors who have suffered loss or damage from the effects of climate change wanted to be compensated by those responsible. Finally, transition risks are the financial risks that could result from the transition to a low-carbon economy. In other words, regulatory changes, technology, and physical risks could cause many assets to be revalued, and the speed with which this reassessment occurs could influence overall financial stability.

The economist William Nordhaus (2007), a pioneer in the modeling of climate change, now recommends that natural disasters and their repercussions on economic growth be included. Today, international reports such as the "Intergovernmental Panel on Climate Change" and the MSCI index are already inspired by the DICE model (Pindyck, 2013), which highlights the cost–benefit of reducing greenhouse gas (GHG) emissions through the global cooperation of all countries. Regulatory bodies are aware of the economic challenges of climate risk and invite countries to adopt international regulations. Thus, the Paris Climate Agreement in 2015 proposed a maximum global warming target of 1.5 degree Celsius, a value which, according to the economist Combes, may remain admittedly laudable, but without effect if countries do not concretely commit to emission reduction policies compatible with such an objective.

In Europe, the Prudential Control Authority and the European Central Bank have thus set up a mechanism for monitoring and engaging financial players in the management of climate risks in accordance with Article 173 of the law of August 17, 2015, on the energy transition for green growth, which provides for increased transparency obligations for investors in taking into account criteria relating to compliance with environmental, social, and governance (ESG) objectives. Likewise, European banking regulations now require banks to hold a capital requirement for provisioned financial resources in order to guard against potential market risks, such as credit, which does not include climate risk. However, the study carried out by the ACPR[1] in 2019 shows a very weak commitment by banks to the policy of reducing the carbon footprint of portfolios or GHG emissions. Indeed, this policy represents only 18 percent of commitments for insurers and 11 percent for banks. Financial institutions do not currently seem to be able to support companies in this transition. In this case, how will companies be able to finance their "sustainable" assets? Can the emergence of this new "climate" market overcome this problem?

Most of the research work focuses on the overall economic consequences through a macroeconomic or microeconomic approach (Colombo & Philip, 2012; Hallegatte *et al.*, 2018; COACCH, 2021), while our research aims to be more meso-economic through the observation of the impact of climate risks on the performance of companies, resulting in a clear disengagement of banks in their support for companies whose investments present major climate risks. The originality of this research work is to reveal, by qualifying the conclusions of the ACPR (2019), that if banks do not actively support the energy transition, these institutions are nevertheless reluctant to support investments whose climatic risks are proven.

The interest of this chapter is to demonstrate the high exposure of companies to climate and environmental risks — risks that impact their performance and their method of financing toward financial

[1] ACPR-AMF 2019, "The climate commitments of French financial institutions."

institutions that undertake to reduce their "polluter" customer portfolios. The objective of this chapter is therefore to assess the impact of weather events on the valuation of a company on the market, which thus determines its overall financial and extra-financial performance. Thus, it is interesting to ask what the impact of climate risk is on the performance of companies. Another major innovation of our study is that we mixed qualitative and quantitative methods: We used the Carbon Disclosure Project (CDP) data from a sample of the world's 500 largest companies and a qualitative method by conducting interviews with 14 senior managers.

Our analysis first highlighted the negative effects of Scopes 1 and 2 CO_2 emissions on the overall performance of 391 large global companies. This chapter also shows that the energy and transport sectors could achieve a low ecological rating despite good financial performance. Therefore, this confirms the link and negative correlation between overall performance and environmental risks, and the results of our qualitative interviews prove the progressive disengagement of banks toward polluting companies.

This chapter is structured as follows. Section 2 reviews the relevant literature on sustainable finance and performance, including the following aspects: the economic nature of environmental risk, environmental risks and corporate performance, Environmental risks and financial strength of borrowers, and sustainable finance, a new mode of financing. Section 3 is about measurement, quantification, and modeling; it includes a qualitative as well as a quantitative approach to green finance. Section 4 is about sustainable investment, performance, and the role of banks; it presents and discusses our empirical results and analysis. The three points analyzed are the dispersion of the environmental rating, perspectives on sustainable finance, and a nuanced analysis. Some concluding remarks are made in Section 5.

2. Sustainable Finance and Performance

2.1. *The economic nature of environmental risk*

The environment was considered a common good by the early theorists of well-being, and any damage to the environment (such as pollution) constitutes a negative externality, harming collective well-being. In order to optimize it, economists evaluate a cost–benefit ratio. Economists estimate this future cost–benefit ratio using a discount rate, but these results remain relative because of the problem of subjective judgment of the implicit values associated with discounting. There remains a level of uncertainty in the assessment of the costs and benefits of risk that would likely incorporate ecological and economic costs and benefits.

Economic studies dealing with the cost–benefit analysis of climate change have come to very different conclusions about the economic policy to be adopted. According to early studies by Nordhaus (2007), "optimal" economic policies for slowing the climate involve modest rates of reduction in greenhouse gas (GHG) emissions, followed by increasing reductions over the medium to long term. We then speak of a gradual rise in power of climate policy, although some studies have recommended more drastic measures.

The debate on the economics of climate change took a turn in 2007 with the publication of the works of Nicholas Stern (2007). Until now, previous economic analyses of climate change have suggested relatively modest policy responses, while the Stern report has recommended immediate and substantial political action. The studies by Stern (2007) and Nordhaus (2007) adopted a standard economic methodology. Stern's approach gives much more weight to the ecological and economic aspects in the long run and uses a low discount rate of 1.4 percent to balance future performance and costs. In the long run, the damage to the environment caused by the behavior of actors on a global scale will have significant negative effects on the economy. But using a standard discount rate had the effect of reducing the present value of significant long-term future damage to a relatively small magnitude.

However, Stern's work has certain limits, as pointed out by Pindyck (2013): the orders of magnitude set out by Stern (i.e., an effective reduction of CO_2 representing 1 percent of GDP in 2050) are contested because they are not supported by robust assumptions and are not based on the economic consequences of climate change. Within the literature, we can observe divergences in the assessment methods and the perceptions of climate risk. The most recent authors are inspired by these models to draw a vision closer to reality.

Recently, the literature has highlighted the main characteristics of climate risk (Andersson *et al.*, 2018). It is presented as systemic and nonlinear (Alessi *et al.*, 2019) and characterized by its uncertainty (Weitzman, 2009). This means that if not addressed in time, it could lead to tipping points in the ecosystem and to prolonged and irreversible socioecological and economic crises (Steffen *et al.*, 2018), with profound implications for the financial stability of organizations. Finally, climate risk is considered endogenous, which means that the realization or not of the worst scenarios depends on the perception of the risk by the agents concerned (for example, political decision-makers, investors, and society) and their reactions to this perception (Alessi *et al.*, 2019). Furthermore, climate risk involves and affects, at the same time (but through different channels), several dimensions linked to food, water, and energy, as well as the socioeconomic activities linked to them. All of this increases the complexity of implementing policy actions (Howarth & Monasterolo, 2016).

The characteristics of climate risk play an important role in assessing macroeconomic policies and the financial consequences of climate change. They influence the design of major scenarios and the conditions of amplification and persistence of shocks. However, traditional approaches have limitations when analyzing the macroeconomic and financial impacts of climate change and climate policies (Dafermos & Nikolaidi, 2021). Indeed, macroeconomic models, such as dynamic stochastic general equilibrium (DSGE) models and computable general equilibrium (CGE) models, which generally adopt strong assumptions on labor and product market compensation, foresight and perfect rationality of agents, as well as the conditions of equilibrium in the economy, are in contradiction with the deep uncertainty, nonlinearities, and endogeneity that characterize climate risk. Moreover, these models relegate the role of money and finance to the background, while they play a very important role (Farmer *et al.*, 2015). Although the role of the financial system has been incorporated into many DSGE models since the global financial crisis, in the vast majority of these models it has been done in the context of "financial frictions" without taking into account the endogenous accumulation of financial fragility (Gali, 2018), currency endogeneity, and the complexity of interconnections within the financial system. Furthermore, in these models, investment decisions are retrospective, as they are informed by price dynamics and resource scarcity that ignore scientific scenarios of the impact of climate change and climate mitigation policies.

Omitting these aspects of real-world financial systems makes it difficult to use these models effectively to understand the financial implications of climate change. In addition, the models can give rise to a false sense of control, on the one hand, over the ability of the economy to shift relatively quickly from carbon-intensive to low-carbon investments to meet the targets of the Paris Agreement and, on the other hand, over the capacity to manage the financial risks linked to the climate. Conversely, coherent stock-flow models (SFC) and agent-based models analyze the macroeconomic and financial system as a complex adaptive system and can easily integrate the role of nonlinearities, interconnections, and imbalances. They also explicitly formulate the endogenous process of money creation, which plays a key role in the emergence of financial cycles.

2.2. *Environmental risks and corporate performance*

This issue raises two questions: one concerns the influence of climate risk on asset prices, and the other relates to the difficulty that financial agents have in perceiving climate risk. First, regarding the influence of climate risk on asset prices, it should be noted that climate change has a significant impact on the economy by reducing business productivity, investments, and innovation in adapting to a changing climate (NFGS, 2019). However, the IMF underlines a poor understanding of the impact of climatic hazards on the production of investors and on the financial markets. The occurrence of a weather event characterized by its uncertainty can lead investors to revise their expected future profits, thus reflecting asset depreciation (Campiglio *et al.*, 2019). Indeed, the study by Bernstein *et al.* (2019) shows that nearshore properties exposed to possible sea-level rise are sold at a lower price than similar properties far offshore.

This result highlights the influence of climate risks on the value of an asset in the real estate sector, but this conclusion can be applied to other sectors. Climate change, particularly weather, affects business production. Thus, for example, a drop in the performance of French companies has been observed in the event of meteorological disturbances (Bertrand & Kaddour, 2009). The weather variable is the second variable explaining the variation in the performance of companies deemed to be weather sensitive. Thus, the weather variable plays a considerable role in the profitability of companies and must be included in the risks facing the company. However, this risk is not sufficiently anticipated by financial investors. The consequences of climate change are not only felt in their industry but throughout the value chain, from production even up to the consumer. We also observe, for example, that a cap on the production of fossil fuels would result in the immobilization of assets in the mining sector, but would also trigger waves of immobilization of assets in other sectors: energies with electricity and gas, coke and refined petroleum products, base metals, and transport, through the input–output structure of the economy (Cahen-Fourot *et al.*, 2021). This indicates that climate risk decreases the capital structure by reducing the optimal leverage of the company and supply because lenders precisely increase the risk margins of borrowing from polluting companies (Ginglinger & Moreau, 2019.) It is therefore easy to formulate a first hypothesis arguing that *climate risks have a negative impact on the performance of the company.*

Second, regarding the perception of risk by financial agents, it should be remembered that climate risk requires a different approach from traditional financial risks because of its characteristics of uncertainty and consequently the difficulty in quantifying such risks. Several studies show that companies have difficulty integrating this risk into the valuation of their assets, which determines the performance of the company. It was noted, for example, that through a study of the behavior of the financial market in the face of climate change during the period 2011–2016, a very high return was recorded by oil companies, despite the meteorological risk. This observation reflects the difficulties for investors to assess and hedge against the risks associated with climate change. The majority of overvaluations are concentrated in the industrial and energy sectors.

The lack of anticipation on the part of investors to integrate their emission factor (EF)[2] in their fixed assets has often been criticized (McGlade & Ekins, 2015). Indeed, fossil fuels are part of the fixed assets of companies and increase their value. This is the reason why

[2]This factor makes it possible to transform a physical activity data into a quantity of greenhouse gas emissions.

companies continue to invest in the localization and development of new fossil fuels. In addition, the ACPR (ACPR-AMF, 2020) observes through a study of 23 management companies that less than a third of the companies questioned have developed a climate strategy, and 46 percent of companies do not plan to integrate this type of strategy. As a result, it seems that the climate risk is not considered sufficiently important by a large number of companies.

But we must also question the relevance of certain expertise capacities. For example, the Palmer Drought Severity Index (Hong *et al.*, 2019) shows that equity markets are unable to anticipate worsening farmland in times of drought. Often, companies actually fear the negative effects of an energy transition on business performance. In terms of the negative impact of climate risk on the value of assets, we observe that if the change is significant, investors will revise their results downward by integrating additional costs borne by the company. A sudden drop in asset prices due to this climatic hazard will have strong economic repercussions and will give rise to the "Minsky effect." This effect indicates that stability breeds instability, especially when indebted investors are rushed to sell their assets. This indicates that capitalism is never satisfied with stability in the long term. Only financial intermediaries can therefore ensure financial stabilization and avoid an economic crisis.

A different vision was proposed by Weitzman (2009). It is based on the long-term effect of the energy transition: integrating the probable climate risks by companies outweighs the possible decrease in investments following the energetic transition. Of course, the measures taken by companies will have effects on GDP, consumption, and employment, which partly explains the reluctance of governments to take drastic measures to significantly reduce CO_2 emissions, but these effects will not be all negative. In order to avoid a repercussion of climate risks on the entire economy, the intervention of regulatory bodies is essential to ensuring that the economy is maintained. Retail banks must therefore integrate climate risk.

2.3. *Environmental risks and financial strength of borrowers*

This issue raises two questions: on the one hand, that concerning the cost of physical and transition risks, and on the other, that concerning the financial soundness of banks. First, regarding the cost of physical and transition risks, note that the physical damage caused by extreme weather events linked to climate change affects the ability of debtors to service their loans. Thus, companies can use other modes of financing, such as the debt market, to borrow (Diamond, 1991). We also observe, by studying a large sample of banks around the world, that banks operating in regions affected by weather-related disasters observed higher rates of non-performing loans and foreclosures than other banks over the past two years following an event. This greatly increases the likelihood of failure of these banks. This effect is maintained when we consider the characteristics of banks that are generally associated with bank failures, such as bank capital ratios or non-performing asset ratios. Weather-related events affect the financial strength of debtors (Klomp, 2014).

Transition costs also have an impact on the financial strength of borrowers (Roncoroni *et al.*, 2021). When one observes the measures taken by the Chinese authorities to promote the transition to a low-carbon economy, it is possible to highlight the impact of transition risks triggered by policies on debt instruments. Such observations show that after the implementation of the clean air action launched by the Chinese government in 2013, the failure rates of highly polluting companies increased by about 50 percent. Conversely, Chinese banks which have a higher green credit ratio, i.e., banks which are less exposed to loans for the benefit of polluting companies experience fewer non-performing loans (Cui *et al.*, 2018).

Second, regarding the financial soundness of banks, it should be noted that if a company is exposed to higher weather risks than others, banks should also take this into account by charging it a higher margin on loans. Against the backdrop of stranded asset risk, one study compared the lending rate banks demand from fossil fuel companies based on their climate policy exposure to non-fossil-fuel companies (Delis *et al.*, 2019). It is observed that before 2015, banks did not set prices for companies' exposure to fossil fuels in accordance with climate policy. After 2015, however, the risk began to be assessed, especially for companies with more fossil fuel reserves.

However, the economic importance of this risk premium is rather low, and it is very unlikely that it corresponds to the potential losses of stranded assets. A shift in the earnings expected by lenders is also reflected in the financial markets, affecting investors and asset owners. Feedback loops between the financial system and macroeconomics could further amplify these impacts and risks. For example, damage to assets used as collateral could create losses for banks to restrict lending in some areas, which would reduce the funding available for reconstruction in affected areas. Climatic vagaries affect the creditworthiness of borrowers, who are faced with difficulty in collecting data, allowing them to design a reliable statistical model. Thus, the Institute for Climate Economics (I4CE, 2019) exposes the limits of financial institutions to model climate risk. First, the time horizons of the standard five-year credit models cannot align with the 30-year climate scenarios. Next, climate data present many variables, which are difficult to quantify and are heterogeneous, making the exercise complex. The scenario tool was designed by measuring probable future situations, which is the opposite of a climate risk characterized by its uncertainty. Integrating scenario analysis into current statistical models seems impossible because scenarios are not forecasts, and it is difficult, if not impossible, to assign probabilities to them (Raynaud *et al.*, 2018). A second hypothesis therefore seems to apply: *banks grant less credit to, and gradually withdraw from, polluting companies.*

2.4. *Toward a new mode of financing: Sustainable finance*

This new method of financing is linked to the emergence of a need for "green" financing but is not without effect on the performance of companies. The need for "green" financing led, in 2007, the European Investment Bank to introduce the so-called "green" bonds. These are fixed- and liquid-income financial instruments that are used to raise funds for climate mitigation, adaptation, and other environmentally friendly projects (The World Bank, 2018). This new market has grown exponentially in a few years, reaching $41 billion in 2015 (Meltzer, 2016). As this market is accessible to the public and private sectors, companies have resorted to this new method of financing, abandoning commercial banks. Very quickly, green municipal bonds became more profitable and better managed than ordinary bonds in the United States (Baker *et al.*, 2019). This proves the efficiency and profitability of these bonds, which, at first, are expensive but will offer higher returns later. Green financing can, at first glance, appear to be a solution to ensure an energy transition while stabilizing the economy. However, these bonds seem to have little effect if they are located in the same sector (Baker *et al.*, 2019). This raises the question of the negative effects of sustainable finance on the performance of companies.

Are issuance yields lower for green bonds compared to conventional bonds? An econometric study finds controversial results (Fatica *et al.*, 2021): while the returns are lower for supranational institutions and non-financial corporations, there is no difference between the returns on green bonds and conventional bonds in the case of financial institutions. Green bond yields are lower if companies issue a lot of green bonds and there is an external review of the green bond certification process. Another finding is that banks that issue green bonds tend to reduce their lending to carbon-intensive sectors. The performance of green bonds should also be studied in the stock market.

Focusing on the stock markets, and more specifically using a sample of companies listed on the STOXX Europe Total Market Index, some analyses observe that investors accept lower compensation for holding shares of companies that disclose environmental data and have a lower emission intensity (Alessi *et al.*, 2021). It is the question of the losses of institutional sectors at the global level that is posed if we consider a scenario in which the actions of companies with a high environmental profile outweigh the actions of carbon-intensive companies. We can see that the losses are not quantitatively large, while a reallocation of assets toward greener assets could even reduce these losses. We can certainly deduce that weather and its derivatives can be useful financial instruments for hedging climate-related risks, but that would lead to a loss of profitability. As for the positive effects of sustainable finance on the performance of companies, it should be noted that they are confirmed by existing research, in particular through the theory of stakeholders, which shows that the interest of companies in meeting the needs of the stakeholders improves their reputation and financial performance (Waddock & Graves, 1997).

A distinction should be made, however, when it comes to green investments, and it is possible to group them into two categories of assets: non-real green assets and real green assets. By comparing the performance of green assets with traditional assets according to their exposure to liquidity shocks on the markets or their sensitivity to volatility, we observe that green assets, in particular real green assets, perform better than traditional assets (Martinez-Oviedo & Medda, 2018). We observe the same trends regardless of the country studied, as indicated by Chen and Ma (2021), who study the relationship between green investments and the performance of listed companies in China from 2008 to 2017. Their research shows a positive correlation with green investment by energy companies. Indeed, in the third year after investing in CO_2 emissions reduction, the financial performance of companies tends to increase. Companies that integrate green investment initiatives designed to reduce carbon emissions can therefore manage their financial performance more effectively (Miliacca *et al.*, 2017). Yufeng and Yanbai (2021) observe the same effects of green investment on the behavior and performance of companies. This is the reason why some authors suggest state intervention on the competition of green companies by the establishment of a taxation for polluting companies in order to maximize social welfare (Sheu & Chen, 2012), thus resulting in prohibitive transaction costs for polluting companies, as suggested by Coase (1988). It can be concluded that green investment, through technological innovations, has positive effects on long-term performance. The action plans implemented aimed at reducing disregard for the environment and promoting environmental performance have the following three positive effects: it improves transparency and image through the rating assigned by the MSCI (ESG); it attracts new investors; and it improves the financial health of the company. This approach is, of course, part of a long-term vision because, in the short term, the fruits of these investments are not necessarily visible. This leads to a third fundamental assumption that *sustainable investing has a positive impact on the long-term performance of a company.*

However, climate risk faces many obstacles, starting with its uncertainty, which is difficult to quantify and assimilate into standard financial risks. However, research has shown the significant impact on the economy as a whole: devaluation of assets, a decline in production, or even higher interest rates linked to loans that could destabilize the global economy. Banks are trying to understand this better, but banking regulations and forecasting models currently appear to be incompatible with climate change. We must therefore ask ourselves whether companies would not be interested in seeking financing methods that are more suitable and favorable to environmental issues. Conversely, this type of substitute market must be regulated in order to avoid disruption of financial stability. Indeed, if companies decide to invest heavily in climate bonds, what will happen to the traditional financial market? This is a question that poses a real dilemma in the long term.

3. Measurement, Quantification, and Modeling

The methodological approach adopted is a combination of qualitative and quantitative approaches in order to highlight both the density of the phenomenon and the meaning of the different perceptions and exposures to risks of the actors concerned. This dual analysis allows us to have an exhaustive diagnosis of the financial and extra-financial impacts of climate risks and their financing leverage, on the one hand, and of the development of companies toward sustainable finance, on the other hand. In other words, we observe the relationship between banks and their professional clients, the impact of CO_2 emissions on the performance of companies, and their long-term investment in sustainable finance.

3.1. *A qualitative approach to green finance*

Regarding our qualitative method, we couple, as recommended by Perch-Nielsen *et al.* (2008), climate models with migration models, because to understand interconnected changes in both natural and human systems, a measure of objectivity in the study of the interactions between these phenomena is useful, if not necessary. The people interviewed benefit from a certain freedom of response, thus leaving room for surprises and unforeseen elements (Mongeau, 2008), and this approach is recommended for research related to questions of traditional ecological knowledge.

Our chapter focused on the new ECB and ACPR regulations toward banks, insurance, or asset management in their climate commitments. Thus, for example, a study carried out by the ACPR has shown that "75% of French banks are committed to reducing their carbon footprint," but 75 percent face difficulties in estimating climate risks. These results have guided our semi-structured interviews with businesses and banks. Our sample includes seven different sectors (forest preservation, banking, insurance, rail, energy, catering, and real estate), and 60 percent of the stakeholders are familiar with the subject of climate risks and work in support functions (financial services, corporate responsibility, project management, etc.). We reserved 40 percent of the sample for operational activities to obtain more subjective and distanced information.

It should be remembered that our research work is based on two hypotheses based on two different visions: on the one hand, the role of banks in supporting companies toward an energy transition and the impacts on their solvency, and on the other hand, the extra-financial impacts of climate risks on the activities of companies and the action plans implemented. Thus, the information collected falls under hypotheses 2 and 3 of our research, respectively: *Banks grant less credit and gradually withdraw from polluting companies*; *sustainable investing has a positive impact on the performance of the company*. The content analysis was carried out using the MAXQDA software through the axial quince method, which takes into account the following categories and sub-categories: CO_2 emissions, renewable energies, climate-related risks, and cost.

3.2. *A quantitative approach to green finance*

Regarding our quantitative method, we use climate data from the CDP,[3] which studies the impact of large listed global companies on climate change. This database is processed by IBM SPSS Statistics software. This database enables future investors and clients to observe the inclusion of environmental risks in companies' strategies and their transparency on their carbon emissions. Their choice of investment will therefore be based on the score assigned by the institution. The rating is between 0 and 100 for the company and varies according to several criteria, including control and monitoring by corporate governance of climate risks, environmental risks and opportunities, targets, and performances over the next five years; transparency and completeness of data on the company's CO_2 emissions, company CO_2 emission rate, and carbon price in the asset

[3] CO_2 emissions of the 500 largest companies in the world by market capitalization (by sector, country, Scopes 1 and 2, and the score attributed to companies).

portfolio and commitment to sustainable development. These data allow us to identify the companies that have implemented an environmental control system, their CO_2 emission rates, and the strategies to reduce their carbon footprint. A high score brings about a considerable advantage, and the transparency of the data provided a proof of authenticity and influences the choice of investors.

International standards, such as ISO 14064-1 and the GHG Protocol, define methodologies for calculating different categories of CO_2 emissions. Each country may have its own classifications, but overall, they are similar. For example, in France, the French Environment and Energy Management Agency (ADEME) distinguishes three categories or "scopes": Scope 1 includes "direct emissions from fixed or mobile installations located within the organizational perimeter..." (combustion, industrial processes excluding combustion, biogas, fluid leaks, nitrogen fertilization, biomass, etc.); Scope 2 includes indirect emissions: "emissions linked to the consumption of electricity and emissions linked to the consumption of steam, heat and cold"; and Scope 3 corresponds to all the other indirect emissions, which are necessary for the activity of any company without the latter being the emitter, such as purchases of products and services, immobilization of goods, waste, transport of goods, and business trips.

Our quantitative analysis makes it possible to measure, quantify, calculate, and analyze variances and covariances and perform multiple and varied regression models. This method makes it possible to measure the exposure of banks to environmental risks based on climate data and the financial performance of companies. This information allows us to answer questions about the systems put in place in the banking and insurance sector to measure their exposure to these climate changes.

4. Sustainable Investment, Performance, and the Role of Banks

4.1. *Dispersion of the environmental rating*

In this research study, the 500 listed companies in 2017 are used as the research sample; 391 companies responded to CDP questionnaires

Table 1. Descriptive statistics.

Number of variables	Number of observations	Minimum	Maximum	Mean	Standard deviation
Disclosure Score	391	2	100	81.43	18.053
Scope 1	339	4.78	181,690,000	8,579,921	25,991,501.86
Scope 2	339	8.8	200,000,000	1,467,240.65	2,734,790.61

and provided their CO_2 emissions index (Scopes 1 & 2). We removed the empty lines and reduced our sample to 391 observations (Table 1).

Based on our first analysis, we can observe a low dispersion of the environmental rating attributed to companies. In other words, in 2017, companies had an average environmental performance of 82/100. The table shows us that the distribution is skewed to the right and a large dispersion of observations to the mean. Of the 391 companies surveyed, 43.7 percent of them obtained a B rating, while 15.4 percent of companies obtained an A rating. In order to better understand the value of the standard deviation, we carried out the *Z* score test to determine where the value of the variable studied in our case, the performance of companies, is located. The *Z* score is an inducer of the dispersion of the observations compared to the mean. Our chapter aims to demonstrate whether, if the *Z* score is positive, the emission of greenhouse gases from polluting companies is near or far from the average in order to determine the severity of their pollution and the impact on their performance. It also allows us to determine which are the most polluting countries and/or sectors in our sample.

First, we determine the companies with the highest Scope 1 level (GHG emissions directly related to the company's activity). Following our analysis, we observe that the three polluting companies in 2017 are from Russia, Luxembourg, and Germany (Table 2): RWE AG is a German company in the energy sector, Arcelor Mittal is a Luxembourg company in the steel industry, and Gazprom OAO is a Russian company involved in the production of natural gas.

We can hypothesize the following: companies whose businesses use and exploit fossil fuels emit the most CO_2. The *Z* scores of RWE AG (6.66), Arcelor Mittal (5.7), and Gazprom OAO (4.9) are above

Table 2. Three polluting companies.

Company	Scope 1 emission (in metric tonnes)	Performance brand	Z score
RWE AG	181,690,000	B	6.66
Arcelor Mittal	158,192,000	B	5.75
Gazprom	154,230,874	C	4.80

average. Arcelor Mittal is at a Scope 1 emission level of 158,192,000 tons of CO_2. Looking at the Z score, we can say that this observation is above average and is 6.6 standard deviations above average. The result obtained is explained by the strong pollution of the company due to its activity, which thus moves its emission rate away from the central tendency indicator from the average.

Concerning the data normality, to check if our dataset follows the normal law, the skewness and kurtosis tests must be carried out. The data for a variable follow the normal distribution if the X is between -1 and 1 and the kurtosis is close to 3.

The skewness test measures the symmetry of the data. In view of the results obtained for the quantitative variables, we can see that the asymmetry coefficients oscillate between -1.91 and 4.24. Kurtosis test results are between 4.57 and 18.81. Thus, the dataset does not follow a normal distribution. For example, the disclosure score distributions are skewed to the right. As the sample size is much greater than 30 ($N = 391$), we can conclude that the distribution of the data of the variables is quasi-normal.

4.2. *Perspectives on sustainable finance*

4.2.1. *Analysis of variances*

Our question is whether the performance of the company differs according to the environmental rating assigned by the CDP. The null hypothesis is that the average performance is the same regardless of the environmental rating, which can be tested using analysis of variances (ANOVA). Conditions are met to conduct an ANOVA. The ANOVA significance test for scope levels 1 and 2 based on the performance of the company is significant at the 10 percent level. The p-value is greater than 5 percent, so we accept the H0 hypothesis:

the difference in the means between the Scopes 1 & 2 (public) levels and the performance of the companies is not significant between the two groups.

4.2.2. *Construction of the multinomial logistic regression model*

Descriptive statistics showed us that the average environmental performance of companies was 82/100. However, the data dispersion and normality tests showed a strong dispersion of the observations compared to the average. Therefore, we hypothesize that the levels of Scopes 1 and 2 have a negative impact on the level of environmental performance. Correlation tests have proven the strong and negative correlation between CO_2 emission levels and the environmental rating assigned to companies. Our first hypothesis is based on the negative impact of CO_2 emissions on the performance of companies. Thus, the variable to be explained is the qualitative "performance brand" variable, not to be confused with the "disclosure" score, which only presents environmental performance. We suppose that there is a relation between the performance of a company (the variable to be explained) and its environmental score (the explanatory variables). Thus, we established a simple linear regression model, which will allow us to answer the following question: By how much does the performance of the company decreases following a low environmental score?

Our final regression model is as follows:

$$PerfBrand_x = \alpha + \beta_1 DisclosureScore + \beta_2 Permission + \varepsilon_x \quad (1)$$

$PerfBrand_x$ represents the overall performance of the company, with ratings ranging from A to E.

DisclosureScore refers to the environmental rating of 50–100, and *Permission* represents the publication of the company's CO_2 emission.

The application of the ordinary least-squares method is based on several conditions to be observed:

- The absence of multicollinearity between the explanatory variables: The levels 1 and 2 CO_2 emissions variables were not added to the model because they had a strong dependence on the explanatory variable "disclosure score." The data are unbiased.

- The data normality tests (KS) carried out during our analyses show that the "performance brand" follows a normal law.

4.2.3. *Interpretations of regression model results*

We illustrate our remarks by interpreting the data from the estimation of the parameters studied (Table 3).

The interpretation of the likelihood model is based on the reference category (E), which is the lowest score. Companies that disclose their carbon footprint are nine times less likely to have an E performance score than those that decide not to show them publicly. Indeed, if a company does not disclose its carbon footprint, it lacks transparency, which calls into question its commitment to reducing CO_2 emissions. As a result, the overall performance score of the company is lower.

Take the example of companies with a performance rating of A. If companies obtain an A rating, they are 64 times less likely to increase their CO_2 emission rate than if they had obtained an E rating (−63, six of which have Sig <0.001). In other words, a company with a high rating will have a lower CO_2 emission rate than a company with an E rating. Indeed, "Leader" companies have a policy of reducing CO_2 emissions in order to ensure the sustainability

Table 3. Multinomial logistic regression table.

Performance brand	**Variables**	***B***	**Standard error**	**Wald**	**ddl**	**Sig**
A	Constant	650.7	6.210	77.243	1	<0.001
	DS*	**−63.594**	3.342	68.137	1	<0.001
	Permission	0.712	0.086	57.809	1	<0.001
B	Constant	678.9	8.364	58.691	1	<0.001
	DS*	−34.034	4.990	46.525	1	<0.001
	Permission	0.501	0.077	42.679	1	<0.001
C	Constant	879.32	12.987	13.499	1	<0.001
	DS*	**−16.199**	4.409	15.259	1	<0.001
	Permission	0.268	0.071	14.345	1	<0.001
D	Constant	987.34	10.342	12.599	1	<0.001
	DS*	**−8.515**	**4.158**	**10.543**	**1**	<0.001
	Permission	0.160	0.068	11.435	1	<0.001

Note: DS* = Disclosure Score.

of their activities in the years to come. Thus, taking into account the environmental factor proves the long-term vision of the company and attracts investors. Conversely, companies whose activities reject high carbon emissions must put in place action plans in order to move quickly toward sustainable finance.

Companies with a performance rating of D are eight times less likely to increase their CO_2 emission rate than if they had obtained an E rating. The probability is eight times greater than if the company had obtained an A rating. Thus, the higher the company performance rating, the lower its CO_2 emissions rate. The results show a negative correlation between company performance and its carbon footprint. If a company has a negative impact on the environment, then its overall performance rating decreases.

Our quantitative approach reveals that a regression model validates our first hypothesis: environmental risks, in our case CO_2 emissions, have a negative impact on the performance of companies, and environmental performance has a positive impact on the financial performance of the company. Non-financial indicators have a major role in the overall performance of the company.

This hypothesis is supported by the literature, in particular the work by Kreft and Eckstein (2014), which measures the level of losses linked to extreme weather events on a country scale. They find that the likelihood of losses from weather events is associated with lower financial flows and lower profits for the companies studied. Thus, our model refutes the studies suggesting an absence of link between the two indicators, in particular the work by McWilliams and Siegel (2001), which proposes a theory according to which there is supply of and demand for social responsibility in a standard microeconomic context, which each leads it to invest socially to meet stakeholder demand. Market equilibrium cancels out the costs and profits successively generated by the offer of social responsibility. This approach leads to the formulation of a hypothesis of the neutrality of the interactions between social and financial performance.

4.3. *A nuanced analysis*

This search for meaning is based on a qualitative analysis this time. Our semi-structured interviews address the following four themes: climate change and companies' exposure to risks, evolution of the companies' performances and long-term strategies, development of sustainable finance, and financing of banks in their activities. The responses of professionals show similarities in the perception of environmental risk and its challenges. However, the risk exposure and the long-term strategies differ according to the business sectors, and the responses are relatively nuanced. The intonations and the lexical field used by the speakers reveal gray areas in their knowledge of their companies' climate strategies.

4.3.1. *Definition of climate risks and their companies' exposure to these risks*

The first theme addressed during the interviews is to define climate risks and determine whether the company is exposed to them or will know about them in the future. These elements are essential in order to observe from the outset whether the operator has a wide or narrow vision of climatic risks and their impact on his activity. Our axial coding presents the keywords linked to climate risks. If the interlocutors use all of the words present in the coding, then they constitute a concise and clear definition of climate risk. This first test is essential to the continuation of our analysis. The results of the analysis, presented in Table 4, show the percentage of all interviews carried out with the corresponding keywords.

The managers interviewed have a fairly similar definition of climate risks; let's now take a look at their exposure. The question asked presupposes that the company is already directly or indirectly

Table 4. Axial coding according to repeated keywords expressed as a percentage.

Coding	**Percentage**
CO_2	100
Energetic transition	96
Natural disasters	100
Global warming	90
Pollution	76
Exploitation of fossil resources	89
Repercussions/Impact/Consequence on biodiversity	67
Internal vulnerability to the organization	40

impacted by these hazards. Therefore, the objective is to observe whether stakeholders are aware of these repercussions on the business of the company.

The results of our analysis show contrasting responses. Of the 14 managers interviewed, five of them were able to explain the financial impact on their activity, in particular the rail network: "Train traffic was severely disrupted this year following numerous bad weather, in particular the storm 'Justine' and 'Hervé,' which heavily damaged the tracks in the PACA Provence in France." Conversely, according to our stakeholders, the textile and catering sectors do not appear to be directly exposed to these risks. "The year 2021 has been very complicated for our sector, we are affected by climate risks if, for example, our suppliers cannot deliver the stock of clothing to us on time." These results reveal uncertainties as to whether natural events are taken into account by the company.

Indeed, the person questioned is involved in an operational function, while the other participants work in support functions. Therefore, this person has a comprehensive view of the risks incurred by all activities in their sector. In addition, studies carried out by Ecoact in 2020 prove that the textile sector is highly exposed to the risks of water stress or flooding in Viscose-producing countries, for example. As for the catering sector, it is indirectly affected by these hazards if agricultural suppliers cannot sell the quantities of fruit and vegetables necessary for their activities following floods, droughts, etc. Our chapter thus takes on its full meaning by showing the imprecisions on the environmental risk and thus pushing us to reflect on the topic.

4.3.2. *Evolution of the company's performance and its long-term strategy*

The first theme showed an imprecision of the environmental risk perceived by companies, the definition of which differs depending on the business sector. Thus, the second theme of the interview aims to show the impacts of these hazards on the overall performance of the company and to observe whether the long-term objectives are geared toward an activity that respects the environment.

The textile, real estate, catering, and rail transport sectors have been severely affected by the health crisis. However, these sectors were facing a decline in their activities due to increased competition not only between different EU countries but also internationally. The French textile sector, for example, faces strong competition from Chinese companies. Companies consider environmental risk as a key indicator of extra-financial performance and, in particular, the expectations of stakeholders.

A study carried out by OFCE in 2018 shows that 85 percent of French people are worried about the consequences of climate change and designate the international community (Guivarch & Taconet, 2020), governments, and private sector companies as responsible. It is essential for companies to be transparent and to commit to sustainable development. All the companies interviewed include climate risks in their long-term strategies, which indicates a gradual awareness of climate-related issues. Companies where there is a pole dedicated to corporate CSR provide in-depth and detailed answers for future actions. The energy sector and the transport network aim to reduce their carbon impacts and change their activities by using renewable energies.

The following is a list of the main action plans mentioned by the professionals, broken down into several categories. We performed selective word coding related to our chapter:

- reduction of the carbon footprint,
- energetic transition,
- renewable energies (wind turbines, electricity, etc.),
- circular economy and partnerships with local communities.

Companies in the energy and rail transport sectors have implemented action plans, particularly in the creation of a hybrid TER "which is distinguished by its performance in terms of costs and maintenance but also by very low energy consumption, we can therefore clearly see here the possibility of reconciling economic performance and ecology." The energy sector has meanwhile changed its entire business model by changing its name and logo in order to have a new image of a green company. In addition, the company was able to generate financing capacity, allowing it to obtain a high MSCI score, positioning itself as the first company in the sector to have a rating recommended for socially responsible investors in ISS ESG assessments.

4.3.3. *The role of banks in sustainable investing*

Companies include action plans in their long-term strategies to reduce their CO_2 emissions by 2030 or 2050, depending on the business sector. These actions entail a high cost, and they need the support of credit institutions to finance their projects but also to protect themselves against possible risks with insurance companies. There are still question marks about this issue: How do banks support their customers in this energy transition? Are their customers who adopt responsible behavior privileged over polluting companies? How can insurance cover the risk at affordable prices?

To answer this, we have produced an interview guide with professionals working in the banking and insurance sector in order to understand how climate risks are modeled in their credit risk. The interest of this study is to prove the gradual withdrawal of banks from polluting companies. Interviewees are credit risk modeling engineers in banks and professional insurance advisors. Our interviews focus on three main areas: the methodology and the constraints of risk modeling and the banks' strategies/commitments in favor of an environmental policy. Our interviews also discuss on three main areas: climate change and the exposure of companies to risks, company performance, and finance and sustainable investment.

Our discussions have shown that financial institutions, particularly insurance companies, have always taken claims related to climate risks into account. Consequently, they have climate data and an analysis method developed, unlike banks, which have difficulty at the start of their work to define the impact of these risks on their activities. Indeed, "banks are impacted by climate risks as a company but also on its customer portfolio." A bank is impacted by climate risks on several aspects (our example illustrates the risk of transition):

- The bank as a company, if it does not take the "green" dimension of its assets into consideration when defining its financing costs; but also to choose a good customer portfolio, because changes in energy efficiency standards are likely to lead to significant adaptation costs and reduce the profitability of the company.
- They run a reputational risk by not taking climate and environmental aspects into account in their business activities and

by sanctioning them in the event of non-compliance with the regulatory requirements of the ACPR and the ECB on climate commitments.

The sector is therefore faced with taking these aspects into account in risk modeling. The risk identification methodology is based on TFCD and ACPR reports and integrates ESG criteria into the management of company performance. Both sectors are committed to reducing their portfolio of "polluting" assets and customers. As a result, they encourage the managers of clients or investor companies to adopt positive changes on climate-related issues. The Paris Agreement implies that CO_2 emissions will have to be reduced significantly.

To alleviate this problem, insurance companies decide to divest from polluting industries, according to our interlocutor: "Our insurance mainly targets mines and coal-fired power stations which continue to develop their activities using coal of more than 3 gigawatts, which extract more from 15 to 20 million tonnes of coal, and the energy sectors where coal represents more than 30% of turnover, you can clearly see our commitment even if it means penalizing industries that bring us money."

We then compared the information from credit institutions to see if the actions mentioned were implemented. One of the interviews with a professional in the energy sector showed that the company had every interest in adopting a climate strategy because financial institutions were able to offer them terms that reconcile economic and environmental performances. In addition, in the event of non-compliance with its rules, they lost investors.

Therefore, our interview with the banks showed that they adopt an environmental approach following regulatory requirements and are gradually withdrawing from polluting companies.

4.3.4. *The development of green finance in financial markets*

Our last hypothesis is based on "green" finance and the positive impacts on its long-term effects for companies. The current economic and societal context following the health crisis favors the expansion of green finance and environmental issues. The interviews highlighted the main mode of financing activities: sustainable finance and SRI bring together different funding methods, such as equities, bonds, and "green" investment funds. Among the people interviewed, several of them triggered an increase in sustainable investments within their companies, which are based on several labels and environmental indicators. The main labels are the "SRI Label" and the "Greenfin Label," which have the green quality of financial investments based on ESG criteria. With the recent financial market being very new, not all companies answered the question related to its valuation with a repetition of hesitant words, although the investment has advantages, especially in renewable energies, since it offers a higher return than conventional investments. The vocabulary used on this subject is optimistic and envisages positive long-term effects on the profitability and performance of companies.

5. Conclusion

To conclude our chapter, we can say that climate and environmental risks are major issues for the economy. Faced with the alarming observation of an increase in natural disasters and global warming due in part to business activities and consumption patterns, drastic measures have been taken to contain less-responsible behavior, even if there are still many controversies. From an economic point of view, the central question is whether we can adopt a growth model that respects the environment while generating high profitability for companies engaged in the logic of international competition. The interest of this chapter is to understand how these hazards affect the financial and extra-financial performance of a company while highlighting the roles of conventional and unconventional financial institutions in the assessment of this risk during the process of granting traditional or green financing.

Our first analysis highlighted the negative effects of Scopes 1 and 2 CO_2 emissions on the overall performance of 391 large global companies. This chapter showed that the energy and transport sectors could achieve a low ecological rating despite good financial performance. This therefore confirms the link and thus the negative correlation between overall performance and environmental risks.

The purpose of our chapter is to provide a critical look at the concept of performance and the difficulties encountered by banks and companies. To do this, we conducted semi-structured interviews, which provided additional information on the companies' strategies and the various action plans implemented to adapt their activities to environmental standards. This qualitative analysis made it possible to show the fuzzy and ambiguous perception of companies' exposure to financial climate risk. As a result, the difficulty of integrating environmental risk into traditional models is partly explained by the resulting misinterpretations, especially for traditional banks. In addition, interviews with stakeholders from different sectors shed light on the different degrees of involvement of companies in the preservation of the environment. The sectors are not exposed in the same way to climate risks, but they must all take corrective actions to reduce their carbon footprints. Of course, not all companies benefit from the leverage of funding that allows them to take corrective actions to conduct an environmentally friendly business. As the costs incurred by corrective actions are high, they further accentuate the inequalities in environmental performance between companies across sectors.

Finally, green finance appears to be a new method of financing that would make it possible to combine competitiveness and respect for the environment. All companies display their CSR strategies in full transparency in order to reassure stakeholders and attract new investors. They are under vigorous pressure not only from consumers but also from financial institutions, which are gradually withdrawing from polluting companies.

So, institutions must financially help and support companies, whatever their size, to move toward sustainable activities. Insurance companies, for their part, must guard against risks by offering investments such as low-carbon and green funds to improve their clients' portfolios.

This work cannot be complete without identifying avenues for reflection. Climate risks are the subject of much debate in the literature because the very definition of climate risk remains unclear and encompasses many aspects. For example, it would be interesting to provide a more detailed analysis of climate risks by distinguishing between climate-related risks (floods, droughts, fires, etc.) and environmental risks (loss of biodiversity, loss of agricultural yields, etc.). In addition, the research could use a common method for studying climate risks by selecting measurement criteria common to each sector. As a result, the problems related to methodological differences would be corrected.

The uniqueness of our research work results from its double vision: that of financial institutions and that of companies. It is indeed useful to no longer separate research work from its complementary actors because financial institutions participate in the development and financing of companies, and companies represent the customer portfolio of banks, which ensures their solvency through outstanding loans. Thus, work on the financial performance of companies should no longer be limited to indebtedness, but should take into account other variables, such as changes in regulatory standards or consumer expectations.

References

ACPR-AMF (2020). Les engagements climatiques des institutions financières françaises. https://acpr.banque-france.fr/sites/default/files/medias/documents/20201218_rapport_vf.pdf.

Alessi, L., Battiston, S., Melo, A. S., *et al.* (2019). The EU sustainability taxonomy: A financial impact assessment. EUR 29970 EN, Publications Office of the European Union, Luxembourg. https://doi.org/10.2760/347810.

Alessi, L., Ossola, E., & Panzica, R. (2021). What greenium matters in the stock market? The role of greenhouse gas emissions and environmental disclosures. *Journal of Financial Stability, 54*, 100869. https://doi.org/10.1016/j.jfs.2021.100869.

Andersson, M., Bolton, P., & Samama, F. (2018). Hedging climate risk, *Financial Analysts Journal, 72*, 13–32. https://doi.org/10.2469/faj.v72.n3.4.

Baker, M., Bergstresser, D., Serafeim, G., & Wurgler, J. (2019). Financing the response to climate change: The pricing and ownership of US green bonds (No. w25194). *National Bureau of Economic Research.* https://www.nber.org/papers/w25194.

Bernstein, A., Gustafson, M. T., & Lewis, R. (2019). Disaster on the horizon: The price effect of sea level rise. *Journal of Financial Economics, 134*(2), 253–272. https://doi.org/10.1016/j.jfineco.2019.03.013.

Bertrand, J. L., & Kaddour, B. (2009). La valeur d'une entreprise peut-elle être sensible à la météo? Une étude empirique du marché français. *Management et Avenir, 28*, 56–72. https://doi.org/10.3917/mav.028.0056.

Cahen-Fourot, L., Campiglio, E., Dawkins, E., *et al.* (2021). Capital stranding cascades: The impact of decarbonisation on productive asset utilization. AFD Research Papers, 204, pp. 1–32. Retrieved from https://www.cairn-int.info/journal-afd-research-papers-2021-204-page-1.htm.

Campiglio, E., Monnin, P., & von Jagow, A. (2019). Climate risks in financial assets. Council on Economic Policies, Discussion Note 2019/2, November 2019. Retrieved from https://www.cepweb.org/wpcontent/uploads/2019/11/CEP-DN-Climate-Risks-in-Financial-Assets.pdf.

Chen, Y. & Ma, Y. (2021). Does green investment improve energy firm performance? *Energy Policy, 153*, 112252. Retrieved from https://doi.org/10.1016/j. enpol.2021.112252.

COACCH (2021). The Economic Cost of Climate Change in Europe: Synthesis Report on Interim Results. *Policy brief by the COACCH project.* Editors: Paul Watkiss, Jenny Troeltzsch, Katriona McGlade, Michelle Watkiss. Published July 2021. https://www.coacch.eu/wp-content/uploads/2018/03/COACCH-policy-brief-2-Sector-results.pdf.

Coase, R. H. (1988). *The Firm, the Market, and the Law.* University of Chicago press, Chicago, USA.

Colombo, A. F. & Philip H. B. (2012). Adaptation, flexibility and project decision-making with climate change uncertainties. *Impact Assessment and Project Appraisal, 30*(4), 229–241. https://doi.org/10.1080/14615517.2012.731189.

Cui, Y., Geobey, S., Weber, O., *et al.* (2018). The impact of green lending on credit risk in China. *Sustainability, 10*(6), 208–216. https://doi.org/10.3390/su10062008.

Dafermos, Y. & Nikolaidi, M. (2021). How can green differentiated capital requirements affect climate risks? A dynamic macrofinancial analysis. *Journal of Financial Stability, 54*, 100871. https://doi.org/10.1016/j.jfs.2021.100871.

Delis, M. D., de Greiff, K., & Ongena, S. (2019). Being stranded with fossil fuel reserves? Climate policy risk and the pricing of bank loans. Climate Policy Risk and the Pricing of Bank loans (September 10, 2019). EBRD Working Paper, (231). http://dx.doi.org/10.2139/ssrn.3451335.

Diamond, D. W. (1991). Monitoring and reputation: The choice between bank loans and directly placed debt. *Journal of Political Economy, 99*, 689–721. http://dx.doi.org/10.1086/261775.

Farmer, J. D., Hepburn, C., Mealy, P. *et al.* (2015). A third wave in the economics of climate change. *Environmental and Resource Economics, 62*, 329–357. https://doi.org/10.1007/s10640-015-9965-2.

Fatica, E., Panzica, R., & Rancan, M. (2021). The pricing of green bonds: Are financial institutions special? *Journal of Financial Stability, 54*, 100873. https://doi.org/10.1016/j.jfs.2021.100873.

Gali, J. (2018). The state of New Keynesian economics: A partial assessment. *Journal of Economic Perspectives, 32*(3), 87–112. https://doi.org/10.1257/jep.32.3.87.

Ginglinger, E., & Moreau, Q. (2019). Climate risk and capital structure. *PSL Research University.* Retrieved from https://papers.ssrn.com/sol3/papers.cfm?abstract_id=3327185#.

Guivarch, C. & Taconet, N. (2020). Inégalités mondiales et changement climatique. Revue de l'OFCE, 165 (2020/1). Retrieved from https://www.ofce.sciences-po.fr/pdf/revue/3-165OFCE.pdf. *In French.*

Hallegatte. S., Brandon C., Damania R., Lang Y., Roome J., Rozenberg J., & Arame T. (2018). The Economics of (and Obstacles to) Aligning Development and Climate Change Adaptation. *A World Bank Group contribution to the Global Commission on Adaptation.* Discussion Paper, Global Commission on Adaptation, Rotterdam, Netherlands.

Hong, H., Li Weikai, F., & Xu, J. (2019). Climate risks and market efficiency. *Journal of Econometrics, 208*, 265–281. https://doi.org/10.1016/j.jeconom.2018.09.015.

Howarth, C. & Monasterolo, I. (2016). Understanding barriers to decision making in the UK energy-food-water nexus: The added value of interdisciplinary approaches. *Environmental Science & Policy, 61*, 53–60. https://doi.org/10.1016/j.envsci.2016.03.014.

Klomp, J. (2014). Financial fragility and natural disasters: An empirical analysis. *Journal of Financial Stability, 13*(C), 180–192. https://doi.org/10.1016/j.jfs.2014.06.001.

Martinez-Oviedo, R. & Medda, F. (2018). Real natural assets: The real green investment alternative. *The Journal of Alternative Investments, 21*(3), 53–69. https://doi.org/10.3905/jai.2018.21.3.053.

McGlade, C. & Ekins, P. (2015). The geographical distribution of fossil fuels unused when limiting global warming to 2°C. *Nature, 517*, 187–190. https://doi.org/10.1038/nature14016.

McWilliams, A. & Siegel, D. S. (2001). Corporate social responsibility: A theory of the firm perspective. *The Academy of Management Review, 26*(1), 117–127. https://doi.org/10.5465/amr.2001.4011987.

Meltzer, J. P. (2016, September 21). Financing low carbon, climate resilient infrastructure: The role of climate finance and green financial systems. In *Climate Resilient Infrastructure: The Role of Climate Finance and Green Financial Systems.* http://dx.doi.org/10.2139/ssrn.2841918.

Miliacca, M., Gastaldi, M., & Cucchiella, F. (2017). The management of greenhouse gas emissions and its effects on firm performance. *Journal of Cleaner Production, 167*, 1387–1400. https://doi.org/10.1016/j.jclepro.2017.02.170.

Mongeau, P. (2008). *Réaliser son mémoire ou sa thèse: Côté jeans and côté tenue de Soirée.* PUQ, Quebec, Canada.

MSCI (2020). Climate risk reporting. Retrieved from https://www.msci.com/our-solutions/esg-investing/climate-solutions/climate-risk-reporting.

NGFS (2019, July). Macroeconomic and financial stability. Implications of climate change. Technical supplement to the first NGFS comprehensive report. Retrieved from https://www.ngfs.net/sites/default/files/medias/documents/ngfs-report-technical supplement_final_v2.pdf.

Nordhaus, W. D. (2007). *The Challenge of Global Warming: Economic Models and Environmental Policy* (Vol. 4). New Haven, CT: Yale University.

Perch-Nielsen, S., B. Bättig, M., & Imboden, D. (2008). Exploring the link between climate change and migration. *Climatic Change, 91*, 375. https://doi.org/10.1007/s10584-008-9416-y.

Pindyck, R. S. (2013). Climate change policy: What do the models tell us? *Journal of Economic Literature, 51*(3), 860–872. https://doi.org/10.1257/jel.51.3.860.

Raynaud, D., Hingray, B., François, B., *et al.* (2018). Energy droughts from variable renewable energy sources in European climates. *Renewable Energy, 125*, 578–589. https://doi.org/10.1016/j.renene. 2018.02.130.

Roncoroni, A., Battiston, S., Escobar Farfàn, L. O. L., *et al.* (2021). Climate risk and financial stability in the network of banks and investment funds. *Journal of Financial Stability, 54*, 100870. https://doi.org/10.1016/j.jfs.2021.100870.

Sheu, J.-B. & Chen, Y.-J. (2012). Impact of government financial intervention on competition among green supply chains. *International Journal of Production Economics, 138*(1), 201–213. https://doi.org/10.1016/j.ijpe.2012.03.024.

Steffen, W., Rockström, J., Richardson, K., *et al.* (2018). Trajectories of the Earth system in the anthropocene. *Proceedings of the National Academy of Sciences of the United States of America, 115*(33), 8252–8259. https://doi.org/10.1073/pnas.1810141115.

Stern, N. (2007). Climate. Stern review: The economics of climate change. *New England Journal of Public Policy, 21*(2). http://scholarworks.umb.edu/nejpp/vol21/iss2/4.

Waddock, S. A. & Graves, S. B. (1997). The corporate social performance financial performance link. *Strategic Management Journal, 18*(4), 303–319. https://doi.org/10.1002/(SICI)1097-0266(199704)18:4⟨303::AID-SMJ869⟩3.0.CO;2-G.

Weitzman, M. L. (2009). On modeling and interpreting the economics of catastrophic climate change. *Review of Economics and Statistics, 91*(1), 1–19. https://doi.org/10.1162/rest.91.1.1.

Yufeng, C. & Yanbai, M. (2021). Does green investment improve energy firm performance? *Energy Policy, 153*, 112252. https://doi.org/10.1016/j.enpol.2021.112252.

https://doi.org/10.1142/9781800614482_0014

Chapter 14

The Establishment of a Gross Ecosystem Product: A Country Comparison

Silvio Andrae
Senior Adviser and Author
andrae@zedat.fu-berlin.de

Abstract

The gross ecosystem product (GEP) has been an alternative to the gross domestic product (GDP) for 70 years. Nature's contribution to economic activity is the primary focus of the GEP. While the concept has gained rhetorical traction, it has not helped significantly change the way we treat nature. The reason lies in its lack of practical relevance. The first approaches to calculating a GEP are now emerging around the world. The UN's "Natural Capital Accounting and Valuation of Ecosystem Services" project is part of such a GEP effort. The article analyzes the first project results for Brazil, India, and China. The comparative analysis shows which particular challenges exist in the practical implementation. GEP provides policymakers with incentives to conserve and enhance ecosystems.

1. Introduction

Ecosystems and their processes create and contribute to the life support of the Earth and provide the conditions for human well-being. Humans and the biophysical environment in which they live form complex economic–social–natural or socioecological systems. Anthropogenic influences alter the conditions of ecosystems that sustain human well-being (Levin *et al.*, 2013). The main goal of socioeconomic development should be to ensure the quality and quantity of ecosystem services. Development depends on the surrounding natural landscape's structure, processes, and functions (De Groot *et al.*, 2002).

Environmental change assessment and resource management are becoming increasingly important (Troy & Wilson, 2007). Therefore, natural capital encompasses natural resources found in nature, such as minerals, petroleum, fish, and timber stocks in forests, water, arable land. However, the services provided by ecosystems are invisible to most people, such as purifying air and water, protecting against flooding or erosion, capturing and storing carbon, and providing habitat for species. Ecosystem services are the benefits that people derive from ecosystems. They can be divided into the provision of tangible services (e.g., food, water supply, hydropower generation), regulating services (e.g., carbon sequestration, flood control, soil retention), and intangible services (e.g., ecotourism, mental health).

Natural capital accounting (NCA) is gaining popularity as a systematic approach to recognizing the total value of natural resources, such as soil, vegetation, wildlife, water, and biodiversity. NCA is currently defined in a variety of ways. The subject of scholarship spans economic, ecological, and sector-specific disciplines (e.g., agriculture, forestry, ecology). More recently, contributions from the social sciences and humanities have also been added to address the contribution of culture-related ecosystem services. Fleming *et al.* (2022) conducted 57 interviews with stakeholders in Australia to promote perceptions of natural resources as forms of capital and the role of NCA in supporting changes in management practices. The authors identify four key critical areas of contestation related to values, complexity, digital technology, and the desired future vision of NCA in society.

Bateman and Mace (2020) define natural capital as:

> those renewable and non-renewable natural resources (such as air, water, soils and energy), stocks of which can benefit people both directly (for example, by delivering clean air)

> and indirectly (for example, by underpinning the economy). These stocks yield flows of 'ecosystem services' such as energy, water, plant and fibre growth, from which people derive benefits. (p. 776)

For the future well-being of the planet, it is essential that we no longer focus solely on standard metrics, such as gross domestic product (GDP). Since 1953, GDP has been the primary measure in a complex system of national accounts overseen by the United Nations. To be sure, GDP possesses many of the characteristics we expect of a good metric: It has established systematic data collection that leads to easy calculation. It is also easy to communicate as a single number or percentage change. The advantage of GDP is its ability to simultaneously measure production output, consumption expenditure, and income in an economy. Finally, as a ratio, it has considerable leverage for decision-making. However, GDP is flawed. It completely ignores nature's contributions to economic activity and human well-being. At the same time, it does not consider the environmental costs (e.g., pollution, overexploitation, and general environmental degradation) that result from our consumption of these essential contributions:

> To put it another way, GDP is like a ledger that will not accept red ink. Like an accounting trick, it has allowed us to vent greenhouse gasses into the atmosphere, destroy habitats, and neglect human well-being without worrying about the consequences. (Onakuse, 2021)

In recent decades, there has been increasing research on how we can complement GDP (OECD, 2018). The goal is to develop more integrated statistics to help us move toward sustainable development. Costanza *et al.* (2014) suggest that it is time for countries to move beyond GDP as an accounting indicator and look for new metrics to more accurately and objectively formulate strategic conservation and development plans. It is primarily about ecosystem services. They include the benefits that people derive directly or indirectly from ecosystem functions.

Many countries are paying increasing attention to accounting for the values of ecosystem products and services. The United Nations Statistics Division (UNSD) is advocating that countries adopt the core framework of the System of Environmental Economic Accounting (SEEA). It involves incorporating the value of ecosystem services into the accounting system to increase enthusiasm throughout society for creating ecological value. Gross ecosystem product (GEP) is a new metric, or ecosystem value, which has become widely accepted. GEP includes both economic value and ecological value. It includes the total value of products and services provided by ecosystems to humans. Ecosystems include forest, wetland, grassland, desert, marine, cropland, and urban ecosystems.

Ecosystem products include traditional economic goods, such as felled trees and caught fish.

The valuation of economic assets generally has a mature theoretical basis and a market price reference. Ecological services are diverse and challenging to value. Nevertheless, the GEP concept attempts to convert the value of ecological production into monetary terms. The monetary value of final ecosystem goods and services in a given region is aggregated into a metric over an accounting period (usually one year).

This chapter aims to evaluate whether GEP is a valuable metric. In the first step, the previous alternatives to GDP are discussed. Then, the GEP concept is presented. So far, studies on GEP accounting have covered different regional scales and ecosystem types, with the former including dimensions such as global, national, and local areas, and the latter including forests, wetlands, grasslands, etc.

The public resonance of socioecological transformation is always context- and milieu-specific. It is shaped by historical experiences, path dependencies, and the respective system structures, interests, and cultural orientations. However, transformation is also closely linked to central social conflicts and the respective experiences of problems and crises. Sustainable development thus means something substantially different in the countries of the Global North than in the countries of the Global South. The purpose of this chapter is to present and compare the activities of Brazil, India, and China. Brazil and India are making the first steps in ecosystem services valuation and are still far from calculating a GEP. In China, national and local governments have launched some pilot projects on GEP accounting. These projects aim to integrate the new concept into real-world decision-making. Many regional studies are available, and their results are summarized and assessed. They show how tailor-made measures for local economic growth and environmental protection better support local enterprises in ecological reforms. The chapter ends with a summary.

2. Alternative Approaches to GDP

Initially, the GDP measure was not intended as a welfare indicator. The precursor of GDP, gross national product (GNP), was first systematically calculated during the Second World War in Great Britain and the United States. It should be used to plan for defense investment funding. Later, GNP became GDP. The latter also includes the output generated by foreigners in a country, which fits better into the age of globalization.

Nevertheless, this did not change the primary problem. Since the 1980s, the correlation between material and social indicators has weakened. Moreover, the burdens on the environment associated with past economic growth have not been taken into account. Even economists believe that the critical measure of well-being needs to change (van den Bergh *et al.*, 2014).

Today, GDP is the best-known and most appreciated key figure. The term is frequently cited by politicians, economists, and statisticians and is ubiquitous in the media. GDP refers to the single aggregate monetary value of all goods and services produced in a given period (usually per year). An excellent example of its prevalence is the impact of the COVID-19 pandemic and the scramble to predict by how many percentage points GDP might fall due to lockdown measures.

Efforts to establish an alternative GDP have been underway for years — the pioneer being the Southeast Asian country of Bhutan. There, gross national happiness was introduced as early as 1972. Since 2008, the population's happiness has officially been more important than anything else. The United Nations launched the Human Development Index (HDI) in 1990. An eight-dimensional resilience index assesses a country's resilience. The index relates to socioeconomic status (GDP and HDI), natural resources and population (arable land and water resources per capita), energy (supply and renewable energy), and environmental impact (greenhouse gas emissions and physical footprint). Countries with abundant natural resources are more resilient in a crisis than others. Conversely, seemingly successful countries, whose advanced economic development (high GDP per capita) allows them to import natural resources from abroad, will prove more vulnerable in the long run (Bolson *et al.*, 2022).

The EU Commission launched the "Beyond GDP" initiative in 2007. The OECD presented its Better Life Index in 2011. Since 2018, there has also been the association of "Wellbeing Economic Governments," to which Scotland, New Zealand, Iceland, Wales, and Finland belong. Together, the states are pursuing the goal of placing quality of life at the center of the national economy. Most existing GDP alternatives have in common that they condense different indicators into one number. The challenge here is to convert various units of measurement, such as life years, CO_2 emissions, or hectares, into euros and thus inevitably weight them (WHO Council, 2022).

It is interesting to look at France. In early 2008, shortly before the outbreak of the financial crisis, Joseph Stiglitz and other Nobel laureates in economics were appointed to a commission to examine the validity of GDP as a measure of prosperity. The 22-member commission met for a year and a half. In their final report of around 300 pages, the economists explained that alternatives could not be conjured up so quickly out of a hat (Stiglitz *et al.*, 2009). However, to measure material satisfaction, we should at least look much more closely at indicators such as income distribution, health, and education. Stiglitz spoke of a "GDP fetishism" that must be overcome.

However, the big turnaround failed to materialize. A law was passed in France in 2015 that obliges the government to report on 10 social, economic, and ecological indicators every fall. These indicators supplement GDP. However, this has no political significance. During the pandemic, a council of economists convened by incumbent French President Emmanuel Macron featured Olivier Blanchard and Paul Krugman, who were similarly prominent as those in the earlier

Stiglitz Commission. By June 2021, the focus was again on significant societal issues. However, the topic of alternative well-being indicators is not echoed in the roughly 450-page report (Blanchard & Tirole, 2021).

The European Commission recently published the Transitions Performance Index (TPI) 2021 (European Commission, 2022). The index, which covers 27 EU states and 45 other countries and thus 76 percent of the world's population, focuses on transitions in sustainability and digitization. It refers to the period 2011–2020 and has the methodological goal of replacing the one-dimensional GDP indicator as an instrument of political control. In this way, the lack of sustainability in the political and economic spheres is to be addressed. With the four thematic areas of the economy, social inequality, environment, and governance, the TPI also aims to cover a large part of the Sustainable Development Goals (SDGs). The environmental transformation reflects emissions, energy efficiency, biodiversity, resource efficiency, and a circular economy. The TPI has many methodological shortcomings. For example, it is surprising that two dictatorships or authoritarian regimes appear at the front of the TPI in fourth place (Indonesia) and fifth place (UAE).

Natural alternatives to GDP include the Index of Sustainable Economic Well-Being (ISEW), the Genuine Progress Indicator (GPI), Real Savings, and Gross Ecosystem Product (GEP). All of these alternatives are proposed to add to GDP the outputs or aspects that it omits. However, the methods and focus of each alternative differ. The ISEW approach generally adjusts GDP for various aspects, including the costs of current and future social welfare distribution, environmental degradation, and social protection (van den Bergh *et al.*, 2014). The GPI approach differs slightly from the ISEW approach in that more calculation categories are included in the equation, including volunteerism, crime, divorce, and unemployment (van den Bergh *et al.*, 2014). Initially proposed by economist Herman Daly and theologian John Cobb, the GPI attempts to adjust GDP for environmental, social, and financial factors that are not adequately accounted for in GDP itself. The GPI has been an indicator of progress in the US state of Maryland since 2015. A bill introduced in the US Congress in July 2021 would require the Department of

Commerce to publish a US GPI and use both the indicator and GDP for budget reporting and economic forecasting. The GPI is also used in Atlantic Canada.

On the other hand, there are genuine saving attempts to distinguish between current and future well-being by subtracting the value of natural resource depletion, pollution damage, economic and health impacts, etc. Although all of these alternatives offer possible answers for improving the GDP indicator, none prioritize the study of ecosystem services and products. Stevenson *et al.* (2021) highlight that the concept of ecosystem services is often challenging to implement in practice. The authors see the problems primarily at the structural, organizational, and agent levels. For individual ecosystems, there are selective tools to make an assessment. For example, Arto *et al.* (2022) propose a novel accounting system for assessing the forest footprint of nations. The method combines multiregional input–output techniques with detailed data from the Food and Agriculture Organization of the United Nations on the production, consumption, and bilateral trade of primary, intermediate, and final wood products. Only the GEP approach considers the integration of ecosystem services.

3. The GEP Approach: "E" Meets "D"

The first step in accounting for natural assets and ecological services or functions for human activities in environmental-economic accounting is to define their spatial and functional dimensions. Measuring and valuing these two dimensions and identifying the interrelationship of these components with human activities, particularly with the economy, enables the integration of ecosystems into an accounting structure. The System of National Accounts (SNA) and the System of Environmental-Economic Accounting (SEEA) are the two accounting standards (see Section 4). They capture the respective values. Measuring well-being is not the focus of ecosystem accounting, although the data integrated through the ecosystem accounting framework can support such a measurement.

The value of an ecosystem is divided into the value of natural resources and the value of ecosystem services (see Figure 1).

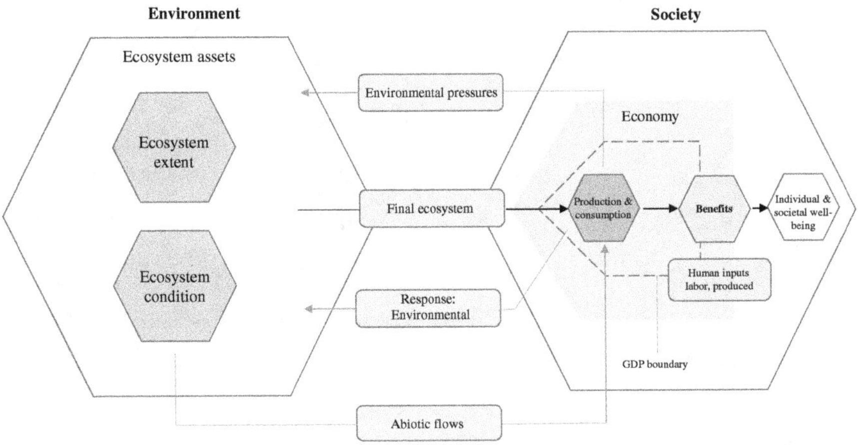

Figure 1. General structure of ecosystem asset accounting.
Source: IBGE (2021, p. 16).

The focus of valuation in ecosystem accounting is on total ecosystem services, including those that contribute to benefits within the current scope of GDP and those that fall outside that scope, i.e., non-SNA benefits. The term "benefits" thus includes:

(a) SNA benefits, which are the products (goods and services) produced by economic units as recorded in the national accounts;
(b) non-SNA benefits are produced by ecosystems and consumed directly by individuals and societies.

The significant advantage of such balancing is that it clearly shows the interrelationship between the economy and the environment. The use of an accounting framework allows the identified ecosystems and the assessed service flows in relation to each other and a range of other environmental, economic, and social information.

The general steps of ecosystem accounting are shown in Figure 2. Ecosystem accounting can provide information on the extent of ecosystems, their condition based on selected indicators, and the flow of ecosystem services. Because of the spatial nature of ecosystem accounting, maps are a standard method for presenting the information. The linkages between an ecosystem and the economy can be represented in physical and monetary terms.

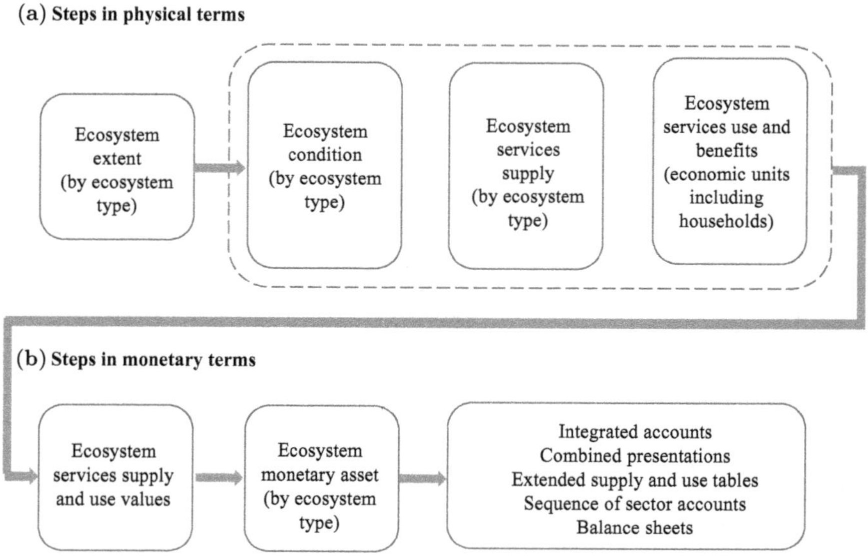

Figure 2. Broad steps in ecosystem asset accounting.
Source: NSO India (2021, p. 16).

The most crucial development in the ecosystem accounting model is the expansion of the production frontier to include a whole range of ecosystem services. Figure 3 provides an overview in terms of ecosystem accounts. These accounts include the extent account, the state account, the supply and use of ecosystem services (in physical and monetary forms), and the monetary ecosystem asset account. As shown in Figure 3, this set of ecosystem accounts provides an overall coherent and comprehensive view of ecosystems:

- **Ecosystem expansion account:** A common starting point for ecosystem accounting. It organizes information on the extent of different ecosystem types with land area (e.g., forests, wetlands, agricultural lands, and marine areas) within a country.
- **Ecosystem condition account:** Measures the overall quality of an ecosystem asset and captures in a series of key indicators, the condition or functioning of the ecosystem in terms of its naturalness and its potential to provide ecosystem services.
- **Ecosystem service accounts:** Measure the supply of ecosystem services and the corresponding users and beneficiaries, classified

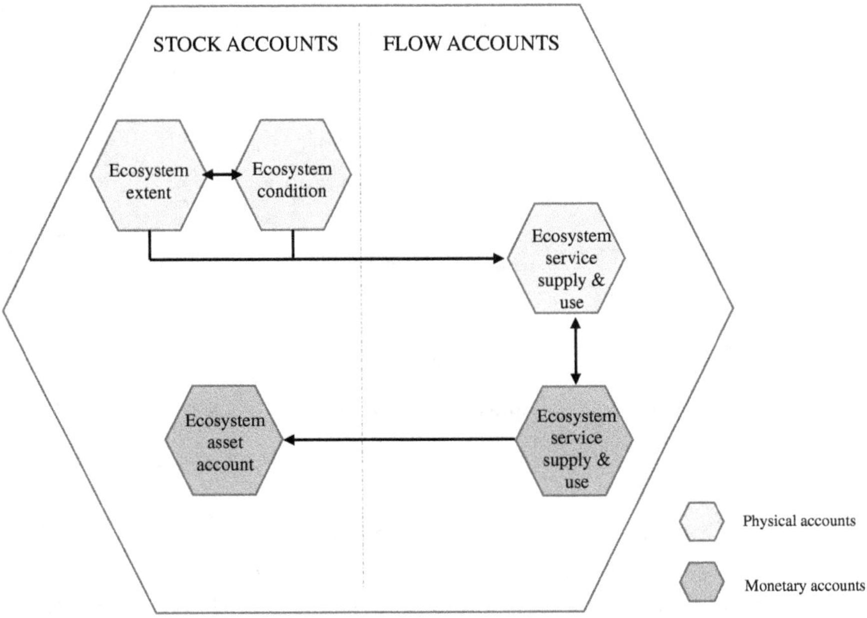

Figure 3. Types of ecosystem accounts.
Source: NBS China (2021, p. 15).

by broad categories of national accounts or other groupings of economic units.

- **Monetary wealth account:** Records the monetary value of the beginning and ending stocks of all ecosystem assets within an ecosystem accounting area and the inflows and outflows to and from these stocks.
- **Thematic accounts:** These include accounts for land, water, carbon, and biodiversity, and are stand-alone accounts on topics important for policy analysis but are also of direct relevance to the preparation of ecosystem accounts.

The IUCN Global Ecosystem Typology (GET) is a classification that distinguishes between ecologically important terrestrial, aquatic, and bioclimatic niches (see Figure 4). Costanza (1997), based on a 1996 research by the National Center for Ecological Analysis and Research (NCEAS), summarized ecosystem value calculation methods and valued 17 ecosystems around the world. It includes a nested

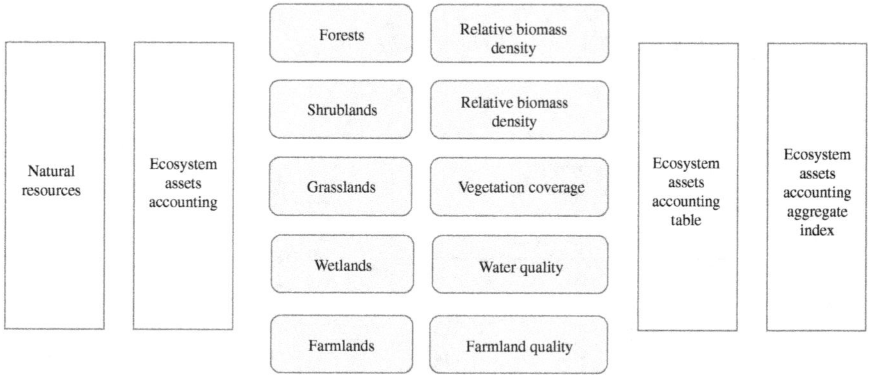

Figure 4. Ecosystem asset accounting framework.
Source: IUCN (2019, p. 3).

hierarchy of units at each level and more detailed classified niches embedded in broader units at higher levels. The three upper levels classify ecosystems based on their functional characteristics, independent of species composition. The three lower levels of classification distinguish functionally similar ecosystems based on similarity of composition and allow for the integration of established classifications that are already in use and incorporated into the policy infrastructure at the national level. It is critical because necessary conservation actions occur at the local level, where most expertise exists. The six different hierarchical levels are (Figure 5):

(1) **Realms:** One of the five major components of the biosphere (land, freshwater, marine, subsurface, and atmospheric), of which each differs fundamentally in ecosystem organization and function.
(2) **Biome:** A component of a domain united by one or a few common major ecological factors that govern the main ecological functions and are derived from the top down through the subdivision of domains.
(3) **Functional ecosystem group:** A group of related ecosystems within a biome share common environmental factors that promote convergence of the biotic features that characterize the group. It is derived from a top-down approach in which lower biomes subdivides into this order.

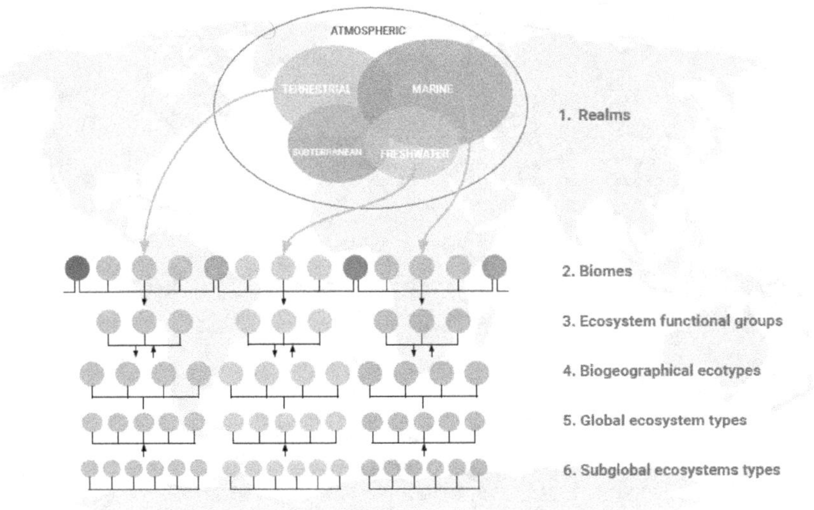

Figure 5. A hierarchical structure of the Global Ecosystem Typology.
Source: NSO (2019, p. 21).

(4) **Biogeographic ecotype:** It is an ecoregional expression of an ecosystem functional group derived from a top-down subdivision of ecosystem functional groups (level 3). They are proxies for compositionally distinct geographic variants occupying different areas within the distribution of a functional group.

(5) **Global ecosystem type:** A complex of organisms and their associated physical environments within an area occupied by an ecosystem functional group. Global ecosystem types, grouped in the same ecosystem functional group, share similar ecological processes but differ significantly in their biotic composition. They are derived from the bottom up, either directly from ground observations or through the aggregation of sub-global types (level 6).

(6) **Sub-global ecosystem type:** A subunit or nested group of subunits within a global ecosystem type exhibit a higher degree of homogeneity in composition and similarity among themselves than global ecosystem types (level 5). These are units of established classifications, in some cases arranged in a subhierarchy with multiple levels, derived directly from ground observations.

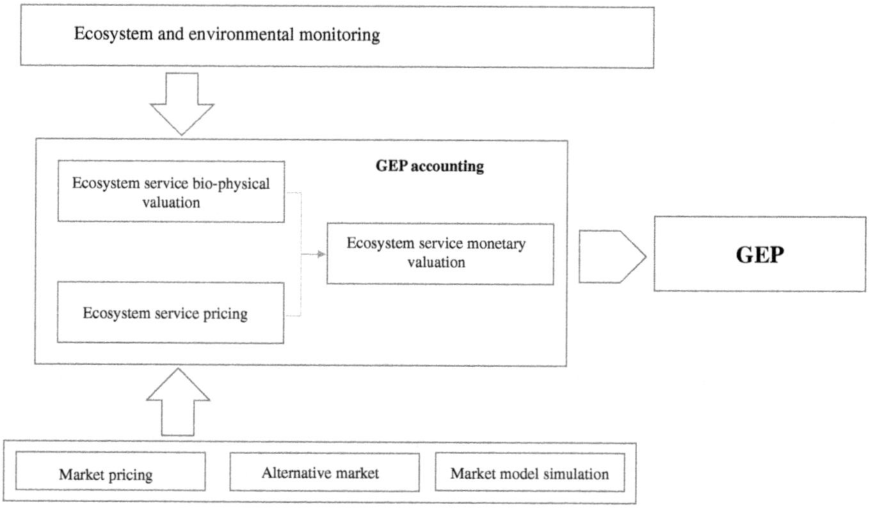

Figure 6. GEP framework.
Source: IUCN (2019, p. 6).

Traditional valuation of ecosystem services usually focuses on valuing a single service or a small group of services. The concept of GEP originates from the economist Hannon (1985). The GEP accounting aims to evaluate all relevant services using an aggregate indicator comprehensively (see Figure 6). GEP is the sum of the monetary value of the final ecosystem services (excluding intermediary or "supporting" services to avoid economic double counting).

The structure of the GEP is not simple. Like the intricate linkages within a country's economy, ecosystem services result from interconnected and complex relationships within the environment and its subsequent functioning. Examples of ecosystem services include providing clean water and food security or the regulation of soil and water quality. One of the significant challenges of GEP is to value services appropriately, identify all services that provide simultaneously, and avoid double counting. It should be noted that these challenges arise everywhere when trying to translate nature into economic terms. For many ecologists, this is one of the sticking points when squeezing nature into accounting systems.

Many methods can be used to value natural resources, the most common of which is divided into market methods, income methods, and cost methods. "If the purpose is to integrate values of ecosystem stocks and flows within the standard national accounts and hence obtain adjusted measures of income and wealth, then the challenge that faces the national and environmental accountant is how the concept of exchange values can be applied in the area of ecosystems and particularly how the broad range of non-market services can be accounted for" (Obst *et al.*, 2016, p. 6). Due to the different characteristics of different natural resources, some methods are not comprehensive and accurate enough. Therefore, adjustment coefficients are applied to correct the value of different resources and compensate for incomplete characteristics.

In the following, the most common valuation methods are briefly presented:

(1) **Methods of evaluation of soil resources:**

- *Market comparison method*: Uses the principle of substitution to compare the land being valued with a similar land traded on the market on the valuation date.
- *Income reduction method*: Estimates the land price by reducing the future expected annual net income (government rent) of the land to a specified land discount rate.
- *Cost approximation method*: Based on the sum of the objective costs incurred in developing land plus objective profits, interest, taxes payable, and value-added land income to determine the land price.
- *Benchmark land price efficiency correction method*: Uses the results of a benchmark urban land value along with the associated table of correction coefficients to compare regional conditions.

(2) **Water resources valuation methods:**

- *Shadow price model*: Values water resources using the constraint optimization approach, assumes maximization of economic benefits and profits of resources as the target value, and uses quantitative analysis of resource use-value by adjusting a unit amount of resources, all else being equal, to calculate the marginal return of resources.
- *Water pricing model*: According to the relationship between the supply and demand of water resources, the price of water

resources is obtained after deducting the production costs and profit associated with the development of water resources.

(3) **Forest resources valuation methods:**

- *Market transaction price comparison method*: Used to evaluate the value of forest land.
- *Expected value method for forest land*: Estimates the value of forest assets; it refers to the discounting and accumulation of net returns in infinite rotation periods under the initial condition of afforestation on non-forest land.
- *Annuity capitalization method*: Calculates the value of forest assets according to a reasonable return on investment using the realization of sustainable use of forest resources as a condition and the stable annual yield of the evaluated forest as the return on investment.
- *Cost value method for forest land*: The monetary value is determined based on the cost required to maintain the forest land and keep the existing condition of the forest land unchanged.
- *Market approach*: Involves estimating forest resource values using market prices, taking the actual price of forest resources traded in the markets as the value of a unit of forest resource assets.
- *Income approach*: The average net returns of forest resources are predicted in the future, an appropriate investment interest rate is selected, and summation procedures are performed after discounting to the valuation date to estimate the value of forest assets.

The following challenges must be considered when applying natural resource assessment methods: Insufficient resource monitoring capacity, availability of environmental data, lack of integration of statistical monitoring data, and lack of assessment parameters.

In terms of research methodology, geographic information systems (GISs) combined with the survey experiment method are mainly used to balance the ecological performance function (Bordt, 2018). In addition, a variety of market means is used to estimate a river's value. Considering the heterogeneity of regional ecological space, which leads to significant differences in accounting parameters, accounting research should use characteristic parameters localized in specific regions; otherwise, the effectiveness of policy management will be affected.

In addition, recent studies have attempted to combine the ecological index and the traditional economic index into a comprehensive indicator to measure the construction of ecological civilization. For example, the green gold index (GGI), the ratio of gross domestic product to GDP, has been used to measure potential regional productivity that converts natural resources into assets (Liang *et al.*, 2021).

Figure 7 shows the GGI framework, which is divided into three scenarios. The slope of the curve indicates the ratio of GEP to GDP, i.e., GGI. Area A (i.e., GGI < 1) is usually the area with rapid ecological development, while area C (i.e., GGI > 1) is usually the area with a high endowment of ecological resources. Area B

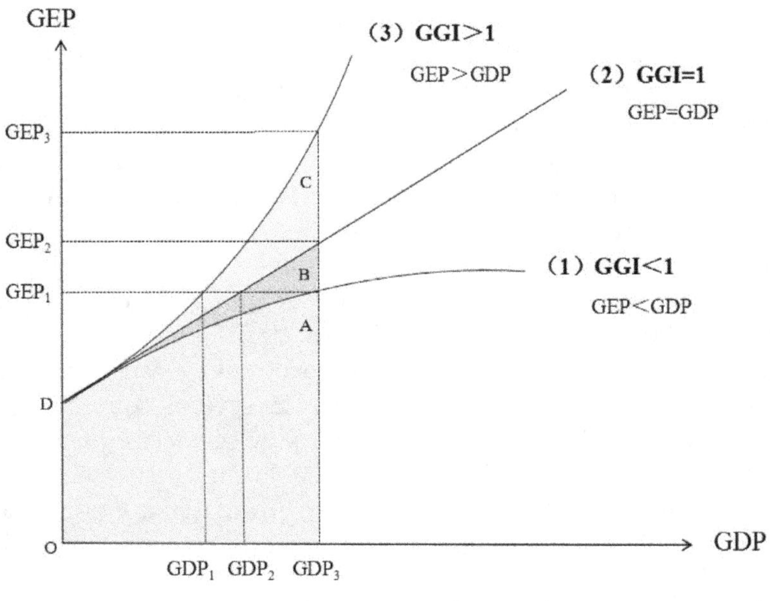

Figure 7. Schematic diagram of the green gold index (GGI, i.e., GEP to GDP). *Source*: Liang *et al.* (2021, p. 5).

(GGI = 1) provides a balance point between the ecological environment and economic development (Liang *et al.*, 2021).

4. Country Studies

An essential step toward NCA was taken with the adoption of the SEEA Central Framework by the United Nations Statistical Commission (UNSC) in 2012 (UN *et al.*, 2014a). This system provides an internationally agreed-upon method, compatible with the SNA currently in place, to account for renewable and non-renewable natural resources, such as minerals, timber, water, and others, in a physical manner. These resources are assumed to be tradable in established markets. In this respect, pricing can be based on known methods of environmental economics.

However, most of the services derived from ecosystems, referred to as ecosystem services, are neither measured nor traded in markets. Therefore, their inclusion in the accounting system requires research and international debate among experts on the methodology to be used in each case due to the complexity and diversity of ecosystems around the world. In 2013, the UNSC endorsed developing and testing a body of work known as ecosystem accounting, summarized in SEEA 2012 (System of Environmental-Economic Accounting — Experimental Ecosystem Accounting, SEEA EEA) (UN *et al.*, 2014b). The SEEA provides a reliable measurement framework that enables a deep understanding of the linkages between economic well-being and natural capital. It integrates economic and environmental information using internationally agreed statistical standards developed and applied by governments worldwide. The new methodology is in the trial phase in several countries, with countries testing different accounts and services according to their priorities and circumstances. It is noticeable that ecosystem service valuation and the GEP based on it are primarily done in emerging economies. Industrialized countries are still struggling with such projects (see Section 2).

The Natural Capital Accounting and Valuation of Ecosystem Services (CAVES) project was launched in 2017 to advance both the knowledge agenda and the development of ecosystem accounting. The project was conducted in five participating partner countries:

Brazil, China, India, Mexico, and South Africa. These five countries were selected as strategic partners of the European Union because of the importance of their natural capital, diverse ecosystems and biodiversity, and their commitment to the obligations of the Convention on Biological Diversity (CBD).

The US has also recently announced its intention to pursue this approach; The Natural Capital Accounts system is designed to measure the correlation between environmental and economic health (U.S. Whitehouse, 2022).

The following are the goals of CAVES:

- improve the measurement of ecosystems and their services (both in physical and monetary terms) at (sub)national level;
- integrate biodiversity and ecosystems into policy planning and implementation at (sub)national level;
- contribute to developing an internationally agreed methodology and its application in partner countries.

The active participation and input of the five CAVES countries contributed significantly to the adoption of the SEEA EEA as a statistical standard by the United Nations Statistical Commission in March 2021. The SEEA EEA is now reflected in the United Nations Common Agenda, which calls on the member states and others to begin implementing the SEEA EEA. The resolution "Accounting for biodiversity: encompassing ecosystems, species and genetic diversity" was endorsed by the IUCN World Conservation Congress (WCC, 2020).

Finally, CAVES has been a significant contributor to the Global Biodiversity Framework for the post-2020 period, particularly in the work package on indicators; SEEA implementation is recognized as SDG indicator 15.9.1.

While the publication of the SEEA documents represents an essential milestone for the national accounts approach, several challenges remain in integrating measurements of ecosystem goods and services into national accounts standards. This point is particularly true for the further development of GEP. China is an exception in this regard, being already very far advanced. The other two countries presented here — Brazil and India — are still at the stage of accounting for ecosystem services.

4.1. *Brazil*

The accounting of environmental services in Brazil is based on the "Sistema de Contas Econômicas Ambientais" (SCEA). The SCEA is methodologically based on the SEEA principles of compiling globally comparable indicators. The Environmental-Economic Accounts (Contas Econômicas Ambientais, CEA) are structured sets of information that integrate environmental data and economic statistics. Specifically for the ecosystem accounting component, the methodology foresees its development under a spatially explicit approach. Therefore, environmental-economic accounts compile in GIS, in which several information layers can be integrated, allowing analyses in different environmental profiles, such as biomes or hydrographic basins.

The Brazilian statistical agency, IBGE, is creating a map of biomes and the coastal marine system in Brazil. With a scale of 1:250,000, the country was mapped in a physical-biological representation. Each biome includes large contiguous areas, respecting the mapping conditions. Methodologically important vegetation interruptions are assigned to the dominant biome. Areas of vegetation contacts are assigned to one of the adjacent biomes, using the dominant vegetation typology in each as a criterion (IBGE, 2021). This grouping is quite simple in the areas with natural vegetation (not anthropized). However, in the anthropized areas of the territory, there were two main problems: a simpler one, where the previous vegetation was not in contact, and a more complex one, where these contacts need to be further investigated using the mapping of the other natural resources as well as literature searches.

Six groups of vegetation types with similar physiognomy are relevant for the assessment. They form the Brazilian biomes: Amazônia, Mata Atlântica, Caatinga, Cerrado, Pantanal, and Pampa. The coastal marine system forms a particular biome due to the fragility of the coastal environment, its particular dynamics, and its enormous impact on the associated biodiversity, which is also strongly influenced by anthropogenic activities. Further activities are needed here in Brazil. Therefore, only terrestrial biomes are currently considered for analysis (IBGE, 2021).

The monitoring of land cover and land use is performed using the following steps. First, satellite images of the entire territory are acquired. Then, each grid cell is assigned to one of the predefined land cover and land use categories resulting from the interpretation of the images using complementary inputs. The availability of data in a statistical grid allows integration and comparison between different types of geoscience and statistical data. It also allows for historical monitoring of the spatialization of economic activities and impacts on natural resources in the country. After each biome was added to the grid, information on land cover and land use were added. Finally, with each cell containing information on the biome and land cover and use, statistics are generated for the biomes for the years analyzed (2000, 2010, 2012, 2014, 2016, and 2018). The compilation is based on statistical data series available from land-cover and -use monitoring in Brazil (IBGE, 2021).

IBGE proposes the change intensity indicator (CII) as a parameter for assessing the dynamics of land-cover and land-use changes in Brazil. This assessment focuses mainly on the transformations of the territory in terms of land use and changes in natural land cover. This analysis makes it possible to identify areas where land-use changes were more pronounced. These areas are also important for land-use planning and the management of national environmental policy. The CII is an essential input to environmental accounting studies because it indicates areas where ecosystem values have changed more or less (IBGE, 2021).

The ecosystem analysis shows that all Brazilian terrestrial biomes had a negative balance in the additions and losses of natural areas from 2000 to 2018. The analysis represents a loss of these areas in several areas throughout the country. It means a total reduction of about 500,000 km^2 of natural ecosystems (IBGE, 2021).

The most significant absolute decreases in natural areas were in the Amazônia and Cerrado biomes, of 269,801 and 152,706 km^2, respectively. An enormous percentage loss occurred in the Pampa biome, where 16.8 percent of the natural area (as of 2000) was converted to anthropogenic uses. The Pantanal was the biome with the minor decrease in natural areas, both in absolute terms (2,109 km^2) and in relative terms (1.6 percent), indicating a lower dynamic of land-use conversion in this region of the country (IBGE, 2021).

A large concentration of change points can be observed between the Amazônia and Cerrado biomes, many of them with high CIIs (2.5 and 3.0), indicating intense changes in the landscape of these regions. The Pampa biome was also highlighted with a relatively high number of high-intensity change points (3.0) in its reduced area, indicating an intense transformation of this spatial unit during the period considered (IBGE, 2021).

4.2. *India*

India covers an area of 3.28 million km^2. It is only 2.4 percent of the world's total land area, but is often referred to as the "land of diversity". India because of its immense wealth of biodiversity, not only in terms of the number of plant and animal species but also thanks to its diverse ecological landscapes, ranging from mountains, plains, plateaus to coasts, islands, and deserts, represented in 10 unique biogeographical zones.

In India, land-cover statistics are maintained by the National Remote Sensing Center (NRSC), the Department of Space of the Government of India, and by a component of the National Land Use/Land Cover Mapping (LULC) under the Natural Resources Census (NRC) project of the National Natural Resources Repository Program.

For accounting purposes, ecosystem services are assigned to individual ecosystem goods (e.g., timber from a forest). When the provision of services is more complex, the contribution of each ecosystem good to the total provision is estimated. For each ecosystem service provision recorded, there must be a corresponding use. Attributing the use of final ecosystem services to different economic units is a fundamental element of accounting. Depending on the ecosystem service, the user (e.g., a household, business, or government) may receive that service while either in the supplying ecosystem good (e.g., fishing from a lake) or elsewhere (e.g., receiving air filtration services from a neighboring forest). The physical flows of supply and use of ecosystem services are captured in physical supply and use tables (NSO India, 2021).

The central valuation concept of the SNA, which is also used in ecosystem accounting, is exchange value, i.e., the value at which goods, services, labor, or assets are exchanged or could be exchanged for money. Valuation approaches used for ecosystem accounting exclude the consumer surplus associated with transactions in ecosystem services. In most cases, ecosystem service values are not reported because they are not priced or traded in markets. Some techniques developed for valuing non-market transactions can be applied to estimate the value of ecosystem service provision and use in monetary terms. However, it should note that there are many challenges in implementing these techniques and interpreting the resulting values. In this respect, the ecosystem service valuation results presented in the report should be considered experimental (NSO India, 2021).

The supply and use of ecosystem services in the monetary form are captured in monetary supply and use tables (MSUTs). So far, six ecosystem services are considered in India: provision of crops, provision of timber and non-timber forest products, carbon storage (from forests), nature-based tourism, and soil erosion control. For each ecosystem service, data sources and appropriate valuation approaches that are conceptually valid were used to determine values consistent with the SNA and facilitate the integration of environmental and economic statistics.

Physical supply accounts are provided for carbon storage and soil erosion control for two selected ecosystem services. Monetary supply accounts have been developed for the provision of crops, timber and non-timber forest products, carbon storage, and nature-based tourism using appropriate valuation techniques. Finally, ecosystem condition accounts focus on surface and ground water quality, the coastal water quality index, and forest and cropland condition accounts.

4.3. *China*

Decades of double-digit economic growth have made China an expanding economy. However, this economic growth, combined with a growing population and rapid urbanization, has meant that the country now faces a major environmental crisis. Not only has the consumption of natural resources increased exponentially, but biodiversity has declined, ecosystems and the services they provide have been lost, and the quality of air, soil, and water has been significantly affected by increasing pollution.

It is not only for these reasons that the Chinese government has increasingly called for a systematic framework to complement GDP in recent years to measure progress toward sustainable development.

In early November 2015, China initiated a national pilot program to compile natural resource balances of land, forestry, and water for 2015 within the general framework of ecological civilization. The National Bureau of Statistics (NBS) of China, the coordinating government agency for this balance compilation, selected eight pilot areas of different sizes (city, township, or province) to participate in the experiment, representing different levels of socioeconomic development and different natural resource endowments. Since then, several more regions have volunteered to participate in the pilot program. Introducing a National Ecological Accounting and Auditing Scheme (NEAAS) has attracted national attention. The NEAAS, which builds on the SEEA, is designed to achieve several goals beyond calculating a GEP (Wang, 2019).

China does not fully adopt the requirements of the SEEA. This point is also valid for the concept of "ecological liabilities," as it is not compatible with the SNA or the SEEA framework. It seems too complex and almost impossible to measure the degree of ecosystem degradation and create the "liability accounts" that capture the ecological restoration and maintenance costs (Wang, 2019).

China is particularly far along in the valuation of ecosystem services. A large number of studies are available. Ouyang *et al.* (1999) first estimated the value of terrestrial ecosystem services in China in the late 1990s using an integrated modeling method that includes organic matter production, carbon sequestration and release, nutrient cycling and storage, soil conservation, water conservation, and environmental purification. The authors calculate an annual value of 30.488 trillion yuan. A large number of studies were added. Most of them were small-scale studies focusing on specific ecosystems (e.g., forests, wetlands, grasslands, and deserts).

China is now a leader in the following areas of sustainable development:

- NCA (e.g., survey and valuation, gross ecosystem product);
- national zoning (e.g., ecological function zones, ecological boundary lines);
- financial mechanisms (e.g., ecological compensation).

In terms of ecosystem service accounting, the forest plays a central role. The forest's ecosystem services are divided into four categories (product provisioning, regulation, culture, and life support). An assessment system with 13 indicators is established, including forest products and photosynthetic oxygen sequestration.

Guangxi a autonomous region, is considered one of the pilot regions in China for ecosystem service assessment and accounting. Located on the southern border of China near the headwaters of the Pearl River, Guangxi encompasses vast and diverse landscapes with terrestrial, freshwater, and marine ecosystems consisting of vital habitats and ecological corridors. Following the requirements of the National Accounts Department of the NBS, the objectives of the pilot work in Guangxi were to value ecosystem services in Guangxi, overcome the technical difficulties in compiling natural resource balances, and develop an ecosystem service valuation that not only meets international standards but also takes into account the specific characteristics of Guangxi (NBS China, 2021).

An assessment of the value of ecosystem services for the whole region was carried out in 2015, 2016, and 2017. The concepts of natural resources, environmental assets, natural capital, and ecosystem assets are systematically classified. Accounting for ecosystem assets and ecosystem services divides accounting for stocks and accounting for values, which can be measured in both physical and monetary forms. Ecosystem values are mainly measured in area, distribution, quality level, etc. The concept, classification, and ecosystem services indicators refer to provisioning, regulating, and cultural services. These indicators are based on the principle of direct contribution to human benefits, which means that only the final and not the intermediate ecosystem services are selected. The ecosystem's services to humans in a year were calculated on the time scale of "years." The extent and condition of ecosystems form the basis for quantifying ecosystem services (NBS China, 2021).

The ecosystem types in the Chinese pilot projects are divided into cropland, forest, grassland, freshwater, marine, and urban subsystems. The accounting system distinguishes only three types of accounts: Natural Resource Asset Accounts, Ecosystem Asset Accounts, and Ecosystem Service Accounts. The methodology for calculating primary spatial data, collecting associated parameters, and using biophysical models to value different types of ecosystem services are standardized. The physical values corresponding to the different types of ecosystem services will be calculated. The values will serve as the basis for calculating the monetary values of ecosystem services. Finally, the valuation methods for different ecosystem services are standardized (NBS China, 2021).

Ecosystem service maps are used to identify critical hotspots for ecosystem service provision over the past decade to identify ecological focus areas for spatial planning (National Ecological Function Zones, NEDC). From the NEFZs, 63 Key Ecological Function Zones (KEFZs) were selected as essential areas for ecosystem service provision.

Based on the accounting of ecosystem goods and services, Chinese scientists have recently developed the GEP. With support from government agencies and the Asian Development Bank (ADB), efforts to develop GEP in China are well advanced. By 2020, GEP calculations were applied in eight provinces, 15 cities, and over 150 counties. The pilot studies aim to develop GEP as a means of assessment in the NEDC. Initial results show that measuring GEP can help assess conservation performance, local government performance, and the effectiveness of ecological compensation and related conservation measures.

Qinghai is a region of particular interest in northwestern China. It is a biodiversity hotspot and serves as the source of three regionally essential rivers, the Mekong, the Yellow River, and the Yangtze, earning it the title of "Asia's water tower." Ouyang *et al.* (2020) undertook the task of calculating GEP for the Qinghai region between 2000 and 2015. This study was facilitated by extensive data collection in China and previous work with the Integrated Valuation of Ecosystem Services and Tradeoffs (InVEST) ecosystem services modeling. The open-source modeling tool InVEST was developed by the Natural Capital Project at Stanford University (Hamel *et al.*, 2021). It is a GIS-based tool that includes models for ecosystem services. The model is applied to determine the spatial distribution of stored carbon in a region based on land classification data and carbon pool values. The recorded ecosystem services provided by nature in Qinghai are then valued using market prices where appropriate. Otherwise, market replacement values are used.

Two essential results of Qinghai's GEP are worth highlighting (Ouyang *et al.*, 2020):

(1) The GEP value exceeded the GDP value of the region. In 2000, GEP was much higher than GDP (81.5 vs. 26 billion yuan), while

in 2015, both values had increased, and GEP accounted for 75 percent of GDP (185.4 vs. 242 billion yuan). These figures show that the value of nature is immense and should play an essential role in decision-making on par with economic considerations. Both GEP and GDP have increased since 2000, indicating that successful investment in economic and environmental values can contribute to the overall growth and development of the region. However, the increase in GDP has been much more extensive, suggesting that investments have been asymmetrically directed toward conventional economic assets.

(2) A significant share (70 percent in 2015) of GEP value was distributed outside Qinghai. While ecosystem functions occurred within Qinghai, the benefits accrued to people in other parts of China, making the region a net exporter of ecosystem services.

Another study refers to nine Chinese cities in the Pearl River Delta. Here, apparent differences between the cities are found. Zhaoqing, for example, has the highest GEP. It is due to the rich ecological resources in this city. In contrast, the cities of Zhuhai and Shenzhen have the lowest GEPs. The ecological service structures in Guangzhou, Shenzhen, and Zhuhai were balanced with regulatory, utility, and cultural services (Liang *et al.*, 2021). Figure 8 schematically shows the GEP determination in the Pearl River Delta urban study.

Zou *et al.* (2020) assess how rapid urbanization affects ecological production, as measured by GEP, at the regional scale and how natural capital can be sustainably managed under such conditions. The authors answer these questions in an interdisciplinary framework by conducting a spatiotemporal analysis of land-cover change in conjunction with an economic assessment. The study focuses on the Chang-Zhu-Tan (CZT) urban agglomeration, located in the central and eastern part of China's Hunan Province and consists of three major cities: Changsha, Zhuzhou, and Xiangtan. The composition of CZT's GEP has changed over the 15 years. In 2000, regulatory services accounted for a large part of the GEP, 88.75 percent, while the value of tangible and intangible services accounted for only 9.78 percent and 1.47 percent, respectively. Fifteen years later, the value of intangible services increased sharply and accounted for 18.53 percent of GEP. This point was because economic development through

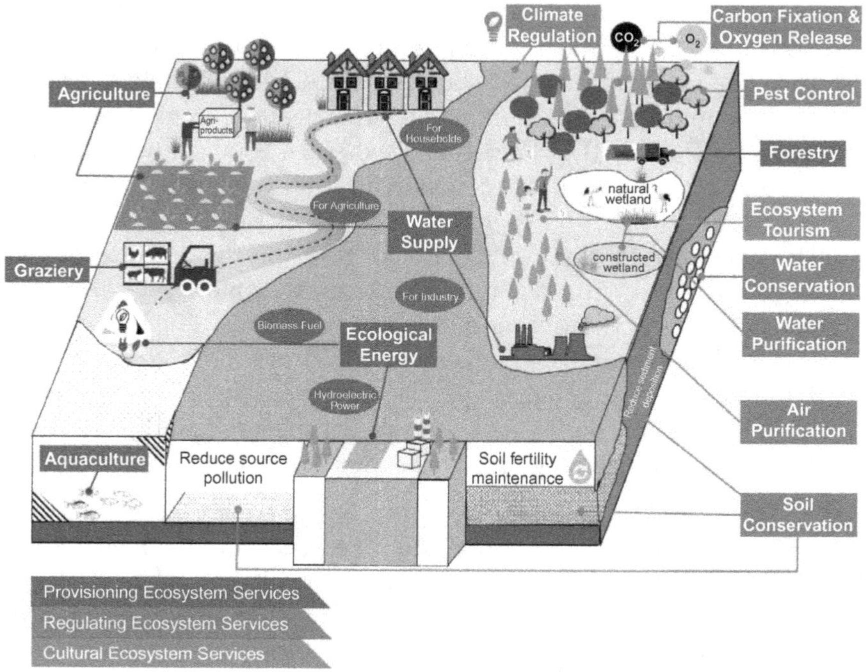

Figure 8. Schematic diagram of gross ecosystem product (GEP) accounting in nine cities within the Pearl River Delta.
Source: Liang *et al.* (2021, p. 4).

rapid urbanization improved locals' living standards and visitors from other parts of the country.

The study by Geng and Liang (2021) examines the ecosystem services of forest resources in Jiaokou County, Shanxi Province, North China, for the year 2018. The forest ecosystem services valuation is considerable and more than 13.85 times the county's GDP. The county's valuation results can provide a pricing basis for a compensation mechanism for forest ecosystem value. However, the authors caution against simply adopting the results.

It is also a logical consequence of such calculations to evaluate the effectiveness of a policy of compensation payments between areas (Shen, 2022). These payments are known as eco-compensation schemes. One obstacle to ecosystem protection is the lack of funding mechanisms to provide households, communities, and regions with incentives and compensation for not engaging in environmentally damaging activities. China has a program for ecological transfer payments. By 2021, the central government has spent over 400 billion yuan on ecological transfer payments to more than 800 counties. The amount of funds is determined at the county level, considering population size, ecosystem types, the spatial extent of major EFZs, GDP, average income level, ecological restoration projects, etc. In China, ecological compensation is considered a policy mechanism to reduce poverty while promoting ecosystem protection. The value of ecosystem services is also encountered in China in the context of fines for violating environmental regulations. Ecological compensation reduces the conflict between development and conservation by having beneficiaries (i.e., urban residents) pay suppliers (i.e., farmers) for ecosystem protection for specific services, such as maintaining clean drinking water. Geng and Liang (2021) summarize:

> In summary, the ecosystem services value is often used in mandatory payments related to the Chinese government, and the recipient of the value paid will be the only one to benefit. Moreover, the natural resource assets value is market-based and fair, which reflects in the exchange of assets. Accordingly, only the natural resource assets value can include in the balance sheet of natural resources. (p. 11)

5. Country Comparison

The analyses of the three selected emerging countries clearly show that they proceed very differently in terms of GEP determination. All three countries are enormous in terms of land area. They have an extensive reservoir of natural capital. However, the degradation of individual ecosystems varies across the three countries. One could conclude that the larger the ecosystems at risk, the greater the political pressure to engage in the valuation of ecosystems and their services (Figure 9).

Brazil presented its first overall review of Brazilian ecosystem accounts in 2021. The analysis provides general results of the conservation status of ecosystems in the terrestrial environment and an evaluation of the corresponding remaining natural areas. Likewise, Brazil evaluates the main land-use changes in these ecological units

Comparative criteria	Brazil	India	China
Planetary condition: large reservoir of natural capital	✓	✓	✓
Economic status: emerging country	✓	✓	✓
Degree of degradation of ecosystems	(✓)	(✓)	✓
Inventory ecosystem accounts	✓	✓	✓
Change intensity indicator	✓	—	—
Valorization of ecosystem services (e.g., ecological footprint)	—	—	✓
Integration into national accounts	—	—	(✓)
Payments for ecosystem services	—	—	(✓)
Nature-based solutions	—	—	(✓)

✓ - Existing
(✓) - Partially present
— - Not present

Figure 9. Comparison of the GEP concepts between the three countries.
Source: Own representation.

in each part of the territory. Through spatial evaluation, it is possible to understand the territorial environmental dynamics of the country and identify the regions where the land-use transformations are more or less intense. Unlike China, where analyses are conducted on a smaller scale, Brazil prefers a large-scale approach. This approach identifies such biomes as Amazônia and Cerrado with the highest proportion of changes. At first glance, this does not seem to be a big surprise. Both biomes are complex ecosystems where the reduction of natural areas — forest and savanna or scrubland and grassland — and the expansion of cropland use, intensive or not, is accurately documented.

The main challenge is to record the stock of natural resources. Landscapes and biodiversity are so diverse in Brazil that the spatial unit always inadequately reflects the biomes. Therefore, in the future, it is essential to move to an environmental profile with a more detailed description of ecosystem types. It would allow production results at larger scales of investigation.

In addition, in order to assess the extent of Brazilian ecosystems, it is important to highlight other possible spatial units of analysis that are relevant to the environmental scenario for Brazil and can also be considered in the accounting framework, such as regions/hydrographic basins and priority areas and conservation units.

It is worth highlighting the CII. This indicator shows significant changes observed in land-use conversions. However, the indicator is not calculated selectively in time and space. Therefore, the methodological improvement of weighting the indicator by ecosystem area and interpreting it over the whole time series could allow for a better interpretation of the state of the environment in an aggregated and traditional way.

There are still significant steps remaining for Brazil to arrive at a GEP. Here, it is recommended — similar to China — to carry out the determination on a small scale.

India, too, is still far from a consistent ecosystem accounting and GEPs based on it, especially when it comes to the transfer of payments for ecosystem services. The discussion on the valorization of ecosystem services has been conducted mainly in the Indian Himalayan states. According to this, a state's ecosystem services that benefit the rest of the country should be valued. These values should then be included in the national accounts.

In the Uttarakhand region, the Ganges River plays a unique role in providing soil and water to the Gangetic plains. Carbon sequestration is a global ecosystem service; biodiversity is regional, national, and global. In addition, the use of hydropower potential and river water storage in the form of multipurpose projects in river valleys with a subsequent detour of water from reservoirs to regions other than the basins is an aspect that requires a larger scale of ecosystem services.

The purpose of implementing GEP in India is not transparent. Is it a simple assessment of the ecological wealth of the state or an assessment of how much it contributes to GDP? Is it an attempt to claim budgetary resources from the central government for the ecosystem services that the state provides to the rest of the country, or is it a process to provide benefits to its residents? Some conceptual work is needed here. China could serve as a model.

The Chinese experience shows that a considerable amount of data can be integrated by applying the ecosystem accounting method under the SEEA EEA. It demonstrates that further work is also needed in China. They concern the estimates, the coverage of socioeconomically essential ecosystem services, and the improvement of the quality and simulation accuracy of the biophysical models.

Biophysical models for measuring ecosystem services enable the production of provincial-level ecosystem accounts and comparison with more minor scales (municipality, county, etc.). The use of spatial information allows the identification of precise locations to provide ecosystem services. This approach helps determine the locations that most need to be modified or protected to optimize ecosystem service provision. It is also essential to have consistent approaches for collecting indicators of ecosystem conditions, as this information is essential for monitoring progress toward the goals set by the government.

It is crucial to emphasize that ecosystem accounting is being introduced gradually and flexibly. There is still a significant gap in the basic information on the environment and its linkage with national accounts. Here, the case of Brazil has shown that large-scale research of biomes brings to light a wealth of information. This information is of great importance for subsequent ecosystem accounting — at whatever level.

The following improvements are being discussed in relation to these national projects:

- Use remote sensing to strengthen monitoring capacity and expand environmental data sources.
- Strengthen the development of statistical monitoring capacity for natural resources.
- Increase government investment at all levels for infrastructure development, such as statistical monitoring.
- Establish a statistical monitoring system for resource data to integrate data monitoring, collection, and processing, reflecting the situation in real time.
- Form a set of parameters for different administrative units and different natural resources to facilitate the selection of correction coefficients and reflect the differences in the value of natural resources among administrative units; this point is a vital issue, especially in China (Zhang *et al.*, 2022).
- Build an information system based on which the primary natural resource data recommends.
- Develop a standardized information platform for natural resources.
- Integrate a system of standardized assessment methods.

Natural capital management has become a national priority for China, so the country has quickly assumed a leadership role in the core areas of sustainable development. Such a national priority cannot be seen to the same extent for Brazil and India.

6. Policy Implications

A key challenge is to integrate SNAs into policy making. It includes raising awareness about the potential benefits of national accounts. Policymakers should be persuaded to move forward with the data collection process. Only in this way can national accounts be further developed into a GEP. The first essential step is to develop the accounts. This step can be done based on the UN's SEEA. China deviates here at various points, which is not very advantageous for comparability between countries.

Nevertheless, the development of the accounts in ecosystem accounting contributes to better and more informed decision-making. The compilation of national accounts of environmental assets or natural capital, their spatial extent, and quality are essential prerequisites for the calculation of GEP. The various case studies in China demonstrate this impressively. It can be concluded from this that GEP balancing should be a constantly evolving process. This process is oriented toward both long- and short-term improvement goals (Hao *et al.*, 2022).

The accounting shows how natural resource extraction and emissions, changes in condition, and the economy's response are captured in terms of environmental protection and resource management expenditures. It provides a system that can help produce a wide range of indicators and statistics with various applications for decision-making.

Scenario analysis has an important policy role. This exploration aims at decision-making. Scenarios are used to assess the outcomes and effectiveness of different policy intervention options. This way can demonstrate to policymakers the utility of newly collected SNA-related information.

GEP can reflect the contribution of nature to human well-being. Long-term trends can serve as indicators of the extent and quality of local and regional ecosystems, providing a corrective or complement to more conventional development measures. For example, if urbanization exacerbates spatial constraints on the management of natural capital, advances in environmental protection and restoration may improve the quality of ecosystems and services.

Accounting for ecosystem services highlights many areas where approaches to valuing ecosystem services and describing the relationship between ecosystem services and ecosystem assets need to be better articulated. These areas include determining the appropriate valuation approach, clearly distinguishing between ecosystem services and benefits, distinguishing between ecosystem services and degradation, and understanding the relationship between restoration costs and ecosystem degradation measurement (Obst *et al.*, 2016).

The development of ecosystem accounting in different countries is far from complete. Some critical conceptual and measurement challenges remain to be addressed. For example, key challenges include (Obst *et al.*, 2016):

- the accounting of low and negative resource rents;
- the derivation of values for ecosystem assets;
- the accounting of regulatory services that provide inputs across multiple spatial domains;
- the accounting of ecosystem services;
- the full integration of ecosystem accounting into national accounts.

The SEEA EEA and GEP are complementary frameworks for assessing the values and benefits of nature-based solutions (NbS). NbS create synergies between biodiversity conservation and societal challenges, such as climate change. Applying GEP helps improve stakeholders' understanding and application of NbS and further embed the concept.

Ambitious deadlines have been set for the future: achieving the UN SDGs by 2030 and reducing net global greenhouse gas emissions to zero before 2050. Revising the SNA, with a new system of national accounts to be agreed upon in 2023 and put in place from 2025, is an essential step toward achieving these longer-term goals. That is why opening up this revision process to broader debate and scrutiny is crucial. As the name implies, national accounts need a consistent, comprehensive, and mutually exclusive set of definitions and classifications. A new framework requires collecting other source data and thus changing the processes embedded in the national statistical offices.

7. Conclusion

How societies have understood and measured progress has changed significantly over the centuries. The GDP concept, which combines technical authority and political utility, has led to "path dependency" and forms of social "lock-in" that are difficult and costly to eliminate. While GDP looks solely at the value of production — or output — GEP instead places a value on nature's inputs and incentivizes policymakers to invest in nature. It would be naïve to simply add the two metrics and a total number. Nevertheless, the two metrics can provide decision-makers with complementary information that could enable the future sustainable economic growth of economies. In short, there is an inherent tension in constructing an alternative to GDP, namely striking a balance between technical robustness and social resonance.

Within the current revision of the SNA and ongoing statistical research, there is some momentum toward measuring inclusive well-being — building on the economics of sustainability summarized in Dasgupta's (2021) recent report on the economics of biodiversity. This framework is likely to achieve broad consensus among economists and statisticians and is already being implemented by the United Nations, starting with the SEEA.

Based on decades of research in environmental science and ecological economics, tools to untangle the complexity of ecosystem services are improving. Efforts to compile national accounts of environmental assets or natural capital, spatial extent, and quality are also helpful for calculating GEP. Statistical modeling, remote sensing, field data collection, GIS mapping, and cost–benefit analysis can all contribute to a more robust GEP calculation. Sunstein (2018) notes:

> In terms of saving money and saving lives. It has stopped bad things, spurred good things, and turned them into better things. However, the revolution remains unfinished. In the fullness of time, it may well turn out to be a transition to something far better, focused more directly

> on measuring human welfare and enlisting unimaginably ambitious strategies to capture and improve the real-world effects of public-sector initiatives. (p. 215)

Creating a GEP for the three countries discussed is a significant step in considering nature's contribution to society's well-being and sustainable development that respects people, the planet, and profit. The article shows how valuable the services provided by nature can be and how great the potential is to invest in natural resources to sustain these flows in the future:

> By placing a value on the benefits that we derive from our natural environment, GEP would also encourage us to think differently about how we manage, maintain, and grow those regions that have been neglected in favour of centralised growth strategies. (Onakuse, 2021)

However, there are also some disadvantages. First, GEP and GDP can overlap significantly in value. For example, when it comes to food provision, this can lead to double counting. Second, care must be taken to determine which ecosystem services are included in the valuation. The total value of GEP may be underestimated. Part of the appeal of GEP is its parallel to GDP as a single, aggregate measure. Many might argue that this distracts from the complexity of ecosystems and promotes a form of "substitutability" of natural assets. It is often referred to as weak sustainability. At the same time, the valorization of ecosystem value promotes complementary measures to economic instruments that have not yet been addressed. By demonstrating that GEP is as significant, if not more, than GDP, this approach could encourage decision-makers to consider nature on an equal footing with economic growth.

The GEP metric will likely be refined and improved as our understanding increases. Untangling the complexity of natural systems to create the GEP is a complex undertaking. However, it is worth remembering that the GDP did not emerge overnight either, with all its flaws and weaknesses. The GEP is undoubtedly one of the new steps forward and in the right direction. However, at least for now, it would not be practical to implement a system like the GEP. Apart from being very complex and largely untested, its introduction would require a global economic consensus, which has not been seen since the creation of the international financial order after the Second World War. Arguably, a more radical shift in thinking is required if the complex trade-offs needed to contain the climate crisis are to be managed.

References

Arto, I., Cazcarro, I., Garmendia, E., *et al.* (2022). A new accounting framework for assessing forest footprint of nations. *Ecological Economics*, *194*, 107337.

Bateman, I. J. & Mace, G. M. (2020). The natural capital framework for sustainably efficient and equitable decision making. *Nature Sustainability*, *3*, 776–783.

Blanchard, O. & Tirole, J. (2021). *Major Future Economic Challenges.* Paris: France Stratégie.

Bolson, N., Yutkin, M., Rees, W., *et al.* (2022). Resilience rankings and trajectories of world's countries. *Ecological Economics*, *195*, 107383.

Bordt, M. (2018). Discourses in ecosystem accounting: A Survey of the expert community. *Ecological Economics*, *144*, 82–99.

Costanza, R., Kubiszewski, I., Giovannini, E., *et al.* (1997). The value of the world's ecosystem services and natural capital. *Nature*, *387*, 253–260.

Costanza, R., d'Arge, R., de Groot, R., *et al.* (2014). Time to leave GDP behind. *Nature*, *505*, 283–285.

Dasgupta, P. (2021). *The Economics of Biodiversity: The Dasgupta Review.* London: HM Treasury.

De Groot, R. S., Wilson, M. A., & Boumans, R. M. (2002). A typology for the classification, description and valuation of ecosystem functions, goods and services. *Ecological Economics*, *41*(3), 393–408.

European Commission (2022, March). Transitions performance index 2021: Towards fair and prosperous sustainability. Publications Office of the European Union.

Fleming, A., O'Grady, A. P., Stitzlein, C., *et al.* (2022). Improving acceptance of natural capital accounting in land use decision making: Barriers and opportunities. *Ecological Economics*, *200*, 107510.

Geng, J. & Liang, C. (2021). Analysis of the internal relationship between ecological value and economic value based on the forest resources in China. *Sustainability*, *13*, 6795.

Hamel, P., Guerry, A. D., Polasky, S., *et al.* (2021). Mapping the benefits of nature in cities with the InVEST software. *npj Urban Sustainability*, *1*, 25.

Hannon, B. (1985). Ecosystem flow analysis. *Canadian Bulletin of Fisheries and Aquatic Sciences*, *213*, 97–118.

Hao, C., Wu, S., Zhang, W., *et al.* (2022). A critical review of gross ecosystem product accounting in China: Status quo, problems and future directions. *Journal of Environmental Management*, *322*, 115995.

Instituto Brasileiro de Geografia e Estatística (IBGE) (2021). Ecosystem accounts: Land use in the Brazilian biomes (2000–2018). Rio de Janeiro: IBGE.

Levin, S., Xepapadeas, T., Crépin, A. S., *et al.* (2013). Social-ecological systems as complex adaptive systems: Modeling and policy implications. *Environment and Development Economics*, *18*(2), 111–132.

Liang, L.-N., Siu Siu, W., Wang, M.-X., *et al.* (2021). Measuring gross ecosystem product of nine cities within the Pearl River Delta of China. *Environmental Challenges*, *4*, 100105.

NBS China (2021). Ecosystem accounts for China. Results of the NCAVES Project. United Nations.

NSO India (2021). Ecosystem accounts for India: Report of the NCAVES Project. United Nations.

Obst, C., Hein, L., & Edens, B. (2016). National accounting and the valuation of ecosystem assets and their services. *Environmental and Resource Economics*, *64*(1), 1–23.

OECD (2018). Beyond GDP: Measuring what counts for economic and social performance. Paris: OECD.

Onakuse, S. (2021). GDP ignores the environment: Why it's time for a more sustainable growth Metric. *The Conversation*, December 13.

Ouyang, Z., Song, C., Zheng, H., *et al.* (2020). Using gross ecosystem product (GEP) to value nature in decision making. *PNAS*, *117*(25), 14593–14601.

Ouyang, Z., Wang, X., & Miao, H. (1999). A primary study on Chinese terrestrial ecosystem services and their ecological-economic values. *Acta Ecologica Sinica*, *19*(5), 607–613.

Shen, W., Zhou, T., Chang, H., *et al.* (2022). Responses of grazing households to different levels of payments for ecosystem services. *Ecosystem Health and Sustainability*, *8*, 2052762.

Stevenson, H., *et al.* (2021). The practical fit of concepts: Ecosystem services and the value of nature. *Global Environmental Politics*, *21*(2), 3–22.

Stiglitz, J. E., Sen, A., & Fitoussi, J.-P. (2009). Report by the Commission on the measurement of economic performance and social progress. Paris.

Sunstein, C. R. (2018). *The Cost-Benefit Revolution.* Cambridge, MA: MIT Press.

Troy, A. & Wilson, M. A. (2006). Mapping ecosystem services: Practical challenges and opportunities in linking GIS and value transfer. *Ecological Economics*, *60*(2), 435–449.

van den Bergh, J. & Antal, M. (2014). Evaluating alternatives to GDP as measures of social welfare/progress. Working Paper No. 56. WWW-for Europe, Vienna.

United Nations (2014a). *System of Environmental–Economic Accounting 2012 — Central Framework*. New York: United Nations.

United Nations (2014b). *System of Environmental–Economic Accounting 2012 — Experimental Ecosystem Accounting*. New York: United Nations.

U.S. Whitehouse (2022). National strategy to develop statistics for environmental economic decisions: A U.S. system of national capital accounting and associated environmental-economic statistics. August 18th, 2022. Washington, DC.

Wang, X. (2019). The national ecological accounting and auditing scheme as an instrument of institutional reform in China: A discourse analysis. *Journal of Business Ethics*, *154*, 587–603.

WHO Council (2022). Valuing health for all: Rethinking and building a whole-of-society approach. Council Brief No. 3. World Health Organization.

Zhang, T., Lyu, X., Zou, Y., *et al.* (2022). Value assessment of wetland ecosystem services in the Da Hinggan mountains, China. *Chinese Geographical Science*, *32*, 302–311.

Zou, Z., Wu, T., Xiao, Y., *et al.* (2020). Valuing natural capital amidst rapid urbanization: Assessing the gross Ecosystem product (GEP) of China's 'Chang-Zhu-Tan' megacity. *Environmental Research Letters*, *15*, 124019.

https://doi.org/10.1142/9781800614482_0015

Chapter 15

Renewable Energy Transition for Sustainable Economic Development: Implications for Green Recovery in the Post COVID-19 Era

Ahmed Imran Hunjra[*,†,||], **Mahnoor Hanif**[‡,**], **Dilvin Taşkın**[§,††], **and Qasim Zureigat**[¶,‡‡]

[†]*Rabat Business School, International University of Rabat, Morocco*

[‡]*University Institute of Management Sciences, PMAS-Arid Agriculture University Rawalpindi, Pakistan*

[§]*Department of International Trade and Finance, Faculty of Business, Yaşar University, Izmir, Turkey*

[¶]*School of Business, Sulaiman Al Rajhi University, Saudi Arabia*

[||]*ahmedhunjra@gmail.com*

[**]*mahnoorhanif289@gmail.com*

[††]*dilvin.taskin@yasar.edu.tr*

[‡‡]*q.zureigat@sr.edu.sa*

Abstract

The COVID-19 pandemic has posed considerable difficulties for the shift to clean energy sources. COVID-19's potential impact on the global energy transition has received scant scholarly attention so far. This research aims to explore the impact of renewable energy consumption and renewable power generation on sustainable economic development

[*]Corresponding author.

in developing countries. We use a panel dataset for developing countries for the period 2000–2021. The fixed effect model (FEM) is used for hypothesis testing, while the system generalized method of moments (SYS-GMM) is employed to confirm the robustness of the results. We found that renewable energy generation and energy consumption have a considerable positive impact on sustainable development in developing countries and confirmed the feedback hypothesis. This research offers a thorough empirical examination of the relationship between renewable energy consumption and sustainable development in developing countries and recommends a post-pandemic roadmap for a low-carbon energy transition in developing economies.

1. Introduction

A "green economy," characterized by reduced fossil fuel use and greenhouse gas emissions, is becoming increasingly urgent as the world attempts to address rising climate change concerns (Pegels & Altenburg, 2020). The worldwide energy transformation has been moving along steadily. For instance, in 2019, the world added more than 200 billion kilowatts to its renewable energy installation capacity (Murdock *et al.*, 2021). The future of the energy shift is questionable, however, because the COVID-19 pandemic has greatly hindered the growth of renewable energy (Elavarasan *et al.*, 2021). How best to encourage the worldwide energy transition in the wake of a global epidemic has sparked heated debate.

Amid rising concerns regarding reliance on traditional energy sources, nations throughout the world have enacted legislation and restrictions. More and more people are stressing the need for global coordination and cooperation on the subject of fossil fuel divestment. Important steps in climate governance, the Kyoto Protocol and the Paris Agreement, laid the groundwork for a worldwide shift to low-carbon energy (IEA, 2016). Governance of the climate works at decarbonizing the economy by shifting its reliance on fossil fuels to renewable sources of energy (Meng *et al.*, 2018). The increasing worldwide need for renewable energy production is reflected in the international climate accords (Xiao *et al.*, 2019). Although many energy policies point toward a bright future for renewable energy development (Wang *et al.*, 2021), the COVID-19 pandemic inflicted an extraordinary shock throughout the whole energy sector, slowing the progress of energy transformation.

After the COVID-19 outbreak was officially designated a worldwide pandemic by the World Health Organization (WHO) on March 11, 2020, several nations entered a new stage of pandemic prevention and control, severely limiting international travel and economic activity (Goodell, 2020). Worldwide energy demand dropped by approximately 5 percent in 2020 and global emissions dropped by 7 percent as a result of a significant interruption in corporate activity; this fall may have lasting effects on energy consumption and carbon emissions in the coming decades (Zhang *et al.*, 2021). Meanwhile, the oil-producing countries' grasp on the energy market was weakened by the pandemic, resulting in a continuing decline in oil prices. In light of the drop in oil prices, traditional energy sources become more cost-effective than their renewable counterparts.

There is no denying COVID-19's growing influence on the expansion of renewable energy sources. Many governments have altered their investment strategy since the pandemic by shifting resources from renewable energy initiatives and tax exemptions to healthcare. Without financial backing from the government, renewable energy initiatives are less likely to be made due to high initial costs and low returns. Many nations are desperately searching for viable methods to revive their economies in the face of current difficulties. Although there has been a rising need for environmentally friendly stimulus programs, most countries' energy investment structures are still heavily weighted toward fossil fuels, and the stated plans have been relatively green (Jiang *et al.*, 2021). A less sustainable and resilient global economy is the inevitable result of an irresponsible recovery mode that weakens the world's ability to adapt to climate change and the energy transition.

Due to industrialization and population pressure, most developing economies are dependent on carbon emissions. To put it another way, developed countries are responsible for just 37 percent of global carbon emissions, while developing countries are responsible for 63 percent, as per 2011 estimates. As a result, developing nations must act promptly on climate change globally. Even more so, it is claimed that oil and fossil fuel resources account for more than 80 percent of energy use in developing nations (Larcher & Tarascon, 2015). As a result, emerging economies are experiencing climatic issues. Energy extraction from fossil fuel usage is noted as having a significant impact on climate change in the Intergovernmental Panel on

Climate Change report (IPCC, 2020). According to the research by Grigoroudis *et al.* (2015), the issue of climate change in underdeveloped nations is entirely a question of government and institutional problems.

To successfully develop economic recovery and an energy transition, we need answers to the following questions. How does the COVID-19 pandemic affect the energy transition, and what are the opportunities and problems it creates? Can we expect renewable energy production to benefit from the international economic revival measures currently being implemented? When a global epidemic strikes, how do we make progress in the energy transition? We answer these concerns and give suggestions for formulating green recovery policies following pandemics and contributing to the framework of the global transition to low-carbon energy. This research offers a thorough empirical examination of the relationship between renewable energy consumption and sustainable development in developing countries and recommends a post-pandemic roadmap for a low-carbon energy transition in developing economies.

The literature review is presented in Section 2, and the data and methods are discussed in Section 3. The statistical findings are discussed in Section 4, and the study is concluded in Section 5.

2. Literature Review

It is a new fundamental concept to link renewable energy and economic growth. It takes into account the impact of energy conservation on a nation's ability to save money. As a result of this discussion, four key hypotheses relating to energy and growth have been presented. The growth hypothesis focuses on the unidirectional link between energy use and economic growth. As a result of the belief that energy consumption is a complementary input alongside capital and labor in industrial production, energy consumption has a positive impact on economic growth (Apergis *et al.*, 2012). It indicates that energy use and economic growth are linked. A lack of progress in technology is a consequence of the economy's heavy reliance on energy. A green structural shift toward the use of renewable energy is needed. Another aspect of a conservation hypothesis is that it emphasizes a one-way relationship between economic expansion and an increase in energy use. This theory recognizes circumstances where real savings take precedence over the ideology of economic expansion. It predicts that the economy will become less reliant on fossil fuels for its energy needs. Third, economic growth and energy use are linked in a bidirectional manner according to the feedback hypothesis. It indicates that as the economy grows, so does our need for energy, and vice versa. According to this idea, the relationship between energy and economic growth is inherently complementary (Apergis *et al.*, 2018). An independent relationship between energy use and economic growth is the fourth foundation of the neutrality hypothesis arguments. In addition, it suggests that energy use and economic growth are interrelated. Conservation and neutrality hypotheses combine to provide a more comprehensive theory of sustainable development that places greater emphasis on the use of renewable resources and reduces the reliance on non-renewable ones.

The literature on the topic of energy consumption and economic growth has been examined in three distinct ways by Mohsin *et al.* (2021) and Taghizadeh-Hesary and Yoshino (2020). The first thread is a collection of verified assumptions about the link between energy use and GDP expansion. Some studies, such as by Destek and Sinha (2020), corroborate the growth concept (Antonakakis *et al.*, 2017). The focus of these analyses is on nations such as the United States, the Organization for Economic Cooperation and Development (OECD), non-OECD nations, the Group of Seven (G7), South American nations, and Vietnam (Lise & Van Montfort, 2007). Data from Turkey (Al-Saidi, 2017) and 82 nations from 1972 to 2002 confirm the conservative hypothesis, and feedback for 53 countries (Shahbaz *et al.*, 2017), data from India (Fuinhas & Marques, 2012), 21 African countries (Belke *et al.*, 2011), 25 OECD countries (Apergis & Payne, 2010), and 11 CIS countries from a variety of periods all confirm its accuracy. The parallel combination hypothesis is also confirmed by Rasoulinezhad *et al.* (2020) and Anser *et al.* (2020).

The second track examines how switching to renewable energy sources affects the economy. There is credible evidence supporting this strategy, including the growth hypothesis proposed by Bilgili *et al.* (2017), Mezghani and Ben Haddad (2017), and Chien and Hu (2007) for India, China, the United States of America, and

45 other nations. Gozgor *et al.* (2018) and Bhattacharya *et al.* (2018) all confirm the feedback hypothesis.

The third strand investigates the dynamic between energy and development; here, both renewable and non-renewable sources of energy are taken into account (Apergis & Payne, 2012; Wang *et al.*, 2021). Numerous studies have used non-renewable and renewable energy resources to examine their relationship with GDP. Economic growth is positively correlated with the use of both renewable and non-renewable energy sources in emerging and industrialized nations (Sekrafi & Sghaier, 2018). The use of renewable energy sources has been shown to hasten economic growth while halting further environmental degradation. However, the quality of the environment cannot be maintained with non-renewable energy sources in either developed or emerging nations. Jammazi and Aloui (2015) found that when looking at the GCC nations as a panel, the correlation between renewable energy and GDP in Germany, Italy, and the United States was positive. Renewable energy does not appear to be stimulating GDP in Canada, France, Japan, or the United Kingdom. The role of renewable energy consumption and high-value-added product creation in the United States' gross domestic product was analyzed (Ozcan & Ozturk, 2019) using the ARDL model. Numerous studies, such as those by Gorus and Aydin (2019) and Pablo-Romero and Sánchez-Braza (2017), have demonstrated the positive impact that switching to renewable energy sources may have on GDP reduction in underdeveloped nations. It has been found that the GDP of 16 of the emerging economies evaluated (except for Poland) is unaffected by RER, which is the result of the author's analysis of the correlation between renewable energy and GDP in 17 developing nations.

The literature evaluates the influence of GDP and energy use on greenhouse gas emissions for both emerging and developed nations. Literature from a variety of regions also emphasizes the importance of renewable energy and its sources in reducing greenhouse gas emissions (Baloch *et al.*, 2020). Greenhouse gas emissions, however, have not been researched in environmental management programs. This research contributes to the literature by highlighting the significance of environmental management regulations, the use of renewable and non-renewable energy resources, and rising per capita GDP in determining greenhouse gas emissions in emerging markets.

Several studies (Armeanu *et al.*, 2017; Adams & Collyer, 2018) have shown that integrating renewable energy into the energy system is beneficial to economic growth. These researchers used numerous econometric models, each with its own unique methodology, and a plethora of control variables, including gross fixed investment, employment rates, non-renewable energy use, production, and institutional factors. Almost all of them concluded that renewable energy generation or consumption contributed positively and significantly to GDP development. The sustained environment, footprint, greenhouse gas, energy consumption, etc., are just a few of the many variables and factors of sustainable development. Pezzey and Burke (2014) have argued that adjusted net saving (ANS) is a good index for measuring sustainable development in several countries that have focused mostly on this variable. The World Bank's Environment Department explains that an economy's genuine rate of saving can be calculated by adjusting for factors including human capital investment, natural resource depletion, and damage caused by natural disasters resulting from contamination by pollutants. Genuine saving, or ANS, is an indicator developed from the ideas of extended national accounts to measure the long-term health of a country's economy. ANS is an attempt to provide a metric for monitoring progress toward a goal of "sustainable" development for nations whose leaders have made such a pledge. To get to the ANS from the standard national accounting measure of gross saving, the following four adjustments are made: deducting the consumption of fixed capital to obtain net national saving; adding the current public expenditure on education to account for investment in human capital; subtracting estimates of the depletion of a variety of natural resources to reflect the decline in asset values associated with extraction to obtain the ANS; CO_2 and local pollution damages are deducted. However, if the ANS rate is negative, the country's wealth will fall, especially if it relies heavily on the export of non-renewable resources.

H1: Renewable energy consumption and renewable power generation are significantly related to sustainable economic development.

The impact of trade liberalization on GDP has been documented in several academic works. Trade openness positively impacts economic growth in Latin America (Roquez-Diaz & Escot, 2018).

Through their research on Sub-Saharan Africa (SSA), Brueckner and Lederman (2015) confirmed this positive correlation. By analyzing data from SSA countries at the threshold level, Zahonogo (2016) confirmed the positive impact of trade openness on GDP growth. On the other hand, Rigobon and Rodrik (2005) used data from European countries to conclude that increased openness to trade has a negative effect on economic growth. When the total trade contribution proxy is taken into account, Ramzan *et al.* (2019) found that trade openness negatively affects economic growth. Moreover, the relationship is positive when considering total factor productivity in the economic model. Those few studies that do address sustainability tend to do so from an environmental rather than an economic view (Murshed, 2020; Nepal *et al.*, 2021).

H2: Trade openness is significantly related to sustainable economic development.

The two methods in which foreign direct investment (FDI) might contribute to sustainable development are explored. According to the supporters of the pollution halo hypothesis, which states that FDI has a net positive effect on environmental quality (Mert & Caglar, 2020), conditions for sustainable development are enhanced by the transfer of green technology alongside increased FDI and enhanced efficiency (Dincer & Rosen, 2011). The correlation between FDI and carbon dioxide (CO_2) emissions has received a lot of attention in the economics literature. It is reasonable to assume that the pollution haven hypothesis (PHH) has garnered similar interest from researchers throughout the world. It points to polluting businesses as key culprits in ecological decline. For instance, after comparing data from low-, middle-, and high-income nations, Shahbaz *et al.* (2015) found that the PHH holds true. The PHH idea was verified by further research in the Asia-Pacific region (Yang *et al.*, 2013; Ahmad *et al.*, 2021).

H3: FDI is significantly related to sustainable economic development.

The world's aging population poses a serious risk to economies everywhere (Dugarova & Gülasan 2017). The relationship between the world's aging population and the SDGs is substantial (World Health Organization, 2015). Sustainable development is affected by the aging population in three ways: the emergence of new channels of inequality, increased poverty, and the quality of life for existing populations. One of the main aims of sustainable development is to strengthen human capacity for adaptability and social cohesion (United Nations Development Programme, 2017). Up until 2050, an aging population poses serious challenges, and it may lead to an increase in human dependence on non-human sources of support. The negative and severe effects of an aging population on sustainable development are also reported by Chapman and Shigetomi (2018). However, there is little current research on how aging populations and sustainable growth interact. Therefore, it is necessary to delve further into the question of whether or not it is important to comprehend the significance of population aging for low–middle income economies in terms of economic sustainability.

H4: Aging population is significantly related to sustainable economic development.

3. Methodology and Data

To find the impact of renewable energy consumption on sustainable development, we use a dataset of 42 developing countries in the unbalanced panel dataset starting from 2000 to 2020, taken on an annual basis. The selection of developing countries is primarily based on data availability. For hypothesis testing, we use panel fixed effect estimation, and for confirming the results' robustness, we turn to the system generalized method of moments (SYS-GMM). We use ANS per capita (Kamoun, 2019; Güney, 2019), which is calculated by dividing ANS by the population rate. The ANS does not include specific emissions damage provided in the World Development Indicator (WDI) data source. Net national savings plus education expenditures, minus net forest, mineral, and CO_2 depletion, as well as specific emission damages, are used to calculate the ANS. The percentage of renewable energy consumption (REC) as well as the renewable power generation (RPG) are used to capture renewable energy an indicator developed by the WDI. Nevertheless, factors such as FDI, economic growth (GDP), trade openness (TO) and age dependency ratio (ADR) serve as controls. Table 1 provides a summary of the variables.

Table 1. Variable description.

Variable	Description	Symbol	References
Adjusted net savings	Adjusted net savings, excluding particular emission damage (percentage GNI)	ANS	Hunjra *et al.* (2022a, 2022b)
Economic growth	Gross domestic product per capita	GDP	Solarin *et al.* (2019); Ntarmah *et al.* (2022)
Renewable energy consumption	Percentage of renewable energy in total final energy consumption	REC	Kamoun (2019); Güney (2019)
Renewable power generation	Electricity production from renewable sources, excluding hydroelectric (kWh)	RPG	Kamoun (2019); Güney (2019)
Trade openness	Trade (percentage of GDP)	TO	Kamoun, Abdelkafi, & Ghorbel (2019)
Foreign direct investment	Foreign direct investment, net inflows (BoP, current US$)	FDI	Solarin *et al.* (2019)
Age dependency	Age dependency ratio (percentage of working-age population)	ADR	Solarin *et al.* (2019)

Notes: ANS (adjusted net saving) and GDP (economic growth) are dependent variables, REC (renewable energy consumption) and RPG (renewable energy generation) are independent variables. TO (trade openness), FDI (foreign direct investment), and ADR (age dependency ratio) are control variables.

The following mathematical model is used for hypotheses testing:

$$\begin{aligned} \text{ANS}_{i,t} &= \alpha + \beta 1(\text{REC})_{i,t} + \beta 2(\text{RPG})_{i,t} + \beta 3(\text{FDI})_{i,t} \\ &\quad + \beta 4(\text{TO})_{i,t} + \beta 5(\text{ADR})_{i,t} + \varepsilon_{i,t} \end{aligned} \tag{1}$$

$$\begin{aligned} \text{GDP}_{i,t} &= \alpha + \beta 1(\text{REC})_{i,t} + \beta 2(\text{RPG})_{i,t} + \beta 3(\text{FDI})_{i,t} \\ &\quad + \beta 4(\text{TO})_{i,t} + \beta 5(\text{ADR})_{i,t} + \varepsilon_{i,t} \end{aligned} \tag{2}$$

where ANS and GDP stand for adjusted net saving and economic growth, respectively, which are dependent variables, α is a constant,

REC (renewable energy consumption) and RPG (renewable power generation) are used as independent variables in the study. Furthermore, FDI (foreign direct investment), TO (trade openness), and ADR (age dependency ratio) represent the control variables included in the model while $\varepsilon_{i.t}$ is the error term.

Descriptive statistics, correlation, a test for multicollinearity, and static and dynamic panel regression were employed for analysis in this study. It is possible to employ descriptive statistics in an investigation to shed light on the most fundamental aspects of the data. Correlation analysis is a technique for determining the degree of association between two variables. The sample correlation between two variables is between -1 and $+1$, and it seeks to evaluate the linear relationship between them. The relationship between renewable energy and sustainable development is analyzed using a panel regression model. Fixed and random effects models are the two cornerstones of panel regression. According to the results of the Hausman test, it is best to analyze the data using a fixed-effect model. The reliability of the findings is further assessed using GMM. González (2013) claims that the GMM has been employed to address issues of endogeneity in independent variables, unobserved variability in characteristics, and autoregressive behavior in a dependent variable.

4. Analysis and Results

Table 2 provides a descriptive analysis of the variables. In terms of the log values of adjusted net saving and GDP, the average value of sustainable development is 6.537 and 9.320, respectively. The average REC is 5.078, and it represents the amount of renewable energy used in developing nations. High mean values of REC suggest a high level of sustainable development in selected developing countries. Considering that the average value of RPG is 1.952, it is safe to assume that this percentage is quite low. It is hypothesized that a less widespread adoption of efficient solutions contributes to a lower overall value of RPG. Our sample of developing countries has a low mean value of TO (4.622) and a low mean value of FDI (3.406). The mean value of the ADR is 11.092, with a standard deviation of 1.760, implying that emerging countries have a high number of dependent workable persons.

Table 2. Descriptive analysis.

Variables	Mean	Median	St. Dev.	Min	Max	Obs.	VIF
ANS	6.537	6.353	1.017	−2.443	10.736	882	1.323
GDP	9.320	8.893	1.532	0.629	18.345	882	1.298
REC	5.078	4.986	0.104	2.053	7.926	882	1.487
RPG	1.952	1.974	1.521	−4.657	7.345	882	1.529
TO	4.622	5.032	1.273	2.218	6.587	882	1.204
FDI	3.406	3.679	0.728	2.767	5.030	882	1.182
ADR	11.092	10.754	1.760	5.854	19.030	882	1.762

Notes: ANS (adjusted net saving) and GDP (economic growth) are dependent variables, REC (renewable energy consumption) and RPG (renewable power generation) are independent variables. TO (trade openness), FDI (foreign direct investment), and ADR (age dependency ratio) are control variables.

Table 3. Correlation analysis.

Variables	ANS	GDP	REC	RPG	TO	FDI	ADR
ANS	1						
GDP	0.067	1					
REC	0.075	0.549	1				
RPG	0.032	0.344	0.215	1			
TO	0.028	0.047	0.073	0.036	1		
FDI	0.088	0.481	0.188	0.054	0.075	1	
ADR	−0.077	−0.036	0.284	0.013	0.505	0.143	1

Notes: ANS (adjusted net saving) and GDP (economic growth) are dependent variables, REC (renewable energy consumption) and RPG (renewable power generation) are independent variables. TO (trade openness), FDI (foreign direct investment), and ADR (age dependency ratio) are control variables.

Pearson's product-moment correlation matrix between the variables is displayed in Table 3. As the independent variables are only moderately correlated with one another, multicollinearity is not a big issue in our panel regression analysis.

The results of the redundant fixed-effect test are displayed in Table 4. It is revealed that the fixed-effect model is preferred over the common correlation model for evaluating the panel data under investigation. The null hypothesis of the redundant fixed-effect test is rejected because the p-value is less than 0.05, which rules out the use

Table 4. Model testing using the fixed-effect method.

	ANS		GDP	
Variables	**Model 1**	**Model 2**	**Model 3**	**Model 4**
REC	1.080^{***}	—	1.086^{***}	—
	(2.78)		(2.84)	
RPG	—	0.112^{**}	—	0.176^{***}
		(2.49)		(2.32)
TO	0.514^{***}	0.504^{***}	0.518^{***}	0.520^{***}
	(7.85)	(6.72)	(7.01)	(7.35)
FDI	0.089^{***}	0.113^{**}	0.109^{***}	0.092^{***}
	(7.53)	(7.14)	(7.30)	(7.76)
ADR	-0.085^{***}	-0.061^{***}	-0.059^{***}	-0.067^{***}
	(−5.47)	(−5.19)	(−5.17)	(−5.16)
Constant	1.427^{***}	1.393^{***}	1.159^{***}	1.343^{***}
	(4.58)	(3.48)	(3.19)	(4.40)
Observations	882	882	882	882
R-squared	0.576	0.540	0.551	0.555
Year fixed effect	Yes	Yes	Yes	Yes
Country fixed effect	Yes	Yes	Yes	Yes
Number of countries	42	42	42	42

Notes: Results in Table 3 are estimated using fixed-effect estimation. ANS (adjusted net saving) and GDP (economic growth) are dependent variables, REC (renewable energy consumption) and RPG (renewable power generation) are independent variables. TO (trade openness), FDI (foreign direct investment), and ADR (age dependency ratio) are control variables, $^{***}p < 0.01$, $^{**}p < 0.05$. Model 1 and Model 2 are estimated with ANS, and Model 3 and Model 4 are estimated with GDP as sustainable economic development measures. The independent variable in Model 1 and Model 3 is REC, and in Model 2 and Model 4, RPG is used as an independent variable to measure renewable energy.

of the common coefficient model. The results of the Hausman test, which determines which of two statistical models — the fixed-effect model or the random-effect model — to apply, are also presented. The results from the Hausman test indicate that the fixed-effect model is used for analysis because the F-statistics are statistically significant. All models have an adjusted $R2$ of around 0.60, indicating a well-fitting model and the explanatory factors' contribution to sustainable development.

Table 4 reports the results of fixed-effect estimation. Model 1 and Model 2 are estimated with ANS, and Model 3 and Model 4 are estimated with GDP as sustainable economic development measures. The independent variable in Model 1 and Model 3 is REC, and in Model 2 and Model 4, RPG is used as an independent variable to measure renewable energy. Both measures of renewable energy (REC and RPG) reveal a significant positive impact on sustainable economic development as measured by ANS and economic growth. The findings back up the concept of the feedback hypothesis, according to which, there is a two-way connection between economic expansion and energy use. It shows that the demand for energy increases in tandem with the economy and vice versa. This finding on the energy–growth nexus is consistent with previous empirical research, including that by Hao *et al.* (2020), Hussain *et al.* (2021), and Islam & Islam (2021), all of which found that increased energy consumption significantly increased sustainable economic development. Positive GDP growth and ANS are associated with longer-term economic stability in developing countries. Our findings suggest that the expansion of these economies is conducive to sustainable economic growth as a result of increased financial competence. This proves that economic growth in these nations has reached a level that can appropriately stimulate sustainable development in the economy. We also discover that the use of renewable energy sources has a large and favorable effect on sustainable development. Because of this, the resource conservation theory is supported (Güney, 2019; Kamoun *et al.*, 2019). The findings suggest that replacing the usage of fossil fuels in the energy production process in developing nations with renewable energy generation is crucial to sustaining energy supply and safeguarding the environment from greenhouse gas emissions.

Furthermore, the results of the control variables TO and FDI reveal a significant positive impact on sustainable economic development with both measures. These findings suggest that trade liberalization policies have a favorable and considerable effect on these countries' ability to achieve sustainable economic growth (Murshed, 2020; Nepal *et al.*, 2021). That is why opening up borders to international trade is inextricably tied to the economic benefits of trade liberalization policies in these nations. Only through such policies will these economies be able to foster technological innovation and knowledge spillover. Since the goal of liberal trade is to replace inefficient industry technology from the economies of trade members, the transfer of green technology is achievable at a time when these economies are undergoing a technological transition. Positive effects on sustainable economic development have been observed in several countries as a result of net inflows of FDI. For this reason, the long-term welfare implications of FDI, especially for natural resources, come with their own set of costs, including to the environment and social infrastructure. The findings lend credence to the pollution halo theory in certain emerging nations (Mert & Caglar, 2020). The ADR reveals a significant negative impact on sustainable economic development. As the world's population ages, it poses a threat to economies everywhere (United Nations Development Programme, 2017). Again, in a selected group of countries, a sizeable population seems to have a negative correlation with progress toward sustainable development, inferring that an aging population poses a bigger threat to these countries' ability to grow sustainably. Due to unhealthy lifestyles and decreased productivity, an aging population poses a threat to the economies that are already struggling to make ends meet. Major targets of sustainable development include fostering inclusiveness and human resilience (United Nations Development Programme, 2017). The negative and considerable impact of an aging population on sustainable development is also reported by studies conducted by Chapman and Shigetomi (2018).

We anticipate that our regression model's endogeneity will lead to biased estimates. There are several ways to estimate dynamic panel models with endogeneity issues. The SYS-GMM proposed by Arellano and Bover (1995) and Blundell and Bond (1998) is seen as a feasible approach to this problem. Our econometric model is estimated using the dynamic panel system GMM technique to verify the stability of our findings. The GMM estimation outcomes are shown in Table 5. The ANS is used for the estimation of Models 1 and 2, whereas the GDP is used for the estimation of Models 3 and 4. Models 1 and Model 3 use REC as their independent variable, while Models 2 and 4 use RPG. ANS and economic growth show a strong correlation with the use of renewable energy, and both REC and RPG contribute to this positive trend. What we observe lends credence to the idea of a feedback hypothesis. The feedback hypothesis postulates that rising energy consumption mirrors rising economic output. It demonstrates that the need for energy grows alongside

Table 5. Model testing using the GMM estimation method.

	ANS		GDP	
Variables	**Model 1**	**Model 2**	**Model 3**	**Model 4**
L1	0.369***	0.371***	0.395***	0.407***
	(5.39)	(5.02)	(5.31)	(5.61)
L2	0.643***	0.597***	0.616***	0.601***
	(5.63)	(5.81)	(5.87)	(5.86)
REC	0.018***	—	0.565***	—
	(2.92)		(2.67)	
RPG	—	0.112***	—	0.081***
		(2.66)		(2.74)
TO	0.330***	0.305***	0.307***	0.289***
	(7.84)	(7.76)	(7.53)	(7.05)
FDI	0.516***	0.538***	0.541***	0.537***
	(7.95)	(7.71)	(7.73)	(7.04)
ADR	−0.079***	−0.067***	−0.063***	−0.074***
	(−5.24)	(−5.13)	(−5.10)	(−5.19)
Constant	0.286***	0.158***	0.164***	0.197***
	(4.14)	(4.95)	(4.49)	(4.28)
Sargan (p-value)	21.694	22.446	21.163	23.487
	(0.986)	(0.996)	(0.975)	(0.996)
AR_1 (p-value)	1.456	1.386	1.383	1.411
	(0.145)	(0.166)	(0.166)	(0.138)
AR_2 (p-value)	0.277	0.306	0.313	0.374
	(0.781)	(0.952)	(0.974)	(0.751)
Year fixed effect	Yes	Yes	Yes	Yes
Country fixed effect	Yes	Yes	Yes	Yes
Number of countries	42	42	42	42

Notes: Results in Table 4 are estimated using fixed-effect estimation. ANS (adjusted net saving) and GDP (economic growth) are dependent variables, REC (renewable energy consumption) and RPG (renewable power generation) are independent variables. TO (trade openness), FDI (foreign direct investment), and ADR (age dependency ratio) are control variables, $^{***}p < 0.01$. Model 1 and Model 2 are estimated with ANS, and Model 3 and Model 4 are estimated with GDP as sustainable economic development measures. The independent variable in Model 1 and Model 3 is REC, and in Model 2 and Model 4, RPG is used as an independent variable to measure renewable energy.

the economy. Hao *et al.* (2020), Hussain *et al.* (2021), and Islam and Islam (2021) all found that higher energy consumption considerably boosted sustainable economic development; hence, our finding is in line with past empirical studies on the energy–growth nexus. In developing countries, longer-term economic stability is linked to GDP growth and ANS. Our research suggests that improved fiscal shrewdness makes it possible for these economies to flourish sustainably as they expand. This demonstrates that economic growth in these countries has strengthened enough to promote long-term growth. Furthermore, we find that the utilization of renewable energy sources has a sizable and positive impact on long-term sustainability. This lends credence to the hypothesis of conserving natural resources (Güney, 2019; Kamoun *et al.*, 2019). To maintain energy supply and protect the environment from greenhouse gas emissions, the results suggest that renewable energy generation should replace the use of fossil fuels in the energy production process in emerging nations. In support of this conclusion, numerous studies have been conducted (Menegaki *et al.*, 2018; Din *et al.*, 2021).

Control variables, such as TO and FDI, have a favorable and significant effect on long-term economic growth. According to these results, trade liberalization policies significantly and positively affect these nations' prospects for long-term economic growth (Murshed, 2020; Nepal *et al.*, 2021). Because of this, liberalizing trade policies in these countries will have a positive effect on their economies only if their borders are open to foreign trade. The only way these economies can promote technological innovation and knowledge spillover is through a trade liberalization strategy. To achieve the purpose of liberal trade, which is to upgrade inefficient industry technology in the economies of trade members, the transfer of green technology must occur during a period when these economies are going through a technological transition. It has been shown that net FDI inflows have a positive impact on economic growth and stability in various countries. So, there are costs associated with the long-term welfare implications of FDI, particularly when it comes to natural resources. These costs can be seen in the form of damage to the environment and social infrastructure. In several developing countries, the results support the pollution halo theory (Mert *et al.*, 2020). ADR indicates a major drag on long-term economic growth. The global economy is in peril from an aging population (United Nations Development Programme, 2017). Once again, in a subset of nations, having a large population appears to be negatively correlated with sustainable development, insinuating that an aging population is a more significant danger to these nations' prospects for economic growth. An aging population threatens economies that are already struggling to keep afloat due to unhealthy lifestyles and lower productivity. Inclusiveness promotion and strengthening human resilience are two of the main aims of sustainable development (United Nations Development Programme Development Programme, 2017). Studies by Chapman and Shigetomi (2018) confirm the negative and substantial effects of an aging population on sustainable development.

5. Conclusion

The COVID-19 pandemic has had unanticipated consequences for the energy transition. Many countries have proposed and implemented a number of initiatives to accomplish green recovery and an energy transition following the pandemic. Nonetheless, despite growing global demand for green stimulus programs, fossil fuel investments continue to dominate half of all stated economic stimulus initiatives. If the recovery paradigm of high energy use and high emissions persists in the post-pandemic age, it will prolong the global energy transition and destroy recent advances in sustainable development. This study provides a rigorous empirical investigation of the relationship between renewable energy consumption and sustainable development in developing nations, and it presents a post-pandemic pathway for developing economies to transition to low-carbon energy.

We discovered that renewable energy production and consumption have a significant beneficial impact on sustainability of developing countries, confirming the feedback hypothesis. There is strong evidence in favor of the feedback hypothesis, suggesting that energy consumption and production is a crucial growth determinant in developing countries. Thus, it follows that a rise in energy consumption can stimulate economic growth, whereas insufficient energy exploitation can slow a nation's economic development. The assumption is that a rise in investment in energy resources and infrastructure will have a beneficial trickle-down effect on the developing countries' economies, while a fall in energy use would have the opposite effect. Optimal use of the nation's energy resources is necessary to achieve the much-desired sustainable development; it must foster green growth by significantly decreasing its use of fossil fuels and increasing its reliance on renewable energy. This research offers practical suggestions for formulating post-pandemic green recovery policies and contributing to the framework of the global low-carbon energy transition. Transitioning to a more sustainable energy source is especially important in the aftermath of a global pandemic. A successful recovery strategy will support the global energy transition while bolstering the economy. Therefore, in the post-COVID-19 age, it is strongly suggested that "green" be effectively integrated into the economic recovery program.

References

Adams, D. C. & Collyer, M. L. (2018). Phylogenetic ANOVA: Group-clade aggregation, biological challenges, and a refined permutation procedure. *Evolution*, *72*(6), 1204–1215. https://doi.org/10.1111/evo.13492.

Ahmad, M., Jabeen, G., & Wu, Y. (2021). Heterogeneity of pollution haven/halo hypothesis and environmental Kuznets curve hypothesis across development levels of Chinese provinces. *Journal of Cleaner Production*, *285*, 124898. https://doi.org/10.1016/j.jclepro.2020.124.

Al-Saidi, M. (2017). Conflicts and security in integrated water resources management. *Environmental Science & Policy*, *73*, 38–44. https://doi.org/10.1016/j.envsci.2017.03.015.

Anser, M. K., Yousaf, Z., Khan, M. A., *et al.* (2020). Does communicable diseases (including COVID-19) may increase global poverty risk? A cloud on the horizon. *Environmental Research*, *187*, 109668. https://doi.org/10.1016/j.envres.2020.109668.

Antonakakis, N., Chatziantoniou, I., & Filis, G. (2017). Energy consumption, CO_2 emissions, and economic growth: An ethical dilemma. *Renewable and Sustainable Energy Reviews*, *68*, 808–824. https://doi.org/10.1016/j.rser.2016.09.105.

Apergis, N. & Payne, J. E. (2010). Renewable energy consumption and economic growth: Evidence from a panel of OECD countries. *Energy Policy*, *38*(1), 656–660. https://doi.org/10.1016/j.enpol.2009.09.002.

Apergis, N. & Payne, J. E. (2012). Renewable and non-renewable energy consumption-growth nexus: Evidence from a panel error correction model. *Energy Economics*, *34*(3), 733–738. https://doi.org/10.1016/j.eneco.2011.04.007.

Apergis, N., Jebli, M. B., & Youssef, S. B. (2018). Does renewable energy consumption and health expenditures decrease carbon dioxide emissions? Evidence for sub-Saharan Africa countries. *Renewable Energy*, *127*, 1011–1016. https://doi.org/10.1016/j.renene.2018.05.043.

Armeanu, D. Ş., Vintilă, G., & Gherghina, Ş. C. (2017). Does renewable energy drive sustainable economic growth? multivariate panel data evidence for EU-28 countries. *Energies*, *10*(3), 381. https://doi.org/10.3390/en10030381.

Baloch, S., Baloch, M. A., Zheng, T., *et al.* (2020). The coronavirus disease 2019 (COVID-19) pandemic. *The Tohoku Journal of Experimental Medicine*, *250*(4), 271–278. https://doi.org/10.1620/tjem.250.271.

Belke, A., Dobnik, F., & Dreger, C. (2011). Energy consumption and economic growth: New insights into the cointegration relationship. *Energy Economics*, *33*(5), 782–789. https://doi.org/10.1016/j.eneco.2011.02.005.

Bhattacharya, M., Inekwe, J. N., Sadorsky, P., *et al.* (2018). Convergence of energy productivity across Indian states and territories. *Energy Economics*, *74*, 427–440. https://doi.org/10.1016/j.eneco.2018.07.002.

Bilgili, F., Koçak, E., Bulut, Ü., *et al.* (2017). The impact of urbanization on energy intensity: Panel data evidence considering cross-sectional dependence and heterogeneity. *Energy*, *133*, 242–256. https://doi.org/10.1016/j.energy.2017.05.121.

Brueckner, M. & Lederman, D. (2015). Trade openness and economic growth: Panel data evidence from Sub-Saharan Africa. *Economica*, *82*, 1302–1323. https://doi.org/10.1111/ecca.12160.

Chapman, A. & Shigetomi, Y. (2018). Developing national frameworks for inclusive sustainable development incorporating lifestyle factor importance. *Journal of Cleaner Production*, *200*, 39–47. https://doi.org/10.1016/j.jclepro.2018.07.302.

Chien, T. & Hu, J. L. (2007). Renewable energy and macroeconomic efficiency of OECD and non-OECD economies. *Energy Policy*, *35*(7), 3606–3615. https://doi.org/10.1016/j.enpol.2006.12.033.

Destek, M. A. & Sinha, A. (2020). Renewable, non-renewable energy consumption, economic growth, trade openness and ecological footprint: Evidence from organisation for economic co-operation and development countries. *Journal of Cleaner Production*, *242*, 118537. https://doi.org/10.1016/j.jclepro.2019.118537.

Din, S. U., Khan, M. Y., Khan, M. J., *et al.* (2021). Nexus between sustainable development, adjusted net saving, economic growth, and financial development in South Asian emerging economies. *Journal of the Knowledge Economy*, 1–14. https://doi.org/10.1007/s13132-021-00818-6.

Dincer, I. & Rosen, M. (2011). *Thermal Energy Storage: Systems and Applications*. UK: Wiley.

Dugarova, E. & Gülasan, N. (2017). Global trends: Challenges and opportunities in the implementation of the sustainable development goals. Joint report by the United Nations Development Programme and the United Nations Research Institute for Social Development. New York: UNDP and Geneva: UNRISD.

Elavarasan, R. M., Pugazhendhi, R., Jamal, T., *et al.* (2021). Envisioning the UN sustainable development goals (SDGs) through the lens of energy sustainability (SDG 7) in the post-COVID-19 world. *Applied Energy*, *292*, 116665. https://doi.org/10.1016/j.apenergy.2021.116665.

Fuinhas, J. A. & Marques, A. C. (2012). Energy consumption and economic growth nexus in Portugal, Italy, Greece, Spain and Turkey: An ARDL bounds test approach (1965–2009). *Energy Economics*, *34*(2), 511–517. https://doi.org/10.1016/j.eneco.2011.10.003.

González, V. M. (2013). Leverage and corporate performance: International evidence. *International Review of Economics & Finance*, *25*, 169–184. https://doi.org/10.1016/j.iref.2012.07.005.

Goodell, J. W. (2020). COVID-19 and finance: Agendas for future research. *Finance Research Letters*, *35*, 101512. https://doi.org/10.1016/j.frl.2020.101512.

Gorus, M. S. & Aydin, M. (2019). The relationship between energy consumption, economic growth, and CO_2 emission in MENA countries: Causality analysis in the frequency domain. *Energy*, *168*, 815–822. https://doi.org/10.1016/j.energy.2018.11.139.

Gozgor, G., Lau, C. K. M., & Lu, Z. (2018). Energy consumption and economic growth: New evidence from the OECD countries. *Energy*, *153*, 27–34. https://doi.org/10.1016/j.energy.2018.03.158.

Grigoroudis, E., Kouikoglou, V. S., & Phillis, Y. A. (2015). Energy sustainability of countries. In *Handbook of Research on Sustainable Development and Economics* (pp. 96–117). IGI Global. https://doi.org/10.4018/978-1-4666-8433-1.ch006.

Güney, T. (2019). Renewable energy, non-renewable energy and sustainable development. *International Journal of Sustainable Development & World Ecology*, *26*(5), 389–397. https://doi.org/10.1080/13504509.2019.1595214.

Hao, Y., Wang, L. O., & Lee, C. C. (2020). Financial development, energy consumption and China's economic growth: New evidence from provincial panel data. *International Review of Economics & Finance, 69*, 1132–1151. https://doi.org/10.1016/j.iref.2018.12.006.

Hussain, S., Yu, C., & Wan, L. (2021). Energy–growth nexus-A case of South Asian countries. *Asian Journal of Economics and Empirical Research*. https://ssrn.com/abstract=3921009.

Hunjra, A. I., Azam, M., Bruna, M. G., *et al.* (2022a). Sustainable development: The impact of political risk, macroeconomic policy uncertainty and ethnic conflict. *International Review of Financial Analysis*, 102370. https://doi.org/10.1016/j.irfa.2022.102370.

Hunjra, A. I., Azam, M., Bruna, M. G., *et al.* (2022b). Role of financial development for sustainable economic development in low middle income countries. *Finance Research Letters*, 102793. https://doi.org/10.1016/j.frl.2022.102793.

IEA (2016). World energy outlook 2016. Retrieved from https://www.iea.org/reports/world-energy-outlook-20162016.

IPCC (2014). *Climate Change 2014 Synthesis Report*. IPCC: Geneva, Switzerland.

Islam, M. M. & Islam, M. S. (2021). Globalization and politico-administrative factor-driven energy-growth nexus: A case of South Asian economies. *Journal of Public Affairs*, e2736. https://doi.org/10.1002/pa.2736.

Jammazi, R. & Aloui, C. (2015). RETRACTED: On the interplay between energy consumption, economic growth and CO_2 emission nexus in the GCC countries: A comparative analysis through wavelet approaches. https://doi.org/10.1016/j.rser.2015.07.073.

Jiang, P., Van Fan, Y., & Klemeš, J. J. (2021). Impacts of COVID-19 on energy demand and consumption: Challenges, lessons and emerging opportunities. *Applied Energy, 285*, 116441.

Kamoun, M. (2019). The effects of inflation on sustainable growth: The case of OECD countries. *Journal of Economics, Management and Trade, 22*(2), 1–9. https://doi.org/10.9734/JEMT/2019/34821.

Kamoun, M., Abdelkafi, I., & Ghorbel, A. (2019). The impact of renewable energy on sustainable growth: Evidence from a panel of OECD countries. *Journal of the Knowledge Economy, 10*(1), 221–237. https://doi.org/10.1007/s13132-016-0440-2.

Larcher, D. & Tarascon, J. M. (2015). Towards greener and more sustainable batteries for electrical energy storage. *Nature Chemistry, 7*(1), 19–29. https://doi.org/10.1038/nchem.2085.

Lise, W. & Van Montfort, K. (2007). Energy consumption and GDP in Turkey: Is there a co-integration relationship? *Energy economics*, *29*(6), 1166–1178. https://doi.org/10.1016/j.eneco.2006.08.010.

Meng, B., Liu, Y., Andrew, R., Zhou, M., Hubacek, K., Xue, J., Peters, G., & Gao, Y. (2018). More than half of China's CO_2 emissions are from micro, small and medium-sized enterprises. *Applied Energy, 230*, 712–725. https://doi.org/10.1016/j.apenergy.2018.08.107.

Mert, M. & Caglar, A. E. (2020). Testing pollution haven and pollution halo hypotheses for Turkey: A new perspective. *Environmental Science and Pollution Research, 27*(26), 32933–32943. https://doi.org/10.1007/s11356-020-09469-7.

Mezghani, I. & Haddad, H. B. (2017). Energy consumption and economic growth: An empirical study of the electricity consumption in Saudi Arabia. *Renewable and Sustainable Energy Reviews, 75*, 145–156. https://doi.org/10.1016/j.rser.2016.10.058.

Mohsin, M., Kamran, H. W., Nawaz, M. A., *et al.* (2021). Assessing the impact of transition from nonrenewable to renewable energy consumption on economic growth-environmental nexus from developing Asian economies. *Journal of environmental management, 284*, 111999. https://doi.org/10.1016/j.jenvman.2021.111999.

Murdock, H. E., Gibb, D., André, T., *et al.* (2021). Renewables 2021-Global status report. Retrieved from https://inis.iaea.org/search/search.aspx?orig_q=RN:52059346.

Murshed, M. (2020). An empirical analysis of the non-linear impacts of ICT-trade openness on renewable energy transition, energy efficiency, clean cooking fuel access and environmental sustainability in South Asia. *Environmental Science and Pollution Research, 27*(29), 36254–36281. https://doi.org/10.1007/s11356-020-09497-3.

Nepal, R., Paija, N., Tyagi, B., *et al.* (2021). Energy security, economic growth and environmental sustainability in India: Does FDI and trade openness play a role? *Journal of Environmental Management, 281*, 111886. https://doi.org/10.1016/j.jenvman.2020.111886.

Ntarmah, A. H., Kong, Y., Obeng, A. F., *et al.* (2022). The role of bank financing in economic growth and environmental outcomes of sub-Saharan Africa: Evidence from novel quantile regression and panel vector autoregressive models. *Environmental Science and Pollution Research, 29*(21), 31807–31845. https://doi.org/10.1007/s11356-021-17947-9.

Ozcan, B. & Ozturk, I. (2019). Renewable energy consumption-economic growth nexus in emerging countries: A bootstrap panel causality test. *Renewable and Sustainable Energy Reviews, 104*, 30–37. https://doi.org/10.1016/j.rser.2019.01.020.

Pablo-Romero, M. D. P. & Sánchez-Braza, A. (2017). Residential energy environmental Kuznets curve in the EU-28. *Energy, 125*, 44–54. https://doi.org/10.1016/j.energy.2017.02.091.

Pegels, A. & Altenburg, T. (2020). Latecomer development in a "greening" world: Introduction to the Special Issue. *World Development, 135*, 105084.

Pezzey, J. C. & Burke, P. J. (2014). Towards a more inclusive and precautionary indicator of global sustainability. *Ecological Economics, 106*, 141–154. https://doi.org/10.1016/j.ecolecon.2014.07.008.

Ramzan, M., Sheng, B., Shahbaz, M., *et al.* (2019). Impact of trade openness on GDP growth: Does TFP matter? *The Journal of International Trade & Economic Development, 28*(8), 960–995. https://doi.org/10.1080/09638199.2019.1616805.

Rasoulinezhad, E., Taghizadeh-Hesary, F., & Taghizadeh-Hesary, F. (2020). How is mortality affected by fossil fuel consumption, CO_2 emissions and economic factors in CIS region? *Energies, 13*(9), 2255. https://doi.org/10.1016/j.enpol.2009.09.002.

Rigobon, R. & Rodrik, D. (2005). Rule of law, democracy, openness, and income: Estimating the interrelationships1. *Economics of Transition, 13*(3), 533–564. https://doi.org/10.1111/j.1468-0351.2005.00226.x.

Roquez-Diaz, A. & Escot, L. (2018). Relationship between trade openness and economic growth in Latin America: A causality analysis with heterogeneous panel data. *Review of Development Economics, 22*(2), 658–684. https://doi.org/10.1111/rode.12358.

Sekrafi, H. & Sghaier, A. (2018). Examining the relationship between corruption, economic growth, environmental degradation, and energy consumption: A panel analysis in MENA region. *Journal of the Knowledge Economy, 9*(3), 963–979. https://doi.org/10.1007/s13132-016-0384-6.

Shahbaz, M., Nasreen, S., Abbas, F., *et al.* (2015). Does foreign direct investment impede environmental quality in high-, middle-, and low-income countries? *Energy Economics, 51*, 275–287. https://doi.org/10.1016/j.eneco.2015.06.014.

Shahbaz, M., Van Hoang, T. H., Mahalik, M. K., *et al.* (2017). Energy consumption, financial development and economic growth in India: New evidence from a nonlinear and asymmetric analysis. *Energy Economics, 63*, 199–212. https://doi.org/10.1016/j.eneco.2017.01.023.

Solarin, S. A., Tiwari, A. K., & Bello, M. O. (2019). A multi-country convergence analysis of ecological footprint and its components. *Sustainable Cities and Society, 46*, 101422. https://doi.org/10.1016/j.scs.2019.101422.

Taghizadeh-Hesary, F. & Yoshino, N. (2020). Sustainable solutions for green financing and investment in renewable energy projects. *Energies, 13*(4), 788. https://doi.org/10.3390/en13040788.

United Nations Development Programme (2017). Aging, older persons and the 2030 agenda for sustainable development. Retrieved from https://www.undp.org/content/undp/en/home/librarypage/poverty-reduction/aging–older-persons-and-the-2030-agenda-for-sustainable-develo.html.

Wang, Q., Zhou, B., Zhang, C., *et al.* (2021). Do energy subsidies reduce fiscal and household non-energy expenditures? A regional heterogeneity assessment on coal-to-gas program in China. *Energy Policy, 155*, 112341. https://doi.org/10.1016/j.enpol.2021.112341.

World Health Organization (2015). World report on aging and health. Retrieved from https://www.who.int/aging/publications/world-report-2015/en/.

Xiao, H., Sun, K. J., Bi, H. M., *et al.* (2019). Changes in carbon intensity globally and in countries: Attribution and decomposition analysis. *Applied Energy, 235*, 1492–1504. https://doi.org/10.1016/j.apenergy.2018.09.158.

Yang, B., Brosig, S., & Chen, J. (2013). Environmental impact of foreign vs. domestic capital investment in China. *Journal of Agricultural Economics, 64*(1), 245–271. https://doi.org/10.1111/j.1477-9552.2012.00370.x.

Zahonogo, P. (2016). Trade and economic growth in developing countries: Evidence from sub-Saharan Africa. *Journal of African Trade, 3*(1–2), 41–56. https://doi.org/10.1016/j.joat.2017.02.001.

Zhang, H., Yan, J., Yu, Q., *et al.* (2021). 1.6 Million transactions replicate distributed PV market slowdown by COVID-19 lockdown. *Applied Energy, 283*, 116341. https://doi.org/10.1016/j.apenergy.2020.116341.

https://doi.org/10.1142/9781800614482_bmatter

Index

K

L

M

N

P

R

V

W

www.ingramcontent.com/pod-product-compliance
Lightning Source LLC
LaVergne TN
LVHW021231160926
848178LV00066B/76
* 9 7 8 1 8 0 0 6 1 4 4 7 5 *